AN ODYSSEY

THE
FINAL
CARTWHEEL

Fourth book in the
CARTWHEELS QUADRILOGY

Lawrence
WINKLER

Note for Librarians: A cataloguing record for this book is available from Library and Archives Canada at www.collectionscanada.ca/amicus/index-e.html

Cover Image:
solarseven, www.shutterstock.com (Image ID: 83814205)

Cover Design:
Jenny Engwer, First Choice Books

Book Images:
"Orion" (p.233) by Emanuel Sungging Mumpuni
© International Editorial board of "Stars of Asia

ISBN – 978-1-988429-08-3

Printed in Canada ♻ on recycled paper

 FIRST CHOICE BOOKS

firstchoicebooks.ca
Victoria, BC

10 9 8 7 6 5 4 3 2 1

For Destiny

Spokes

End of Strife
The Road to Mandalay
Burmese Days
String of Pearls
Slow Boat to China
With its Back to Heaven
Songs of the South
Stone Forest
Dire Straits on the Yangtze
Landscapes Clear and Radiant
Sinews of Our Fathers
Frank Li
Fairy-Land
Back in the USSR
The Narrow Road to the Interior
The Route of Seeing
Spiders and Snakes
Be are All Abailable
Rice Mixed with Sand
Eating the Wind and Moon
Shadow Puppets
Fair Dinkum
Beyond the Black Stump
Bearing the Southern Cross
Coromandel Gold

Alpha and Beta Centauri pointed to the Southern Cross, from the bottom of the Otama night sky. Moonlit breakers crashed on the shore below the shack.

"Tell us the rest of the story, Uncle Wink." Said Millie. She and Sam were not sitting at the picnic table; they were on it, for eye level contact.

"Where did I leave off?" Asked Uncle Wink. "Had I told you about Orion the constellation and the myth, and the different kinds of heroes, and vision quests, and the Buddha?"

"Yes." Said Sam. "You were just about to fly into Burma."

"Alright." Said Uncle Wink. "Let me just finish my lamington."

"Did you find anything special on the last part of your adventure?" Millie asked.

"Many things were waiting on the Final Cartwheel, Millie." Said Uncle Wink. "Roads of lizard skin and silk, a stone forest and a white castle and water buffalo houses, mountain parrots and flying foxes, a giant gecko and a manta ray above, dragon boats and cargo boats and racing sloops, and outriggers, kung fu monks and clay warriors and shadow puppets and bootlegged Buddhas, gold mines and tree ferns, boiling mud and smoking volcanoes, raving poets and barons and painters and wizards, and typhoons and love.

"And Auntie Robbie? Millie asked.

"You'll just have to wait and see, Mil." Said Uncle Wink, taking the last bite of his cake.

And they squirmed on the table, to find comfort.

The Final Cartwheel

is an inaccurate name for this story, of course. Not many things are ever final. Success is not final, failure is not fatal: it is the courage to continue that counts.

It had been 3 years, 7 months and 20 days since my thumb first carved an arc in the prairie sky. It had been that long since I had last seen my family. In exchange for a normal existence, I had followed Orion's Cartwheel down through South America and up through Africa, traced a second European Grand Tour clockwise through the history of Western Civilization, and turned a third Hind Cartwheel around the mythical mystical Indian subcontinent.

But there are four cartwheels on a carriage, and Orion and I would need one more through the Far East, Southeast Asia, and the Antipodes, to close the last compass points on my chart, and to complete the five-year circle.

With a final cartwheel you get commitment, completion, and closure. You get the odyssey you signed up for. Push on through to the other side. *The Final Cartwheel*, it is.

End of Strife

I landed in Burma when it was still Burma. I landed in Rangoon when it was still Rangoon. I landed in a military dictatorship, in humidity, decay, and cigar smoke.

It could have been Havana, if my revolutionary reincarnation had gone through more crucifixion. The Cuban marriage of Catholicism and Communism was about the extinction of the self, through submission to collective control; the Burmese union of Buddhism and Socialism was about the extinction of the self, through the individual attainment of enlightenment, through an impossible contradiction.

The ratio of corruption to competence was encouraging. The smiling faces of the inept immigration officials cleared the middle path for me out of the terminal, where a hopalong Indian babu loaded me into his taxi for the drive to the YMCA.

We drove by the 300-foot spotlit towering temple spire of the Schwedagon, a seven ton golden hypodermic tipped with 5,448 diamonds and 2,317 rubies, injecting karma into the night sky. The Schwedagon was twenty-five hundred years old, the oldest pagoda in the world. During his visit in 1889, the golden dome had made an indelible impression on Rudyard Kipling.

"This is Burma." He said. "And it will be quite unlike any land you know about."

Legend has it that the eight strands of Gautama's hair the Shwedagon contained, were brought from India to Burma by two merchant brothers. When King Okkalapa opened the golden casket in which they were transported, *'there was an incredible tumult among men and spirits ... rays emitted by the Hairs penetrated up to the heavens above and down to hell ... the blind beheld*

1

objects ... the deaf heard sounds ... the dumb spoke distinctly ... the earth quaked ... the winds of the ocean blew ... Mount Meru shook ... lightning flashed ... gems rained down until they were knee deep ... and all trees of the Himalayas, though not in season, bore blossoms and fruit.'

My own reception at the YMCA was somewhat more subdued. The Fat Man provided the only sleeping space remaining, on the stage floor beside the piano. I drank Vimto and played Beethoven, until the fatigue worked its way down my arms and into my fingers.

My last ounce of energy extinguished the floodlights. A squadron of mosquitoes and a wounded grandfather clock chimed two hours off my life. *Big-bong Bing-chunk... Big-bong Bing-chunk.*

I was still semiconscious in the Gold Kazoo, when a large pair of mirrored sunglasses shook my shoulders. I looked up into a green Burmese jungle hat, and a smiling black moustache on a tanned mustard face. He was just like they said he'd be.

"MingaLAba." He said. "I'm Roy."

"I'll bet you are." I said. "Where you been?"

"MandaLAY." He said. "You got the duty free?" I handed him a bottle of Vat 69 whiskey and a carton of 555 cigarettes. In Bangladesh, they had told me it would pay for my entire week upriver and incountry. Roy looked it over, and tapped me twice again on the shoulder.

"Ready to go?" He asked.

"I just got here." I said. It was four in the morning.

"You only have a week." He said. "Burma big country." I rolled up the Gold Kazoo painfully, wondering why I had just paid six kyat to play a piano.

Rangoon was a British bastardization of Yangon, which in the local dialect literally meant 'to run out of enemies,' or the 'End of Strife.' My strife was just about to begin, in its dark humid low altitude decomposition. Because electricity was intermittent, there was no reliable power to run elevators.

2

Other than the Schwedagon, no buildings were constructed higher than the set of stairs you could climb in the heat.

I stowed Serendipity in favor of a smaller bag that Roy provided. Room in the truck would be at a premium. He suggested I buy a ticket from 'Tourist Bummer.' *Tourist Burma.*

"Why?" I asked

"To show them you go somewhere." He said.

"But I am going somewhere." I said. He told me our trip was 'special,' and a train ticket would cover our tracks. He prodded the Fat Man to accompany me to Tourist Bummer. I bought passage to Mandalay, for a dollar.

My upcountry adventure travel companions were waiting impatiently, back at the 'Y.' This was the group I would spend the next week with, crammed in the back of a yellow pickup. Introductions began with Tony, a friendly 32 year-old hairdresser from Los Angeles, recently divorced, and deep in heartbreak. There was Jo, an English naturopath, hosing down the planet with her alternative remedies and lifestyle choices, as a talisman against impending menopause. Her partner, Vivian, was an older mother of two, afflicted with a more advanced case. Christianne was a bitter Belgian with a jutting jaw that led every one of her efforts to get a bargain on everything she would consume.

And finally, and not many things are ever final, there was Dominique, a 26 year-old French Napoleanne, traveling the Far East for the previous four years, who had made a small fortune as a stripper in Japan, and collected addresses, just like Button Nose in Darjeeling. Dominique had a nose ring, before transflesh metal was a more universally accepted artistic form of individual expression. You could tell it was there to provoke anyone into pulling her around by it. She could turn her charm and accent on and off like a rivet gun and, by the time we returned to the end of strife, I would be riven with rivets. It was going to be a long week.

Roy introduced us to our drivers, James and Henry.

"Aren't you coming?" Jo asked of Roy.

"No room." He said. Reexamining the iron cage behind the cab, I think he meant that for at least three of us.

Leafy avenues led us around corner teashops and along *fin-de-siècle* colonial architecture, to the Strand Hotel, in an abortive attempt to buy more export quality cigarettes. There would be no more change in American cash.

We turned north in our yellow truck, just before noon. Whatever few traffic signs there were, were facing the wrong direction.

No one spoke at first, but the ice gradually melted as the sun rose higher, past waving Burmese, semiarid rice paddies, receding pagodas, and the realization of the adventure before us.

*   *   *

> Burnett: "We need to get upriver."
> Rambo: "Where are you going?"
> Burnett: "Into Burma."
> Rambo: "Burma's a warzone... I don't go that far north."
> Rambo 2008

If Burma was a war zone, it was because of the traffic. There wasn't much, but it had been given a colorful local handicap. Drivers in America sit on the left side of the car and drive on the right side of the road. In England, they sit on the right and drive on the left. Burma, as a former British colony, had right hand steering and a left wing despot.

In 1970, despite the right-hand drive, all traffic was moved to the right side of the road. General Ne Win's wife's astrologer thought the country would be better off, and the General always made decisions based on omens and horoscopes. When his soothsayer warned him of an impending bloodbath, he would stand in front of a mirror and trample on meat to simulate the blood, then shoot himself in the mirror, to avert the possibility of an assassination attempt. When his astrologer told him he would live to ninety if he demonetized the country, he introduced banknotes in awkward 90 kyat denominations. He married six times, and lived to ninety-two. His name meant 'Brilliant as the Sun.' When Burmese University students protested, he dynamited their student union building. When he was younger, failing to get into medical school, he became a postal clerk. When his picture later appeared on the stamps, the Burmese began spitting on the side without the glue.

James and Henry, like most Burmese with access to a gas pedal, drove fast. Separated as they were from most of the roadway, they could only guess at the identity of the animals they were running over. In the first half hour north of Rangoon, we hit a chicken, a duck, and a pig. The fact that none of the tires had any tread remaining may have given them a fighting chance. We didn't dream of stopping. They didn't seem to mind passing on blind corners, as they were the least likely tribal members to be killed for a miscalculation. It was a good thing we were shoehorned in the back of the Yellow Terror, and couldn't see forward. Not that it would have mattered if we could. On the rare occasion when I got to sit up front, I realized that there was so much ankle-deep dust coming off the dirt road, they couldn't see either. Only the occasional thump gave away our position in space and time. We may have been driving the country's main highway, but it was still only wide enough for one conveyance at a time. Every time another vehicle appeared out of the powdered air, we swerved onto the shoulder, hoping they would too. We passed ox cart trains as high as a house.

Our first stop was Pegu, home of the largest reclining Buddha in the world. Built in 994, and lost when Pegu was destroyed in 1757, the smiling Shwethalyaung was rediscovered under a cover of jungle growth in 1881. At 181 feet long and 46 feet high, they must not have been looking very hard.

My first real glimpse into the souls of the travelers lining the wooden benches in the back of the Yellow Terror came at lunch. Inside a rattan hut, we sat on a bamboo mat, at a low table. Bowls of soup and steamed rice came with *hin* main dishes of curried chicken, salt fish, vegetables, and green tea.

Tony asked for a fork and ate everything. Christianne did likewise and ate what she thought cost the most. Dominique asked for chopsticks and picked at her food. And Jo and Viv, with a superior knowledge of how the Burmese eat, rolled their rice into little balls, and mixed them with vegetarian morsels only. I reached for a second helping of chicken.

"You're not going to eat that, are you?" Asked Jo. I told her that yes, indeed I was.

"You know that meat is bad for your health." She said, like she shouldn't have to explain it. I told her that I'd seen no data to that effect, at which point she hauled out her professional qualifications.

"Well, I'm a certified naturopathic doctor, and I'm afraid that eclipses any information you're unaware of." I told her that I was a real one, and that eclipsed any dim light she was basking under. I was lucky she was trapped under a low table. It was not the end of strife. Tony had a second helping of chicken. I had an ally.

We left to visit the thousand year-old Shwemawdaw Pagoda, a slightly smaller version of the Schwedagon temple in Rangoon. It looked so much like a gigantic golden bell, I wanted to reach up and ring it. Inside, there were allegedly two more hairs from Gautama's head. Like pieces of the true cross, I was beginning to suspect that, with respect to messianic relics and body parts, early devotees were probably splitting hairs.

The sun was so mercilessly hot on our exit from the shrine, we ran to the shaded canopy of the Yellow Terror's trucked. James and Henry fired up the beast, and we reentered a purgatory of dust.

It was midafternoon when we arrived at a long train crossing. Several packed olive green Chinese-built army trucks pulled up behind us. Tony made the observation that everything seemed to be packed in Burma, even the laborers digging in the trench beside us. Locals appeared on bicycles, also waiting to cross. Lithe women with open umbrellas, flowers in their jet black hair, and mesh bags full of produce, sang stacked nasal tones to each other. Young uniformed schoolboys with long dark pants and starched shirts, far too white for the dust clouds they lived in, gathered around Tony and I, seeking inspirational sources on their path to masculinity.

They suggested it was hot. Tony and I agreed, the first success in the search for a common vantage point. They suggested that we needed a beer. It was the mother lode of brotherly love. Tony and I left the Yellow Terror and followed them into town, to the only place that sold Mandalay Strong Ale. Their obvious pride, in strutting us down the main street, was precious.

Not so precious was the silent sisterly love waiting in the back of the Yellow Terror, on our return. It wasn't completely clear, but I think that Jo and Viv were upset that we partook of a dangerous indulgence, Christianne was upset because we left the vehicle, and Dominique was upset that we didn't bring one back for her. Rambo had been right. *Burma's a war zone.*

The gears ground and shifted through the hours, the temperature started to drop a little, both outside and within the Yellow Terror. Tony and I bought some nut-filled sweetmeats for the sisters, as a peace offering. Some of the façades crumbled with the pastry flakes.

Dinner was a bit like lunch, except when the watermelon surcharge arrived, and Christianne went onto fully automatic. The poor Burmese proprietor withdrew in pain, until Tony and I lingered to make it right for him. The bad karma still permeated the trucked, however, and Christianne droned on about how she had been right to object. She would have spent an order of magnitude more on a coffee back in Belgium, but in Burma, principle was indistinguishable from privilege. The fortunate must not be restrained in the exercise of tyranny over the unfortunate.

All of this had affected Tony more than me. We were becoming better friends, and he confided to me how he lost his wife. He had come to Burma to heal, but I wasn't sure the company was going to be all that conducive to a cure. In a rest stop later that evening we found ourselves among a small group of Burmese army recruits. I entertained them on their guitar and they, in their appreciation, passed a bottle of government Mandalay Army Rum into the back of the Yellow Terror, as we departed.

Tony and I were in, as was Dominique, and even Viv, but Christianne was still sputtering about dinner, and Jo was having none of it. I pointed out to her that the libation contained quinine, an effective herbal antimalarial. She still wasn't having any of it. I told her that the smoky notes came from its aging in yamanay wood, from the gamhar tree, *Gmelina arborea*, and her eyes lit up ever so dimly. Tony passed me another swig.

"In Ayurvedic medicine, it's used to promote hair growth, and in the treatment of vaginal discharge." She said. The first one explained the profusion of Buddha's relics, but there was no way I was going near the second. But Tony, under Mandalay Army influence by now, couldn't resist, and Burma was a war zone again.

I looked over to find him making forays into Christianne's clothing. If you don't know where you're going, any road will get you there. Viv was holding my left arm, and Dominique had found her way onto my lap. The trance-inducing lights of oncoming truck grills passed us like Spielberg UFO's in the night.

"It's also used for snakebites and scorpion stings." I said.

The Road to Mandalay

'There's a Burma girl a-settin', and I know she thinks o' me;
For the wind is in the palm-trees, and the temple-bells they say:
I've a neater, sweeter maiden in a cleaner, greener land...
On the road to Mandalay... On the road to Mandalay.'
Rudyard Kipling, *Mandalay*

Her name was Aye-Aye. As in what you'd say to the captain,
if you could find the words. Her skin was gold on saffron and
her long hair hung in a vertical black waterfall over my head.
She was sublime.

"Tea?" She asked, already pouring. I had no recollection of
how I ended up in this rattan bed, or in the Min Chan Myei
Guest House in Pagan.

"You drink Mandalay Army?" She asked.

"At least a division." I finally said.

"Very strong." Said Aye-Aye.

"Very strong." I agreed.

"I am your guide for today." She said. That was good.

We had apparently arrived in Pagan about three am. Jo was
banging on my door now at eight, anxious to get moving.
Aye-Aye left so I could dress. She was sitting demurely with
most of the others outside, when I finally emerged into
daylight.

I bid them good morning and left to have a shower.
Dominique's contoured movements were reflected in the
cement tubs on the other side of the rattan screen.

Jo had already left to see the temples on a bicycle, by the time
I was clean. Aye-Aye had arranged horse carts for the rest of
us and, after a catfish broth and noodle *moh hin gha* breakfast,
two of them pulled up to the guesthouse. Tony, in his search
for reaffirmation and affection, jumped into Dominique and
Christianne's cart, and I accompanied Viv and Aye-Aye in the
second.

Pagan had been the capital of the first Burmese Empire. At the height of its glory in the 12th century, it was known as the *City of Four Million Pagodas*, the *Land of Copper*, the *City of the Enemy Crusher*, or the *Parched Land*. If the Burmese seemed to have had a lot of enemies, clipclopping around Pagan, they certainly had more parched land. We rode through a hot and dusty plain, on the eastern bank of the Irrawaddy, the water road to Mandalay. In 1057, King Anawrahta set out to establish a truly cosmopolitan center of Buddhist studies. Thousands of temples, pagodas, and other religious structures, dotted an area of over forty square kilometers. But time had not been kind. In 1287, when the Burmese refused to pay tribute to Kublai Khan, the Mongols turned the place into a crumbling ruin of bricks and sandstone. The earthquake that arrived nine years before we did almost finished it off, and the military junta's haphazard attempts at restoration only made it worse. In Buddhism, impermanence, along with unsatisfactoriness and selflessness, is one of the three marks of existence. In both ways, there wasn't much left, to prove the point, in Pagan.

Additional proof was in evidence in the back of our cart by Aye-Aye, who reached for my hand, selfless, unsatisfactory, and impermanent. *On the road to Mandalay, Where the flyin'-fishes play, An' the dawn comes up like thunder outer China 'crost the Bay.*

Vivian was in the front, expostulating on enlightenment, unaware that Aye-Aye and I had already achieved it behind her.

A young monk at the Myoe Daung Monastery went into rapture over a gift of a ballpoint pen. We took our own pleasure from a delicious soup in a small café. Christianne and Dominique returned to tell us that theirs had been thirty cents cheaper.

Our horse drawn procession continued, connecting as many dots of the two thousand remaining temples, as we could fit into a scorching afternoon. The magnificent oversized Buddhas, cramped inside their Manuha temple enclosures, represented the imprisonment and desire for release of a Mon king, and the suffering of existence itself.

In a small shop, I found an old cylindrical *pan yun* incised lacquerware box. I drank too much of their green tea, and smoked too many of their complimentary cigars, before Aye-Aye finally convinced me to buy it. Upon our return to the Min Chan Myei at sunset, Christianne told me she had seen a less expensive better one, in another part of town. I told her that she was living proof density can exist in a vacuum.

As black night invaded the dying orange dust of the day, the Yellow Terror travelers gradually went off to bed. Aye-Aye and I held hands outside, watching the constellations come onto the field. I pointed out Orion, and told her of my odyssey. She told me a story from her youth.

There was once a young man and woman who were very much in love. Their names were Cohn-sawn-law and Nahn-ooh-bean. But Cohn-sawn-law's stepmother didn't approve, and tried to drive them apart. Because of the constant harassment, the couple decided to move to another village.

Just after Nahn-ooh-bean became pregnant, Cohn-sawn-law received a message from his stepmother. She had apparently experienced a change of heart, and implored them to return.

But it wasn't true. Still determined to separate them, she sent Cohn-sawn-law off on a long business journey. He was gone for a long time, and Nahn-ooh-bean missed him terribly. In her weakened condition, she miscarried. In her anguish, she died of a broken heart.

When Cohn-sawn-law finally returned, he, too, died of heartbreak.

Friends of the couple built a funeral pyre and lay the two lovers together. As the smoke rose into the blue-black sky two groups of stars appeared, Cohn-sawn-law and Nahn-ooh-bean, together at last, in the night sky, forever.

But while their friends weren't looking, the stepmother quickly approached the fire. She placed a three-segmented piece of bamboo between the couple. As the smoke rose again, the three bamboo segments become three stars that to this day separate the two lovers.

Aye-Aye pointed to the three stars of Orion's belt. Sometimes

I think of her.
She changed my constellations.

'Is there anything in the world more graceless, more dishonouring, than to desire a woman whom you will never have?'

George Orwell, *Burmese Days*

*   *   *

'Only the guy who isn't rowing has time to rock the boat.'

Jean-Paul Sartre

We left for the northeast early next morning, maneuvering through the matrix of two thousand temples, so as to remain undetected. I wasn't completely convinced that Henry's ABBA tape collection was helping our invisibility.

We ascended a narrow winding road, lined by flowering trees and hazy views. Jo and Vivian were carsick on the curves. It was refreshingly quiet.

Eight hours later, we arrived at Inle Lake, in the Shan Hills. The Intha people here lived in houses of wood and woven bamboo, on high stilts above the water, in small villages along the shore. They ate the lake carp, and tended floating gardens made from lake-bottom weeds, anchored by bamboo poles. They loved their tomatoes and tamarind and chilies and fermented bean cakes and cheroots. Lotuses were pulled, stripped, and woven to make fabric for Shan bags, and Buddhist robes.

We checked into Inle Lodge and, after a shower, Tony and I meandered through the markets. We both bought Burmese jungle hats, Tony in a shop, me off a local. Back at the guesthouse, Christianne told Tony he got the better deal. Dominique wanted to play Patti cake, but the innkeeper's brother produced two friends, a bottle of Mandalay Army, and an invitation to a poker game. The army uniforms should have been a warning, but I never gave it much thought. Neither Tony nor I figured these guys for card sharks. The beautiful thing about poker is that everybody thinks they can play. Tony thought he could, and lost. The army boys thought so too. I slept with my back to the wall.

The morning found us in a long tail outboard dugout, riding slow and hot through the weedy canals to more open water. Unlike the road traffic we experienced on the way, boats still passed each other on the left.

We had come to watch the local fishermen, who were known for their distinctive rowing style. This involved standing at the stern on one leg, and wrapping the other leg around the oar, allowing them to see above the reeds. They looked like awkward dogs, trying to scratch a flea in slow motion.

But it was inside the fabulous wooden Nga Hpe Kyaung monastery, idyllically situated on the far side of the lake, where the true acrobats of Inle lived. Beyond the gold and semiprecious Buddhas in the atrium, square streams of sunlight lasered a yellow patchwork quilt onto the ancient brown hardwood floor below. Four smiling monks brought green tea and jaggery sweets, and a herd of jumping cats. The monks would hold up a hoop, and the cats would jump through. They had apparently taught the monks to feed them. If they had seen the fish in the open water toilet, they might have devoted their acrobatic energy to more energetic protein sources.

"One pen. One pen." Whispered along the middle path as we left.

Back in the dugout, we floated into and among the tall pointed stupas, stilts, yellow parasols, conical hats, and long flat-bottomed boats of the Shan floating market, where I found an old set of opium scales, and a set of rooster-shaped weights, to make them functional.

I was lucky enough to have visited Inle before the boom in population, agriculture and tourism. In 2010 the water level of the lake would drop so low that the floating market was in danger of disappearing, and drinking water had to be brought in from elsewhere. The lake was about to lose thirty percent of its open water. Slash and burn farming, logging, and untreated sewage and wastewater would flow directly into the lake, causing run-off, silt and sedimentation, eutrophication, and pollution, and the promotion of weed and algae growth.

All boats were strangely required to bring in a specified amount of rapidly growing water hyacinth, which would rob native plants and animals of nutrients and sunlight. Non-native fish species, such as the Grass Carp, would be added to the soup. The floating gardens would become solid ground.

Noise pollution from the cheap unmuffled diesel engines driving the stern drive propellers would end the tranquility I had been fortunate enough to experience.

Our landing was decorated by a group of giraffe Kayan women, their necks appearing elongated by stacks of brass coil rings, deforming their collar bones and compressing their rib cages.

"Protection from bite of tiger." Said James. Dominique grabbed her neck.

I roared, just a little.

Burmese Days

'Mandalay is rather a disagreeable town — it is dusty and intolerably hot, and it is said to have five main products all beginning with P, namely, pagodas, pariahs, pigs, priests and prostitutes.'

George Orwell, *Burmese Days*

Tony and I split some bamboo poles, in an attempt to make the back of the Yellow Terror more comfortable, for our ten-hour marathon to Mandalay. James and Henry put the additional opulence onto the speedometer, and Vivian's vomiting once again promoted her to a seat in the cockpit. The rest of us watched the flowering trees and mountains go by at light speed, until even the last of that died with the sun. At the Kyaukse turnoff, we finally stopped for soup. Flickering figures chanted Country and Western songs in Burmese, on the small black and white television tube inside. The townsfolk gathered to peer through the windows at the tourists. Tony gave a local barber his first Hollywood hairstyle, while the entire neighborhood looked on. It was the end of the buzz cut in Kyaukse.

When we finally arrived in Mandalay, Christianne insisted we search for more inexpensive accommodation than the Man Shwe Myo had reserved for us. James and Henry returned with her two hours later. Tony had already scurried upstairs to be with the girls upstairs, and the Chinese proprietress asked if I would share a room with two Burmese. To be away from western travelers was a blessing. I fell asleep at once.

James and Henry arrived at my sidewalk coffee next morning, bringing our guide, Kokoji. He was followed by Tony and the sisters, and finally by Dominique, who seemed to require increasingly longer intervals to become presentable. I told her I had never met a stripper who took longer putting her clothes on. She snarled. I grabbed my neck.

Kokoji piled us into the Yellow Terror and took us to the healing statue of the Mahamuni. Inside was a venerable old verdigris bronze figure, burnished to a shine where supplicants had rubbed their malafflictions. His feet and knees and nose and mouth and breasts and solar plexus were polished copper. The eyes were worn through to darkness. There was a hole where the liver should have been, but the biggest gaping breach was his crotch. Torments of the eyes, the liver, and the groin. The ancient Burmese were connected to and like the rest of us.

The market was a black one, replete with expired pharmaceuticals from around the world. With my Burmese jungle hat and cheroot, Tony said I was starting to look like a local. In a nearby Chinese restaurant, we had the prawns, and watched Christianne gulp down a lobster. She then complained about the food, but we got the bellyache.

Over seven hundred kilometers from Rangoon, Mandalay seemed to be a backwater of dusty streets and bicycles. As Orwell had noted in his *Burmese Days*, there were pagodas, 700 of them. There were pigs. There were priests, if the endless procession of saffron clad monks, holding giant pink parasols, passing by us, qualified. I told Dominique I had only encountered one prostitute and she, in her turn, was busily turning me into the only pariah.

The town was named after the eight hundred foot high Mandalay Hill. We began out climb through the lion figures at the southern stairway. Stalls lining the *dazaung* halls sold flowers, pennants and umbrellas for the Buddha, and refreshments for the pilgrims. Almost at the top was the image of the ogress, Sanda Muhki, who had nothing to offer the Buddha but her breasts. Tony became the second pariah by suggesting to Dominique that she had more to offer. The ornate gold and aquamarine and pink Sutaungpyei pagoda at the summit provided a superb panorama of the mountains, the town below, and the adversity faced by the Gurkhas that finally stormed and dislodged the Japanese here, in one of the fiercest battles of the war.

We descended to the oldest teak monastery in Burma, and the Kuthodaw Pagoda, containing the world's largest book, 729 slabs of stone inscribed with the entire Buddhist canon, each in its own white stupa. The incredible Buddha inside the main hall dripped gold and inertia. Tony and Dominique had their palms and stars read here, while I rolled my eyes on the sidelines. When Dominique had kept us waiting for a third time that day, I asked if it was possible to be more aware of the group. Jo came out of nowhere like an Antichrist banshee, Each missile she launched was tipped with multiple poisonous warheads. There were issues.

We returned to the Man Shwe Myo for a late afternoon nap. I found Tony having an implosion across from me, when I awoke. His wife had left him for someone else. He hadn't known anything until he arrive home to the note on the kitchen table. I spoke to Dominique, who spirited him off to the night market. Following later, I bought a buffalo handle cane for two dollars, on my way to meet the group for dinner. Kokoji turned the brass clip at the top, and unsheathed the sword inside. With a twist of the wrist, it had just morphed into checked baggage. We ate soup and beef and rice and mango pickle and white bean paste, and drank green tea, and took a stroll. A local rock band named 'Shell' played until after midnight, until the power failed, and we all went home. Dominique knocked on my door a short while later. Jo was getting a massage, and she just wondered. I sent her back. Between the mosquitoes and the howling dogs and the news that we were leaving for Rangoon at five, I got about an hour's sleep. It was an hour more than Tony got. He woke me by locking himself out, and we went to a teahouse around the corner to watch the sunrise. A Chinese cook from Shanghai bought us coffee and flatbread, and we thanked him for it. It wasn't necessary.

Three days after our visit to Mandalay, a fire destroyed almost three thousand buildings, and made 23,000 people homeless. The Chinese would come in and buy the ashes outright. The Burmese days were over.

"Mandalay has its name; the falling cadence of the lovely word has gathered about itself the chiaroscuro of romance."
Somerset Maugham, *The Gentleman in the Parlour*

.   *   *   *

"Seven days is the length of a guest's life"
Burmese Proverb

James and Henry hadn't materialized by sunrise, so Dominique and Christianne went off to find them. They were asleep. My Chinese amah gave me an owl as a goodbye gift, Tony slipped into his bag onto the split bamboo floor of the trucked, and we shot off on the long haul back to Rangoon.
If the return road kill reckoning was any indication, James was in a hurry to get home, consigning a chicken, dog, pig, and duck, to new incarnations on the way.
We pulled up to the YMCA about 6 pm, took a final group photo and checked into a bunk on the fourth floor. After a shower upstairs and a soup downstairs, Tony and I went out to score some Mandalay Army rum. I was doing my laundry upstairs when everyone came up. They finished the bottle and

fell asleep where they sat, leaving me to entertain what was still conscious about Jo. A man goes to heaven for the climate and hell for the company. Tony was drooling on his sleeping bag when I hit the lights.

I hugged them all goodbye next morning, and took a black market rickshaw to the airport. I left the Golden Land of Gems as underweight and overexposed as my photos.

String of Pearls

'In diving to the bottom of pleasure we bring up more gravel than pearls.'
Honoré de Balzac

"What's the plan, Wink?" Had been Tony's last question, at the airport in Rangoon. I told him the plan was to take my last Biman flight to Bangkok, another to Hong Kong, a ship to Macau, and a slow boat to China.

I landed in the longest place name on the planet, Krung-dēvamahānagaraamararatanakosindramahindrāyudhyāmahātil akabhavanavaratanarājadhānīpurīramyauttamarājanivēsanama hāsthānaamaravimānaavatārasthityashakrasdattiyavishnukarm aprasiddhi, or, as the locals knew it, *The city of angels, the great city, the eternal jewel city, the impregnable city of God Indra, the grand capital of the world endowed with nine precious gems, the happy city, abounding in an enormous Royal Palace that resembles the heavenly abode where reigns the reincarnated god, a city given by Indra and built by Vishnukarma.*

"First time to Bangkok?" He asked. I was on bus #59 to downtown, and this guy was ancient. He told me his name was Ewan. I asked him how old he was.

"Sixty-nine." He grinned. I asked him what had brought him to Thailand.

"Pearls." He said. "Bangkok is the City of Treasures gracing the Ocean." I asked him if he was a dealer. He told me he was a disciple, and that he wasn't talking about precious stones, he was talking about the nightlife. I felt a wave of motion sickness, as we turned the last corner to the Democracy Monument.

Like Ewan, the monument was a contradiction of itself. Its commission in 1939, evicted innumerable locals and Chinese shopkeepers, with sixty days notice. The widening of Ratchademnoen Road, to create a ceremonial boulevard, required cutting down hundreds of shade trees, with serious consequences in the days before air conditioning, in Bangkok's torrid climate. The monument was constructed to commemorate a coup that resulted in a military dictatorship, the ideology of which was represented by the panel 'Personification of Balance and Good Life.' Like Ewan, however, the mythical stone Naga snakes at the corners, poised to strike, more realistically portrayed its essence.

Dominique had arranged for us to share a room, and Ewan pointed me in the direction of her hotel, down the backpacker ghetto of Khao San Road, the Place to Disappear, *a short road with the longest dream in the world.*

"Sawatdee!" Said the desk clerk, before asking me to pay, as she apparently hadn't. Upstairs, I unlocked the door to find a mattress in a box. There was a man in our bathroom.

Richard was from Montreal, and worked for Via Rail. He had an evangelical pattern of speech, something a little difficult to tolerate, given the circumstances. He had just been discharged from a Bangkok hospital with a heart rhythm disorder and, in his discovery of my vocation, was a sudden fascination with my knowledge. It was becoming an obsession when it was suggested that I was tired and hungry.

We went out for noodles and chicken. Richard had a bottle of something back in the hotel room.

"Sabai Sabai." He said. *Happy happy.* Normally a more complex Thai welcome cocktail, Richard's version was a tumbler full of Mekhong whiskey. Mekhong was to whiskey what Colonel Sanders was to Michelin stars. Made from sugar cane and rice, the Thais sometimes mixed it with cobra blood, for longevity. If it worked at all, it must have been the cobra blood. It certainly wasn't working for me that day. I fell asleep quickly.

Dominique was in my bed when I awoke. Richard was gone, but something was not right. I still had my powers of observation. When he did arrive, Richard and Dominique had a long whispered conversation, while I showered. We went across Khao San for breakfast. There I met Farida, a Swiss cynic, losing fast, and Michel, who had taken an overnight bus from Ko Samui, just to meet Dominique. Life is really simple. But we insist on making it complicated. Michel and Richard decided to have an argument over who was going to be the King of Siam. I felt left out, and out, I left. Dominique once told me she wanted to be in my book. I remembered that.

On my quest to find alternative accommodation, I picked up my mail at the Canadian embassy. Among the garden of letters I discovered there was an old reminder from the program director of my Internal Medicine residency. I had forgotten he existed.

> "Where are you going?" We both waited for it.
> "I was thinking of hitchhiking around the World".
> He didn't even blink. "How long do you think you'll need for that?"
> "About five years, give or take".
> Then he paused, and played a bit with his beard.
> "Call me from Bangkok. We'll see what we can do."

I called him from Bangkok. The connection was full of static. He sounded older.

"Have you kept up?" He asked.

"I'm right on schedule." I said.

"That's not what I mean." He said.

"I know what you mean." He told me if I could be back by the beginning of the following July, he would provide me a position as a second year resident.

"Don't make me look bad." He said, and hung up. I may have cried.

A large quiet room would greet me at the Bonny Guest House, but I had to wait hours, for the inhabitant who had arrived in the middle of the night to vacate. When I finally found out that he had left at five that morning, I inherited his wall mirrors and a ceiling fan, spinning air and nihilism.

*   *   *

'As Calcutta smells of death and Bombay of Money, Bangkok smells of sex, but this sexual aroma is mingled with the sharper whiffs of sex and money'

Paul Theroux

Sex and money. I was probably the only white male traveler in Bangkok destined to leave without either. Worse, at breakfast, I had to listen to Farida's blithering about what a new age liberated feminist Dominique was. The other guy at the table was an old loud fat smoking drinking belching egotistical Aussie, on his way to North America through every cheap hooker in Thailand. Farida didn't see him lining up on her.

I returned from PJ Travel, after paying for my hundred-dollar flight to Hong Kong, to find Ewan in the Bonny lobby. He had come to tell me it was his seventieth birthday, and he was planning on showing me the seamier side of Bangkok, later that night. I told him I thought I had already seen it. He told me I was wrong.

Patpong Road had started as the Rest and Recuperation hub of the Vietnam War cartwheel. Its name came from the family that owns much of the area's property, the Patpongpanich family of Chinese immigrants from Hainan Island, who purchased a plot of land on the outskirts of the city, in 1946. The original small canal and a teakwood house were connected by road to shophouses, which they rented out. By 1968, the bars and explicit sex acts that went on inside had driven away the other businesses. Ewan assured me that I had never seen anything like it. Bus 201 took an hour an hour to get us there, and two decades to get me back. Ewan prepared me for what was to come by describing the activities that went on in the red light district. Most Patpong go-go bars featured women dancing on a stage. The dancers (and occasionally the serving staff) were available to customers willing to pay a bar 'fine' to take them out of the establishment; fees for sexual services were negotiated

24

separately. Some places advertising 'massages' were disguised brothels, and a few famous 'blowjob bars' still offered oral sex at the main bar, or in back rooms. Several upstairs lounges still featured illegal sex shows, with women performing exotic feats, involving their genitalia and projectile table tennis balls. Some second-floor nightclubs were run by scam artists, who lured tourists with initial offers of low prices, and later presented a wildly inflated bill, along with a threat of physical harm should it go unpaid. Some Patpong bars employed post-operative transsexual kathoey *ladyboys*. Ewan told me he could tell the difference.

Our first stop was the Pink Panther. *'More than 40 charming hostesses and go go dancers in a relaing atmosphere.'* Inside were numbered table girls, who immediately hung all over us, and fondled anything that looked like an appendage. After seven months in the Indian subcontinent, my senses were unprepared for the onslaught of music, lights, half-naked women, and 35-bhat beers. I looked over at Ewan, and wished I hadn't.

We left for a nearby massage parlor, ushered upstairs in front of two huge plate glass windows, like fathers in a deluxe maternity ward. There were about fifty women in each room, seated on sofa terraces, turning their smiles off and on for each new customer.

"The girls on the left give only a massage." Said Ewan. "Those with the big tits on the right cost a little more."

"How much more?" I asked.

"That depends." He said.

"On what?" I asked.

"On how much more you want."

I left with a strange mixture of fascination and repugnance. It was wilder than Gloria Steinem's worst fears, and my most elaborate fantasies. I was ready to quit, but Ewan had already hailed a cab. The driver took us halfway across Bangkok, to a hotel with neon Thai script.

We were guided into the lobby, the owner snapped his fingers, and twenty women of various ages and states of undress, strutted into our presence.

"I'll take that one." Said Ewan. "The sultry bitch with the fire in her eyes." And then he and the owner looked at me.

"Well, uh, ahem, I mean..." Was all I could muster. The owner started tapping his toes, and rolling his eyes around like a Siamese version of Al Jolson.

"You have to decide, Wink." Ewan said. I almost closed my eyes and pointed, but some of who was on the other side of the room was downright frightening. Hesitantly, I selected a short young girl with coal black hair that fell like a horse's mane below the rest of her. Everyone was suddenly gone, except for Ewan and I, and the two women. And then he and she were too.

"Goodnight, Wink." He said. "Don't hurt her."

"Happy birthday, Ewan." Was all I had. And then we were alone together, truly alone together, in a great room with a soft bed, mirrors on the wall, and a full bath.

Her name was Nim. She was twenty, from Chang Rai, signed up for a year by daddy, who had been surrounded by too many daughters since mama died. Her English was as good as my Thai. She disappeared, and I was almost relieved. But she returned in fifteen minutes, with three kinds of soap, shampoo, baby powder, massage oil, toothbrushes, toothpaste, and other fragrant packets I didn't recognize.

She put me in a tub of hot water, and sang to me, and shampooed my hair, and bathed me, and giggled, and powdered me, and put me to bed with a romantic Thai comic book, while she showered. Nim returned with Goosebumps, and snuggled next to me. And then we both simply fell asleep. And that was fine.

When we both awoke later, we read her comic book together. In one of the frames was a starfield with Orion. I told her about its cartwheels, and Aye-Aye's Burmese story of the three nodes of bamboo separating lovers as the belt stars.

26

"Dao Kharn Sarm Tar." She said. *Three-joint Bamboo Shaft Star.*
It was the same story in Thailand, except that the heroine's
name was Upem, the 'most beloved child of father.' As it was
all over the world. Romeo and Juliet. And we tried, slow and
sweet, but she was either too small or I wasn't. And that
didn't matter either.

I left her at dawn, wandering aimlessly through waking
Bangkok, watching markets thaw, motorcycles hatch, and the
morning sun catch fire. I finally gave in and caught a bus
back, to a wink from Bonny, and an omelet and coffee. I
spent the rest of the day retrieving my plane ticket to Hong
Kong, mailing my Burmese souvenirs home, and playing
guitar with the Bangladeshis next door.

Mold growth is ubiquitous in Bangkok, but the locals simply
ignore it. Like the sex and the money, and the angels, and the
most beloved child of father.

> "One night in Bangkok and the world's your oyster
> The bars are temples but the pearls ain't free
> You'll find a god in every golden cloister
> And if you're lucky then the god's a she
> I can feel an angel sliding up to me."
> Murray head, *One Night in Bangkok*

*   *   *

Men grow old, pearls grow yellow, there is no cure for it.
Chinese Proverb

I landed in the world's most vertical city, vertically. The flight from Bangkok was breathtaking.

Air Lanka's L-ten-eleven TriStar had conjured up cool towels, wine, duck, beans, potatoes, a roll with Danish butter, smoked ham salad, cake, two coffees, and a brandy. I had my own music console. But the breathtaking part was what the pilot had to do, to land across the Pearl River Delta, in the Pearl of the Orient.

The old Kai Tak airport was ranked the 6th most dangerous in the world. Runway 13 was infamous, reclaimed from Kowloon Bay, and the only way in and out. Skyscrapers and rugged mountains rose to the north. Victoria Harbour, and then more mountains surrounded the other three sides. The pilot took a descent heading northeast, passing over the crowded port, and the densely populated area of Western Kowloon. He found a small hill marked with a red and white checkerboard, made a precise 47° visual right turn, to line up with the runway at a height of 650 feet, and exited this 'Hong Kong Turn' low altitude crab angle at 140 feet, on a final approach, through northeast gusty mountain crosswinds and typhoons, without an instrument landing system. The *feng shui* was all wrong, but the glimpses of the flickering of televisions, though the apartment windows we flew by, were wild. The intercom breathed a sigh.

"Welcome to the Pearl." He said.

The pearl appeared to have a few flaws. After being robbed with a hidden commission at the moneychanger, I got on the wrong bus, and came face-to-face with Cantonese hospitality. I asked for directions, and received only raised noses and index fingers. There may have been some lingering resentment, from the British squeezing their Qing Dynasty opium receptors, two hundred years earlier. I began to take random buses, until the third one, 5C, took me right down

Nathan Road, Lieutenant-Colonel Matthew, second son of Jonah and Miriam Jacob.

The driver let me off where he thought I wanted to go, the Kowloon Walled City at 36-44. *Chungking Mansions.*

Built in 1961, Chungking Mansions was seventeen stories of legend. If Hong Kong was one of the most densely populated areas on Earth, Chungking was one up on Hong Kong. Five blocks of low budget guesthouses, curry restaurants, African bistros, clothing shops, and foreign exchange offices, housed over four thousand inhabitants from over 120 countries, mostly South Asians, Arabs, Nigerians, Europeans, and Americans. It was a postmodern Casablanca under one roof, with fugitives, drug traffickers, illegal aliens, petty criminals, scammers, forgers, gold smugglers, fake roles peddlers, mules, and donkeys. But the building itself was more likely to kill you. The electrical wiring was ancient, the staircases blocked, security nonexistent, conditions unsanitary, and ownership and management structure as labyrinthine as the place itself. Less than four years after I arrived, a fire trapped and killed a Danish tourist. Elevators took fifteen minutes to arrive, and would only take you to even-numbered floors. The bedbugs spoke your language. Public safety was an oxymoron. It was the kind of place you could buy Afghan heroin for your tryst with three illegal sex workers from as many different countries, in a five-dollar room rented by a sari salesman. *The Economist* compared it to the Spaceport Cantina in the original *Star Wars.* None of this mattered to me. It was the cheapest place in town.

By the time I found Travelers Hostel on the 16th floor of "A" block, an obnoxious New Yorker had taken the last good bunk. I got stuck in an overflow closet beside the flickering television, the one blaring the American sitcoms that the he had traveled 13,000 kilometers to watch all night. Like the resident bedbugs, my only other roommate drank my duty free, climbed all over on my bed sheets, and crapped on my copy of *China Off the Beaten Track.*

"Name's Steve." He said. "From Canada. What are you?"
"Embarrassed." I said. And told him to get off my bed. Steve
wore hippie sunglasses with round yellow lenses, in what was
hardly a well-lit space. He had been languishing in Chungking
Mansions for the last five months, summoning the courage to
get on with it.
"I'm going to Tibet to find the secret of eternal life, man."
He said. "Nobody minds if I change the channel, eh?"
Nobody did, except the Yank.
I called home for the first time in five months. My father
answered the phone. He sounded older, and tired.
"Your grandmother died." He said. "I'll let you talk to your
mother." *Nobody minds if I change the channel.* My mother was
gentle, resigned. She made me feel that there was still a better
world to return to, if this one failed to produce the secret of
eternal life. She didn't have to try hard.
I moved out of the Mansions, into a trance and the Princess
Guest House, next morning. The following two days were
taken up with writing letters, getting my Chinese visa, doing
my Chinese laundry, and recharging my depleted nutrients at
the Choi Kun Heung vegetarian restaurant. I went to the
local branch of Credit Suisse, to close the account I had
opened in Bern, twenty months earlier. I would need every
last Swiss franc in it, to get me through China and the rest of
the Far East to Australia, where I hoped to find work. It was
a giant risk, and a bigger secret.
When I finally picked up what was left of the transfer, I
remembered the words of Herr Betrüger.

"Ja, und how much would you like to invest, Herr Winkler?" He asked.
"That depends, Herr Betrüger." I said.
"On what, Herr Winkler?" He frowned.
"On what kind of interest I can expect." I said, assertively. Herr Betrüger
looked stunned.
"Herr Winkler, Vee do not pay you." He said. "You pay us."

I had been planning to continue my odyssey by the skin of

my teeth, but I was now down to my teeth.

After picking up five bucks worth of film, a fifteen-dollar watch, and some coffee and noodles, I hiked Serendipity down to the 'fragrant harbour,' and the Macau dock. The good people of Hong Kong went to Macau to gamble. As did I.

'But in Hong Kong, we don't know how to count. Everything we do is a guess. If you've got the guts, you do it. All of my stuntmen have gotten hurt.'

Jackie Chan

Slow Boat to China

'Pearls around the neck, stones upon the heart.'
Yiddish Proverb

'Out on the briney, with the moon big and shiney
Melting your heart of stone,
I'd love to get you on a Slow Boat to China, all to myself alone.'
Frank Loessner, *Slow Boat to China*

I sailed through the second century on the twentieth. Seven dollars bought me passage on a hydrofoil, streaming to the far side of a flotilla of multi-masted Chinese junks in Kowloon Bay. Two white wakes sprayed out against the misty mountains, on the Jinghai *Mirror Sea* path to Macau.

There was no room at the Vila Jing Jing, so I walked across the country to the Hotel Cantão. It was my first experience with the open screened ceilings between rooms, in Chinese hotels. A thermos full of boiling water, for tea, sat on the night table. It would become a constant expectation at the end of every long day in China.

But I needed to get there first, and I was planning a back door entrance. The bureaucracy that ruled foreign devil *Gwai Lo* ghost man entry to the Middle Kingdom in 1984 was the Chinese International Travel Service, CITS, except it should have begun it with a 'sh.' In China, in 1984, 1984 was still 1984. Solo travel was actively discouraged, yea verily punished, in favor of group tours, and points of entry and exit were rigidly controlled. While it was technically possible for a foreigner with a tourist visa to sneak into the country on a slow overnight boat from Macau, no one had done it. But I was in the Monte Carlo of the Orient, and the dice were mine to throw.

The Portuguese arrived in Macau in 1535, and paid an annual rent of 44 pounds of silver. The name came from what they thought the Chinese were calling it. *Inlet Gates.* These were ones I was looking for.

I started with the CITS in the Metropole Hotel, but it was closed. The three clerks behind the reception desk told me that the only way for me to enter China from Macau was by organized tour with the Friendship Tourist Bureau at the ferry dock. As I turned to leave, one of them wondered out loud in Cantonese. This was followed by immediate, agitated, hushed scolding, from the other two. If a wind comes from an empty cave, it's not without reason. I returned to the desk. "So, it is possible for me to sail overnight to Guangzhou." I said. They looked at each other.

"It is possible, but not recommended." The oldest one said. I asked him why not. He couldn't say. We slapped each other's hands, I patted myself on the back, and left them for the best meal I'd had in a year.

Tucked into a corner table of the Estrella do Mar, was four dollars worth of Macanese ox tail soup, bacalhau, potatoes, kale and egg tart, and a bottle of white wine. It was a place with the kind of atmosphere I intended to breathe forever, if I lived long enough to step off the black line. I returned to echoes of Chinese tones, rising and falling with the fluorescent light migrations, along the screened mesh walls, beginning half way to the ceiling. There came dreams of pandas and pagodas and parchment, garden lanterns and dragons, and rice and tea. I awoke in a drenching sweat, trying to get over the Great Wall. Chairman Mao had been pushing me off.

It was raining torrents next morning and, after pão and café, I sloshed down to the boat dock to see if they would sell me a ticket for the night voyage to mythical Cathay. And, despite the accompanying whispers, they did. I had the rest of the day to explore. I wandered around Fortaleza Monte, St. Pauls, and the Museum. But the most fascinating place of all was the old Protestant Cemetery.

The British East India Company had established it in 1821, in response to a refusal of both the Portuguese and the resident Chinese to accommodate dead heathens. Before the land was purchased, Protestant burials were a secret nocturnal ritual, between the city walls and the barrier gate, and ran the risk of Chinese confrontation or later desecration, if discovered. There were no shortage of rogues, traders and unfortunate seamen. John P. Griffen had died *'By a Fall from Aloft, Age about 35 Years,' and* his gravestone had been *'Erected by his Messmates.'* Then there was R.V. Warren, *'Aged 22 years, Who was Murdered on Board The Schooner "Kappa" By Chinese Whilst on Her way to Whampoa from Macao...'*

I bought a T-shirt that was made in China, before everything else was. *Better to travel 10,000 miles than to read 10,000 books.*

Late in the afternoon, I hoisted Serendipity, a can of mackerel, and a small loaf of fresh pão, down to the wharf where my vessel was tied.

It was March 22, 1984. The cold fog penetrated right through my anorak. I had left Canada three years and eight months behind me, and had met the worst that the planet could throw at a mortal. I was very tired, very lonely, and very broke.

She was called 'Red Star 242.' All the buildings I had seen in these Oriental pearls had been devoid of any identification containing the number 4, due to its similarity to the Cantonese word for 'death.'

But there was one crazy son of a bitch on the waves that night, rocking and rolling in bunk #44, who not only didn't seem to care, but was as high as a hard-winged kite, on a slow boat to China.

'Pearls lie not on the seashore. If thou desirest one thou must dive for it.'
Chinese Proverb

With Its Back to Heaven

'As the port of Canton is the only one at which the Outer Barbarians are permitted to trade, on no account can they be permitted to wander and visit other places in the Middle Kingdom.'

Imperial Edict of 1836

The color of truth is gray. It was the color of the cold dawn, the morning after, and the dreary color the sky would be, throughout the whole of China. Mao had done that. The backyard steel furnaces of Great Leap Forward had eaten the rest of the birdsong, turned the rivers orange, and stirred the sky into soup. Speed kills color. The gyroscope, turning at full speed, looks gray. Like the dirty beach sand on the moon. My celebrity status on the slow overnight boat from Macau, was replaced by the panic of the first Red Guard, who had pushed back the Gold Kazoo covering my face with the muzzle of his Type 56 rifle.

"Gwei Lo!" He shouted to the others. *They said I looked like a foreign devil; they said I spoke like a foreign devil.* I had my passport and visa ready for them. Disarming turned to charming.

I had arrived in Canton on the same South China Sea as all the other *Ghost Men-* the foreign merchants that Huang Chao massacred in 878, the Persian women in the 10th century, the Portuguese in 1514, the Manila Spaniards and Arabs and Indians Muslins by 1690, the French and English soon after, the Ostend General India company in 1717, the Dutch East India Company in 1729, the Danish in 1731, the Swedish East India Company in 1732, the Americans in 1784, and the Australians in 1788. By the mid 18th century, under the Thirteen Factories, Guanzhou had emerged as one of the world's great trading ports, and one of the top three cities in the world.

But I had arrived in the morning mists of 1984, to the sounds of revolutionary martial music and a flotilla of foghorns. I walked out of the port in flip-flops, freezing, with the faint red streak of a throbbing foot infection where the old Munich one had been, drawing a new line up my leg. Poor timing.

The crowds were as colorless as the sky. Old people were exercising in slow motion, amidst the mud and bicycle bells. My gyroscope took me instinctively across to Shamien Island, where I found the Government Service Worker's Hostel, which I understood had just begun accepting ghost men. They wanted to give me my own room. I pulled my empty pockets inside out and they laughed, and put me into the billowing smoke and flying sputum of the worker's dormitory. The Chinese spat everywhere and all the time, even on the rugs. Twenty-five years after I met my roommates, Guangzhou introduced a law that would confiscate homes, from residents caught spitting in public, within a two-year period. But I arrived in the Golden Age of Expectoration. Evil spirits lived in their throats, or maybe they were all just trying to get rid of Mandarin's hard-edged taste.

For six yuán, I was graced with a soft mattress, duvet, towel, and thermos of hot water, but only intermittent ice-cold water out of the taps, in a bathroom that seemed like it had been under construction since the Cultural Revolution.

One of my first words in Mandarin was the one for 'bus.' *Gong gong qi che.* I loved the sound. My good leg took me onto Gong gong qi che #5 to the Civil Air Administration of China (CAAC), to purchase a ticket for a flight to Guilin the following day. I paid for it from the proceeds of a Black Market transaction I had initiated, only minutes earlier outside the Linhia Hotel across the street. The Kenyans would have had him for breakfast. Which is where I inadvertently ended up, in my efforts to find the Huaisheng Mosque.

When I finally pushed my way off Gong gong qi che #7, I was clearly in the middle of nowhere, if that was ever possible in a country of a billion people.

38

My first glimpse of daylight was a sidewalk noodle stand. I hadn't eaten anything since the bread and mackerel of the day before and, despite the strange medicinal smell of the steam coming off the cart, evil spirit saliva began to rise in my throat. I sat on one of the stools. The Golden Horde of Batu Khan was a small garden party, in comparison to the throng that instantly materialized around this tiny soup wagon. The proprietor, with an eye for potential franchise expansion, ladled out a bowl of his finest and, reaching through the toxic cloud coming off his decoction, pulled out an elongated coil of vermilion flesh with a flourish, splashing it quickly into my dish, so as not to burn his fingers too badly. I looked down at a pig penis, and up into the thousand expectant eyes that surrounded me. The owner was clearly proud of his largesse, but I paddled around it, until the crowd deflated.

Heavens opened up on me as I left, but I really wasn't sure what I was being punished for. Whatever the Gods required in the way of propitiation in this People's Republic, was bound to be nasty. I random walked to the rhythm of the pulse in my foot, through pissing rain and bustling commerce, bicycles and buses, sidewalks, animals, and Oriental life. I bought a Frisbee-sized five-cent almond cookie, which dissolved into sand in my mouth. Finally, after a brief interlude in a musical instrument shop, I found one of the oldest mosques in the world. Bare heels protruded out of hunched backsides under the huge angled entrance sign above them. Women were covered in long white shawls.

"Salaam Aleichem." I offered, to the deep-creased, bow-legged, skull-capped old Han Chinese man, guarding the rows of shoes.

"Are you a Moslem?" He asked, in almost flawless English.

"Almost." I replied, and was ushered into an exotic atmosphere of the faithful, kneeling west to Mecca on a Friday afternoon. The Lighthouse minaret was an indisputably Chinese edifice, stark and stubby, poking into the clay-spattered Far Eastern sky, not so unlike the deliberateness of what had protruded from my bowl a few hours earlier.

Hundreds of burning joss sticks smoked around the corner, in the stunning nine stories of the Flower Pagoda, a 180 foot high Buddhist tumescent tower, 200 years older than the mosque's minaret masculinity, and 1500 years older that that of my pig. It belonged to the Temple of the Six Banyan Trees, named by the Song Dynasty poet, Su Shi.

His words came to haunt me later, after dodging bicycles in the crowded streets on the way back to the hostel, after my icy shower, and final almond cookie. My heartbeat pulsed the antibiotics into my swollen leg. I faded in and out of ghostman consciousness, desperately missing my Destiny in Chinese whispers.

> 'I'd like to ride the wind to fly home.
> Yet I fear the crystal and jade mansions
> are much too high and cold for me...
> Why does the moon tend to be full when people are apart?'
> Su Shi, *Shui Tiao Ko Tou*

*   *   *

> 'People's attitudes have been changing over the past 15 years,
> but China is still the world's biggest consumer of dogs.'
> Jill Robinson

Nature abhors a vacuum. For Canton, she held a Golden Age of Execration. The Japanese hadn't helped. They had sucked the life out of 12,000 Chinese men, women, and children and infants, Russian and American POWs, Southeast Asians and Pacific Islanders, in several Kwantung Army Divisions of the Epidemic Prevention and Water Purification Department or, as it became known in Guangzhou, Unit 8604. A special project known as *Maruta*, German for 'medical experiment,' or Japanese for 'log,' was formed, as in 'how many logs fell?' Prisoners were subjected to vivisection without anesthesia, after infecting or traumatizing them. Stomachs and parts of brains, lungs or livers were removed while patients were awake, so as to preserve the experimental purity of the *in vivo* results. Limbs were frozen and thawed to study the natural history of gangrene, or amputation. Extremities were severed to study blood loss, and sometimes reattached to the opposite sides of the body.

Human subjects were tied to stakes and used to test the effects of grenades or flamethrowers at various distances, chemical weapons, or germ-releasing bombs. They were infested with fleas, or inoculated with syphilis, gonorrhea, cholera, anthrax, tularemia, plague, cholera, smallpox, botulism, typhoid, or combinations of the above. Scientists in protective suits would examine the dying subjects. Poisoned candy was given to children.

In other experiments, prisoners were infused with sea water or animal blood or urine or air, spun to death in centrifuges, exposed to lethal x-ray doses or gases or high pressure in various chambers, burned, or buried alive. After the war, MacArthur secretly granted the perpetrators immunity, in exchange for the 'data.' They were still conducting experiments on unwilling Japanese subjects in 1956. It was MacArthur who had once said that 'you are remembered for the rules you break.' Not enough.

But Guangzhou was also the annihilation antechamber of God's other creatures, if what I witnessed in the Qingping market next morning could be believed. Fortunately, I was only able to down a final almond cookie before pushing out into the pouring rain to find it.

My nose arrived first, and filled with the overwhelming stench of body odors and excrement. Creatures live or dead, skinned, freshly gutted dead, dried, and wrapped in newspaper. Chain-smoking street butchers on small stools spat smoke and sputum and prices, beginning at dawn. I roamed through the mobbed alleyways, past a mile of stalls, vending the entire food chain, all the DNA biodiversity they could find. For here was the cradle of one of the finest cuisines in the world, one of the 'Four Great Traditions' of Chinese food. The Cantonese will eat anything with four legs, except the dinner table. An old proverb validates their belief that 'anything that walks, swims, crawls, or flies *with its back to Heaven*, is edible.'

Here, dried bugs were scooped for frying. Scorpion ladies tilted seething barrels of hundreds of black and grey scorpions towards me, looking for a sign to pluck one out with tweezers, and dip him into a hotpot, or roast him alive. Up through the centipedes and starfish and seahorses, and goldfish and carp, and lungfish and shark fins, and frogs and bundled strips of shredded toads, snakes were skinned for roasting, and turtles dismembered for soup. And on to ducks and black chickens and owls and hawks and badgers and pangolins and civets, you could 'have your zoo, and eat it too.'

"Fresh." Said one vendor, pointing to his collection of puppies and kittens. It was likely his only word of English, because it didn't matter.

Dogs hung from hooks in the downpour. I saw one cut in half for an impatient motorcycle helmet. There were *yewei*, 'wild flavor' restaurants, whose patrons believed that eating wild creatures would make them *fan rong*, prosperous. A tiger paw lay in front of me, disconnected.

But Nature still abhorred a vacuum. And as these coarse traders in the endangered and the near extinct pushed the void harder, in the filth and the blood and guts, and the feces and the urine, dripping through the stacked cages of moaning cats and rabbits, she would exact her vengeance with a fury. In November of 2002, a corona virus that had quietly gone from bats to humans to civets through a long period of exposure contact, jumped the cages and species in the

Qingping market. The civets gave it back to the humans, causing 800 deaths, and ten times that number of serious infections. I saw my first case of Severe Acute Respiratory Distress Syndrome (SARS) back in Canada. You are what you eat. If you were eating Cantonese at the beginning of the 21st century, whatever you were swallowing was going down with its back to heaven.

"Where did Orion come from, Uncle Wink?" Asked Sam.

"Well, isn't that just the question, Sam?" Said Uncle Wink. "To speak of where they, and the other stars and galaxies, and life, in the Universe came from, we needed a man with no nose."

"Who was that?" Millie asked.

"His name was Gaston Julia, Mil." Said Uncle Wink. "He was struck by a German bullet in the face in 1915 and, after many unsuccessful and painful operations, he resigned himself to the loss, and wore a leather strap across his face for the rest of his life. From his hospital bed he carried on his work in the mathematics of chaos, which later developed into the Mandelbrot set, and the ability to precisely model the entire natural world algebraically. The universe is fractal at all scales. All matter and skeletal structures are assembled from nanotubular blocks, as cartwheels and tubules, from subatomic dust and electrical discharges to hail and tornado formation to the billion-ton clouds of gas that make up solar coronal flares, and the crab nebula. They are all the product of fractal dynamic fields."

"So how does that explain where stars come from?" Sam asked.

"When massive stars explode as supernovas, they leave behind neutron stars and black holes. The black holes, or quasars, are fractal generators, and like Shiva, are creators and destroyers. They produce their future host galaxies through something called jet-induced star formation."

"Are there any black holes producing baby stars in Orion?" Mille asked.

"Yes, Mil." Said Uncle Wink. "A whole nursery full."

Songs of the South

'Witness the man who raves at the wall
Making the shape of his questions to Heaven.'
Pink Floyd, *Set The Controls For The Heart Of The Sun*

Abandonment and personal isolation. That was what had impelled Roger Waters to create *The Wall* for Pink Floyd. But it had been the suicide of the poet who originally raved at it, that had incarnated dragon boat races, 2300 years before breast cancer was survivable, and Roger felt anything. His rant was of abandonment and personal isolation, and broken China.

My flight to Guilin took off with a complementary handkerchief, boiled sweets, and a foil bag of lychee nectar, mislabeled as orange juice. Two CITS agents herded me onto a tourist bus into town, and tried to steer me into the most expensive hotel. Instead, I hobbled my healing foot to the Kweilin hotel lobby, where an elderly German named Stephan, offered me the other bed in his room, for what I had paid in Guangzhou.

Stephan had been in the Hitler youth, a radioman on the Bismarck, a refugee in Danzig, and a Bundesrepublic accountant until his retirement, whereupon he converted his Deutschmarks to Buddhism, yoga, meditation, and naturopathy. He gave lotions and an abrasive salve for my foot. It may have done some good. In appreciation, I bought him a dinner of deep-fried dofu and beer, and fell unconscious listening to a German revving the dharma wheel, like he was driving it on the autobahn.

I had come to Guilin to get to Yángshuò, famed for its *karst* limestone peaks, rising like dragon's fangs along the Li River. Whenever my parents would take us out to eat, in the only Chinese restaurant in my Northern Ontario hometown, I always got to sit under the large traditional "ink-and-wash" brush painting of a landscape so exotic, that I couldn't possibly believe it was on the same planet. It had come from an imagination that had painted the essential poetry of Nature into a shifting perspective of tranquility and timelessness. Below the carbon calligraphy was a scarlet seal, like an eye of a dragon. Traditional brush landscapes originated here, around the same time that our poet was raving at the wall, when silk was giving way to paper, in the Era of the Warring States, in the 3rd century BC.

I needed to see isolated tower peak forests and *fengcong* link-based tower peak clusters of the karst landscape, to see if it was real, and to see if it would evoke the same peaceful foreign feeling that it had over my Chow Mein, two decades and half a world away.

Stephan handed me some almond cookies as I left next morning. Two friendly cloisonné dealers from Peking burned out my English-Mandarin dictionary, and warmed the bus, through the misted limestone pinnacles. I found a three-bed dorm in an unnamed *fàndiàn* guesthouse, and set out to find sustenance and scenery. Both were authentic. For a dime, I ate a bowl of meaty soup and a string of dried tofu.

The most spectacular karst topography in the world, for the brushstrokes I was enamored with, possessed four fundamental characteristics. It was hard, compact carbonate Devonian limestone. Second, it had come from the strong uplift collision of India with Asia, to form the Himalaya. Third, it had a Monsoon climate of high moisture during the warmest season. And finally, the area had never been scoured by glaciers. The magical mountaintop pagoda high above me was the same one I had sat under, growing up wondering, in the Ho Ho Café.

There was a Dane in my room when I returned. Jens owned a farm in Jutland. His welfare cheques paid for his travel. He had just returned from an excursion, with embroidery from the old Kingdom of Dali, and Mongolian silk from the Ta'ersi Tibetan monastery, near Xining. I filed the names away.

Jens had already left when I awoke. In his place, in the lobby, was Lars, a Swedish journalist I had briefly met in Hong Kong. We treated it as a fated event, and agreed to meet after I changed my accommodation. The friendly Xi Fang Hotel was so new, I spent some time helping them correct the English spelling of the sign they were hanging in the lobby.

After a breakfast soup, Lars and I hiked off into the drizzle, thinking we were on the road to Wuzhou. Miles of truck dodging through wet mud brought us to the realization that we were headed back towards Guilin. Retreating all the way back to breakfast, we waited over noodles, until the torrential rain lifted to a downpour.

We stopped briefly, to watch two old men sculpting characters into a gravestone, and arrived under a thousand year-old Banyan tree, where we took a pole-propelled boat across a pond, and a trek to and through a cave, to admire the view of a village set among the jagged karst outcroppings. The cave was actually a barn, and Lars and I skied through mountains of soft hay to break our descent. Faded red Red Guard graffiti stood out on muddied whitewashed brick walls in the village. Sewage ran down both drains lining our alleyways. A large white pig with a black head poked his snout out of the door of one of the houses as we passed. The ferryman haggled unpleasantly for our return trip, so we made a circuitous escape to Moon Mountain, to a wide arch with a semicircular hole punched through it. Lars said it was also called 'Immortal Hill,' and we could climb it. I told him that, in my flip-flops in the deluge, there wouldn't be much immortal about it.

A water buffalo came rampaging across our path along the banks of one of the rice paddies, with two young village girls in pursuit, clutching their *du lì* bamboo hats to their heads, as they ran.

We returned to Yángshuò through the market. A young Mao-suited patent medicine vendor entertained with a herd of trained rats, which he rotated on a turntable, it hub spinning around inside a large glass bottle. Another stall was manufacturing Ming coins, while you waited. There were card sharks and booksellers and profound poverty, and a painful, unhygienic dentist, climbing immortal hills. Lars and I bought a couple of thousand year-old oranges, and returned to the Xi Fang, to make Nescafé on my stove, and played the first of many tournaments, on my Sudanese chess set. We ate pork and edible fungus in a nearby local eatery later, antagonized by an Italian vagrant, who raved about living on the dole for two years in Vancouver. And I was the Wall.

Lars and I had rented bikes to explore the countryside next morning, but the continuing deluge flooded us into the noodle shop, to play chess, discuss philosophy, peruse the execution posters, and discuss philosophy some more.

The sun arrived as we left Yángshuò the following day. The rain had glistened the countryside into a watercolor. We climbed on top of the roof of a flat-bottomed sampan that lifted us back in time, and down the slate blue ribbon of the Li River, flowing south along a mountain spine of jade hairpins. Volcanic yellow sprays of bamboo erupted out of its banks. Farmers followed their water buffalo. Women kneeled on the foreshore, washing clothes. An old fisherman with a wisp of a white beard, poled a flat bamboo raft, and wrestled the outstretched necks and beaks of his cormorants, for the fish they had surfaced with. Animal forms jumped out of the geology, from a landscape of giant cliff turtles, leaping stone frogs, and galloping horses. There were waterfalls. Another sampan, a Persian slipper draping laundry over its layered decks, passed us, leaving the sonorous scratching from the two strings of an *erhu* bowed zither, reverberating across the oiliness, in its wake. We drank tea.

"China." I said to Lars.

"Spectacular." He said, and plugged my head into the Walkman he had just bought in Hong Kong. Faure's *Pavane* floated me past rice fields and rust clay villages, and downstream to some of the most tranquil moments of my odyssey. The sun glided sideways onto our landing in Yanti.

Lars and I decided to push on to Guilin. The boat crew pointed to a forlorn looking piece of communist metal sculpture idling on the jetty. We were on it before we realized we were for it. A Mao-capped Blue Meanie climbed over the back 40, to where we had found the last two seats. She introduced us to the most important word in Mandarin.

"Meiyou!" She shrieked, the last syllable nose-diving into a fiery crash. She seized with indignation, almost uncontrollably, at our inertia, and her increasing inability to change it. A Mao cap seated next to us translated what he could.

"She say this bus is for workers only." He said.

"He's a worker." I said, pointing to Lars.

"She say this bus go to Yángshuò, not Guilin." He said.

"OK. We'll go to Yángshuò." Said Lars.

"She say you pay 5 yuán." He said.

"We'll pay the driver." I said. Our smiles stayed rigidly polite, until the driver returned. Flicking his cigarette out of the entrance he had just climbed, he turned over the engine, closed the door, and whipped a face around to us.

"Guilin?" He grinned, lit up another fag, and pulled off into the mountains and dusk.

The Chinese word for karma is 'ye.' Ten kilometers outside Guilin, the Blue Meanie's *ye* gushed oil from under the engine cowling, all over her. Smoke began flying out of the radiator.

"Zài jiàn." We said, the final tone falling with us, as we vacated the stairwell. My thumb carved an arc as an initial maneuver outside the bus. A Guilin-bound coal truck slowed long enough for Lars and I to climb on. He looked at me in awe. I blew on my thumb, and saw him smile.

We looked back to find two Chinese girls running to join us. Except for the back muscles we put into it, pulling them onto the coal bed, they would have split their heads, on the abandonment and personal isolation racing under us.

"China." I said to Lars.

"Spectacular." He said.

*　　*　　*

'公看呵壁書問天。
Plain though it is, I fear that you still doubt me.
Witness the man who raved at the wall
as he wrote his questions to Heaven.'
Li He, *Don't Go Out of the Door*

Roger Waters got his Pink Floyd line from a demonic genius that had written about our wall-raving suicide poet over a millennium later. Li He's poetry was tightly woven and extremely emotional. He had been excluded from civil examinations because a Chinese character in his father's name had the same sound as the character for the name of the exam. Naming taboos were common in the Tang dynasty, like the naming of G-d had been for Hebrew scribes. By the age of 26, Li He was writing his questions in Heaven.

The Blue Meanie's cousin was the bluebird of happiness. Her name was Jane and she was the Alice Capone of Guilin. She owned the hotel, the restaurant in which Lars and I were eating our hot and sour soup, and the travel commission business that was busy getting us tickets for the 36-hour train trip to Kunming the following evening. Jane put us in a three-bed room with an Austrian, whose tobacco consumption finally lost the race to his mouth with his *Sanhua jui baijiu* rice fragrance 'Three Flower' liquor ingestion. *Let a hundred flowers bloom, let a hundred schools of thought contend.* Little by little the night turned around.

Jane presented us with tickets for two hard seats, over our noodles next morning. Lars complimented her on the taste.

"Horse meat." She said.

"Spectacular." I added.

"China." Said Lars.

We left her, past the Lala Café, with its own caged zoo outside, down springtime streets lined with Sweet Osmanthus trees. The mist turned to rain, as Lars and I came upon an iconic scene. In the foreground drizzle of a gray concrete station on a gray cement plaza, were a dozen men, in blue pants and olive green jackets and Mao caps, running hoses in tight formation between carmine colored fire trucks.

"Chinese fire drill." I said to Lars. In the early 1900's, the original pejorative meaning of the term had originated from an actual fire drill, on a ship staffed by British officers and a Chinese crew. The bucket brigade had drawn water from the starboard side, and threw it onto the fire in the engine room. A separate crew hauled the accumulated water to the main deck, and heaved it over the port side. When the orders became confused in translation, the bucket brigade began to skip the intermediate step, and threw the water they had taken from the starboard side overboard on the port side, without passing through the engine room at all. It was a metaphor for the way I was going travel through the Middle Kingdom.

Gong gong qi che #3 took us, and most of the rest of Yunnan province, to the Reed Flute Cave, an amazing underground labyrinth of surrealistic limestone drippings, perverted by the immense size of our Chinese tour group, the gaudy colored spotlights, and the appellations of the individual formations. In the poetic vernacular of China, the Crystal Palace, the Dragon Pagoda, the Virgin Forest, and Flower and Fruit Mountain, could have been stalactites, fireworks, or heroin.

Back at the Lala, I changed traveler's cheques, and took on new company. Annie was a 28 year-old English rose, with thorns of palmistry, astrology and homeopathy. She had a deep conviction about everything but the rational, and desperate to provide the scientific proof of it. We backtracked to Jane's hotel, and found that Lars had acquired a new American friend, Michael, a 35 year-old Southerner, whose travel stories were more Midwestern corn. We all left together for the North Station, to find our hard seats.

China Rail's promotional posters of their most recent train wreck carnage didn't improve the dark macabre that pervaded the place. My attempt to brighten it with some harmonica blues lasted until the battle began.

Shunted into the hard seat section of the train, as it chugged to a stop, our Gang of Four gravitated to the dining car, in an attempt to escape the expectorating multitude in our designated carriage. The Chinese bureaucratic standoff that ensued was only resolved by our taking soft sleepers for the student price of six times what it first cost me at the Government Service Workers Hotel in Guangzhou. We shared a four-berth compartment, with Lars and Michael up top, and Annie and I below on the lower bunks. We spent until 3 am in the corridor, discussing our avowed philosophies and celibacies. And then we returned to our soft sleepers, and didn't sleep. On my stove, I made Nescafé for me, and tea for her. And threw them over the side without passing through the engine room at all. In the quest for life's essences, hypocrisy is the homage that vice pays to virtue.

My right eye opened first, into a six year old face of mischief and devilry. She was taking my picture, with my camera, and had already appropriated Lars' Walkman, Michael's writing material, and Annie's heart. No one knew how this China Doll had invaded our compartment, or whom she belonged to. Her ragged black bangs jiggled as she laughed, and she was always laughing, in a high hoarse whinny. Her front teeth were silver, and the rest of her was all peasant piss and vinegar. Despite the protestations of the three males, Annie adopted her for the rest of the train trip. Michael and Lars and I had no choice but to teach her how to play poker. Not that she needed lessons. Her grandfather did come to claim her that evening, and Annie and I continued our chaste chitchat, until Lars and Michael were asleep again. We came onto the southern Silk Road.

"China." I said.

"Spectacular." She agreed.

The conductor woke us at dawn, but we didn't pull into the lake and limestone hills of Kunming until around seven. Marco Polo knew the Yachi Fu people to have used cowrie shells for cash and eaten their meat raw.

We took Gong gong qi che #2 to the Green Park Hotel. A score of ancient Chinese were moving in Tai Chi slow motion outside. We ate plum pastries and eggs and lychees and mandarins, but there was no vacancy. We met Barbara, a 30 tear old barmaid from Toronto at the Kunming Hotel. This was too expensive so we all crammed into the scuzzy four-yuán dorm at the Kun Fu, for hot bucket baths.

A human amphitheatre of spectators encircled a street performer strongman, on our way to secure permits to visit Dali. We watched him prepare to perform his feats, but he never actually got around to it. The situation wasn't much different in the Public Security Office, until I suggested we were actually more interested in traveling to Tibet. The Dali permits materialized within minutes.

We drew straws to see who would have the privilege of buying bus tickets for the Gang of Five at the Western Bus Station. I got the short one, and Annie and I waited almost an hour to buy passage to Xioguan, which was as close as we could get. When we got back to the Kun Fu, the dorm and luggage had been rearranged, and Lars and Michael and Barbara were gone.

Annie and I went out for *guò qiáo mǐxiàn* Over the Bridge Rice Noodles, a chicken soup dish under a thin layer of oil or, in our case, a thick layer of grease under thick walls of concrete. It had been invented by the wife of a student studying for the imperial exams on an island a short way from his village. She discovered that she could keep his food hot by layering the broth with oil. The others similarly layered when they reappeared back at the dorm after midnight. I didn't tell them that their bus trip to Dali was going to be twelve hours long.

Annie and I mustered them mightily next morning, and almost missed the bus. They fell asleep with their heads nodding in free space, moments after we pulled out of Kunming. We passed rice paddies and flowered fields, curvilinear roofed houses and monasteries, and up the Cangshan mountain passes, along the winding road to Xiguan. A station attendant guided us through staring throngs, and onto another bus, which ground along beside Erhai Lake for one more hour, until we pulled up at the majestic and quintessentially Chinese old South Gate of the ancient city.

*   *   *

'Ere light and darkness merged in space, Who can fathom what took place? That great axle could suspend? Who the planets' course defines? Or who chose the zodiac signs? Set the sun and moon on high? Constellations hung nearby?'

Qu Yuan, *Heavenly Questions*, in *Songs of the South*

The man who raved at the wall, who inspired Li He to inspire Roger Waters, was a lawmaker and poet who lived around 300 BC, in the Era of the Warring States.

Seven kingdoms had been fighting for dominance of the known world. Located in a Yangtze valley area of exotic plants and shamanistic religion, on the fringes of Chinese civilization, Chu was the southernmost.

It was ruled by King Huai, more interested in women and alcohol, than preserving his realm from the aggressive designs of the northwest dusty warlike state of Qin. Qu Yuan was a court minister who tried to influence his ruler into forming an alliance with other threatened states, and acting against Qin. Like most human hierarchies, however, Huai's court was rife with corrupt and jealous political rivals, who maliciously slandered and undermined Qu Yuan. King Huai listened to them, and banished Qu Yuan to the north shore of the Han River.

During this exile, Qu Yuan wrote some of the greatest poetry in Chinese literature, in an expression of his fervent love for his country and concerns for its future, and the hope of bringing Huai to his senses. Instead, the king, deceived into attending a summit meeting with the Qin ruler, was killed, and a third of Chu was invaded.

Huai's son, Xiang, ascended the throne, reclaimed the lost territory, and reappointed Qu Yuan to a prominent position. But the acorn hadn't fallen far from the tree, and King Xiang became increasing involved with women and alcohol. His court intrigue conspired against Qu Yuan once more. This time, when the Qin king invaded Chu, he spun it into terminal decline.

Qu Yuan was heartbroken, and wrote a series of patriotic poems, in response to his betrayal. These became the main constituents of the classic *Chu Ci* anthology, 'Songs of the South.' At the age of 62, he waded into the Miluo River holding a great rock, and committed ritual suicide. The townspeople went out in their boats, combing the river in a vain effort to find and rescue him, beating drums, splashing paddles, and throwing silk-wrapped rice dumplings into the water as an offering, to distract fish and dragons and serpents and evil sprits, away from his body. They were too late, but ever since, on the fifth day of the fifth month of every year, dragon boat festivals around the world commemorate the anniversary of his suicide.

Prior to his abandonment and personal isolation, Qu Yuan had always believed that Heaven decided a man's destiny on the basis of his moral character. Qu Yuan had acted not only as the instrument between the perfect way of the ancient kings and the ideology of the state, but as the actualization of his individual character. When he was cast adrift, the reliability of the perfect way of the ancient kings and the ideology of the state came under scrutiny, as did his identity as the medium. After his treacherous exile trials, Qu Yuan began to doubt the foundation faith in the inherited concept of cosmological justice, a skepticism that moved his worldview from religion to rationality.

Qu Yuan's 'Heavenly Questions' demanded 173 answers to new uncertainties about the universe, the creation of the heavenly bodies, the earth, nature, myths and legends, and historical events.

The poet's 'raving questions' were written on the walls of the shrines of former kings and the ancestral halls of the nobles of the state of Chu. In the time that Qu Yuan was thinking about the meaning of existence, of the Cosmos and life and love, he received no answers. But after 2300 years, and over three and a half years on the road, I was converging on them. There were two other conclusions I was closing in on, when we arrived at the fandian inside the South Gate. The first was that the China Doll had broken my camera. I was in one of the most picturesque villages in Yunnan, the site of the ancient Kingdom of Nanzhou, and my Olympus XA was as dead as a Qingping dog. The second was the rate of intensity developing with Annie. I pulled back, and arranged a three-bed dorm with Barb as a buffer. She asked me if I really wanted the company. I told her I did. This required an explanation for Annie, who was upset at the unplanned twist in the tryst. It was the first of April. I told her that I was a fool. In the absence of walls, she raved at me.

The next morning was peaceful and quiet. Annie had forgiven me, and she and Barb and I went down to the Garden restaurant for a greasy approximation of hash browns and eggs, before setting off between the Yunnan pure white marble, fenestrated fences, veined with red, light blue, green and milky yellow, along the path to the two lions guarding the Southern Gate entrance to the 'scented wonderland' of the Old City. The magnificent roof projections above us stood ready to spear any evil spirits contemplating a landing on the bow shaped crossbeams, open-carved gargoyles or close-mouthed travelers below.

Down ancient cobbled streets, we passed whitewashed walls with inset black tile paintings of animals and other natural images, dark elegant clay sculpture, woodcarvings, stone inscriptions, and marble screens. Potted bonsai and pink geraniums lined up on their high edges. Banks of three-tiered small windows flowed along the second stories of old brick and wood buildings, with screen walls of brick and stone, and sloped tiled roofs, sagging in the middle with antiquity, above open shops below.

Ink brush paintings jumped off black house doors, their top and side lintels streamed auspicious with pink paper calligraphy, and blood red notices on adjacent white walls. Propaganda paintings and posters of ethnic women broadcast their primary colors from the bulkhead panels of the government office, to discourage any raving at their wall.

The bamboo that bends is stronger than the oak that resists, and everything useful and used in Dali, like the women, was made of bamboo. Yoked baskets bounced hundreds of pounds on small shoulders. Women pulled two wheeled carts with beds of large horizontal woven bamboo cylindrical baskets, full of produce. Woven bamboo sleeves protected the bark of young tree trunks. Bai ladies lined up at the common water tap, carrying box basket backpacks as large as they were, like they could have harvested whole vineyards in Provence.

The snow, the moon, the flower, and the wind- their costume incorporated their symbols. They wore blue and pink wrapped fringed cloth headwear, festooned with red pompoms. Their trousers were blue and loose, their sleeveless jackets were trimmed with red, blue or black collars, and their dresses and cloth belts and shoes were all made from embroidered white cloth. Tibetan tones were set off with silver bracelets and earrings.

We walked by the beauty parlor, containing a spaceport of stationary head top hairdryers that could have been a vacuum cleaner showroom. Street sweepers used large straw brooms with no handles, in wide strokes.

The sound of argument told us we were approaching the market. We turned a corner into a street of stacked hand-cut firewood, the thin horses that had brought it, loose chickens, and tribal raiment. I approached a young Bai woman, wearing a beautiful apron, and complimented her on it in Mandarin.

"Piào liàng." I said. *Elegant and bright.* A crowd formed. How much was I willing to pay? I told them I was just admiring the brilliance of her embroidery. The crowd divided into two factions. What would be my best offer? Neither she nor I had much say in the ensuing proceedings. One camp argued for the time and work she had put into its creation, and the mastery of the result. My side pointed out the social correctness of the compliment, and the decorum that should govern the final price. For 22 yuán, a cultural genocide was enacted. I now have an apron off the loins of a Bai woman from Dali, and all the guilt that comes with it.

We left the throngs in the market to meet up with Lars and Michael, at the Garden Restaurant. The owner and his family made fun of my apron, and supplied steaming plates of tofu stew, and sweet and sour pork. I looked off into the rows of conforming communes in the shadow of the Cangshan Mountains on the horizon, and wondered what they were having for dinner.

My camera was dead, but I still had a roll of Ektachrome. Annie loaned me her camera for a couple of hours early next morning, so I could create a photographic memento of Dali. There were Bai women carrying loads of straw so large you couldn't see them. A dust storm swirled around the South Gate, as I tried to draw its essence. Edges blunted, peaks eroded, stars fell, and dream mists cleared, like a pocket watch melting over a branch of the old Banyan tree. In the need for my own salvation, I found a Salvador in Dali.

Clay feet, brains and tongues made it to the spider-eyes bus, lying in wait at the South Gate early next morning. I had discovered a trove of the same hawthorn flakes that had sustained me during medical school, and distributed them to our cadre. *Eternally vigilant is our motto.* But a bottle of what I though was grape juice, turned out to be a bad Chinese version of wine. The short furry American Rasputin sitting behind me commandeered it, and with far too rapid consumption, his neurosis began travelling faster than the rest of us.

The driver dropped us back in Kunming, where Mao's statue used to stand. We checked into the Kunming hotel, and the most luxurious suite of my odyssey. There were quicksand beds, mirrors, flasks of tea, towels, carpets, and a bathroom with a European toilet and the most singularly imaginable feature of all- a bathtub with hot running water. I spent the rest of the day in it, playing with the taps, the fir trees on my fingertips, and cleaning everything I owned, over and over again. When it isn't clear if you'll get another chance, a man needs to stock up. Barb swears she heard me, raving at the wall.

Stone Forest

'Where is the forest that has grown from stone?'
Qu Yuan

The dragon boat suicide poet knew of our destination, 2300 years before we got there. Unlike Qu Yuan, we took the bus, stopping once in a poor and paranoid and polluted factory town of dread, and a second time across the bridge from Shilin. It had taken four hours and a bag of biscuits, to reach the four-yuán dormitory on the edge of the Stone Forest, and the high water mark of my desperation.

A photographic record of my odyssey was not of much importance to me at the time. I was on a vision quest of another kind, and it really didn't occur to me that the pilot light of my memory would flicker dim as I grew older. My Buddhist bent wasn't interested in preserving images, and I confess that I harbored no small contempt for those fellow travelers who were preoccupied with its art and science, choosing to believe that they were trading the actual living experience for a second hand static record of their camera's two-dimensional optics. Strangely, therefore, how my Luddite clumsiness would eventually make those few poor images I did collect all the more valuable and evocative. But I knew enough, on the edge of the Stone Forest, to realize that looking through a viewfinder made me think about what I was seeing. I needed a new camera and, despite how easily the China Doll had broken my Panamanian Olympus XA rangefinder, and the bad judgment the first one demonstrated by being stolen in Belize, I loved the machine, and yearned for another.

I posted a notice on the corkboard in the dorm lobby.

Wanted to Buy
35mm single lens reflex camera. Mine is dead and I'm desperate.
Room 209, Block #7
Wink

The answer was under my appeal, when I awoke next morning.

How many do you want?
Mao

Written by a Swedish couple, Leif was a self-employed computer geek, and his girlfriend, Uke, a pretty medical student. She brought out their extra camera. It was an Olympus XA.

The cheap flip-flops that had served me well enough from the Indian subcontinent through Southeast Asia had become a dangerous frugality in the cold wet spring of the Chinese mainland. Soggy chilblains had accompanied my ankle sprains, overpronation injuries, tendonitis, strap friction ulcers, and stubbed toes, and feet that were never warm. But none of this would compare to the trauma that was about to be inflicted by the sadistic razor sharp South China karst of the Stone Forest.

Four hundred years after Qu Yuan, another poet committed suicide in middle age, also after writing *On the Nature of the Universe*. Between fits of insanity, halfway around the world, Lucretius observed the fall of dropping water wearing away and hollowing out stone. It had been wearing away the limestone here, for 270 million years.

Every step by step of my steep ascent, past countless precipitous drops into infinity, along the precarious path to the panoramic perch of Darth Vader basalt peaks and pinnacles, was paid for with sudden deep gashes into rubber and flesh, sliced by the water-honed rock. My Barefoot Doctor feet were a mess at the top.

But the magnificence of the 350 square kilometers of petrified tree stalagmites emanating from the ground, tens of meters high, had been worth the climb.

In 1712, the early Qing Dynasty Annual of Lunan Prefecture described the landscape as well and as vividly as I found it.

'...numerous grotesque stone pillars standing densely, looking like a large contingent of troops; the suspended rocks and notches are breathtaking. Dark gray in color, the delicately structured stone forests are extensive. There are also subterranean rivers, cool and tranquil.'

According to legend, the forest was the birthplace of Ashima, a beautiful local Yi girl. After falling in love, she was forbidden to marry her chosen suitor, and instead turned into a stone in the forest that would bear her name. *The observer, when he seems to himself to be observing a stone, is really, if physics is to be believed, observing the effects of the stone upon himself.* Her stone was a monument to a lover's quarrel with the world.

An old weathered wrinkled woman sweeping the narrowest pass left us laughing, whipping out her embroidery and toothless smile as Barb and I approached.

We all met for the 'Yi People dinner and dance show' after sunset. The set dinner served to the Gwei Lo travelers was paltry enough by itself, but the sumptuous feast enjoyed by the Overseas Chinese at the next table made our meager rations look like the Great Chinese famine. We had apparently paid for the dancing, but this was undernourished as well. Thin costumed Yi grinning puppet girls spun and whined like robotic floor polishers gone berserk, while their male partners mechanically bobbed in place, shy and nervous, and clearly wanting to be somewhere else. The performance, even with the moth-eaten lion, went on far too long, but the well-fed Hong Kong crowd ate it up as well, competing for position with their telephoto tumescences. The sign on the back of our dorm door summarized our status most eloquently.

Notice
Please check out before 8:30 am or you will be punished.

A street stall noodle breakfast set the mood for our ramble through Shilin village next morning. Ramshackle thick-walled orange mud brick huts, garlanded with long strings of drying chilies and corncobs, lined streets of pigs' feces and pantless snotty-nosed children, and an aura of overwhelmingly resigned destitution. We recognized some of the Yi male dancers from the night before the way we had recognized the restaurant waitresses as the female dancers. They were dressed in same clothes they had worn the previous night, and invited us into a their houses, to drink lychee juice, and browse the embroidery they sold to survive. It was a Special Economic Zone.

The desk clerk back at the Kunming Hotel was named Mr. Li. He greeted us warmly, and gushed effusively over the Canadians. I asked him if he had been to Canada. "Only in my dreams." He said. We invited him to the dorm, to play his guitar. He brought his understudy, Jerry. Mr. Li sang *Edelweiss*, like Captain Georg Ludwig van Trapp would have, if he had been Julie Andrews. I sang *Hotel California*. He and Jerry were horrified.

We had two more days in Kunming before our night train would take us to Chengdu. The next evening bathed us in the last warm milk of the common man in China, a traditional Kunming teahouse, where tobacco and tea and tones and tunes washed over the congregation. Before Mao had shut them down, *cháguǎn* teahouses had been the neighborhood pubs of the Middle Kingdom, dens of poetry and debate, precisely why Mao shut them down. The one that Barb and Lars and Annie and I stumbled onto, may have outlived Mao because of its slow heartbeat. Caged crickets chirped in a corner. Old men played board games, ate kilos of sunflower seeds, and smoked black cheroots, planted upright in ancient brass and bamboo opium pipes. Each guest had his own vacuum bottle, cup and green tea, and paid for his hot water out of a little window. We were given seats, new boiling water, and old loamy tealeaves.

One custard-colored light bulb cast a diffuse glow on a brood of off-hours instrumentalists and a lone female soprano, echoing quietly, like a cat with stillborn kittens. She sang the same opera for more than an hour.

We returned to the hotel to find that Mr. Li and Jerry had prepared a more formal evening of intercultural entertainment in our dorm. Three more Chinese friends had been invited, and were plainly excited to have been included in the planned festivities. They had arranged a table with pastries, and large bottles of what they referred to as 'vermouth.' There was no dry martini on the planet that wouldn't have choked to death with its addition, although after a few hours of internal application, our hosts would come out just as white and shaken. Jerry appropriated the role of Master of Ceremonies, and I was to learn that even the smallest dimly lit gathering, between the Chinese and foreign guests, was a formal ceremony of diplomatic détente. Poetic introductions were made for each song sung, punctuated by metronome applause at the end. We alternated between Chinese and Western song performers. The clapping for my ballads was decidedly polite. But then the vermouth kicked in. Mr. Li had obviously practiced *Edelweiss* relentlessly overnight, in anticipation of even more exuberant appreciation. He had no way of knowing that the *Sound of Music* had burned it to a cinder a decade earlier, and our recognition fell short. Not as short as the open criticism of one of the invited anointed, however, whose vermouth verbosity turned up the tonality of the exchange. Another self-styled Sinostar performer became jealous, when a younger, newer, and more natural comrade upstaged him with his vocals and guitar playing. The wrath in the vermouth bottle was unleashed, along with their human frustrations and failings, and we finally called a truce around midnight. After the customary address exchanges and mandatory group photos, each culture went off to their respective cults, secure in the knowledge that the East was red, the sun would rise, and we were the only ones leaving the Stone Forest.

Lars was the first to recognize it next day. We had been looking for it ever since we heard of its existence, on our arrival in Kunming. On our return from a morning of wandering the neighborhoods, near the movie theatre with a giant pastel billboard of the Lone Ranger, at the intersection of two bicycle-jammed streets, the aroma hit us broadside. Upstairs, above the dusty powder blue cement walls and corrugated tin roofs of the market was an airy table with a view of the navy masses, Sunday dressers, courters and strollers, and tiny-footed ladies hobbling below. In a fantastic Sichuan café, we ordered a mouthwatering mountain of sweet and sour pork, spicy tofu, and tangy Szechuan chicken, with flat *Pijou* beer and a black-market exchange rate offer of less than we were willing to accept.

Lars and I said goodbye to Annie and Barb, and boarded Gong gong qi che #23 to the train station, for what we hope would be two hard sleepers on the 1100 kilometer journey to Chengdu. We dutifully boarded with a million others, and waited for the arrival of the seat allocation conductor. He growled into the carriage, a short belligerent little bastard, with an obvious hatred for Westerners. The two *gwei lo* girls in front of us, en route to Emi Shan, were refused sleepers. It was our turn.

"Meiyou!" He shouted, and with obvious relish handed the last six sleepers to the most ingratiating Chinese, before leaning back, lighting up a cigarette, blowing the exhaust in our general direction, and grinning a tarry yellow-brown smile. For no reason clear to me, he grabbed my wrist as we walked by him, heading towards the restaurant car. I brought the thumb of his left hand down, hard and square, onto the wooden edge of the counter. He squealed into the food car, securing us no service for the rest of the trip. Lars and I retired to the smoky, sticky hot, airless, noisy and unhygienic confines of our seats. We had resigned ourselves to a sleepless night. Around one in the morning, I'd had enough, shazammed into the Gold Kazoo, and crawled under one of the seats, until just before dawn. I tried not to open my eyes because, every time I did, it was raining sputum.

'The finest workers in stone are not copper or steel tools, but the gentle touches of air and water working at their leisure with a liberal allowance of time.'
Henry David Thoreau

*   *   *

'Women hold up half the sky.'
Mao Tse-Tung

The wheels of my diurnal cycle had been thoroughly punctured by the time I had squirmed out from under my hard seat, and we had emerged from a seemingly endless series of tunnels, onto the fertile Chengdu Plain. The *Land of Abundance*, Tiānfǔzhiguó, was also known as the *Country of Heaven*. The Chinese have a fascination for all things to do with Heaven, possibly because it is the home of the poor in spirit, and there is no humor. Lars and I were on a stairway to a stone forest of another kind. Heaven prohibits certain pleasures but one can generally negotiate a compromise. Ours came in the form of duck eggs, oranges, and flour-fried crusted peanuts provided by the other passengers, who treated us with a light dusting of awe, after my interaction with the smoking seat allocator. The two *gwei lo* girls tried to lure Lars and I off in Emi Shan, but we were committed to our arrival in Heaven.

Chengdu pulled up beside us, twenty-four hours after leaving

Kunming, just after seven in the evening. Rat shadows darted under the train on the adjacent track. We ran our own martial maze to the station entrance, through the rickshaws, to the accordion-hinged caterpillar of Gong gong qi che #16. It was stuffed. The driver steered through dismal miles of bicycles into a sterile black emptiness, along vast Stalinesque runways, lined by gray Rubric-cubed apartment blocks and chintzy trident-shaped streetlamps. The three thousand year old City of Brocade and Hibiscus and Turtles and Lao Tzu and Giant Pandas, had undergone a giant vasectomy of the senses.

Lars and I were extruded from the back end of the caterpillar at the Jinjiang fandian, exhausted and craving water and sleep. Alas. The Clark Kent clerk at the desk was a Party enthusiast of the planned economy. The dorms were full, but he could provide us with a double room for a month's salary. We told him we would go out to find something to eat, and hoped he could find a solution by the time we returned. He broke a smile, but not the ice.

Lars and I were only three minutes up the road when the ambush occurred.

"Hello." Was all she said. I looked to my right, and down at a plain Chinese girl, age indeterminate, Coke-bottle eyeglasses, little blue Mao suit, eyes averted, neck-length slightly unkempt hair.

"Sorry." I said. "We don't want to change money."

"No, thank you." She continued. "I'm a student and I'd just like to practice my English." Flashing lights, buzzers, sirens and battle stations.

"Well, Lotus Flower, Lars and I have been enjoying hard seats on the People's Express for the last twenty four hours and we're really not in the mood for a jam session." I'm afraid my tone was indelicate. "Perhaps some other time." She didn't flinch.

"How about tomorrow?" She asked, politely, pointedly, without hesitation. "What time would be convenient for you?" She must have seen my mouth fall open.

68

"How about seven tomorrow evening?" I suggested.

"Fine." She said. "Please meet me at this bus stop. I would be happy to show you around our city. Thank you, and goodbye until tomorrow." Lars and I walked on for a while before speaking. He was first to break radio silence.

"Are you really thinking of going?" He asked.

"Probably not." I said. "But any lady that's brave enough to arrange a meeting this secretly under the pretext of first, learning English, when she speaks it like a UN interpreter, and secondly, showing me around her lovely city, which is even more of a shithole after dark, must want something pretty bad. I might not be up to finding out what it is, but I'm curious." And then we forgot all about her, in our search for sustenance. Lars and I walk for blocks, past the closed Furong Restaurant ('God's will that you try our heavenly dishes'), down a side street to a café directed to us by a misguided local, who was chastised by three more directed party members he had asked for confirmation. We were greeted boisterously, and Lars was looking forward to his first taste of real Sichuan food. He ordered Mapu Dofu. I asked him if he was sure.

"You're a Swede, Lars." I said. "You have no genetic resistance to what this dish can do to a man." But he was indefatigable in his determination to try the Mother of all Szechuan dishes, on its home turf.

Grandma Chen's Mapu dofu, or *Pockmarked-Face Lady's Tofu*, is bean curd, fried in peanut oil with minced beef, sugar, soy, and ground Sichuan pepper, served with a sprinkling of scallions. And, in this Country of Heaven, a full blast of Hellfire. No relation to black or chili peppers, *hua jiao* Sichuan 'flower pepper' is the outer husk of the fruit of the prickly ash tree, and the inner secret to general neurological confusion. Its active ingredient, sanshool, can simultaneously kill off your toothache and your roundworms, in one swallow. It's a little like biting into a pungent bar of lemon soap, connected to a nine-volt battery. Cold braised goose and two steaming platters of mapu dofu arrived at our table, and Lars made for the thin, oily, bright red suspension of doom berries and disbelief.

I noticed his eyes well up, just before his face went red, and his nose began pouring mucus from an open tap. He drank his beer in a single gulp, dousing the scream that had tried to escape. His chopsticks were abandoned, for handfuls of steamed rice mouthfuls, and his clothes were drenched through with sweat.

"Good, eh?" I said. He couldn't speak.

"ABBA." I said. "You come from the homeland of ABBA. You shouldn't fuck with this stuff."

While Lars was still furiously blowing his nose and wiping his eyes, I took a photo of our chef with my new Olympus XA. It came out burnt. Chengdu was the birthplace of the first widely used paper money in the world, during the Northern Song Dynasty, around 960 AD. It cost me 3 yuán for the meal, the thousand-year history lesson, and amusement of watching Lars deworm himself.

Back at the hotel, Clark was again adamant about having no space, so Lars and I collapsed on the single sofa in the amphitheatre lobby. We had nothing left. Minutes later, one of Clark's protégés hurried over to tell us the good news. He had written out instructions to a nearby hotel not normally open to Westerners, and they would take us at a reduced rate. I opened one eye.

"Call them to see if they have room. Ask them how much. Tell us how far. Get your note translated before your shift changes. Then we'll go." And closed it again.

He ran back to Clark with the counter offer, but he was back in seconds with another idea.

"Tomorrow..." Was as far as he got, my eye chasing him back to home plate. His third attempt had a chance.

"We have to wait until a certain lady returns. If she agrees, we will move her to another room and you can sleep in hers.

"Great." I said, and, gwei lo and behold, she arrived from the bowels of the hotel within minutes, completing the transaction. Lars blew on his fingers.

*   *   *

'Love is of all passions the strongest, for it attacks simultaneously the head, the heart and the senses.'

Lao Tzu

It takes one year to form a community, two years to form a town, and three years to form a capital. Cheng du literally means 'become the capital,' as it had been since Kaiming IX, the king of ancient Shu named it 2300 years before. It was the only major city in China that had not changed its location or name for over two millennia. Marco Polo wrote of its bridges, the Mongols slaughtered almost a million and a half inhabitants in 1279, and Mao tore down its Qing dynasty fortress wall, ten meters high and thick, and eleven kilometers long, after his only visit to the city in 1958.

Lars and I missed the wall, by a quarter century and a breakfast, when we entered the hotel restaurant next morning.

"We would like some breakfast, please." Said Lars.

"You'd better have lunch," Came the reply.

"Okay, we'll have lunch." I smiled.

"Twelve O'clock." She sneered, and went back to her book. So I fired up my stove and Lars and I had Nescafé, before we trekked down to the station to buy tickets for the following night to Chongqing. I lost my first ticket and waited in line to buy another, while Lars sourced out a package of fermented fruit flower cookies. Outside the tile roof pointed projections and moon windows and yellow walls of the Wen Shu Monastery, was a candy artist, constructing a three-foot vertical amber dragon from molten treacle. He began to recreate the DNA of other animals as we carried on south,

71

down the Tudor-lined Wide and Narrow Lanes, taking in the busy markets, blackcurrant pastilles, and two smiling vendors, cigarettes dangling, rolling *pídàn* thousand-year-old eggs in a black mud of clay, ash, salt, lime, and rice hulls, a sludge so alkaline and caustic they had to change their gloves frequently.

Sulfur lifted to jasmine on our long march past a teahouse, to a bookstore in the shadow of the outstretched arm of the hundred-foot high statue of Mao, presiding over Tianfu square. A giant poster girl with pigtails, on a nearby corner billboard, embodied his one-child only policy.

Inside the shop, I found *The Dictionary of Americanisms*, a rather pathetic collection of some neurotic New Yorker's idea of epithets the Chinese should be interested in. Under 'mother,' it said '*see mother-fucker.*'

Lars reminded me of my appointment with the plain Chinese girl from the night before. He told me I had made a promise, and that he would go to the opera. I looked up at Mao. We promise according to our hopes and perform according to our fears. The night's darkness fell hard.

I arrived at the bus stand, ten minutes late. I didn't see her at first and, when I did, I didn't recognize her. A lovely smile beamed under a streetlamp, from a young Asian girl, hair piled high, wearing a pink dress and polished shoes. Her glasses were gone.

"I'm sorry if I misunderstood the time." She said.

"No, not at all. It was my fault for being late." I offered.

"I'll just park my bike. Please wait for me at that corner." I complied, and waited ten minutes for her. We were even.

"Please, follow me." She said. We walked, neither of us sure in which direction. And we talked, haltingly at first, exchanging niceties and reassurance.

"Is this dangerous for you?" I asked.

"Some Chinese are afraid that all foreigners are spies." She said.

"And?" I asked.

"I have no secrets." She said. "I don't know any secrets." I switched over to more personal interests. Her name was Joan. She was thirty years old, worked half-time in 'propaganda' relating to communal hygiene on some obtuse level, lived with her parents, made about twenty dollars a month, had never been out of Chengdu, had one other friend, no male friends, and had been learning English for two years on her own. We exchanged information about Canadian and Chinese education, healthcare, employment, and social structure. She told me that, despite the promise of the iron rice bowl, there was no real Social Security in China. Young people were frustrated and confused about job opportunities, and the biggest generation gap in the world.

And still I wondered. What does this girl really want? Joan said she knew of a nearby ice cream parlor. I forced her to have both ice cream and coffee, insisting that for me it wasn't an extravagance. When she brought it to the table, and the crowd that had gathered to stare at me caught sight of her, they practically tripped over each other, trying to flee. We were both ignored and intensely scrutinized, from that moment. The coffee and ice cream were both flat and watery, but her first question was anything but.

"How does a girl meet a boy in Canada?" She asked. Between the eyes.

"Uh, well, that is..." I stuttered, trying to remember myself. "Well, in many ways, I suppose at work, in public places, through friends..."

"How long before they sleep together?" I choked on my coffee. "Well, sometimes the first night, sometimes never." I said. "What about in China?" I asked, changing the subject, just a little.

"The same." She said calmly, and went on to explain in depth about contemporary Chinese mores. Couples apparently lived together in increasing numbers, more in urban areas than in the countryside, where arranged marriages were still common. Contraception was less foolproof than in the West and abortions were mandatory for illegitimate conceptions, and recommended for women under the age of twenty-four. Housing was not provided for unmarried couples.

"Don't Western men find Asian women more attractive?" She asked. "Don't Asian women make better wives? Asian women prefer foreign men, tall, dark and handsome. Chinese men are like girls, not very manly, don't you think? If a Chinese girl married a Canadian, would she be accepted by his family and his society?" And flames blazed on overturned boats, and fireworks reached to Heaven, in the climax of our Chinese opera. Joan wanted to marry a Westerner and leave China. She wanted to go anywhere at any price, and the sooner the better. She explained the technical legalities and logistics like she had written them, and served a high lob over my center court. I winced at her honesty and goodness and generosity of spirit. It didn't matter if her fiancé wanted a divorce after she was out. If he did, she would give it to him, and if he didn't, she would make him a good wife. And then she stopped talking, and looked at me.

"I don't often get proposed to on a first date," I said, and tried to explain how these happy-ever-after things are supposed to work. She didn't flinch. And how naïve had I been to underestimate her desperation and the risk she had taken, just to have a chance at the sort of real freedom I took for granted. We walked a little, and I told her I would try to arrange something in Sydney, but no promises. Did I think I would come back to Chengdu? No, I didn't. We exchanged addresses.

Two blocks from my hotel, she left me with a nervous handshake, a warning to write in very cryptic terms and maintain the most guarded secrecy, and a scene I have never forgotten- a lone resolute Joan of the arc light, peddling her 'Double Happiness' cycle into the ghostly damp night mist, under a slow flicker waltz of amber-haloed lamplight marking her retreat into the horizon, and silver tears streaming back to me. Her name was Joan, and she had made so little impression the previous night I had no intention of going. I wasn't quite sure what happened or anything happened. Maybe it was some Kodachrome dream jolting a grayed-out prisoner from his wet cement slumber. But I would leave her behind, in the Stone forest. I had thought it would be easy to sleepwalk through this country. Apparently, I was mistaken.

Lars returned from the opera around eleven pm, an amorphous red inebriated blob of happiness. He hung the 'Do Not Disturb' sign on the door.

"How was your date?" He asked.

"China." I said.

"Spectacular." He clamped on his Walkman, and boogied until three.

The gigantic pig-tailed poster child for the one descendant family looked down on the God's will of our Bang Bang chicken and Dan Dan noodles, at the Furong restaurant next day. A pockmarked-face Swiss ICU nurse and a loud blue-haired Queen Bess Aussie, smiled at us over their mapu dofu. They said they would meet us on the train to Chongqing that evening. Lars and I spent the afternoon inside the rust red walls lining the bamboo forest, with the trees and flowers and bonsai and teahouse of the Wu Hou Si Temple. We searched for Zhuge Liang's tomb, in vain, wandering instead through a rock garden where Chinese newlyweds pretend posed for paradise. Lars thrashed me in several games of chess, under my distraction and the mimosas.

His reward came that night in the form of the talkative company of Queen Bess, sharing the top bunks of our hard sleeping car. He lay with his back to Heaven. On the lower tier, I met Brian, a balding blond Canadian Airlines pilot from British Columbia, returning home from two years in the Sudan, on his own inspired Grand Tour. We spoke of the Cosmos, lives of dignity, and unrequited love. The rails rocked me to sleep, long into the night.

'Somehow everything comes with an expiry date. Swordfish expires. Meat sauce expires. Even cling-film expires. Is there anything in the world which doesn't? If memories could be canned, would they also have expiry dates? If so, I hope they last for centuries.'

Chungking Express

Dire Straits on the Yangtze

'In the Yangtze River waves push the waves ahead; so in life new people constantly replace the old ones.'

Anon

The journey would begin at the intersection of primary colors. Far down below our vantage point, the blue Jialing River collided with the ochre Yangtze, spinning green eddies into the confluence.

"That must be her." Said Lars. "I wonder how she got her name."

The boat's stern markings were in Mandarin and English. 东方红. *The East is Red.* The Mao suit next to us ignited a Red Golden Dragon cigarette with his electronic Mao lighter. A tinny tune emerged with the flame.

"You hear that?" I asked. Lars nodded.

"It's the same song they blare from every PA system, at dawn and dusk, in every city and village we've been through." He said.

"Like a conch Triton's trumpet." I said. "'*The East is Red.*' Some farmer, who got all warm and fuzzy about Mao during a northern Shaanxi morning sunrise, changed the lyrics to an old song. *The Communist Party is like the sun, Wherever it goes, it is bright.* I liked the original ones better. *Sesame oil, cabbage hearts, Wanna eat string beans, break off the tips, Get really lovesick if I don't see you for three days.*"

"Why was it such a big hit?" He asked.

"To answer that, you need to know what happened during the four years of the Great Leap Forward, and how Mao lost face and ground, because of it. Twenty-five years ago, he seized control of agricultural production, thinking that he would be able to rapidly industrialize the country with the proceeds of the crime. He banned private farming, and persecuted the displaced. Hundred of thousands of starving peasants died like flies in the 'killing fields' of poorly engineered massive irrigation projects. Villagers were forced into producing low-grade pig iron out of their pots and pans, in backyard smelters. The countryside was denuded of wood along with the doors and furniture of houses. Forty per cent of all the houses were turned into rubble, to make fertilizer, straighten roads, to punish their owners, or 'to make a place for a better future beckoning ahead.'

Crops were planted using principles of Soviet agronomy, which declared that 'Socialist seeds' could be sown close together, because they would not compete with each other. Local 'feudalist' customs, like weddings, funerals, markets and festivals, and any celebration of humanity, were banned. Public criticism sessions, beatings with sticks, and other forms of violence were deployed on an increasingly malnourished population. Ears and noses were lopped off, and hair ripped out. Victims were injected with cattle syringes of salt water, forced to ingest excrement and urine, labor naked in the middle of winter, doused in boiling water, thrown bound into ponds, or buried alive.

One of the first actions of the Great Leap Forward was particularly foolish, in its exaltation of ideology over rationality. The Great Sparrow Campaign was an edict issued to annihilate the 'animal enemies of the people.' Mao identified the need to exterminate mosquitoes, flies, rats, and, sparrows. Failure was not an option. Almost all birdlife became extinct. By the time Mao realized that sparrows ate insects as well as grain, and replaced them on the list with bedbugs, it was too late. Then came the locusts, and poisons and pesticides. Pressured local officials inflated their grain quota performance results, while grain was exported, or rotted in public granaries, and people died outside, waiting. The resultant famine killed over thirty million people. Mao described the mass starvation as *'a few cases of illness and death: it's nothing! It is better to let half the people die so that the other half can eat their fill.'* Cannibals, and those who could digest leaves, were more likely to survive. Those labeled as 'black elements' were given the least food. Tibet lost twenty per cent of her population.

Four years after Lars and I stood on the Yangtze riverbank, the 'Four Pests campaign' was resurrected in the 'oven city' of Chongqing, this time with cockroaches substituted for sparrows. Two dozen years later, Beijing officials would set a limit of two flies for every public toilet. *Every Red Heart Shines Toward the Red Sun.*

Queen Bess caught up with us. She arrived with 'Vulgar,' a twenty-year old biology student from Frankfurt, whose nose dripped continuously, even without the Sichuan flower peppers. Lars went into a blue funk, or maybe it was the green dysentery.

I managed to talk us through the giant hardwood boatsheds randomly crowding the muddy sand of the Yangtze foreshore ferry dock, and found the ticket office, and a counter clerk who sold Lars and Vulgar and I passage to Wuhan on *The East is Red*, scheduled to leave the next morning. We met Brian along the sandbanks, and trudged back up into the city. On the rooftop of the cavernous Russian-built Chongqing guesthouse, we camped out for hours, drinking tea, eating mediocre dumpling soup and egg pancakes, and watching the poor polluted ugliness below. It all needed a new coat of lead paint. Brian left, and agreed to meet us off our boat, in Wuhan. Queen Bess departed for another destination.

I suggested to Lars and Vulgar that it might be possible to sleep on the boat overnight. They were reluctant, but agreed to let me try. We hoisted our packs once more down to the sludge, and were refused entry by a sequence of three Harbor policemen. But when other passengers charged by us to board, the fourth, neck veins bulging, issued us three sleeping tickets, and we were welcomed as heroes, onto *The East is Red. Hurrah, there the people are liberated!*

The steward introduced us to the captain, allotted us window side bunks in fourth class, promised a superior brand of beer, and persuaded me into giving an impromptu guitar recital for the drunken cook and his comely courtesan, entranced by our foreign devilry. Back in our bunkroom, we met Sheh, an engineer who had studied at Laval and spoke *patois* French, and an impressionable youth. I curled up with Golding's *Lord of the Flies*, finding profound parallels for the events of the era, out of which came the name of our vessel. A sailor drew his bow between the two strings of a feline instrument, as we floated to the orchestral accompaniment of Lars' Swedish sleep talking, Vulgar's sonorous nasality, and the blasts of distant foghorns, till all was white noise in a yellow world. *A shore of thin reeds in light wind, A tall boat alone at night, Stars hang over the barren land, The moon rises out of the Yangtze.*

When I awoke we were already moving downstream, along the course of the longest river in Asia, four thousand miles from the Tibetan Plateau to Shanghai. It would take me a week to sail all the way back to the East China Sea, through its history of blood flukes and floods, and gorges and gunboats.

Vulgar was complaining about a pain in his left ear, and I took him onto the top deck to look for the ship's medic, so I could borrow an otoscope. The quest, that began to preserve his hearing, was to finish with the vision I found in the clinic. The barefoot doctor exercising on the roof was wearing shorts and a halter neck. Long black hair streamed in cascades of liquid squid ink. She looked up, and I fell into cat's eyes and ivory. She peered into Vulgar's ear and pronounced him neurotic. And then my eyes, and smiled. We spent the day together, seeing sick passengers, pouring over her Chinese textbook of Western Medicine, and comparing notes. I was fascinated to see her collecting money from her patients, something that I had never done as a Capitalist roader back in Canada.

The East is Red pulled into Wanxian late afternoon, to spend

80

the night. The river rapids ahead were best tackled in daylight. An old woman in the local market sold me a large intricate bamboo basket for a dollar. I asked her how long it had taken to weave.

"一个月. Yīgè yuè." She said. *One month.*

The meals served up on *The East is Red* were either mostly rice, greasy turnips, and pork fat, or pork fat, greasy turnips, and mostly rice, so we stuffed ourselves with sesame biscuits, Vulgar's German chocolate, and many Nescafés from my butane stove. Lars and I played chess, and I began to win a few.

That evening the comely courtesan, together with her radio room friends, organized a disco party with Lars, Vulgar, and the impressionable youth. We drank *Tsingtao*, danced the night away, and endeavored to have a good time, despite their cautious concern.

Our voyage down the Yangtze began only a few years before the Three Gorges Dam would destroy the wildly beautiful and precarious passage we were about enter, before the lakes were cut off and the towns flooded, before the pig farm waste, and the single species carp fish ponds, and the algae, and the large scale untreated sewage and industrial pollution.

I found my doctor on the roof next morning, exercising barefoot, with her eyes closed. I placed the earphones of Lars' Walkman, and watched her break into the most graceful Tai Chi set in the Middle Kingdom. She was as spectacular to watch as the scenery around her.

As we entered the Qutang Gorge, she pulled the tape out, and ran it, and me, up the metal stairs to the radio room. The operator took it tentatively, and eased it into the drawer of the ship's intercom tape deck. And then he hit the button.

Dire Straits entered the Three Gorges, as we entered the dire straits of the Wushan Gorge. The rising sun and the refrains of *Love Over Gold* reverberated in synchrony, off steep forested cliffs faces of Sorceress Mountain, and her rushing ravine river rapids. Everyone saw God.

81

'Your footsteps are forbidden
But with a knowledge of your sin...
And you go dancing through doorways
Just to see what you will find...
And when you finally reappear
At the place where you came in
You've thrown your love to all the strangers
And caution to the wind.'

She asked me to bring the tape back to the radio room that night.
We danced down the Yangtze Gorges. She had papered over the windows, so no one would know.

'It takes love over gold
And mind over matter
To do what you do that you must
When the things that you hold
Can fall and be shattered
Or run through your fingers like dust.'

*   *   *

'In China, we hold the welfare of the state above that of the individual. We have six times the population of your country, Mr. Moore, and one-tenth the crime rate. Tell me, who is right?'

Shen Yuelin, *Red Corner*

"I still don't understand the name of our boat." Said Lars. "What does *The East is Red* have to do with the Great Leap Forward?" It was the end of the day, and our ship was pulling into the smog of Wuhan.
"It was here eighteen years ago." I said. "Mao enjoyed a fifteen kilometer swim, at the age of 72. At least that's what *The People's Daily* reported, along with the smiling photo of him in his bathrobe." It was a message to his enemies. Mao

had seen how Khrushchev had denounced Stalin for his excesses, and feared the same thing was about to happen to him, for the 30 million who had died because of his Great Leap. In his bathrobe, he took another. Instead of throwing in his towel he flicked it at new categories of class enemies-those of money, mind, morals, and motive. From the shore of Wuhan, Mao launched the Cultural Revolution.

Landowners with 'bourgeois tendencies' and large houses were squeezed into single rooms, their possessions smashed by Red Guards, and poor families moved into every remaining space. Their children were thrown into trashcans.

In the Cultural Revolution, learning was a crime. The crackdown on teachers, professors and intellectuals was nasty. Red Guard rabble broke into their homes, and stayed for a month, conducting humiliating 'struggle sessions,' before branding their victims bourgeois reactionaries, and shipping them off to be incarcerated for indeterminate periods of time. Mocking students ordered their teachers to wear dunce caps, cultivate cabbage, and spend entire days standing in the kowtow position, performing grotesque loyalty dances, or reciting 'I am a cow demon,' and begging for forgiveness. Pupils at a Beijing girls' school beat their vice-principal to death with nail-studded planks. University professors were humiliated, and crippled, for not doing manual labor. The intellectual elite had half their hair shaved into *Yin-Yang Heads*, dirty gloves stuffed in their mouths, ink and paint splashed on their faces, and insulting signs hung around their necks. They were beaten bloody with leather belts, and then the metal buckles, before being sent to labor in the dark corners of *cowshed* prison camps. They saw one thin slice of meat a week, and their spouses one thin night a year, during the only annual conjugal visit allowed. If the wind was strong both were blown away. When Nixon arrived, they got to eat three slices, and bitterness.

One professor started each day with an order to write a six-page essay on 'Why I Like Dickens,' only to be told afterwards it was rubbish and to write six more pages. Another was forced to work as flycatcher and keep the dead flies in box. Every day, after counting the hundreds of flies in his box his Red Guard supervisor told him to 'kill some more.' An artist was imprisoned for painting a portrait of Mao at a slight tilt so that only one ear showed, implying that the Great Helmsman listened only to a select few. As the banner of tyranny over the mind rose high, Shakespeare, Tolstoy, Dante, and any literary works of human truth, goodness, beauty and warmth were banned, regarded as poisonous weeds of the feudal and bourgeois classes. Pens were beaten into daggers, and thrust into the throats and chests and convictions of their practitioners. The Red Guards smashed musical instruments, and the fingers that played them. In the West, a mind was considered a terrible thing to waste. In Mao's Cultural Revolution, a mind was considered a terrible thing.

The Red Guards didn't discriminate against any one religion. They persecuted all of them. Crosses were ripped from church steeples, and Catholic priests forced into labor camps. Muslim madrassas were turned into pig slaughterhouses. But the most severe repression was directed at the Buddhists, especially the Tibetans. Nothing infuriates a communist conformist like an individual on a path to personal enlightenment.

The Cultural Revolution arrived in Lhasa in July 1966, with an order. 'Smash the feudalistic nests of monks!' Those nests that weren't destroyed with dynamite and artillery, were chalk marked to death. Brick by brick, timber by timber, over ninety-nine percent of Tibet's 6,000 religious monasteries, temples and shrines were looted, totally destroyed, or made into barns and barracks, factories and pigsties. The contents of their libraries, hundreds of thousands of sacred Buddhist scriptures and rare books and paintings, were burned or used as wrapping paper or to make shoe soles. Then they smashed the monks. Festivals and pilgrimages were banned. Tibetans were tortured, and forced to cut their hair, to wear blue Mao suits, to speak the new Sino-Tibetan 'friendship language,' and to work for years digging vegetables.

Anyone could become a class enemy for anything innocently simple- being seen in the company of a foreigner, wearing Western clothes, forgetting a slogan from The Little Red Book, seeking repayment of a debt, hoarding a piece of meat, or owning a Canadian-made alarm clock. People started to smoke, to give them time to think.

On an April Sunday afternoon in 1984, *The East is Red* floated under the long expanse of the First Yangtze River Bridge, and pulled into the 'Chicago of China.' Vulgar had left us the day before in Yueyang, but Brian was waiting for Lars and I on the dock. I said goodbye to my barefoot doctor and ship comrades, and we set off down the street with my Wuxian basket, to find a boat to take us to Shanghai. What could have been another Battle of Red Cliffs turned into the *Romance of the Three Kingdoms*, thanks to the ministrations of Porter #1180. He spoke without breathing to the ticket vendor behind the cage, securing us passage on boat #13 for early next morning, and pointed out a favored noodle shop for replenishing our lost glycogen. He later arranged for us to sleep on boat #14 next door, and introduced us to the captain, who ensured that our bunks were stripped and remade with clean sheets. I settled in with my bunkmates, and *Lord of the Flies*.

"How much worse did it get?" Asked Lars.

"What?" I asked.

"The Cultural Revolution."

"It got maniacal." I said. "There was mass property destruction and mob violence, beatings and public humiliation, struggle sessions and labor camp exile, torture, executions, cannibalism, misery, and suicide. It ran amok."

In their determination to wipe out China's past and create a new society, Red Guards burned and destroyed temples, historical buildings, precious paintings, vases, pottery, calligraphy, embroidery, statues, books and any other works of art they could their hands on. Two miles of the Great Wall were disassembled into stone blocks, to construct army barracks. Owners destroyed their own stuff to avoid getting caught with it. Hundreds of thousands were expelled from their homes and hundreds more killed daily. People were kept in cupboards for years, and then thrown off buildings.

Children of unpopular party members were gagged and executed, as other children denounced their parents, and neighbors informed on neighbors. The accused 'rich peasants' and 'bad elements' had their tongues cut off with scissors or their jaws dislocated so they couldn't speak in their defense, and then paraded in packed stadiums, forced to bow in front mobs that spit and screamed at them, and then beheaded. Corpses were mutilated in order to fit into coffins.

Hordes of naked beggar women, smeared with soot and mud, solicited food from male passengers in small railway stations. Officials established quotas of victims targeted for violence. Counter-revolutionaries were tortured to death and eaten by local party members, as a demonstration of their 'class feelings.'

Thousands were humiliated and abused to such an extent that they took their own lives. Even this wasn't easy. There were no skyscrapers to jump off, and most were too poor to buy poison. So they chose the railway, jumping in front of the trains, on a section of track they called 'Death Road.' One man tried to commit suicide by killing and eating hundreds of flies. Others killed themselves by hammering nails into their own skulls.

What began as Red Guard factional rampages, fighting each other for the 'Purification of the Class Ranks,' over the honor of being the purest Maoists, became feuds for local power, and ultimate 'revenge fests.' What started with sticks and clubs, stone slingshots and wooden spears, became revolvers, hunting rifles, automatic rifles, hand grenades, mortars, rocket-propelled grenade launchers, and artillery. One group welded steel plates onto the body of a tractor to convert it into a tank, while another simply looted real ones from the People's Liberation Army. Factory fought factory, school fought school, and the local police and army were ordered not to intervene in the resultant house-to-house street battles. To prove their loyalty, Red Guards would wear their Mao badge, by pinning it to their skin.

By the time the Great Helmsman finally sent in groups of local workers, backed by PLA troops, to shoot the Red Guard down and restore order, almost a million and a half of his disciples had become victims of 'abnormal deaths.'

Mao had unleashed an unprecedented reign of terror, in which the youth of China were freed from parental and societal constraints, to perpetrate assault, battery and murder upon their fellow citizens, to the extent their barely formed consciences permitted. The resultant nationwide juvenile state of nature condoned this violence and suffering, a Maoist shrug of acceptable collateral damage.

"It was an order of magnitude allegorier than the microcosmic allegory of the boys in this book." I said.

"What's the book?" Asked Brian. I handed it down.

"But Golding wrote *Lord of the Flies* long before the Cultural Revolution." He said, looking inside the cover.

"1954." I said. "But it was a brilliant, if inadvertent, foreshadowing of what Mao's terror.

The central theme is the conflicting impulses toward civilization, the struggle between the desire to live by rules, in peace and harmony, and Nietzsche's will to power. Golding wrote subtext themes of the tension between groupthink and individuality, between rational and emotional reactions, and between morality and immorality. It was the Cultural Revolution of a small group of adolescent boys stranded on a remote island.

Ralph is the directness of Mao's 'genuine leadership.' In his obsession with being popular, he represents the debilitating effects that corruption has on even the brightest mind and, towards the end, forgets the initial reason for maintaining the signal fire.

Piggy represents the Intelligentsia, relying on the power of social convention, and dying for it.

Jack and Roger form the Red Guard tribe, and represent the most primal childish desires. Lured by the promise of meat, play, and freedom, they epitomize the worst aspects of irrational human nature, unrestrained by society, and lead their blind followers into intertribal violence, punishment, torture, murder, and chaos.

Simon is the defeat of Morality and Reason, and peace and tranquility and positivity. His murder is the loss of truth and innocence and common sense. He is the Christ and the Buddha they persecuted.

The Conch is the assembly anthem of *The East is Red*."

"So what's the Beast?" Brian asked, thumbing through the book in the bunk below.

"Ah, the Beast." I sighed. "Isn't that the question? Is the Beast the first rumors of its existence? Is it the corpse of the fighter pilot entangled in the jungle foliage, or the movement it made when gusts of wind billowed its parachute, or the gusts of wind themselves? Is the Beast the severed pig's head, on the stick sharpened at both ends and stuck in the ground, that the boys created as an offering to the Beast, once a clean, loving, and innocent mother sow, and then a bleeding head case of horror, a Lord of the Flies, with a grin 'six feet across?' Is the Beast the flies, or their revenge? Is the Beast what they mistake Simon for, or is the Intelligentsia the Beast? Or is the Beast the Beast inside them all, which allowed them to create the Beast. The name, 'Lord of the Flies,' is a literal translation of Beelzebub, the 'fiery serpent' fallen angel of the Hebrew Seraphim, who presides over the Order of the Fly. He is the demon of pride, gluttony, an object of supplication, and the prince of false gods and demon possession. His name came up at the Salem witch trials, among the Pharisees, and in Milton's *Paradise Lost*. Or

was the Beast the smiling Mao in his bathrobe?"
Brian read from the book.

'We've got to have rules and obey them. After all, we're not savages.
Here, invisible yet strong, was the taboo of the old life.
The world, that understandable and lawful world, was slipping away.
You're not wanted...
The desire to squeeze and hurt was over-mastering.
The creature was a party of boys, marching...
Kill the beast! Cut his throat! Spill his blood!
There were no words, and no movements but the tearing of teeth and
claws.
Which is better--to have laws and agree, or to hunt and kill?
After all we aren't savages really...
Maybe there is a beast.... maybe it's only us.'

*   *   *

'The function of the artist is to disturb... In a world terrified of change, he
preaches revolution--the principle of life... He is an agitator, a disturber
of the peace – quick, impatient, positive, restless and disquieting.'
Norman Bethune

*Over the distant, dark-blue mountains, a pale, faint line of light appears
in the east. In an hour the sun will be up.*
The day began with some Chinese ex-marine kicking in our
door with his brush cut. It was 5:15 am. Time to leave. I had
been dreaming about being a lone Indian soldier on the
Ladakhi frontier, and looking down to find the entire
People's Liberation Army, advancing up my hill. By the time I
had focused up into brush cut's eyes, the cold sweat had
soaked my sheets.
Porter #1180 was waiting outside, to show us our new
window side bunks next door, in lucky boat #13. I parked

Serendipity, and Lars and Brian and I set off to find breakfast. We had two hours before our ship would sail.

Our search took us along the opening shops and early morning streets of Wuhan, into the lobby of the Xuangong Hotel. We asked the sleepy-eyed desk clerk where the restaurant was.

"Seven o'clock." He said.

"That's when." I said. "We'd like to know where."

"Seven o'clock." He said.

Halfway back down the street, I suggested returning. We slipped quietly through the lobby, and climbed to the second floor. The restaurant was open, and we tucked into a delicious breakfast of pseudospam and eggs, toast, butter and jam, canned mandarin slices and coffee. Lars and Brian headed back to the boat, while I tried to absorb the last of Wuhan. Along the river it came on the sea, of a hundred venerable men and women, in Tai Chi slippers and slow motion synchrony, within a public square. As he passed me, a tough old Chinese jogger led out of bloodcurdling 'Hnyaaaaah!' And we boarded, and waved goodbye to Porter #1180 from our portals, as ropes released us into the Yangtze flow. His last act was to provide us with a list, in Mandarin, of cafeteria recommendations, which is how we discovered the existence of the organ meats in sauces, dofu, seaweed and rice, that would not otherwise been made available. The organ meats made for more bizarre dreams- of hitchhiking to Lhasa from Turfan, Western women, Northern lights, Southern nights, and Eastern days of sneaking our cassettes into 1984 loudspeakers. But Lars had become indisposed to loan his tapes or Walkman or attention. He was increasingly distant and moody, and his blue funks were growing funkier, like he'd had enough pleasure, and it was time to stop. It was as if the Nordic climate and the Lutheran Church had come to reclaim his silent stoic sullen sunless sea level Swedish soul. Or maybe it was that Brian and I seemed to have more in common. And we were both Canadians. Somewhere on the river, there was just a simple shift in allegiance. But not completely.

Down in a stairwell, between the 1940's deco forward lounge and the rest of the boat, was a large painting of Mao and one of his iconic minor deities. The other man in the painting started life as someone who couldn't have been more Canadian. His reverend great great grandfather had established the first Presbyterian church in Montreal. His great grandfather had been a Hudson Bay Company explorer and fur trader, and Toronto alderman. His grandfather was a founder of the University of Toronto School of Medicine. And his father was a small town pastor in Gravenhurst, Ontario. Norman, himself, had volunteered at remote lumber and mining camps in Northern Ontario, was wounded as a stretcher-bearer in France during World War I, joined the Royal Navy as a Surgeon-Lieutenant, and became an FRCS surgeon in Edinburgh. After spending his new wife's inheritance on a Grand Tour of Europe, he worked so hard in Detroit, that he contracted tuberculosis. He divorced his wife because he thought he was dying, saved himself by collapsing his lung, and remarried her, for a short while. He became a surgeon at the Royal Vic in Montreal and, in 1935, became a committed lifelong communist, after a short visit to the Soviet Union. The next year he went off to the Spanish Civil War, and developed the world's first mobile blood transfusion unit. In 1938 he went off for the last time, to join Mao's Eighth Route Army, as a battlefield surgeon. He wrote poetry and, in return, Mao wrote a poem of him. Norman Bethune died of blood poisoning a year after he arrived. The adoration and accolades and awards have been endless.

But I believe his blood has poisoned us back. Bethune was a hero, by any measure but mine.

Perhaps it was the 'fear of being mediocre,' instilled into him by his emotionally strict father and domineering mother that had turned Norman into an impatient, intolerant, crusty, nasty-tempered, heavy drinker. Bethune didn't go to China to help humanity, but to help Mao's communist army. Like Mother Teresa's not tending sick people, but souls for the scoreboard, Norman didn't tend sick people, but wounded communist soldiers. His dedication to communist ideology was fanatical to the point that he specifically refused to work with Chiang Kai Shek's Nationalists.

Bethune called for the extermination of the alternative.

'What do these enemies of the human race look like? They are the respectable ones. They are honoured. They call themselves, and are called, gentlemen. They are the pillars of the state, of the church, of society. They support private and public charity out of the excess of their wealth. They endow institutions. In their private lives they are kind and considerate. They obey the law, their law, the law of property. But there is one sign by which these gentle gunmen can be told. Threaten a reduction on the profit of their money and the beast in them awakes with a snarl. They become ruthless as savages, brutal as madmen, remorseless as executioners. Such men as these must perish if the human race is to continue. There can be no permanent peace in the world while they live. Such an organization of human society as permits them to exist must be abolished. These men make the wounds.'

But aren't there two ironies? The first is how he has been manipulated - by communists to get deals with capitalists, and by capitalists to be favored by communists.

The use that China makes of Bethune to teach Chinese children the 'value of helping humanity' is disingenuous, since everything China does is based on self-interest. The market for body parts of people executed for crimes, of Falun Gong dissidents, the sale of unwanted girl babies to foreigners willing to pay, the kidnapping and imprisoning expatriates from neighboring countries, and the persecution of Tibetans, hardly constitutes the definition of 'helping humanity.'

The Chinese deification of Bethune has commercial and psychological value in dealing with Canada. Every trade delegation and tourist got the 'homage to Bethune' treatment. Canadians also realized that, by publicly revering Bethune, they gained an advantage with the Chinese. One Canadian ambassador in Beijing, Michel Gauvin, buttonholed the Chinese foreign minister, who had proposed a toast to Norman Bethune, after his first official banquet.

"I would appreciate it," He said, "if for the duration of my time in China as Canada's ambassador, there be no more toasts in my presence to Dr. Bethune. I feel I must tell you that I do not consider Dr. Bethune a Canadian patriot, but hostile to the values of my country." The foreign minister stared at him for a moment, and broke into a big grin. It was the last time the Chinese mentioned Bethune to him. Despite Norman's unwavering commitment to collectivism, he is the quintessential tourist attraction on both continents, and good for business.

The second irony is that, even as they fulfilled Norman's ideal image of communism at the time, I'm sure he was absolutely delighted to have his own bourgeois ego gratified and deified, in ways that only communist cults of personality are capable of.

I watched Norman Bethune and Mao all the way to Shanghai, through the rain and dreams of organ meats. *And the same pallid moon tonight, Which rides so quietly, clear and high.*

Landscapes Clear and Radiant

'Shanghae is by far the most important station for foreign trade on the coast of China... No other town with which I am acquainted possesses such advantages; it is the great gate - the principal entrance, in fact, to the Chinese Empire.'

Robert Fortune, *Three Years' Wanderings in the Northern Provinces of China*, 1843

The Western paint-by-numbers of Mao and Norman on boat #13 had been a static window of limited perspective, framed with Marxist sharpness. My trip through China was wider, smoother and more gradually revealing than that, flowing like a Qing Dynasty scroll. I controlled the edges, rolling what I had encountered up behind me and making it disappear, and uncovering forward what was about to happen next, living like a mighty river of experience.

In 1684, Qing Emperor Kangxi reversed the previous Ming Dynasty prohibition on ocean going vessels entering the Yangtze delta. The massive mobile madness that Brian and Lars and I awoke on seemed to contain every boat since the ban had been lifted. We cruised past a flotilla of old Chinese junks and an armada of new Chinese submarines, to dock in the largest city in the world, the '*Harpoon Ditch*' of its ancient residents, and the '*Paris of the East*' of its invaders. It had been the first and last fortress of the Cultural Revolution, but for me it conjured up Marlene Dietrich, Rita Hayward and Orson Welles, Errol Flynn's yacht, and the shady foreign intrigue of the 1940's. I carried images of forced child labor factories, back alley frozen corpses in winter, and the infamous sign at the Public Garden entrance, *Dogs and Chinese Not Allowed*. Its name became associated with the coercive 'crimps' that kidnapped unsuspecting conscripts as sailors, using fraud, violence or intimidation. *Shanghai*.

We bounded through the dockyard gate, and headed for the best known street in the Orient, the dark conspiratorial romantic Huangpu riverfront of black marketers and hawkers, seamen and diplomats, coolies and deformed beggars, and the businessmen of the great banks and trading houses that rose along it. We were on the Bund, looking for the Peace Hotel. It had once had been Sassoon House, built by Sir Victor Sassoon, the Iraqi Sephardic Jew, who had aided twenty thousand of his coreligionists to survive the Nazis, in the Shanghai Ghetto. Lars and Brian and I were simply looking for a room. They insisted that it was closed, despite the cruise ship in the lobby. The Swiss Miss in the bookstore burned out both of Brian's eyes, and most of his seminal vesicles.

"You need more than luck in Shanghai." I said, with a Bogart inflection. He returned the volley.

"Some people can smell danger. Not me. Maybe I'll live so long that I'll forget her. Maybe I'll die trying. The only way to stay out of trouble is to grow old, so I guess I'll concentrate on that." We crossed the bridge to our second choice, the Puxiang. The Lone Ranger 'Service Desk' clerk began his eight track speech about no dorm beds, but we were in too much of a hurry to see the place. We piled our packs on the counter and told him we'd be back.

Shanghai had been built on mud and was growing sideways. Brian and Lars and I had arrived in the least exciting time. Before we came, Shanghai had been a polyglot parlor of lowlife and high fashion. After we left, Shanghai would become a polyglot parlor of lowlife and high fashion. We were the unsavory foreign fillings in the decadence sandwich in between, and everyone was still wearing baggy blue suits. It was a year before the Spiritual Civilization program would kick in, with its campaigns of The Five Talks of politeness, civil behavior, morality, attention to social relations, and attention to the hygiene of one's surroundings, and The Four Beauties of beautiful language, beautiful behavior, beautiful heart and beautiful environment. If, as reputed, the millions of Chinese on the sidewalks, were comforted by crowds,

Shanghai should have been a scroll of serenity, but we were stuck in impenetrable slob mobs, in noisy, smelly stifling streets of makeshift market stalls, spilling over into the gutters.

We took refuge in the soot-covered Shanghai Club, gloomy and indestructible, with its massive Italianate first floor Grand Hall, and the twelve-foot ceilings supported by colossal Ionic columns. There had been a billiards room, a dining room, a smoking room, and a library with more books than the Public Library. A serpiginous climb up the curving marble staircase brought us to the level of what had been the world's longest bar. The 110 feet of unpolished mahogany had been the measuring stick of class, with the prime Bund-facing *Tai-Pan* and banker territory at one end, tracing the hierarchical class gradient falling in social scale, as one moved down its length. Noël Coward laid his cheek on the Long Bar, and saw the curvature of the Earth. There was Art Deco lamps, fluted cornices and teak paneling. The Japanese had occupied it during the war, the Maoists turned it into the Seamen's Club and, after we had long bar long gone, a Kentucky Fried Chicken, and then the Waldorf Astoria Shanghai.

We crossed a bridge to the 'Friendship Store,' where I finally traded my flip-flops for a pair of brand new running shoes, two pairs of socks, and a large replacement jar of Nescafé. Lars shifted into blue funk mode, leaving Brian and I to lemon meringue pie at a student worker's café, and an afternoon of shopping along Nanjing Road. I bought some refills for my black pen, and a copy of the Ming Dynasty *Journey to the West*, a 16th century allegorical tale of an adventurous individual, journeying towards spiritual insight and enlightenment. I told Brian I had already come from there.

"You've been traveling around the world too much to find out anything about it." He said.

There were rumors of an all-Chinese Jazz band that played in the Peace Hotel nightly. Brian and I entered the bar to find my armchair traveler's vision of old Shanghai- six old grinning musicians with a love for American jazz, shut down in 1947, and reincarnated four years earlier than our entrance. We sat with two Aussie librarians, who bought us cold beers, and swung us around the dance floor. The big one pulled me in a little too close, when they broke into 'In the Mood.' *It took more than one man to change my name to Shanghai Lily.*

Our second day in Shanghai began like the Han Dynasty transparent bronze mirrors we later found in the History Museum, throwing previously invisible illuminated complex patterns when hit by the sun. Lars threw a tirade about how I treated different people differently, while he treated everyone with the same detached indifference, or something like that. I still remember him fondly, but it was the seismic shift that ended our relationship. Brian and I took Gong gong qi che #42 to the Long Hua Jade Buddha Temple, to view the peach blossoms, the *cloth bag monk*, and the four heavenly Disney kings. Later that afternoon we ran a road race, to see the Chinese acrobats, who amazed us with contortions through small-diameter pipes, spinning plates and juggling bowls while standing on their heads, and air balancing enough liquor cabinets, lit lamps, and bartenders, to open a sky tavern. We left for the atmosphere of Peace Hotel Jazz bar, where an American Jazz band had come off the cruise ship on which Elizabeth Taylor was paying $8000 a night for four suites. When they took the stage and played Duke Ellington's *Take the 'A' Train*, I noticed tears in the eyes of the old Chinese musicians. In the opium den of iniquity that Shanghai had been, Elvis may have left the building, but Jesus was back in the temple.

'You're in China now, sir, where time and life have no value.'
Henry Chang, *Shanghai Express* (1932)

*   *   *

98

'Taking, therefore, all these facts into consideration, the proximity of Shanghae to the large towns of Hangchow, Soo-chow, and the ancient capital of Nanking; the large native trade, the convenience of inland transit by means of rivers and canals; the fact that teas and silks can be brought here more readily than to Canton; and, lastly, viewing this place as an immense mart for our cotton manufactures, which we already know it to be, there can be no doubt that in a few years it will not only rival Canton, but become a place of far greater importance.'
Robert Fortune, *Three Years' Wanderings in the Northern Provinces of China*, 1843

The Jesuits had been here before. In 1689, Emperor Kangxi embarked on an inspection tour of his Southern Provinces, a journey of over two thousand miles. He brought his mother, the dowager empress, his imperial wives, children, concubines, bureaucrats, and thousands of soldiers, down the Grand Canal.

His climb to the top of Mount Tai, the *Cosmic Peak of the East*, and a site sacred to the three Chinese religious traditions of Buddhism, Confucianism, and Daoism, was the ultimate Qing Dynasty photo op, sending a message to his subjects that he didn't intend to rule as a Manchu conqueror, but as a traditional Chinese monarch. Unlike Mao's ham-handed beastly strategy three hundred years later, Kangxi sought to enlist the southern provincial intelligentsia as his advisors.

The method he chose to commemorate his tour was perfect format for documenting such a long journey. He commissioned the creation of twelve linear landscape hand scrolls. End-to-end, the story spanned the length of three football fields. The artist he chose was given fine silk and the minerals to create a blue-green palette. Wang Hui's emphasis on the monumental grandeur of the landscape, without attention to perspective or scale, became known as the Orthodox school. There was no attempt to separate the foreground and background. *'I must use the brush and ink of the Yuan to move the peaks and valleys of the Song, and infuse them with the breath-resonance of the Tang. I will have a work of the Great Synthesis.'* The result was a fusion masterpiece, and the Emperor bestowed upon Wang Hui the honorific name

'Landscapes Clear and Radiant.'

Six decades later, in 1764, grandson Qianlong repeated the tour, and the commission. But the Jesuits, meanwhile, had brought their western perspective, the blue-green palate was gone, and the previous grand sweep of landscapes were depicted in relation to the measurable scale of the human figure, in a detailed rendering. The Orient's spirituality of Nature had been usurped by the Occident's desert monotheism of Man.

For Brian and I to begin our own Southern Inspection Tour of the Grand Canal, we needed to take the 'A' train to Hangzhou. He returned from a counter encounter at the Peace Hotel without tickets. I hiked Serendipity back with him, and managed to extort hard seats for that evening's train. Two Han warriors tried to commandeer our reservations, and failing, proffered sunflower seeds as a post-Peace peace offering. The pile of shells on the floor was gargantuan by the time we arrived in the 'River-ferrying Prefecture' downpour. Gong gong qi che #7 took us to the Hangzhou Hotel. Despite the orchestra and Overseas Chinese cocktail party in the lobby, and an imposing computer terminal the clerk was hiding behind, we managed to secure dorm beds in a comfortable room with tea and an immense bathtub. We joined the festivities, but the trumpet and tenor sax were locked in a death spiral, and we withdrew early.

The rain continued to teem down the next day. Brian and I went in search of boat tickets for our overnight trip down the Grand Canal to Suzhou on the following night. On the way we climbed a hill to a stark gray pagoda, for a misty view of the lake, and stayed for tea and almond cookies. We got lost on the way to the Canal dock, and ended up at the overseas Chinese hotel downtown, for expensive bland coffee and the realization that the day was flawed. Frustrated, we tried for some sightseeing on a jammed tourist boat to the Island of Three Pools. It took us two more boats and a class struggle to

100

get back to the mainland in the deluge.

The only success of the day was to be found in the museum's Ming Dynasty 'Brazen Bowl,' a large round bronze vessel, with two square handles and four tentacled fish embossed on the inside. When the shop worker rubbed her wet hands back and forth on the handles, the fish tentacles sprayed streams of water in high arcs, and into the bowl. *The people are like water and the army is like fish.* The army of waiters in the first two restaurants we tried on the way home refused to swim anywhere near us, but we managed to find Dongpo pork and Jiaohua Young chicken and tofu on our third try. The three noisy Hong Kong adolescents that cloudburst into our dorm stormed room were the perfect end to a downpoured day. During the time of the Southern Song, Hangzhou, with its large population and densely crowded multistoried wooden buildings, had been particularly vulnerable to fires. It was hard to believe.

What the 14th century Moroccan explorer, Ibn Battuta, referred to as 'the biggest city I have ever seen on the face of the earth,' had already been described in similar terms by a Venetian, a hundred years earlier. Marco Polo wrote of 12,000 stone bridges, some so high that ships could pass beneath them. The main street was 200 feet wide, and the markets saw fifty thousand people shopping for 'roebuck, red-deer, hares, rabbits, partridges, pheasants, quails, fowls, capons, and of ducks and geese of infinite quantity.' Musk came from Tibet, ebony, sandalwood and spices from the Indies, silk from southern China, and a hundred times more pepper from Indo-China than it to the whole of Europe. Mansions named 'Pure Delight' or 'Bamboo Chambers' stood on wooded islands in a lake thirty miles across, filled with hundreds of barges for 'a-pleasuring.' Quinsay was, according to Marco, 'beyond dispute the finest and noblest city in the world.'

Daylight brought some sunshine, but it was a Sunday in China, and we were alone with the masses. Brian and I rode our rented Double Happiness bicycles, first to the boat dock to buy tickets for the night boat to Suzhou, and then to a factory noodle shop for breakfast. The owner charged us two fen for parking, and another two for the noodles. And then we peddled to the sights of the *vague and indistinct expanse of water and clouds, where lotus leaves merge with weeping-willow branches.* Our introduction to Lake Abundant was the Jingci Temple, closed for renovation, having been completely ravaged by the Red Guards. It was clear by now that the Cultural Revolution had not been a radical innovation of culture, but a destructive mutiny against it. We passed a young couple popping corn in an overkill pig iron hand turned furnace forge, before Brian tore off, leading me on a rubber-burning speed chase to the north bank of the Qiantang river into what was originally the south orchard of the Five Dynasties Wuyue king, at the foot of Yuelun hill. The nine-storied octagonal Six Harmonies Pagoda, almost 550 feet high, rose steep and grand above us, alternating layers of light on the upper surfaces and shade underneath. Over two hundred carvings of pomegranates and lotuses, lions and phoenixes, peacocks and parrots, and unicorns and fairy maiden protruded from its embossed brick ceilings. It had been built as a lighthouse, and an oblation to calm the tidal bore of the river. *In the pagoda... there is a hideous aspect which we execrate and a sublime aspect which we venerate. So great a subject for spiritual contemplation, such measureless dreaming- the echo of God on the human wall.* The human wall of flag-waving Sunday parades swamped the pagoda, and drowned God.

Back on the West Lake, we didn't fare much better. Built in 1090 by the poet Su Shi, and two hundred thousand helpers, it seemed that they had all returned to celebrate, and occupy every inch of the three kilometer Su Causeway. Qing Emperor Qianlong of the second set of Southern Inspection Tour scrolls thought it was singularly attractive in the early morning of the springtime, but the key word here is singular. Our own *Spring Dawn by Su Causeway* was a Monty Python 'spring surprise.' There could be no *Viewing the Fish at Flower Harbor* when we couldn't get near the water, no *Lotus in the Breeze at Crooked Courtyard* when we couldn't see the ticket office for the crowds, no *Lingering Snow on the Broken Bridge* because we had arrived too late in the year, no *Orioles Singing in the Willows* because they had eaten them all, and no *Evening Bell Ringing at Nanping Hill, Leifeng Pagoda in Evening Glow, Autumn Moon over the Calm Lake,* and no *Three Pools Mirroring the Moon,* because we had a night boat to Suzhou. Of the ten classical views of the West Lake, the only one we managed to see was that of the *Twin Peaks Piercing the Cloud,* because Sunday in China couldn't clusterflock or eat either of the components. There was a moment when the sun brightened and the throngs thinned, where Brian and I experienced, for a time, Ouyang Xiu's Spring Day on West Lake. *The lovely spring breeze has come Back to the Lake of the West. The spring waters are so clear and Green they might be freshly painted. The clouds of perfume are sweeter than can be imagined. In the Gentle East wind the petals fall like grains of rice.*

We parked our bikes, to catch a bus to the Lingyin Monastery. Through an incongruous gauntlet of multicolored beach umbrellas, mirrored sunglasses, Mao caps and Mickey Mouse gloves, Brian and I entered the Temple of the Soul's Retreat. At the peak of the Wuyue Kingdom around 1000 AD, there were nine multistoried buildings, 18 pavilions, 72 halls, and 1300 dorm rooms, inhabited by over 3000 monks. Three of their dharma descendents almost throttled me for sneaking a photo, after Brian's feeble attempt to distract their attention. We moved more quickly and quietly, past the largest wooden statue in China, the Shakyamuni in the Grand Hall of the Great Sage, the largest bronze Buddha in the world, and the carved pilgrims of the *Journey to the West.* Outside was the craggy limestone 'Peak that Flew Hither,' with its ceiling crack sliver of silver sunlight 'one thread of heaven,' and the rich Buddhist carvings in the surrounding grottos. An open-air hypertension clinic was underway, when

103

we reemerged, with long queues of chain-smoking Mao men, waiting their expectorating turns expectantly. We didn't bother. Our pressures were bound to be high.

We returned our bicycles walking, balancing our backpacks on the handlebars. Gong gong qi che #51 took us to the boat dock, where Brian and I found a Chinese friend, from the previous night's restaurant. He ordered for us, West Lake sour carp, steamed pork rice, lotus root pudding, and Xi Hu Long Jing tea. Then he wouldn't let us pay.

In 1276, a Southern Song poet wrote about the West Lake:

> 'Green mountains surround on all sides the still waters of the lake.
> Pavilions and towers in hues of gold and azure rise here and there.
> One would say a landscape composed by a painter.
> Only towards the east, where there are no hills,
> does the land open out, and there sparkle, like fishes' scales,
> the bright coloured tiles of a thousand roofs.'

Just before Kublai Khan laid siege to it.

Brian and I laid siege to Boat 535, half a millennium later. We boarded it like pirates, and like we had learned to board other boats in China. The captain gave us the V berth cabin, in his very small and very slow vessel. The sun set pink and yellow and low on the Grand Canal. Wool was once so scarce here that the boatmen in winter wore stockings of human hair. The one out of our porthole stood high on the timber cargo of his massive barge, guiding its trail with a tiller ten times his size. The water traffic and neighborly snoring would make sleep impossible. But it didn't matter. The full moon and soft filtered lights from the shoreline courtyards rolled along the canal. Brian and I rolled out our sleeping bags anyway, and entered the next section of the Southern Inspection Tour scroll.

> 'Heaven Above, Suzhou and Hangzhou below.'
> Old Chinese Adage

∗   ∗   ∗

'Be born in Suzhou, live in Hangzhou, eat in Guangzhou, die in Liuzhou.'
Chinese Proverb (Suzhou was renowned for its civilized citizens, Hangzhou for
its scenery, Guangzhou for its food, and Liuzhou for its *nanmu* wood coffins
which delayed decay)

The bucket toilet was six hours late and overflowing, when we finally docked in the 'Venice of the East,' at midday. Brian and I had stood in the galley most of the morning, staring at the commissary coolie, until he found us some rice.

We made our way along Youyi Road to the lobby of the Suzhou Hotel where, the predictable awaited. Behind the front desk were three stalwart clone Mao suits with grim countenances. We asked for dorm beds.

"Méi yǒu!" They blurted in unison. Go fish. We told them we would come back later and placed our bags on the counter, requesting that they keep them until we returned. As Brian and I turned to leave, there was a resounding implosive 'thud' that seemed just a little too consequential, in the carelessness they had applied to the gravity on their side of the counter. I didn't know that it had come from Serenity.

Brian checked out the bed status at the Nan Lin across the street while I paid a visit to Public Security, to get a visa extension. Our paths reconnected across the tracks at the Pagoda of Auspicious Light. But this was where the luminescence began to go out. My stomach contracted in pain. I couldn't find my passport. I told Brian that I must have left it at the Public Security Bureau, and ran we ran the full distance back. But they didn't have it, and my insides contracted further, as they ushered me further inside. I waited for a few minutes, until a polished young officer, uniformed in green, wearing a checkerboard banded peaked cap and white tie and gloves, entered the small room. He took up a position behind the desk, and neatly laid out paper and pen and seal. Smooth.

105

"How did you lose your passport?" He asked in perfect English. I told him the story of my morning glory, drew him a map of all the places that Brian and I had been, and let my head fall into a spiral silence.

"Return tomorrow morning at nine." He said. "Do not move from the Suzhou Hotel." And that was it. I was about to ask him what the odds were that he would find such an item, in a city of almost a million people, when I caught his return look. *There is no need to ask questions.*

Brian sensed my devastation, and suggested a special dinner to celebrate the misery, near the Temple of Mystery. The Manchu emperor of the second Southern Inspection Tour scrolls, Qianlong, used to eat at a restaurant that still existed on Guanqian road, two hundred years later. It looked like they hadn't cleaned the place since, but the 'Crane and Pine' *Song helou* food was brilliant. We ate sweet-and-sour Mandarin fish, and dofu with big, black, ugly delicious mushrooms. The two beers may not have been such a good idea.

We returned to the Suzhou Hotel, calm and contented, unaware that the rest of the Auspicious Light was about to go out.

"Good evening, gentlemen." Brian said. "Have you managed to find the dormitory yet?"

"Full!" They blurted in unison. I tried to explain, as graciously as the circumstances allowed, the Public Security officer's instruction to stay nowhere else, but they had already switched to shun mode.

"Fine, thank you." I said. We'll wait." And we sat in the comfy chairs across the room, but nothing happened. I began to pull out the Gold Kazoo, and Brian headed for the exit. Nothing happened. I took off my new sneakers. Nothing happened. I took off my shirt. The lobby filled with a busload of Overseas Chinese. The desk phone rang, and I looked up into three grimaces of grim determination.

"For you!" The one with the phone said, handing me the handset. It was Brian. He had scored two beds in the sitting room of the Nan Lin, and was desperate to avoid an international incident. I had my shirt and shoes back on, by the time he returned to collect his pack, and me. But the Auspicious Light was still dim. When they handed me my pack, I found my immense jar of Nescafé, shattered and strewn through Serendipity's interior. Robotic eyes darted back and forth, looking for their faces, and a way to save them. Eventually, a small jar of 'Sunflower' brand instant coffee surfaced, and hands were shaken. We walked.

"What is essential in war is victory, not prolonged operations." Said Brian, on our way to the Nan Lin.

"Sun Tzu?" I asked.

"He who knows when he can fight and when he cannot will be victorious." He said. "You didn't stand a chance." And he was right.

I fell asleep in the sitting room, to the lunar illumination of a Tang Dynasty poem from the Cold Mountain Temple, its calligraphy dancing over Brian's head.

'While I watch the moon go down, a crow caws through the frost;
Under the shadows of maple-trees a fisherman moves with his torch;
And I hear, from beyond Su-chou, from the temple on Cold Mountain,
Ringing for me, here in my boat, the midnight bell.'
Zhang Ji, *A Night Mooring near Maple Bridge*

The knocking on our door was insistent next morning. The desk clerk delivered an order for me to present myself to Public Security as soon as possible. So it was.

The smooth young agent who had hosted my carelessness the previous day greeted me with no small anxiety. He wanted to know what had transpired at the Suzhou Hotel, the previous evening. I asked him why. He told me he had received an irate call that morning, accusing him of 'meddling.' I had trouble understanding the dynamic. It was like the FBI getting mauled by Howard Johnson's.

So I explained story of the Siege of the Suzhou, and offered to write an account exonerating him of any responsibility for my psychosis. I asked if he had my passport. It had been found at the Pagoda of Auspicious Light, and he was waiting for it to be delivered from a peripheral station. But I caught a glimpse of it in his portfolio, as he handed me paper and pen, accepting my offer of a confession. I was about to experience my own Orwellian 'struggle session.' After thirty minutes I had my first draft. Slowly and diligently, we went over each of the words for comprehension and appropriateness. He made me recopy it twice, each time rearranging the order of the paragraphs, for both of us to gain new and deeper introspection. It was a masterpiece of mutual exoneration. With a satisfied grin and averted eyes, he reached into his case, and pulled out my passport with a flourish, and three messages for me to absorb. In future, I must try to control my temper. I was now witness to the benevolence and efficiency of the Chinese Public Security apparatus, a system which does not exist in any meaningful way in 'capitalist countries.' And, finally, Happy Trails.

"They must've X-rayed and tortured everything between the train station the pagoda." Said Brian, waiting outside. He handed me a cigarette from a packet with a hydroelectric station design. And we ventured into the 2500 year-old Marco Polo neighborhoods of silk and stone, pagodas and canals and elegant bridges, and gardens. In a reflection of recent events, we floated through the round portals, half moon bridges, and upturned pointed eaves of the Humble Administrator's Garden. It was my turn to buy train tickets, and I went off to arrange transport to Kaifeng for the following night. The next roll of the scroll assured, we spent another evening with the classical Chinese cuisine and feminine beauty in the Song helou. Back at the Nan Lin, a large blue-haired American tour group with big luggage was doing standup comedy in the foyer. They were shepherded by a flustered young American girl, trying to conduct a geriatric symphony with chopsticks. Her Mandarin was impressive.

Deidre was a Harvard major in Far Eastern studies, with a minor in Oriental bureaucratic disentanglement. We poured her beer, and she poured out her frustrations. There were tales of the Chinese collective mind, the inertia of tenured positions in the tourism, of transport halted to search for 'stolen chopsticks,' and of cigarette and Swiss Army knife bribery to get planes off the ground.

"They returned one man's laundry with one sock unwashed." She said. Brian asked why.

"They said they couldn't wash just one sock, because where was the other one." She said. I asked for her most profound insight about the Chinese.

"I've been studying them for a decade, and still don't understand them." She said. Diedre showered us with American Fig Newtons and plastic cheese, and left us to put out another cultural conflict.

Our unanticipated initial experiences turned our last day in Suzhou into a mad tour. We had to go slowly through the metaphysical masterpiece of the Master of the Nets Garden. A synthesis of art, nature, and architecture, the combined perfection of dimension, contrast, foil, sequence, depth, and borrowed scenery, it was a tranquility base of clouds and pines and water and stone.

The Great Wave Pavilion was the oldest Suzhou garden, with its walls of 108 fenestrated viewpoints, overlooking a lotus pond formed by a branch of the Fengxi Stream. It was named after a *Fishermen* verse from Qu Yuan's *Songs of the South* poem. '*If the Canglang River is dirty I wash my muddy feet; If the Canglang River is clean I wash my ribbon,*' alluding to an honest official who removed himself from office, to avoid corruption.

A long march brought Brian and I to the very ruined Ruigang pagoda, set in a field overgrown with weeds, and the remnants of an old factory. We lingered in the Lingering Garden outside the Changmen gate, *clean cold color of bamboo, limpid green light of water*, but retreated hastily from the sea of white bucket hats and sunglasses massing in the West Garden Temple next door.

Later than evening in the station, waiting for the Kaifeng Express, I thought of how the Suzhou garden names had echoed my experiences of recent Landscapes Clear and Radiant- *Humble Administrator... Master of the Nets... Lingering... Great Wave.*

Brian gave his dictionary to a tipsy mechanic, and I met an old man who had worked for the American Tobacco Company in Shanghai, back in the 1930's.

"Things are different now, I guess." I offered.

"Oh yes." He said. "Very, very different."

'The Chinese have a strange way of finding out things that we miss.'
Sir Frederick Bruce, *Behind That Curtain* (1929)

Sinews of Our Fathers

'...visiting the sins of the fathers upon the children, and upon the children's children...'

Exodus 34:7

The sweetheart carriage attendant woke Brian and I for breakfast, stirring us, and the dining car staff, to a state of mutual sustenance. Just before noon, we arrived on the southern bank of the Yellow River flood plain, in one of the seven ancient capitals of China and, as an 11th century Northern Song branch of the Silk Road, the largest city on the world.

Located at the junction of four major canals, Kaifeng was known for steaming pie and dumplings, and for a rare community I had come to find traces of. According to three ancient stellae found in their house of worship, they had arrived from India during the 2nd Century BC Han dynasty, and they, and the soldiers and officers they contributed to the Chinese army, had been 'boundlessly loyal to the country and Prince.' The *Hwuy* foreigners living here were named by what they ate. Christians were known as '*Hwuy who abstain from animals without the cloven foot*,' Moslems were called '*Hwuy who abstain from pork*,' and the Jews of Kaifeng were referred to as the '*Hwuy who extract the sinews*.'

It wasn't just any sinew that the description referred to. It was the sciatic nerve, the *gid hanesheh*, which had named a people. My mother had told me that Jews were forbidden to eat the hindquarters of certain domesticated animals, because it was considered 'unclean.' The real story, like most Judaic narratives, was more complicated, and richer in allegorical imagery. The tradition had come from Jacob, the third Patriarch of the tribe, after Abraham and Isaac, and his all-night wrestling match with the angel of his brother, Esau. As morning approached, the angel realized that he had to act fact, for his power would dissipate with the sunrise. He struck

111

Jacob's thigh, 'from which all sexual desire extends,' wounding his sciatic nerve, and permanently crippling him. But Jacob prevailed, and forced the angel to grant him the name of 'Israel,' *he who prevails over the divine.*

Symbolic of man's struggle with his darker side, Jacob's victory over evil urges, and the preservation of his rational and religious scruples, required the literal crushing loss of his potential for visceral arousal. The removal of this sinew, and the acrobatic cartwheels the Hasidic followers of my great ancestor, Baal Shem Tov, spun into, were a commemoration of the birth of a people. Jacob's grappling was the cosmic battle of duality, the spirituality of Israel versus the materiality of Edom. The night of conflict is the 4000 year long and dark *galut* exile, wrestling the Egyptians and Canaanites and Babylonians and Persians and Romans and Inquisition Spaniards and German Nazis and Islamic terrorists. Jacob's descendants were condemned and chosen to suffer physically and in spirit, but ultimately emerge with a new identity, and a journey on to wholeness, *Shalem*. Jerusalem.

The Chinese understood.

> 'They were funky China men from funky Chinatown
> They were chopping them up and they were chopping them down
> It's an ancient Chinese art and everybody knew their part
> From a feint into a slip, and kicking from the hip.'
> Biddu Appaiah, *Kung Fu Fighting*

The Silk Road had ended in the cotton mill we passed, and the crowds we drew at the bus stop followed us for a short a distance through a semi desert park, to the Iron Pagoda. After the original burnt down a thousand years earlier, the Song had reconstructed the two hundred feet masterpiece, in more than fifty kinds of multicolored glazed bricks, appearing iron-grey from a distance. There were over a hundred bells hanging from the eaves, and more than 1600 standing monks and flying dancers, and lions and dragons intricately carved into the exterior. Inside were frescoes from the *Journey to the West*. In almost a thousand years, it had survived 38 earthquakes, six floods, and a Cultural Revolution.

Ugly smokestacks, electric cables, thick air, and industrialized proletarian poverty had replaced whatever wealth and beauty Kaifeng had enjoyed a millennium earlier. We watched exhausted women pulling a road train of laden carts through dusty streets. Emperor Kangxi's Dragon pavilion had been slain. The Yanging Taoist Temple had been obliterated, except for the blue and green tiled red brick faience Jade Emperor Hall, inside a nasty factory yard, overgrown with weeds and abandoned machinery and broken glass. The ten-foot compassion of the Xiangguo monastery's Guanyin Goddess of Mercy was strained, but her thousand hands and eyes had been carved from a single ginkgo tree, taking sixty years to carve, and cover in gold.

Brian and I returned to the Kaifeng Guest House, and made the mistake of asking the desk clerk where to eat. The sign inside the Yuoyixin restaurant should have been the giveaway. 'Comrade Please!' It was captioned, with a short hair female cadre cartoon, in a white numbered lab coat and abattoir hairnet, pointing into the bomb shelter with her outstretched palm. The rice and pork fat and garlic shoots were turbocharged in grease and price. I pointed out that we didn't consume the delicious soup they were adamant we ordered. But it was there on the bill. The myth about the Chinese symbol for crisis and opportunity being identical hit the bomb shelter wall head on, as we were forced to pay for the privilege of, instead of licking our fingers, licking our wounds. In Pearl Buck's novel, *Peony*, she wrote of a 'Street of the Plucked Sinew.' But Brian and I never found one. We were three hundred years too late. Even in 1605, when the Jesuit priest Matteo Ricci found them, the Kaifeng Jews were 'well on their way to becoming Saracens or heathens.' They certainly hadn't waited for me, in the inevitability of their assimilation.

'He was part of a whole, a people scattered over the earth and yet eternally one and indivisible. Wherever a Jew lived, in whatever safety and isolation, he still belonged to his people.'

Pearl S. Buck, *Peony*

*   *   *

'The heavy earth cart
Rumbles by
Peonies tremble.'
Yosa Buson

Brian and I arrived in the geographical center of China, the *First Under Heaven* 'City of the Peony,' ten days after the beginning of its Second *Sho Yu* Festival. The traditional flower symbol of China had been thought to been created by the moon goddess, to reflect her beams at night. During the Middle Ages, 'lunatics' had been covered with peony leaves and petals, in the belief that this would cure them. There weren't enough peonies on the planet, to cure the lunacy of the heavy earth cart that rumbled over us on the night we arrived.

Brian and I had initially left Kaifeng on a three-hour bus ride to Zhengzhou, intending to spend a day there. The gritty thickness of the orange incense masquerading as air catapulted us onto another conveyance, heading to where the sun shone on the *yang* north side of the Luo River, Louyang. But not before Brian picked us up some greasy sesame-coated rice donuts, and I braved the worst *cesuo* public toilet in China. Broad slow milky streams flowed reluctantly around frightening uroliths, into uric acid-encrusted drains. I wondered what they ate in Zhengzhou.

"Time to go." Brian shouted. And I was right behind him.

Right behind us were two animated young English teachers, rapturous with the sudden opportunity to practice their craft. The older one with the Mao cap blew a long trumpet blast on

Sino-Canadian friendship, something about Norman Bethune. It didn't seem to have the desired effect.

"What do you think of China?" He asked.

"What do you think of China?" I answered, like a Kaifeng Jew. Too open-ended, they changed the subject.

"What do you think of Afghanistan?" The younger, more tentative one asked.

"What do you think of Afghanistan?" Asked Brian.

"Very bad." He replied, surprised that I didn't know. "Cultural imperialism."

"What do you think of Tibet?" I asked, closing the trap.

"Tibetans are Chinese, like Chinese." He said. "Except for Indian Tibetans. Bad people." I went for the mind probe.

"Because of their beliefs?" I asked. "Can't people who think differently live together in harmony?"

"There is no God." Said the Mao cap. "Only modern man." I asked if they thought that tolerance of individual beliefs and personal freedom were basic rights. The younger and more troubled companion thought so, and disagreed with the older android.

"So you have a difference of opinion." I asked. "Is that good or bad."

"Bad." Said the Mao cap.

"Neither good nor bad." Said the questioning one. We had arrived at their stops, physical and metaphorical. They withdrew, leaving tidings of international friendship, and taking the seeds of dissent, as they departed.

"Well, they're done." Said Brian. And we rolled on into the dusk, past a Sung dynasty ruin, lined with boulders carved in human form.

The lunacy of the heavy earth cart met us in the late night darkness of Luoyang, crushing all flowers and moonbeams in its path. The ground outside the station began to tremble, as it rumbled around the corner, nearly colliding with the bus shelter we were waiting in. As if they could have been shelter. This was the infamous Gong gong qi che #2, the bus carved in human form, careening by at light speed, with Guanyin's thousand handholds grabbing our human forms and backpacks, and inhaling us whole into its entrance, before passing us backwards into its crushing alimentary tract. It didn't matter that we had no air, as we were squeezed so tight that we had no way to move it anyway. Brian and I relinquished the last of our breath to preserve what was left of our circulation. We couldn't have fallen if we had wanted to. The monster spat us out, down a Leviathan airport runway. The scale of public works in China was designed to continually remind you of your individual significance. Personal beliefs were inconsequential. The state was all that mattered. Several kilometers later, we entered the lobby of the Friendship Hotel. The young clerk behind the desk found us a guitar, and escorted us to the spacious fourth floor dorm. He opened the door to a voice from another train.

"Hi Wink." Said Annie from Kunming. "Welcome to the Friendship." I knew she meant it.

"Who's that?" Asked Brian. I told him. The wind picked up through the trees outside.

"Bai liang jin." I said. "One hundred ounces of gold." That's what the locals used to call Luoyang peonies, and the monopoly they maintained. Unsuspecting visitors used to pay enormous fortunes for dead plants which had their roots boiled. A problem with beauty. *Pity the girl of the flowery house, who is not equal to the blossoms of Luoyang.*

> 'From whose home secretly flies the sound of a jade flute?
> It's lost amid the spring wind which fills Luoyang city.
> In the middle of this nocturne I remember the snapped willow,
> What person would not start to think of home.'
> Li Bai, *Hearing a Flute on a Spring Night in Luoyang*

We took the next morning early and easy, slurping jarred mandarins and chewing the dry glutamate buns that Brian had ventured out to procure. Out of our dorm window, we watched other local foragers, bringing back little peony

116

cuttings from their 'mountain combings.'

Later, Brian and I went south into the *Dragon's Gate* limestone cliffs that flanked the Yishui River, and the hundred thousand Buddhist statues of the Longmen Grottoes. Some were less than an inch high. Others soared sixty feet above us. But heads had been lopped off and sculpture disfigured, and it wasn't clear whether most of the damage had by done by Japanese looting or the home team vandalism. Despite the desecrations, especially in the Lotus Flower and Medical Prescription Caves, you could still feel the magnificence, tamer than my memory of Ellora, more imposing.

It had taken 800,000 workers twenty-three years to create the Middle Binyang Cave alone. Empress Wu Zetian contributed 'twenty-thousand strings of her rouge and powder money' to include her 'Chinese Mona Lisa' face, on the quintessential *Vairocana* Buddhist sculpture of the Fenxian Ancestor Worshipping Cave.

The ongoing devastation was occurring in the souls of the visitors, if they had any. The longer we stayed at Longmen, the more what should have been a spiritual grotto became a mobbed carnival scene of white hats, dark sunglasses, ghetto blasters, and vendors. Many of the ancient Buddhas at Longmen were two-faced, but nothing like their modern Han visitors. I grieved for the reverse direction that human evolution had shifted into. *Heart of the flower sadness about to break but how could we know this from such spring colors.*

Back at the Friendship, Brian and I met the two faces of Annie's new friends, Liz and Jamie, Peace Corps volunteers fresh from Samoa, caught in the headlights of a hundred flowers blooming. I left to book hard seats to Xi'an and, upon returning found two new-faced additions to our dorm room. The Australian with the T-shirt emblazoned with 'Stand Up for Your Rights,' could have been Germaine Greer, if Germaine had been immature forever. Her partner, although that particular euphemism didn't exist yet, was an even more hob-nailed, opinionated and outspoken American.

Unusual physical occurrences that are harmful to human beings are called catastrophes; unusual occurrences that are merely startling but do no harm are called phenomena. Brian and I tried to harmonize the vital forces of heaven and earth with some guitar playing, but catastrophe was up to bat. The feminazis wanted to talk politics. Brian produced a bottle of bad Chinese whiskey, and the black ants came crawling out over the green fists of the peonies. I may have become a little effusive, but I did manage to change the course of the discourse.

I told them of Ouyang Xiu, the Song Dynasty Renaissance man, the 'Old Drunkard' who had written the *Luoyang mudan ji*, an account of the tree-peonies of Luoyang. His catalogue of the forms and colors of Elegant Plum, Cranes in-Harmony Red, Inverted Sandalwood-Heart, Nine-Stamen True Pearl, Doe's Womb Flower, Licorice Root Yellow, Jade Tablet White, Crimson Peach, Auspicious Jade Lotus still evokes their wild and pristine hunger for life, and their transience. Ouyang Xui had been undisciplined as a youth, stepping off the path, for pleasure, before returning to a more noble focus.

"Just like you some day, Wink." Said Brian.

We all fell asleep drunk with flowers, butterflies swirling in our dreams.

'We had a drinking party to admire the peonies.
I drank cup after cup till I was drunk.
Then to my shame I heard the flowers whisper,
'What are we doing, blooming for these old alcoholics?"
Ling Huchu, *Drinking with Friends Amongst the Blooming Peonies*

*   *   *

'India Conquered and dominated China culturally for 20 centuries without ever having to send a single soldier across her border.'

Hu Shih

There had been one soldier that crossed her border. Just as my pilgrimage through Europe had traced the evolution of Western civilization and the travels of Benjamin of Tudela, my path to the epicenter of Zen in China had followed the man who brought it.

Traditionally depicted as an ill-tempered, bearded wide-eye barbarian, Bodhidharma had come from Tamil Nadu in Southern India, via Canton and the Yangtze River, to the Shaolin Temple. In 547 AD, according to the record of the Buddhist monasteries of Luoyang, he 'sees the golden disks reflecting in the sun, the rays of light illuminating the surface of the clouds, the jewel-bells on the stupa blowing in the wind, and the echoes reverberating beyond the heavens.' But this is where our paths diverged.

Bodhidharma, either refused entry or ejected after a short time, moved into a nearby Song Mountain cave to meditate. He 'faced a wall for nine years, not speaking for the entire time.' The Wall-Gazing Brahmin fell asleep after seven years and, angry with himself, cut off his eyelids to prevent it from happening again. As his eyelids hit the floor, the first tea plants sprang up, providing the stimulant to keep his subsequent students awake during their own meditations. After nine years of sitting, his legs had atrophied so badly, that Japanese Bodhidharma dolls have no legs.

When I opened my eyes at 5:30 am, they hurt all the way to my hair. But Brian and I were determined to visit Shaolin monastery, and clattered out the dorm door and into the Luoyang streets. The searing sunlight had cut off my eyelids, and the thousands of automaton early-morning joggers were too much for the rest of my head. It was 1984, hardcore, and hard to ignore.

"Someday we'll need missiles on the BC coast." I shouted to Brian as he tried to keep up with a runner, trying to get directions to the bus stop, between gasps. We shoehorned onto Gong gong qi che#2, exhaled at the station and secured tickets for the 7:30 am bus to the temple. The liquid craving in our heads found a jar of lychees and a glass of tea at a roadside stand, before we boarded. Brain was seated in the very back, but I was given the engine cowling next to the bus driver, which I shared precariously with several army recruits. The rattling engine and body heat, and the Mandarin chattering around me, were perfect turbulent complements to the runaway chainsaw inside my skull. The echoes reverberated beyond the heavens.

To make matters worse, it was a Sunday, the full impact of which struck even the Chinese tourists, when we spotted the fleets of buses in the Shaolin lot. David Carradine would have lost it, and the Indian Brahmin monk would have headed straight for the cave, without stopping at the monastery.

After his ninth year of meditation, the Bodhidharma had made a hole in the cave wall with his stare, leaving behind an iron chest. When the monks opened it, they found two books, the *Bone Marrow Cleansing Classic*, and the *Sinew Metamorphosis Classic*. The first has long since disappeared, but the 'Yi Jin Jing' Sinew Change Classic, inspired by the poor physical shape the Bodhidharma had initially observed in the Shaolin monks, had been preserved and guarded for centuries. The techniques contained within have been taught intensively and, as a result, the monks of Shaolin have become famous for their fighting skill, *Shaolin-do qigong*, more widely known as Kung Fu.

Brian and I walked under the calligraphy hanging over the Heavenly King Hall, written by Emperor Kangxi, of the first Southern Inspection Tour scroll, and a Shaolin benefactor. Inside red earthen walls and yellow peonies, were blue kung fu frescos, deep depressions in the stone floors made by centuries of martial art practice, innumerable portraits in stone and paint of the founder of Zen, and disciplined killer monks in a magical place. One gave me a rubbing of Bodhidharma, which I still have in my office today. Another gave me a gift of sweet yams, which fortified me for the gristle-grinding, sinew-stretching return to Luoyang. We passed an immense billboard, advertising Shaolin Rheumatoid Anodyne Powder, too late.

We left the 6th century cave of Bodhidharma for his evolving successive renditions, as Daruma or Da Mo, founder of Zen and kung fu, a convergence back to my own path, and more in harmony with what I wished to become. From the 17th century onwards, Japanese paintings and woodblock prints depicted the ill-tempered, bearded wide-eye barbarian as a living eminent monk, not a rarified dead deity. Daruma had become identified with the daily sufferings of the common man, and just as weak and acquisitive and vain. Instead of staring at a cave wall, like a Plato allegory, he seeks to bring compassion and wisdom to his community. To reach the great truth of Zen, and gain salvation, he would *throw himself down into a bottomless abyss, and this, indeed, is no easy task.* With mirth and laughter, let old wrinkles come.

Later that evening, after noodles and duck, the clerks from the front desk brought their guitars and friends to our dorm room, and the spirit of international harmony was rejoined. Just before we turned in, well after midnight, one of the comrades asked me to improvise a spontaneous song, to commemorate the enduring friendship of our peoples. The echoes of the applause reverberated beyond the heavens.

> 'Everybody was kung-fu fighting
> Those cats were fast as lightning
> In fact it was a little bit frightning
> But they fought with expert timing'
> Biddu Appaiah, *Kung Fu Fighting*

Frank Li

'A youngster when I left
And now grown old I return;
Still with my country dialect,
But with my hair thinning;
None of the children know me
And they laughingly ask,
'Traveler, where do you come from?"
He Zhizhang

Those who would have you believe that natural selection is anything but random, had never tried to board a train from Luoyang to Xi'an in the 1980s. The largest human experiment in the eradication of individual variation had gone prime time, and the smallest stations in the hinterland cities of the farthest flung corners of the Middle Kingdom, were rainbows of chaos. Nietzsche's remark that you must have chaos within you to give birth to a dancing star saw Brian and I reborn, on the morning we left the Friendship, as Fred and Ginger.

It began with a violent bus stop scrimmage, and a steep climb to the train station. A blue zoot Mao suit pointed us to the stadium-sized parking lot that served as an antechamber. When the train pulled in, it triggered a frenzied stampede of rabid lemmings, kicking and elbowing to get the last seat on a nightmare. Brian and I plowed through car after cramped car, sweating, cursing, and exuding international harmony, until we found our hard sleeper carriage. The mandarin in charge perused the funny colored stamps in our passports, and the reservations we had worked so hard to obtain.

"Meiyou!" He said. We had been officially unnaturally deselected.

Instead of the recumbent repose we had looked forward to, Brian and I played chess and drank tea, on hinged seats, in a haze of tobacco and a hailstorm of flying sputum, striving on with diligence.

Half a day later, we arrived in what had been the ancient capital of Chang'an, the eastern terminus of the Silk Road, and city of 'perpetual peace.' It was destined to come very close to mine. The special virus, lurking in the biochemical murkiness of whatever we had been breathing on the death transport, was another dancing star, waiting in the wings. Brian and I checked into the cheaper annex of the Jiefang Hotel, and the noisiest, dustiest, dingiest, double room in China. Across from a view of ubiquitous gray smokestacks, power lines, cranes, NeoStalinist concrete architecture, and a lone basketball backboard, I lay on my bed and decided to be ill. As Brian left to change some money, another rainbow appeared, bringing a high fever, sinew-wrenching rigors, muscle pain, stuffed sinuses, a rib-searing cough, and a headache that pounded me prostrate with every heartbeat. But the cotton that had arrived in my ears wasn't quite enough to block the Chinese corridor cacophony, the sounds of taxiing expectorations, blaring televisions, and the incessant nasal revolutionary feline female loudspeaker whining outside our window; the mercury that had arrived in my own nasal passages wasn't quite enough to block the aromas of stale urine and MSG-saturated feces and industrial fallout and saltpeter cigarette smoke. For the first time in the odyssey, I wondered if I would make it home alive. Soot powder blew in with the homesickness, through the windows. By the time that Brian returned with dumplings, I was already comatose. He told me later that I had slept for 36 solid hours, interrupted only by his administrations of aspirin, jarred fruit, gunpowder tea, and nursing care.

Somewhere above the factory floodlights and the smog of Smaug, was one of the oldest Chinese constellations, *Shen*, sometimes associated with punishment. During my first two days in Xi'an, I needed no further proof. Shen had been a rainbow of dancing stars. But ancient Chinese astronomers had visualized Shen in the exact same way as the same European constellation, which had propelled me this far around the globe, right down to the antagonism of the Scorpio constellation on the other side of the sky. Shen was Orion, the hunter. In his final form, he not only had the four traditional outline stars, the three stars of the belt and three in the sword, but an additional subconstellation, imagined as the various army generals for a warrior chief.

That he rose again on the third day, according to the scriptures, because we had come to Xi'an to see the various army generals of another warrior chief, the first emperor of China. In 210 BC, Qin Shi Huang, was interred in a necropolis complex of three pits, containing 130 chariots, 6700 horses, and over 8,000 clay soldiers, officials acrobats, strongmen, and musicians. It took 700,000 workers a century, to construct what a contemporary poet had described as possessing a hundred rivers flowing with mercury, under a ceiling decorated with heavenly bodies, and land features of palaces, towers, and wonderful objects. The terracotta army had been assembled in parts, on the same assembly line that manufactured drainpipes. The figures were placed in precise military formation, according to rank and duty, and painted in bright pigments. The weapons discover inside were coated with chromium oxide, a technology that wouldn't be developed in the West until two millennia later. The crossbows had a range of half a mile.

Brian and I arrived only ten years after a group of farmers digging a well had discovered the Terracotta Army. We climbed the 1300 meters of Mount Li, Black Steed Mountain, said to 'shine like a beacon in the evening sunlight.' Lí Shān was said to be the place where the goddess, Nüwa, creator of mankind, repaired the wall of heaven. Frankly, I confess a small incantation.

Two days before our visit, the army had played host to another warrior, whose red carpet was still visible, weaving through the pits. We had a less auspicious welcome than Ronald Reagan had enjoyed, our views obscured by the People's Liberation Army, and our exit delayed by the Hong

Kong throng, buying out the entire collection of miniature replicas in the shop.

The chancellor of the Qin dynasty that had built this, and the real force that unified China, was from the same Chu state that our raving wall poet, Qu Yang, had taken his own life over the loss of.

As a young man, Li Si had observed that outhouse rats were dirtier and hungrier than barn house rats. He concluded that values are determined by social status, and that was determined by randomness. Honor was a relative commodity. He moved to Qin, and convinced Emperor Qin Shi Huang not only to lure intellectuals to his jurisdiction, but to also send out assassins to kill important scholars in other Warring States. And then had him kill his own.

Li Si instituted the totalitarian policy of Fénshū Kēngrú, the *Burning of the books and burying of the scholars.* All the classics of the Hundred Schools of Thought, including key Confucian texts, were burned, except for the few legalistic works he needed to achieve complete autocratic control. History and poetry archives disappeared, and anyone ever associated with them was buried alive, along with their families, along with those who failed to report known associations, and their families. Those who failed to burn the listed books within 30 days were banished, to work as convicts on the Great Wall. The rats had taken over the barnyard.

Li Si created the prototypic militarily successful efficient Chinese bureaucratic state, systematizing written language, currency, weights, and other measures. Axle lengths were made uniform, so Qin cartwheel ruts were all the same width, and all carts could travel all the roads of the empire. He even standardized the form of capital punishment and, in 208 BC, discovered to have ratfinked the chief eunuch that gained power, was executed with his own *Five Pains.* First, his nose was cut off, followed by a hand, and a foot. Then he was castrated, and finally cut in half by way of waist slice.

Southwest of Xi'an is a pattern of large ancient clay pyramids that mirror the belt stars of Orion. Even behind the Bamboo Curtain, were constellations, and cartwheels, and chaos.

> 'Thirty spokes on a cartwheel
> Go towards the hub that is the center
> – but look, there is nothing at the center
> and that is precisely how it works!'
> Lao Tzu, *Tao Te Ching*

*   *   *

> 'Thread in the mother's hand
> Sewing for her journeying son
> Stitching finely, carefully,
> Because she fears he will wander
> Long; who says
> That the grass' green
> Well rewards
> The sunshine of spring?'
> Meng Chiao, *A Traveler's Song*
> (Postcard to my Mother, Xi'an, 04 May 1984)

The echoes reverberating beyond the heavens were from thunder. Shen's punishment pelted us with Nüwa's rain, as we descended to the base of Mount Li, and the Huaqing Hot Springs. After two days in the Jiefang annex, Brian and I needed the cleansing. Beyond the two towering cedars at the entrance, in the middle of a small lake, was the white marble statue of a perfect female form, magnificent in her voluptuous proportions.

"I've almost forgotten about them." Brian said. "Who's that?"

"Yang Gufei." I said. "One of the four great beauties of China. Her exquisiteness was thought to shame flowers. *Xi*

Shi sinks fish, Wang Zhaojun entice birds falling, Diaochan eclipses the moon, Yang Guifei shames flowers. Mirrored in the lotus-dotted lake, punctuated with rocks and willows and lotuses, was the Frost Flying Hall, no snow surrounding it in winter, because of the hot steam rising within.

"What was her story?" Brian asked one of the guides.

He told us of the love story that also rose within, in the bedroom of the Tang Emperor, Xuanzong. Yang had originally been the wife of his son, *Li* Mao, but Xuanzong took her as a replacement for the loss of his favorite concubine. Her mother was given the title of Lady of *Li*-ang. Yang was attended by the eunuch, Gao *Li*-shi, who brought her favorite *li*chee fruit by pony express from southern China. After chancellor *Li* Linfu died, crown prince *Li* Heng's eunuch, *Li* Fuguo, accused her of treason, and ordered her strangled. The emperor wanted to bury her properly, but his official *Li* Kui spoke against it.

"Certainly a love-li dol-li." Said Brian. And the game was afoot.

"But a beast-li anoma-li from a dastard-li bul-li." And so went the rest of the day. We left the high spots of Mount Li Palace where *The Song of Everlasting Sorrow* had entered into the azure clouds, for the underground Neolithic excavations of Banpo village, before my pounding head crashlanded me back in the ug-li confines of the smel-li Jiefang.

I was feeling better by next morning, and Brian and I climbed the two hundred feet, to the top of the Big Wild Goose Pagoda, for a misty view of an amusement arcade that had been carved out of an old bomb shelter. We crossed the moat, which had once surrounded sixteen miles of fifty-foot thick walls, enclosing the Sui dynasty city of fourteen square miles, once, like so many others, the largest in the world. In 1911, the revolution that overthrew the Qing Dynasty, massacred the Manchus living in the northeastern zone, within the city ramparts. An impressive Confucian temple garden, a memorable Tang Uiguar military edict in the museum, and the somber terra cotta of the melancho-li mosque, overrun with rain and ruin, lead us back to fetch our packs, for the eleven hour train journey to Xining.

A day of chess games, box lunches and lethargy finally pulled us into the largest city on the Tibetan plateau, the *City of Peace in the West*. Xining had a large Islamic population, and a reputation for the heaviest alcohol consumption in China, *due to the cold climate*. Brian and I had a beer and *gan ban* noodles, in a Moslem café across from the station. A midnight marauding tuktuk tuk us through a bitter-li cold wind, to the Xining Hotel. The desk clerk wore a suit and tie, both of which were two sizes too big for him. He promised to book our exit train to Hohot, and checked us into a room. The Japanese guy, fast asleep on the cot, hadn't been mentioned. Lucki-li for him, we were friend-li, and tired.

*   *   *

'In the land of China, people hardly got nothing at all.'
Forrest Gump

Emerging into the high altitude aridity transported me back to the Altiplano, or Ladakh. The Silk Road sun was glorious. Brian and I hoisted our packs, and boarded a bus, near-li empty, to what we thought was going to be just another disappointing destination from another dead dynasty. But when the snow-clad mountains buoyed up over the horizon, they made the sound of two low whistles. We were headed for the source of the Dane's Mongolian silk in Ta'ersi, through ridges and passes, and meadows of wildflowers. The only detraction was Israeli Izzie, who knew everything about everywhere, and his older Australian consort, who didn't know anything about anywhere, and didn't care.

A steep kilometer climb took us to the lamasery pilgrim

guesthouse. Brian and I checked in, leaving Izzie haggling over the black market exchange rate, and his princess cutting her nails onto the office floor. After a dumpling soup and a jar of mandarins in a market food stall, we set off further up the hill, to find the Mongolian silk. I bought an old bone opium pipe from a vendor, whose bones were likely as old, and in the final establishment, a tiny wooden working abacus, from an aging Muslim figure with a long sparse white beard. His wife stood behind him, and whispered in his ear, and behind her stood their grandson, the shrewdest of the lot, whispering in hers. Brian caught me looking at the small Buddhas, corroded with time, on his back shelf. He saw me spread my hands, inquiring if there might be a bigger one. The old man glanced around at his wife furtive-li and, receiving a nod, ushered us behind the curtain in the back of his shed, dusted the chairs, poured out the tea, and proffered the tobacco. We had arrived. But I wasn't prepared. What he removed from the bottom of a wooden chest threw me 400 definite years into the past, and my like-li future forever, in a Chinese prison. The look on Brian's face was sheer terror. Sitting on a newspaper covered makeshift table, in all his verdigris poise, was the most magnificent bronze Buddha in the world. After three cups of tea, countless saltpeter cigarettes, and innumerable inquiries as to the health and variety of the fami-li members, I finally summoned up the courage to ask the price. Brian fell of his stool but, after almost four years of globetrotting, I knew the rules of the opening gambit. In Latin America, it was three times the asking price; in darkest Africa, it was twice; in Islamic cultures, it was the moon. I sent out a lunar probe. It went back and forth, as the old man and his whispering wife and grandson dropped an order of magnitude, but it was still too much. We receded into stalemate and a need for contemplation, and agreed to return the following day. *Salaam Aleichem. Aleichem Salaam.*

On jel-li legs, and the weakness of the dying sun, we hiked to the Golden Tiled Temple of the Kumbum monastery, and context. Under the reflection of the solid gold roof plates, in the courtyard of an ancient lamasery, on the flagstones of an invaded people, sat a hundred monks. The sea of crimson robes and shaved heads was like a crustacean reunion. Brian and I sat in a corner and listened to the deep otherworld-li chanting, monotonous melancholic moaning minor-key marrow-penetrating mantras to the end of existence and suffering, an aspiration to which the Han Chinese seemed more than happy to contribute. In an otherwise spiritless land, we had found a voice, and it resonated like a sad wind through a medieval ruin.

Younger monks pinched and threw water at each other during the ritual, and the older lamas seemed more bemused than angry at the hijinx. A devout but mischievous novice snatched us from our vantage point, to show us how to spin the bank of giant prayer wheels lining the cloister. He grabbed each handle and flicked his prayer into space with a wink, like he was flipping a hockey puck into an unguarded net, in a game which had gone too far into overtime, the last good fight of a white pawn on a black-dominated board, just before checkmate, the high chaparral of the cosmos and life and love.

Brian and I put our hands together and moved out, up the hill overlooking the monastery to the north, and the snow-clad range to the south. We found a rock at the highest point of the freshly furrowed clay, and sat. And wondered at the emptiness, at the dirt track weaving into infinity towards Tibet through impassable peaks, and especially, most poignantly, at the silence. We had survived six weeks in the most cacophonic country on Earth, and the sudden serene sanity was paralyzing. When we broke it, it was softly, with gentle thoughts of small mountain farms, Tibet, existence, the universe and home. And we stayed in our aerie until the wind picked up, and then wound our way down without speaking.

In a small Muslim shack below the Lamasery, the lady of the

dirt floor establishment conjured up the best homemade noodles in China, with hunks of air-dried mutton shank, condiments and Oriental devotion. We returned to the guesthouse to find two new Danes, Jasper and Thomas, who would turn out to be much fun, and more reckless. Our sleep was interrupted first by Izzy's guide to impecunious travel in India, embellished by banal tales from the princess, and then Brian's racing mind.

"Frank-li, I think it's a bad idea." He said. When people start sentences with 'frankly,' there are no other sentences that will matter.

"Besides, since when does a Jew buy a Buddhist relic from a Moslem?" He asked.

"Since I've already given him a name." I said.

The monastery was named *Kumbum*, after the '100,000 enlightening bodies of the Buddha' on the leaves of the holy sandalwood *Tree of Great Merit*, that had sprouted from drops of the Yellow Hat sect founder's birth blood. Built in 1560, it was known as the *Pistil of the Lotus*, a sign of the eight-spoked dharma wheel, and ranked in importance as second only to Lhasa. Alexandra David-Neel, the anarchist Belgian explorer, visited the monastery in 1918, and stayed for three years. She found four thousand lamas living in complete silence, except for the sound of Tibetan long trumpets, calling them together.

'We were taken first to the great kitchen where priests were brewing Tibetan tea in great copper cauldrons ten feet in diameter, beautifully chased with the Buddhist symbols. The stoves were the usual mud affairs and the fuel nothing but straw, which younger lamas continually fed to the fire... Terrible hailstorms would often break over the monastery, due, said the country folk, to the malignity of the demons who sought to disturb the peace of the saintly monks.'

The demons broke over the monastery with a vengeance, ear-li next morning. The mountains had bare-li forced the clouds to turn back, and a sea of white mist enveloped our return to the old man, and his secret. He and his wife welcomed us with tea, cigarettes, chairs and no small measure of expectation. After the customary interval inquiry after our mutual wellbeing, I offered 300 yuán. Their demeanor told me they were disappointed, but not crestfallen. The counter came in at 400 yuán. The split difference placed the four hundred year-old Buddha in my hands. It was warm.

But not as warm as the conversation with Brian, on the way back to the refuge. He was troubled about my exchanging money for something that belonged to Kumbum, about the risk I was assuming in trying to smuggle it out of China, and the bad karma I was creating by materializing something so inherently spiritual.

"It would be a noble gesture for you to return it." He said.

"Yes, it would." I agreed. "If I was sure that its return would result in its protection, and that it wouldn't take the same detour off the middle path that resulted in our finding it in the back of a Moslem trafficker's shack in the first place. Besides, this is one of the hundred thousand Buddhas this place is named after."

"You're contributing to the illicit trade in antiquities." He said, and asked me if I didn't think that the Tibetans hadn't been 'fucked over enough.'

"Absolutely, but I didn't do it, and whose to say that my actions aren't more like Elgin protecting the marbles of the Parthenon. It's not as if the Chinese have been a paragon of cultural custodianship." He asked me if I would give it back if the Chinese began to treat the Tibetans more humanely.

"Yes." I said. And we both knew it would be awhile.

"What are you going to call him?" He asked. I told him that the meaning of 'li,' in Mandarin, was 'decorum' or 'rules of conduct,' as referred to in Confucius' *Liji*, Book of Rites.

"You're going to call him Li?" He asked. I told him that the original word 'frank,' meant, among other things, 'to enable to pass or go freely, to facilitate the comings and goings of a person.'

"You're going to call him Frank?" He asked.

133

"Frank." I said. "Frank Li.'

"And how do you propose to get Frank out of China?" He asked.

"Look, Brian. The Bodhidharma brought Buddhism to China. These monks and this monastery came here through Mongolia. That's how I'm taking him out, physically and metaphysically, back out the way he came in." He looked shocked.

"You'll never make it. What makes you think you'll make it?" He asked.

"One more Frank, Franklin D. Roosevelt. *Take a method and try it. If it fails, admit it frankly, and try another. But by all means, try something.* Besides, Frank Li is a protection *mudra* Buddha, dispelling fear, and only useful to those who have achieved enlightenment. What could possibly go wrong?"

The rest of the day passed into a confused guilt. Brian beat me in chess for the first time, as if to revisit his rectitude. We watched pilgrims from afar, prostrate themselves a hundred times on the porch of the Golden Tiled Temple, wearing the boards and stones into grooves where their feet and hands landed, burying themselves in the dust of their ancestors.

Inside were silk brocade thangkas, an enormous gold figure of Tsongkapa, and thousands of small burning butter lamps, mystical-li gleaming relief onto temple vessels and saint-li faces of the Buddha. Brian and I bought turquoise, and made a pungent fruit cocktail from jarred oranges and mummified pears. In Thomas and Jasper's departure, we requisitioned their quarters and, if it hadn't been for the guilt of Frank Li, and Izzy waking me to borrow my map, we might have slept more than we did.

We should have missed the last day at Kumbum. It was as if the monastery was determined to show me the tragedy I was contributing to. On our hilltop vantage point, a young monk asked me for, and received, that rarest of blessings, a pen. Outside the Golden Tiled Temple, twenty of Gautama's children rose and fell in a rhythm, stirring up a dusty revolution the only way they knew how. A young Tibetan girl of about sixteen, on her knees, pierced me through with a doe-eyed stare. One of the senior monks inside asked me, in passable English, about Canada. I told him that our sympathies were with his people. He nodded, and a thousand butter flames wavered in the semidarkness. But the real darkness was back outside.

Buses had unloaded hordes of Mao suits and white caps and sunglasses, carrying countless blaring ghetto blasters, which competed with the megaphone-amplified patter of their tour guides. They climbed over relics, jammed their clicking cameras in the monks' faces, and gawked at the Tibetan devotees, like they were tadpoles hatching. They laughed and spat and shouted abuse at the prone pilgrims approaching the temple entrance. I asked one what was so funny.

"They are like cave people." He grinned. I didn't do what I wanted to. Perhaps it was Frank's protective mudra. Instead I went back to the guesthouse, and penned a letter to Norman Bethune.

Dear Norm,

Hope you're comfortable in your hard seat Hall of Heroes. I congratulate you and the Great Helmsman for bringing so many human beings from a brutal feudal system of unimaginable deprivation, to a staggering utilitarian material advantage. A billion people, on the revolutionary road to the future, now have food, housing, electricity, health care, and transport. Quantitative security has been achieved, at the cost of their souls.

They have enough food, but there's no joy in its preparation; they have Housing, but it's uniformly gray and shabby; they have electricity, but for what purpose? They have transport, but where are they going? The sparks of creativity and love had been expunged. Their gaze is so firmly fixated in the mythology of the future, they've destroyed their past, their inertial frame of reference, tripping over themselves to eliminate that most important of temporal entities, the present. And here and now, the collective Modern Man, screams and streams over anything that requires the spontaneous impulsive intuitive artistic flame of the individual, dousing it with a society of devastating mediocre sameness.

You have purged the planet of its life, beauty, and quality, for a world of uniform visceral function. But while the dissenters can be overwhelmed, their ideas will endure. With paintbrushes and pens and violins, we can still bring back some of the poetry and birdsong and consciousness you didn't need to sacrifice.

Frank Li, Unimpressed.

He asked me if I would give him back if the Chinese began to treat the Tibetans more humanely.
"Yes." I said. And we both knew it would be awhile.
Thirty years on, and Frank still looks out from my mantle.

"Where is the star nursery in Orion, Uncle Wink?" Asked Millie, looking up as if to find it.

"You see the smudge just beyond the last star of his sword?" Uncle Wink asked. Sam and Millie nodded.

"That's M42, the Orion Nebula, almost 24 light years across, and 1500 light years away, but still the closest region of massive star formation to Earth. It weighs two thousand times more than the Sun, but is just a blister on the invisible Orion Molecular Cloud, spanning from above his head to far below his feet. Supersonic gas bullets, each ten times the diameter of Pluto's orbit and tipped with glowing bright blue iron atoms, pierce the dense hydrogen clouds of the Nebula. The stellar nursery is lively, but is chaotic, seriously overcrowded, and not well run. Orion has rock stars, which live fast and die young. Young stars emit more than 110 spectacular individual gas jets of hydrogen molecules in all directions from their poles, each travelling at hundreds of miles per second, extending across trillions of miles of interstellar space. In the heart of the Nebula is the Trapezium Cluster discovered by Galileo in 1617, two thousand stars within twenty light years diameter. For understandable reasons, he missed the runaway black hole a hundred times more massive than the Sun.

Nearby is my favorite nebula, the Running Man, and nowhere near him is my favorite galaxy, a product of the chaotic collision of two galaxies, one exactly like our Milky Way, which caused a wave of star formation to move out from the impact point like a ripple across the surface of a pond."

"So what's so special about that galaxy, Uncle Wink?" Sam Asked.

"Its creation, out of a pure chaotic collision, produced a large number of neutron stars and black hole binary X-ray sources, which quickly produced billions of massive new stars. You need to look in the direction of the constellation Sculptor, to see it, and its shape."

"What is it?" Asked Millie.

"It's called the Cartwheel Galaxy." Said Uncle Wink.

Fairy-Land

'Unfortunately this earth is not a fairy-land, but a struggle for life, perfectly natural and therefore extremely harsh.'

Martin Bormann

The earthquake, that had flattened and fractured Xining in 1927, measured 8.6 on Richter scale, and killed 200,000 of its inhabitants. It had probably felt a lot like Frank and Brian and I, leaving the tranquility of Taer'si.

We made it back to the hotel for a late afternoon repast of canned soybeans, bread, radishes and fruit from a jar. Our door, also ajar, that had opened to admit the laughter from down the hallway, suddenly closed again, with three young travelers bouncing on our beds, and chirping like the last birds in China. There was Kerry, a tall pockmarked Vancouverite, recently returned from a hard Tokyo escort experience, Chantel, a French student learning Mandarin in Peking, and Mary, a martini mixer from Minneapolis, tripping the light fantastic, from the edge of Qinghai province, to the middle of my chest. We made promises to each other until two am, long after Frank and Brian had turned in.

We awoke well after sunrise, but our train to Lanzhou wouldn't leave until evening. It took half the day to find a bank where I could change money, to pay Brian back for Frank. We ate *zasui tang* soup of lamb and oxen entrails, and some other 'plateau flavour,' made from caterpillar fungus. We fell off a pile of logs in the expansive courtyard of the Dongguan mosque, in our attempt to take photos, and made a hasty exit from the noise and confusion we had created, bowing and salaaming, and bumping backwards into the devout, on our way out. Brian and I separated in the market, to defuse the curious crush of the Muslim mobs. It was the same innocent inquisitiveness I remembered from Pakistan, but just as stifling. Just like sharks, I knew that if I stopped, I would drown. When Brian and I finally found each other again, it was only by our smiles. Both of us were sporting a brand new pair of large black plastic Chinese sunglasses, to help us blend into the crowd.

"No, Ma'am. We're Musicians." I said.

"We're on a mission from God." He replied. Brian had bought five jars of fruit, four bars of chocolate, and a coveted treasure. Desperation had tormented him for over a week, in his pursuit of instant coffee. Out of his pack, with a proud flourish, he pulled out a package labeled 'Coffee,' confident that his suffering would soon be over. But when the thermos of hot water arrived with us, on our hard seats to Lanzhou, he poured it into what were little bricks of sugar, peppered with recycled grounds, cloying and tasteless, and dragging him through most of his other purchases before our train left, just before midnight.

As bad as some of the poisoned places we had seen in China had been, nothing prepared us for the toxic terminus we stepped in, three hours later. Lanzhou was the world's most polluted city, but you couldn't see that immediately. Even in the middle of the night, you couldn't see anything, except an orange glow. But you could smell the raw sewage silted stink of the Yellow river, the clogged coal dust and petroleum mist from the factory chimneys, and the dust from the Gobi desert. It had been suggested that the mountain of Lanshan, rising straight up along the city's southern rim, should be bulldozed to let in some fresh air, but it was lost in the haze of Mao's pride. *The machines are rumbling and smoke is rising from the factories.*

Rearmed with sunglasses and anorak hoods, we emerged into the acidic smog. I had told Brian of Sora, my Japanese friend from the hostel in Paris, who had spent only a single twenty-four hours in each European capital city, before catching his next flight.

"Rundai?" Asked Brian.

"Rundai." I confirmed. Our desk clerk in Xining had made

arrangements for us to pick up tickets to Datong, from the CITS rep in Lanzhou. At 4:30 in the morning, we crossed two kilometers through bus fleets and empty mud lots, to one of a dozen gray apartment blocks. On the second floor of the one on our makeshift map, was a man in his pajamas, right on time. We hobbled back to the Lanzhou hotel, for a lukewarm chemical bath, and a short nap. It was just as well. If we had slept any longer in Lanzhou, Brian had observed, we would have woken up dead.

Unfortunately, Pajama Man had given us both top bunks for our exit and, in the time it had taken for Brian to digest his Xining market comestibles, he had developed a case of flatulence so gruesome, as to launch Lanzhou's air pollution index into the immediately lethal range. The inhabitants of the middle and lowers bunks coughed with the kind of precise delay after each discharge, it would have been possible to plot the diffusion coefficients on a log-log curve. I was grateful to be lying beside, and not under his berth, although the reflective waves in the confined space were almost as asphyxiating.

Gigantic squares of hay checkerboarding recycled the desert landscape all the way into the infinite horizon, as we awoke to the sunrise. Hohot went by like the ancestral ghosts that had created it. A full day after we had left Xining, we pulled into Datong, to the frantic gesticulations of a young American, waving out the window of an adjacent train.

"Where are we?" She shouted.

"Datong." I said. "Where are you going?" She hesitated, and then laughed.

"I don't know." She said. We wished her a pleasant journey.

Near the Yanmenguan Great Wall pass, to Inner Mongolia, we disembarked into the Twilight Zone. Across from the station was a large square with busy bicycle racks, framed with a large edifice of red flags and banners, and jumbo Mandarin characters towering over its name in English. *Fairy-Land*. Welcome to Fairy-Land.

*   *   *

'Don't you know that everybody's got a Fairyland of their own?'
P.L. Travers, *Mary Poppins*

After the usual confusion, we boarded Gong gong qi che #15, for the marathon ride to the hotel.

"We'd like two beds in the dormitory, please." I said.

"Certainly." Said the desk clerk.

"Amazing how we've had no problems with accommodation since the Siege of Suzhou, Wink." Mused Brian. Amazing, I agreed. And we ascended to our quarters to find a neckless Thai, waiting to pounce on us.

"Number one same same." Was all we could get out of him, initially until, with a little probing, we were able to determine that he worked as some sort of restorer of Buddhas. And Frank glowed red inside Serendipity. After a bath, some coffee-speckled sugar, and a brief peruse through the China Daily, we bid Neckless goodbye to do some sightseeing.

Two buses got us to the 252 Buddhist temple grottoes of Yungang. The transcendental art and fifty thousand statues in its 5th century vaults had been better spared from the excesses of the Cultural Revolution. The detailed colored genius in cave 6 was still vivid. After a visit to the richly decorated Liao dynasty upper and lower Huayan monasteries, we met up with our Danish gnomes, Jasper and Thomas, back in our dorm room. Their snoring kept all of us awake, even beyond the furniture-moving Olympics that the hotel staff were engaged in, on the floor above us.

Our morning began at the train station, in an increasingly distressing attempt to secure tickets on the night train to Beijing.

"Meiyou!" Came the echo, at every ticket window. We left to regroup.

"Put your glasses on and your anorak hood up." I said. And

142

we walked back in.

"Wǒmen jùyǒu fēijī jiānádà míngtiān." I said. *We have an airplane to Canada tomorrow.* Two tickets came back out under the wicket opening. And two Blues Brothers looked up, and saluted the great shining portrait of Chairmen Mao above us, watching over the hall of the people. We took in a sidewalk strongman act, and hiked to the 600 year old fire-glazed Ming colored tiles of the Nine Dragon Screen. Twenty-six feet high and 150 feet long, the dragon reflections on the pond in the foreground, did ferocious dragon dances in the breeze.

Brian and I spent the rest of the day wandering the old well-preserved neighborhoods, and narrow streets lined with single story houses of intricately carved eaves, hopscotch windows, and birdcages. We made our way around the horse-drawn carts, to the custodian of the otherwise closed Syrian Orthodox Church, who opened it for us to wonder why it was here, and where they all had gone. We asked him where we could eat something, before our train, and he told us about the cake factory. We told him we didn't feel like cake. He told us it was no longer a cake factory, but a restaurant, and directed us to Fairy-Land.

What he hadn't told us was that Fairy-Land wasn't only a restaurant, and a former cake factory, but one of the most extensive anti-nuclear bomb shelter complex of tunnels in China. Brian and I dropped deep, down four levels, to a corner where the shadow of the walls met together. It was Edgar Allan Poe. *Dim vales– put out the star-light With the breath from their pale faces. Comes down–still down–and down, And buries them up quite In a labyrinth of light- And then, how deep!–O, deep! They use that moon no more And so come down again.*

The table we took, in a secluded part of the kitchen, eventually produced a pale, boyish waiter, from among the young comrades who selected him. He brought us plates of bad garlic shoots, pork fat and rice, and told us of how these caves had come to be. When Mao had given the order to 'Dig tunnels deep, store grain everywhere, and never seek

143

hegemony,' the 335 workers in the factory worked for the next four years, without pay, to dig a mile of tunnels. I told him that the Yungang grottoes were more beautiful, but he disagreed. For they had been dug by the exploiting ruling class, which had used their beliefs to imprison people's minds.

I told him that the penalty you pay for growing up, is having to leave Fairy-Land behind you. And if you fail to find the exit, it will become a hell.

'The idea of fairyland fascinates me because it's one of those things, like ...dragons, that doesn't really exist, but everyone knows about it anyway...We go there because we can; we come back because we must. What we see there becomes our tales.'
Patricia A. McKillip, *Firebirds Rising*

*   *   *

'I visited Peking about thirty years ago. On my return I found it unchanged, except that it was thirty times dirtier, the smells thirty times more insufferable, and the roads thirty times worse for the wear.'
Admiral Lord Charles Beresford, *The Breakup of China*, 1899

It hasn't been quite thirty years since I arrived in Peking, but I'm sure I would have the same impression if I returned. There is actually no desire to, as I left it all there the first time. My first impressions were likely distorted by the seven hours of sleep I missed, sitting upright overnight, on the hard seat near the carriage door. The night was cool enough to shiver in. Secondly, I was not mentally prepared for the main train station of the 'Northern Capital.' China is a big country, inhabited by many Chinese. And here, in 1984, they had all come to welcome us.

The kilometer that Brian and I needed, to wade through the crowds and the bicycles, opened up on the happy Danish troll faces of Jasper and Thomas, strolling outside the Chongwenmen hotel. While we waited for the CITS office to open, we all sat down for breakfast, and were quickly joined by three more travelers. Kim was a bright-eye Brisbanite. She had been traveling with a lighthearted longhaired Iranian refugee, Mahmoud, and John, a crazy Ocker who was even funnier drunk that he was sober, which apparently wasn't often. When the CITS doors were finally unlocked, we were admitted to the third floor sanctuary. I booked passage on the trans-Mongolian express with the trolls for the following Wednesday, and secured us all rooms at the Qian Yuan Hotel, in the southwestern part of the city. Trolley #106 deposited us within ignoring distance of their efficiently indifferent desk staff, who booked me into Room 333 with the Danes, and Brian with a Vancouverite who still thought that China was the Temple of Heaven, and an American Pakistani girl, planning on returning to New York over the Great Wall. I would end up seeing one attraction, and not the other, missing Heaven and raving at the Wall. It was a metaphor for the country. Brian disappeared after our *fanguan* meal of egg, fungus, water chestnut and rice and, in an inebriated stupor, arrived back late with news. Beyond the temple wall is often Heaven's gate.

He had found Mary, who would be at the Beijing Hotel next evening.

Jasper and Thomas and I dogged it to the Russian Embassy next morning. We produced the required number of photos and dollars, in exchange for our little pink vouchers of happiness. Mine could be exchanged for train transport through Mongolia and the Soviet Far East, a night in Irkutsk, two nights in Khabarovsk, and a flight to Niigata, Japan, which I would, hopefully, be able to exchange for a boat from Vladivostok instead. But that plan was already doomed.

The mail at the Canadian Embassy was full of sad news. My parents business had suffered a fire, my middle brother had lost his job, and my Kashmiri walnut box had arrived in splinters. I waited for Mary under the sign at the Beijing Hotel that evening. *We have Friends All Over the World*. But Mary didn't appear, or appear to be one of them. Back at the Chongwenmen, Brian and Jasper and Thomas and I drank hot cocoa, and smoked triple fives. We named ourselves the Four of Gang.

At the Friendship Store next morning, I bought *The Starship and the Canoe*, all my dreams in one book. We rented bikes across the street, and peddled through the Inner City into the Imperial City, and through the Imperial City to the golden doornails, in the gates of the Ming dynasty Forbidden City. Inside were ten thousand rooms of two million artifacts, in 980 buildings on 180 acres. Its construction began in 1406 AD, had taken fifteen years, and required more than a million workers. Whole logs of rare Phobe zhennan wood, now worth more than $10,000 per cubic meter, were used, together with hundreds of tons of marble, and specially baked 'golden bricks' from Suzhou. We saw it before the Starbucks was added.

Brian was keen to cycle down to the Beijing again that evening, so the Four of Gang remounted their bikes. We found Mary there, surrounded by a cadre of young male traveler admirers. The tension was like we had just arrived at a high school dance, and Brian and the trolls diverted me for dinner. Nearby were Mahmoud and John and Kim, who shouted for us to join them. After dinner she asked me to help her look for her keys, which I couldn't find, and we returned to find Mary, sitting in my chair, talking to Brian. She stared at me, Kim stared at Mary, I stared at Brian, and he stared into space, where no one can hear you scream. Within a half an hour, Brian had diverted Kim's attention enough for Mary and I to steal away. We held hands and kissed in alcoves and promised each other to each other, lifelong lovers on Thai beaches. And she peddled me in the carrier of her bicycle under the lamp haloes, through the deserted streets of the Forbidden City, and we were in love, and found each other under our clothes in a spring night in China. I kissed her goodnight at her room door, and returned to the interrogation from the rest of the Four.

Jasper and Thomas and I needed Mongolian transit visas. At their embassy next morning, I tried for one to visit instead. After working my way through two officials, I found myself on the telephone with the voice upstairs.

"You must be in touch with our tourist bureau." He said.

"Where's that?" I asked.

"Ulan Bator." He said.

"How do I contact them?" I asked.

"Telephone or telegram." He said. I asked him if he had the number.

"No number." He said

"Why no number?" I asked.

"No telephone." He said. I asked him if he had the address.

"No." He said. I asked him how long I would have in Ulan Bator, if I got a transit visa.

"Half an hour." He said. I asked him if there was any way I could leave the station during that time. There was a long pause.

"That could be difficult." He said.

I located Brian back at the Beijing, and he had located Mary. She was leaving to visit Chantel, with a French guy, and an American with a faux British accent. Everyone was far too friendly, and Brian began channeling Charlie Chan.

"This mystery is appropriately Chinese." He said. "What's not there seems to have just as much meaning as what is there." We ate as hot as we could stand it, at the Sichuan restaurant, Brian licking his fingers, and I licked my wounds. Back at the Chongwenmen, we found Jasper and Thomas had found a little spice of their own. Not so little, actually.

"Guess what we got for 12 yuán?" Asked Jasper. We were

sure we had no idea. So he pulled a large white plastic bag out of his knapsack and, as he opened it, the aroma knocked us both off our feet. Whatever it was, it was strong. We looked inside, to find several large bricks of tar pitch hashish, sticking together in large fragments. As I began to swear at them in Danish, Brian's echo followed, in our first language. We told them they were crazy to be fooling with this stuff, in a country with the death penalty for drug possession. We told them that they were putting us all at risk with their stupidity. We asked them how they expected to get through a lifetime supply of cannabis, when they were supposed to be getting on a train to the Soviet Union in three days time. Then we fired one up, and asked them why it was so cheap. They just did their Danish grin thing, and handed us a slab for the road. The Four of Gang went to the Great Wall of China next morning. Slowly, but not so slow that we didn't win our price of admission, in a proletarian poker game with the Special Economic Zone of locals in our carriage. CITS may have still exerted absolute control over the drones in the package tours, but they had no weapons against the explosive havoc created by solo travelers. We were the seeds of the new revolution, the law of supply and demand, the reason for the currency black market, the actual delivery system of Deng's zhìfù guāngróng. *To get rich is glorious.* We were ephemeral, evading the main roads, distaining the Hilton accommodation, penetrating across all the boundaries, interacting with the locals, inspiring their initiative. We were an infectious inoculum of individualism, in a sluggish Sino-socialist bloodstream.

A million workers had apparently died, building the first Qin dynasty wall, but it was the Ming who were responsible for most of the 5500 miles of stone and brickwork, transformed from what was initially a rammed earth barrier. After almost four years of traveling, I stood there in the mist, on the enormous, majestic, silent and terrible Great Wall of China. In two days time, I would cross it, Li He's *thousand miles of moonlight*, north into the Mongolia it was built to defend against. But Mary was there with the French guy, and Brian held me back, raving at the wall.

I met her that night, in the lobby of the Beijing. I had to ask. She told me that, although she was sleeping with Chantel's friend, she actually liked me more. Brian just shook his head.

"It's OK, Captain." I said, as we cycled back to the Chongwenmen. "Even Reggie Jackson realized that when he struck out, a billion people in China didn't care."

"Dignity is the doomed man's final refuge." He said, pulling away.

Brian left the next morning. I wouldn't see him again for two years. He would be wearing his Chinese sunglasses, and bearing the gift of a Japanese glass fishing float, which had floated all the way across the Pacific.

My Inspection Tour scroll had reached the end of the roll. Frank and I would drift away now, like a wandering cloud.

'To truly find yourself you should play hide and seek alone.'
Chinese Fortune Cookie

Back in the USSR

'My life was too short to achieve the conquest of the world.
That task is left for you.'

Genghis Khan

On the morning of Wednesday, May 23, 1984, the trolls and I crawled into a taxi and boarded the Trans-Mongolian express for Siberia. My last act in Beijing was to flush Jasper and Thomas's gigantic golden brick lifetime supply of Uighur hashish down the toilet, in our room at the Chongwenmen. I didn't tell them about Frank, glowing red in the bottom of Serendipity. And they didn't tell me they had another brick.

We would spend two delightful days on the train, meeting homeward-bound European travelers, fretting over border crossings, and trying the fare in the various restaurant cars, which changed daily with the countries. Adjacent carriages carried Mahmoud, a Finn with a guitar, a bearded Swede who I played chess with, two electric Dutch girls, and two Aussie sheilas, one of whom would have an impromptu birthday party, just before the Sino-Mongolian border.

The Chinese border guards were inquisitive.

"Have you any antiquities?" She asked, striking in her green uniform. A hum resonated loudly from the bottom of my pack. Luckily no one else heard it.

"I have this ring." I said, showing her my Kaifeng knuckleduster. The Mongolian Peoples Republic authorities didn't even put in an appearance, and Frank was through his first major hurdle. Jasper bought some of my Mongolian tögrögs at a favorable exchange rate, reappearing with several bottles of *kumis* fermented mare's milk. I entertained the troops with the Finn's guitar, and the songs rolled by. As did the Gobi desert, and the treeless steppes of the Mongolian Plateau nomad grassland grazing for their *five snouts*. The herders' horses and oxen and sheep and goats and Bactrian

151

camels, huddled around their remote yurts, gradually crossed the Hentiya Mountains, and became the factory smog and Soviet concrete apartment blocks of Ulan Bator.

Before its foundation as a Tibetan Buddhist yurt monastery in 1639, Ulan Bator had been the site of the brick palace of Ong Khan, a Nestorian Christian monarch who had been identified as the legendary Prester John by Marco Polo. Followed by Genghis Khan in the 13th century, the Mongols nicknamed the place Aziïn Cagaan Dagina, the *White Fairy of Asia*. From here he ruled the largest contiguous land empire in world history, covering 22 per cent of the Earth's total area, and having a population of over 100 million people. In 1797, a decree from the monastery's 4th Jebtsundamba had forbidden 'singing, chess, usury, smoking, and playing with archery.' If I had remembered to bring my longbow and arrows, I could have broken all the rules.

And I would have needed it, had I been living here, when it was still called Niislel Khüree, or Urga, on January 31, 1921. For that was the night that the Chinese garrison became concerned that something was seriously wrong, when the bonfires were lit. Hand grenades destroyed the city gates, and the machine guns, rifles, bayonets and meat cleavers destroyed the Chinese. The two thousand hungry, homeless, and destitute White Russian deserters and displaced Mongolian troops who engaged in the attack, were led by a sadistic psychopath. He claimed descent from Attila the Hun, believed himself to be the reincarnation of Genghis Khan, and, with the delivery of the Bogd Khan from the Chinese, had taken the title of God of War. The exposed blood vessels exposed by the terrible broad forehead saber wound, received in the WWI, pulsed red with rabid fury against his two sworn enemies- Bolsheviks and Jews.

Baron Roman Nikolai Fyodorovich von Ungern-Sternberg, born into a thousand-year old lineage of Baltic noblemen, was afflicted, like Hitler would be, with 'Borderlands Syndrome,' an extreme, zealous nationalism affecting a nonnative citizen raised on the fringes of empire. The Mad Baron was fanatically devoted to Imperial Russia, and his mercenary army had roamed Central Asia, in a desperate attempt to restore it. He was ruthless, shooting all new recruits with any sign of a physical defect, and strangling, whipping to death, dragging behind vehicles, or roasting enemies alive.

When he finally ordered a stop to the three-day rampage of his troops, it was only to implement a more organized legalized *pogrom* liquidation of the Jews of Urga. The methodical military operation was led by his commander Sipailov, and aided by the division's physician, Dr. Klingenberg. Cossacks, wearing silk robes over their rags, hit Jewish men in the face with wooden blocks until they died. Women were gang raped and killed. Those who had taken a vow of chastity butchered the women first. Half-naked bodies hung outside shops. Decapitated heads that lay in the streets were fought over by the Urga dogs. A Mongolian nanny of one Jewish family slaughtered by Cossacks, fled with the baby and had him baptized by an Orthodox priest at the Russian consulate, succeeded in saving the infant, but was cut to pieces by their sabers. The very few Jews that survived only did so, because the Mongols didn't really understand.

Ulan Bator's name means 'Red Hero,' in honor of the brave warrior that finally liberated Mongolia from von Ungern-Sternberg. The Mad Baron was executed by firing squad, after a trial lasting six hours. I'm not really sure what took them so long.

I almost didn't make it back on the train in time, finding out how long it takes to mail a postcard home from the Ulan Bator railway station. It showed a smiling Mongolian cartoon boy with a Soviet Young Pioneer's red necktie, carrying a briefcase and a large bouquet of lilies, walking a wide boulevard lined with modern cars and high-rises, under a full sun. They had painted his eyes blue. He was clearly lost.

And our train would be late, arriving at the Russian border. Jasper and Thomas were playing chess, and the 'B' side of the

153

Brewer and Shipley cassette on their tape recorder. Jerry Garcia's steel guitar rang out behind Mongolia's Iron Curtain.

> 'Oh mommy
> I ain't no commie
> But I hate to bust your bubble
> Cause there's gonna be some trouble... Soon.'

I was about to become more in tune with the Grateful Dead. The trolls were like young frogs in a mason jar. They flipped the cassette over, and the 'A' side, Hunter S. Thompson's favorite song.

I closed my eyes and smiled, thinking about how naïvely it had been performed by 'Gail and Dale,' on the Lawrence Welk show as a 'new generation gospel song...a modern spiritual ballad.' It was undoubtedly the source of the joke.

Q: What's the difference between the Lawrence Welk Orchestra and a moose?

A: On a moose, the horns are in front and the asshole's in the back.

And the smell hit me just ahead of the realization that I had been one brick shy.

> 'I'm waitin' for the train that goes home sweet Mary
> Hopin' that the train is on time
> Sittin' downtown in a railway station
> One toke over the line.
> One toke over the line sweet Jesus...'

Sweet Jesus. I opened my eyes to find Jasper and Thomas lighting up a massive joint, in a hermetically sealed railway carriage, on a train decelerating onto a land border of the Union of Soviet Socialist Republics. Hunter Thompson's fear and loathing in Las Vegas was suddenly insignificant. I tried to be gentle.

"Are you out of your fucking minds?" I said. Or something like that, as the train jerked to a standstill. Thomas told me they had been nervous about crossing the frontier with a brick of hashish, and decided they didn't actually want to be

154

there when it happened. I began to hear the dissonant sound of compartment doors slamming open and closed, and deep official-sounding Russian voices.

"No problem." Said Jasper, sliding our own door tight. The Pullman had filled with smoke. My life passed before me, very slowly. Three Soviet border troops, wearing broad visored military caps and big greycoats with hammer and sickle patches, tapped on our glass, and skated the door back open. Billows of fumes rolled into the hallway. The old senior officer clicked his heels, and grinned like a Siberian tiger. He looked a but like Yuri Gagarin, if Gagarin had lived long enough to have consumed a lifetime supply of vodka, and had taken an ice pick to his own face. He was built like the brick internment camp I imagined we were headed to. It grew warm.

"Доброе утро, господа. Паспорта, пожалуйста." *Gvidye, Tvariche. Pasport, pozhalsta.* He said, swift and polite. We handed him our passports.

The word 'toke' had come from the Spanish *tocar*, through the Vulgar Latin *toccare*, to touch. I was bracing myself to be touched by reality, but it never came. To this day I have no idea why we didn't end up in Siberia forever. Captain Gulag scrutinized my immigration form, and then my customs declaration.

"Buddha?" He asked. "Dva Buddha?" *What Buddha.*

"Yeah, what Buddha?" Asked Jasper and Thomas, in unison. Frank emerged from his wrappings, clearly pleased to be out of China. I felt him exhale. Thankfully, no smoke came out. Captain Gulag looked at the price I had written down in rubles, then at Frank, and furrowed his brow. And then his mouth opened, his eyes looked up, he clicked his tongue on his palate, and he slapped his thigh.

"Replica!" He declared disdainfully, handing him back. And his two comrades laughed out loud with him, and they went on to the next carriage.

The trolls rushed off the train to change money, and I

followed them in the downpour to find the bank. Inside was a lone American ranger.

"Savages took my bibles." He said. "We oughtta nuke 'em." And I wondered what would have happened at the American border, with a four hundred year old Buddha and a brick of brand new hashish.

"Ever seen Lawrence Welk?" I asked.

*   *   *

> 'On the wild steppes of Transbaikalia,
> Where people dig for gold in the mountains,
> A vagrant, bemoaning his fate,
> Is wandering with a bag on his back.'
> Ivan Kondratyev, *Brodyaga (Бродяга)- The Wanderer*
> *(On the Wild Steppes of Transbaikalya)*

We awoke to one cuddly elephant of a babushka in the dining car next morning. She tussled my hair, squeezed my shoulders and brought me kefir and coffee, eggs and chleb, butter, and a packet of Kosmos. And I fell in love with the big bear all over again.

A station break in Ulan-Ude surrounded me with a demure group of chubby young girls with frilly aprons, and giant white carnation pompoms on each side of their heads. We reentered the lazy morning, chugging through the sunshine and the taiga, along the curve of Lake Baikal.

The 'Pearl of Siberia' is the oldest, deepest, clearest, and most voluminous lake on Earth, containing twenty percent of the world's fresh water. Russian Cossacks conquered it from the local Mongol Buryat tribes, who could still be seen herding their goats and camels and sheep, on the eastern side of the *Rich Lake*. When they destroyed the Russian garrison at Bratsk in 1634, unaware of how firearms worked, they burned the muskets along with the dead Cossacks. The guns went off and killed a few Buryats, creating the legend of Russian invincibility, seemingly able to fight even after death.

We travelled the 200 bridges and 33 tunnels, constructed around the southwestern end of the lake at the end of the 19th century. Here, in the Russian Civil War of 1920, thirty thousand soldiers of Admiral Kolchak's White Russian Army, with the Red Army in hot pursuit, fled across the frozen lake with their families, their possessions, and the Tsar's gold, through the Arctic winds of the Great Siberian Ice March. Their frozen bodies remained in a macabre winter tableau, until the spring thaw dropped them into a mile of water.

The outstretched arm, on the gigantic statue of Lenin in Karl Marx Street, welcomed us to the Paris of Siberia. I said goodbye to the trolls, and waited for my Intourist connection to arrive at the Irkutsk station. My déjà vu detector lit up red, as I recalled my first experience with Soviet travel logistics, and the Finns' accurate predictions, a year earlier.

'Back on board, they looked at my itinerary, and told me that no one would meet me at the station. I told them that would be highly unlikely. Our train pulled in to the most western city of Russia, the most northerly metropolis of over a million people, and the home of the Hermitage, the largest art museum in the world.
No one was there to meet me.'

Unlike the Russian artists, officers, and nobles, exiled to Irkutsk for their part in the Decembrist revolt against Tsar Nicolas I in the early 19th century, no one was there to meet me. I presented my credentials and vouchers to the most proximal uniform.

"Taxi." He said. So I jumped into the nearest one, already full.

In America, you can always find a party. In Soviet Russia, the Party will always find you. The two rustic mafia in the back proffered simultaneous cigarettes over my shoulders, even before I had landed in my front seat. A young Irena giggled and squirmed between them. The glint from the driver's gold

157

tooth initially deflected me from the realization that he was sizing up my new Chinese sneakers. Yegor had a black belt in karate, but I didn't know that yet. He pulled away from the curve like I should have. I wondered how he knew where I wanted to go. It wouldn't matter.

"Страна?" He asked. *Strana.* I knew that one.

"Canada." I said. And they all looked around at each other, and broke into song.

"Wayne Gretsky!" They shouted in unison. And I thanked the holy game of hockey and the Edmonton Oilers for my deliverance. This was cause for celebration, of course. It wasn't every day that someone from the same country as *The Great One* landed in Siberia. Our first stop was for vodka. From the number of bottles purchased, I just naturally assumed that we were expecting company. But, no, we were each provisioned with our own lifetime supply. The caps came off at more than the speed limit, until I realized there likely wasn't one. Pretty wooden houses, adorned with ornate hand-cared decorations flew by our windows. We rippled over cobblestones to our next destination. A young Buryat emerged from a building with a large box of newspaper-wrapped smoked *omul* salmon. Of the 1700 species of plants and animals found around Lake Baikal, two thirds of which are found nowhere else in the world, this one was the tastiest. After another hour, and numerous stops for other comestibles, I thought we were set, but I was wrong again. We were missing white wine. There would have been no point in arguing. By the time that Yegor realized that I wasn't going to part with my shoes, and the mafia gave up on trying to score my watch, we had arrived on the shores of a pleasant picnic spot, in the May sunshine. It felt like I was back in Northwestern Ontario, except I didn't speak the language.

It didn't matter. We ate fresh bread and salmon, toasted Wayne Gretsky and world peace, and consumed far too much white wine and vodka in the process. I shuttered to think of what the Irish would have done with this stuff, and wondered if anyone had ever seen this country sober. It didn't matter. Shortly after noon, Yegor piled us all back into his Lada, and drove me to where he thought I should be staying. Yegor clearly expected a reward for returning me to my rightful owners, and I chose to agree with him, in front of the Intourist delegation. Despite my heroic speech, they ushered Yegor out another door, and lectured me about not taking rides with strangers. I left Serendipity in my room, and set off to see the town.

After the marzipan Epiphany Cathedral and the Governor's Palace, I found the Irkutsk Synagogue, and an inscription inside in English. *Nobody is forgotten...nothing is forgotten.*

I walked through the soft light of the Siberian springtime to the 'Baikal' Restaurant, where they seated me in front of the live band, and laid on a feast of delicious fried fish, meats, and salads. I tried to turn away the cognac, but they wouldn't hear of it. Sitting in this delightful summery café, I wondered momentarily what all this Siberian exile fuss was about. It was one of the most pleasant untroubled days of my life, where illusion and delusion coexisted in the same rare place.

I strolled along the sunset reflection in the Angara River, and returned to the hotel dining room. The fruit compote I was having for dessert was interrupted by an invitation from a rowdy American ex-Marine named Arthur, and Andre, a visiting Moscovite, to join their table. They were sitting with Bila, a twenty year-old girl from Norway, and her Danish friend. I missed Denmark but not, as it turned out, as much as Ulla. When I spoke to her in Danish, her big round eyes grew bigger. I told her of my trip, and Frank. The band began to play Beatles, and the girls wanted to dance. Arthur had long faded into the shadows of his vodka, so Andre danced with Bila, and Ulla danced with me.

'Been away so long I barely knew the place
Gee, it's good to be back home
Leave it till tomorrow to unpack my case
Honey disconnect the phone
I'm back in the USSR...'

By the time the tempo slowed, I had come adrift in an ocean of long chestnut hair, and warm embraces. It had been a long time.

"Jeg ønsker at se Frank." She said. *I want to see Frank.* And so she did. Until later, when Bila barged in and, despite our resistance and Andre holding her back, managed to tear off our blanket.

"We're waiting for you in our room." She giggled. And we went to their room. *Kill off all my demons and my angels might die too.*

At 5 am the telephone rang and door banged in unison. Some sources say that the word Siberia originates from the Turkic for 'sleeping land.' No one had told these guys. I may not have been met at the station, but there was no way they were going to let me be late for my train to Khabarovsk.

Dawn broke across the river.

'Even in Siberia there is happiness.'
Anton Chekhov

*   *   *

The original Turkic inhabitants of the Siberian Khanate steppes identified the three stars of Orion's belt as deer, antelope, or mountain sheep, and Betelgeuse was regarded as their arrow point, in a variant of the universal Cosmic Hunt myth that seemed to follow my companion constellation around the world.

Later Lake Baikal locals believed that Christ had once paid a visit to a nearby summit, and looked down on the surrounding region. After blessing most of what he saw, he apparently turned east towards TransBaikal Dauria, waved his hand, and made a pronouncement.

"Beyond this there is nothing." He said. And that is where I went.

A paltry breakfast of kefir, cheese, and a frankfurter, rushed me into a van to the Irkutsk station. I was bunked in with s geophysicist named Misha, and two civil engineers. We played chess.

The Trans-Siberian Railway is the longest railway in the world, spanning over nine thousand kilometers, seven time zones, and eight days, to get to the Sea of Japan. But that is not where I went.

The Russians lost the Russo-Japanese War because of this railroad. The single track would only allow train travel in one direction. And that is where I went.

The engineers were interrogated and removed at a rest stop by a vodka-lubricated two-star military official of some kind, apparently displeased with their command of the Queen's English. I migrated to the dining car for smoked sturgeon and chleb. And the architects of my own Siberian exile.

There was Nikolai, the alcoholic locomotive engineer who fell in love with my Sanyo watch, and drenched me in cognac until I gave it to him. There was Vladimir, a rotund Ukrainian who tried to trade me one of his farm tractor femme fatales for foreign currency. And finally, there was the porter, another karate enthusiast, who produced prodigious amounts of vodka and bread and cucumbers, so we could all toast to peace and international trade some more. I blame Ronald Reagan for my exile. If we hadn't needed to propose so many toasts to peace, I might have preserved my judgment enough to decline a game of cards with these thieves. I might have maintained enough wherewithal to have refused to play for money. I may have not deceived myself into thinking I could win. With lies, you may go ahead in the world, but you may never go back. But that is not where I went.

There were fifty-three cars that made up this particular train, rolling along at full throttle through the Trans-Siberian night. The momentum must have been observable from space. I was down forty rubles and forty dollars when I realized I was being cheated. I'm not sure I meant to reach up and pull the cord above me, or whether I was just balancing myself for an important announcement to my fellow card sharks. But the feeling of ten thousand tons of train grinding to a ear-splitting screeching screaming halt, in a mile-long cyclone slipstream of sparks, could only have produced two words from my lips. "Oh, shit." I believe I said. I hadn't stopped just any old train in its tracks. I had stopped an unstoppable legend, one touch over the line.

The diplomacy took refuge back into the paneling. My right wrist seemed to bent back too far to be mine. Instead of Misha, there were three different colors of military uniforms hanging on the rocking walls of my *kupe* sleeping cabin, and as many sets of discordant snoring erupting from adjacent bunks. This was probably not going to look good on my résumé.

I no longer had my watch. We were still on Moscow time but it felt about five in the morning. The taiga went by as if nothing had happened.

162

The volcanic eruption that formed the Siberian Traps 250 million years ago killed off ninety per cent of living species at the time. It was called the 'Great Dying,' but it was nothing compared to what was doing in my own sweltering Siberian Gulag camp bunk, toddling into the Archipelago. And that is where I went.

Morning light carried us into Khabarovsk, at the confluence of the Amur and Ussuri rivers, and the place I thought I would be able to negotiate an alternative way out of the USSR to Japan. But it was already too way out for any alternative way out. *Els dirigents passen, l'Arxipèlag perdura.*

The militia handed me over to her far too nonchalantly. But then I looked hard at her, and she looked far harder back. Her name was Ludmilla, my soul link to the Free World. She had a link, anyway. Ludmilla was the head of scarlet lipstick and thick glasses, on a stocky torso of determined efficiency. In fluent French, she informed me that my visa had been cancelled, I was confined to the hotel, and that I would be flown to Japan in two days time.

"What about the boat?" I asked. She said something about pirates, and I didn't dare mention airplanes. I put a call into the Canadian Embassy in Moscow to see if they could help. The connection was almost as clear as the message.

"We sell a lot of wheat to these people." It left me relieved I had only stopped one of their trains.

Downstairs in the dining room I met Yuri, a construction worker from Odessa, and another Misha, an internist from Alma-Ata, who chatted about the risks of nuclear proliferation and the cost of living, and Vietnam. The next day I met to British diplomats at the same table.

"They never apologize for anything." One said. "They never do." We were joined by Sergei, who told me he liked my Chinese sneakers. I had already lost my watch to Nikolai, so there was no point in hanging on to the only other thing I'd been trying not to lose, since I was back in the USSR. I handed them over.

"If these people ever rediscover Capitalism, they really will bury us." I told the diplomats. They nodded into their cognacs.

The next morning, Ludmilla banished me from Siberia. I still have her business card.

"You can never come back to our beautiful country." She said.

"I'll manage." I said. I passed one of those organized spontaneous peace demonstrations on the way to airport. And then the sun and I rose high in the sky, over the Sea of Japan. My CCCP-85220 'Crusty' Tu-134 landed across the rice paddies of Niigata less than two hours later.

"We look forward to serving you again soon on Aeroflot." Echoed through the cabin. But I couldn't say when, since they had taken my watch; and I didn't know how, since they had taken my shoes.

'I think my escape from the Siberian Transport was my most difficult performance.'

Harry Houdini

The Narrow Road to the Interior

'Days and months are the travelers of eternity. So are the years that pass by…I myself have been tempted for a long time by the cloud-moving wind-filled with a strong desire to wander…'

Basho, *The Narrow Road to the Deep North*

"Welcome to Japan." Said the immigration man. He clearly hadn't heard the news. Every day is a journey, and the journey itself is home. But I was a stranger in a stranger land than I had left, so overwhelmingly technopolite, and surgical suite clean. The sudden efficiency had fired me out of the airport too fast. I had left my bearings, and their cartwheel axis inflection points, inside. The new direction of my 're-Orient-ation' was south. I hiked to a nearby roadside restaurant. It was empty. A middle aged short-haired Japanese woman appeared, with a smile and an apron and one of those female singsong voices.

"Ohayō gozaimasu!" She said, bowing low. I thought I got the first part, and said 'Hi' back, bowing lower. Her face went red.

"Is this the way to Tokyo?" I asked.

"Hai!" She said, bowing again. Perhaps I hadn't greeted her properly.

"Hi." I said, "Is this the road to Tokyo?" And bowed even deeper. Her cheeks grew crimson.

"Hai!!" She said, bowing more tentatively this time. I thought we had done this.

"Hi." I repeated, pointing out the window this time. "Tokyo?"

"Ahhh, Tokyo desu ne." She said. "Hai." And shook her head no. So it was not to be, and we both backed away from each other, separating like wild geese lost in the clouds.

Back outside, the first bus that would stop dropped me at the train station. I picked the shortest queue.

"Tokyo?" I asked, when it was my turn.

"Hai!" She said. Here we go again.

"Tokyo?" I tried again.

"Hai!" She said. "Shinkansen?" It was my turn.

"Shinkansen?" I asked. "Tokyo?"

"New trunk line." She said in English. "Tokyo."

"Hai." I said, figuring it sounded faster. She asked for nine thousand yen. For that kind of coin, I thought, it had better be.

The narrow road to the interior had changed considerably, two years before I arrived in Niigata. The first bullet train service on the Joetsu line had begun to rip along the rails to the ancient capital of the Land of the Rising Sun. For forty bucks, I bit the bullet, and found myself flying at light speed, past rice paddies and tall white farmhouses with slate grey tiled roofs, attended to by meticulously manicured mannequins, meting out my mandarin microsegments. Moelm would have loved it.

Just a little over two hours later, I hobbled out of Ueno station into the Tokyo twilight, like a newborn giraffe. I made a phone call.

"She's in Indiana and I'm her roommate. Thanks for the postcard." Said the voice at the end of the new trunk line.

"You're welcome." I said. "Know of a cheap place to stay?" She told me of the Green line to Ikebukuro district, and spelled *Kimi Ryokan*. I emerged in the dense swarming urban nightlight, found a police station for more directions, and finally located a small traditional inn, down a steep set of stairs. There were calligraphy scrolls and ikebana and, sitting in the lounge in a black silk robe and bright-eyed twinkle, was the other Kimi, from Beijing, via Brisbane. She asked me if I could help her find her keys, and we laughed, remembering the time she had lost them. But here there were no keys, just a Japanese *ofuro* bath, and soap and gentle hands and white

166

towels, and futons on tatami on wooden floors, and *rainstorm-a wildflower blooms at my pillow.*

I awoke to a stream of diffuse sunlight through the shoji, illuminating Frank's verdigris nobility. He had apparently needed air. Kimi was stretched out naked before his serene countenance. They were undeniably enamored with each other.

"Where in the hell did you find him?" She asked. I told her the story.

"You're lucky they didn't put you in jail in four countries." She said. I told her about stopping the Trans-Siberian. As she turned Frank's face to the wall, her own countenance became serene.

*   *   *

'Where there are humans,
You'll find flies,
And Buddhas.'
Kobayashi Issa

When we finally emerged into the world's largest metropolis, I began to develop a subtle appreciation for why the Japanese were always trying to destroy it in their horror films. The Edo emporium pachinko parlor down the street was a smoke and noise factory, fueled by cigarettes and millions of little metal balls. The prizes for playing well were more cigarettes and millions of little metal balls. Death DNA. Kimi showed me a nearby *kapuseru hoteru* capsule hotel.

"It's cheaper than our room at the Kimi." She said. "And you get your own television." If the cell matrix was refrigerated rather than heated, it could have been a morgue conveyor tray unit. Each capsule was 2m by 1m by 1.25m. I pointed out that there wasn't room for both of us to move in, in the ways we had found we needed room to move in.

167

"Truly a Japanese concept that will stay in Japan.' She said.

We left behind window displays of plastic food, for masses of young girls in identical school uniforms eating ice cream in Ueno Park, and Shinto priests walking under skyscraper-sized television screen facades.

In the city with the most number of Michelin stars on Earth, we could barely afford pizza. Back at the Kimi, we met a likeable slow Aussie named Sleek Deek, and Chris, a German professional one-man band, who had been traveling the world with his hybrid instruments for the previous four years, and making a decent living from it. We all ended up in a local bar, entertaining the locals with our karaoke.

The next day was for embassy surfing. My first stop was at the Canadian, to pick up mail, and inquire after the reason why I had received no assistance in my Soviet disunion. I was ushered in to meet the First Secretary, Call-me Bob, a corpulent facsimile of what might have otherwise been a useful functionary, save for his preoccupation with the feathers in his own nest. The expensive suit and two gold rings were the first clue. He pointed to the 'uniqueness' of his floor-to-ceiling art collection, the wall of his Kenyan safari photos, and the erudition of his jazz collection, and the system he had been provided to enjoy it on. I asked him again about the issue I had come to speak to him about. Call-me Bob shuffled through his files and papers for a while, hemmed and then hawed, and asked if I'd be interviewed for a position with Toshiba. *My house is burned but the cherry tree in my garden scatters its blossoms as if nothing had happened.*

The visa application at the Australian Embassy would have been more like the job interview I had been offered at my own, if it hadn't actually been an interrogation.

"I notice that you've spent a lot of time in Eastern Bloc countries?" Said the young attaché, perusing my passport. "Does that reflect your political ideology?" I told him it didn't.

168

"Did you encounter any drug abuse in the relatively long time you appear to have traveled on the Indian subcontinent?" He asked. I told him I hadn't (not that I really could have been expected to remember).

"This book you're writing, will there be anything in it on Australia?" He asked. I told him that it was entirely up to him.

"And you're single, is that correct?" He asked. "Do you have any plans to marry an Australian?" I told him I didn't, as it would be unlikely that she would be compatible with my Destiny.

"How much money do you have?" He asked. I showed him my Swiss bank account card. He stamped my passport so I couldn't reapply, and told me that, barring anything unforeseen found on a routine criminal background check, I could expect to pick up my tourist visa in Kuala Lumpur, in a few weeks time. A mental image of the Trans-Siberian, shearing into a stratospheric plume of sparks, exploded across my windscreen, and I crossed my fingers on the way out.

My final destination of the day was the 'Association for Far Eastern Relations,' a faux shop front for Taiwanese entry documents. They were just glad to see me.

I cooked dinner for Kimi and I, a savory concoction of tofu, graded bonito, green peppers and noodles. We spent the evening watching the surreal juxtaposition of *Apocalypse Now*, with the interspersed Japanese television commercials for *Cream Sand Biscuits*, *Pocari Sweat* soda, *Mouth Pet* oral rinse, *Creap* powdered coffee whitener, and *Charmy Green* dishwashing soap, *for beautiful human life*.

The next morning I picked up my photos from *Hope Developers*, and rediscovered that you can't see the whole sky through a bamboo tube. Kimi and I took the train to the sea, and what had been the fourth largest city in the world in the 13th century. We strolled through a temple-dotted suburbia, past a couple of boys playing baseball outside an unnamed shrine, a swallow's nest above a corner store door, and a boutique colony of quaint shops, one of which contained an old Samurai with a new Seiko, intently instructing the art of sword appreciation. Beyond was the Kannon Temple, dedicated to the 30 foot-high gilded waves of the 'Goddess of Mercy' bodhisattva, patron deity of travelers.

But we had really come to see Frank's big brother, the 44 foot 800 year-old *Daibutsu* Great Buddha of Kamakura, 93 tons of bronze Amitābha, once covered in the Kōtoku-in Temple and gold, both washed out to sea in a tsunami, and back in again by a tidal wave of Japanese schoolchildren.

Kipling had written his famous tribute to the 'Japanese idol' here in 1892:

'O ye who tread the Narrow Way By Tophet-flare to Judgment Day, Be gentle when 'the heathen' pray To Buddha at Kamakura...
And whoso will, from Pride released, Contemning neither creed nor priest, May feel the Soul of all the East About him at Kamakura...
But when the morning prayer is prayed, Think, ere ye pass to strife and trade, Is God in human image made No nearer than Kamakura?'

Under the image of Buddha all those spring flowers seemed a little tiresome. We walked along the beach to the sublime Zen and lotus gardens of Kōmyō-ji Temple and then, by contrast, ate a noisy video-enhanced Styrofoam meal within the pink plastic décor of the LA burger stand across the street.

"Japan is like this." Kim said. "Contrast contrasted against contrast. Their hearts are in Shinto but their stomachs are in Shakey's."

The world of dew is the world of dew. And yet, and yet we saw the thousand year-old ginkgo tree next to the great stone stairway of the Hachiman-gū, a quarter century before it was finally uprooted by a storm. The oblique sunlight on the nearby Kenchō-ji raccoon-dog temple slid us back onto our return to Ikebukuro, in time to send Frank away, on his final Journey to the West. That night I dreamt of him, looking down on his big brother, as he flew overhead.

'If only you and I could go far, far away, to the other side of the sky...'
Inariya Fusanosuke

*   *   *

'Each and every master, regardless of the era or the place, heard the call and attained harmony with heaven and earth. There are many paths leading to the top of Mount Fuji, but there is only one summit - love.'
Moriheo Useshiba

Reflected in the dragonfly's eye- mountains. And at the end of the week, Kimi and I left Tokyo, on a southwest narrow road to the interior, a hundred kilometers by bus, weaving around the lakes to the shores of Shoji-ko, and a random walk to a quaint and quiet *minshuku*. Mt. Fuji hid behind the rain. The proprietress was just as shy. But we were potential guests, and she overcome her fear of language and *gaijin*, and invited the outsiders inn. A short, stocky rustican, possessed of an undeniable delicate alabaster beauty beyond her strength, she politely and unconsciously reassured us, in Japanese and body language, that we would be accommodated to the utmost of her ability, as though hairy barbarians had not suddenly appeared on her doorstep. She showed us our slippers, and the dividing line between exterior and inside of her hospitality. She took us into the *ofuro*, and made sure we understood that, under no circumstances were we to enter the steep sunken hot pool, until we had thoroughly used the hand shower, and especially on our hairy parts. She wrote out the price of admission in large numbers, obviously wondering if we had the means to avail ourselves of the comforts on offer. And only then did she show us to

171

our room, and opened our shoji screen on Shoji lake, to reveal what would have been, on any other day, a view of the most perfect volcanic cone in the world.

We had come to Fuji because of the *Ukiyo-e*, the 'pictures of the floating world,' a genre of Japanese woodblock prints first produced in the 17th century, that allowed poor townspeople their first access to art, affordable because they could be mass-produced. They gained entry into a realm of fleeting beauty, like a gourd floating along with the river current- evanescent, impermanent, entertaining, and divorced from the everyday responsibilities of a mundane existence. On offer were pleasures of the theatre, wine, and women and song, snow and maple leaves and cherry blossoms, and landscapes. And the most wonderful landscape in Japan was on the peak of the highest mountain where, in *The Tale of the Bamboo Cutter*, the Emperor Mikado, smitten with *Princess of Flexible Bamboos Scattering Light* Kaguya-hime, heading back to her home on the moon, had placed her elixir of life.

The most perfect pictures of the floating world were Hokusai's and Hiroshige's *Thirty-Six Views of Mount Fuji*. A rare complete original collection of the first artist had been in the wellness spa of the Costa Concordia, before it was lost when the ship ran aground in 2012. The captain was accused of being distracted.

The Japanese had other *Ukiyo-e* pictures of the floating world called *shunga*, explicitly depicting such distractions. Kim and I spent the day in our own pleasure quarters. The rain poured down on the only chance we would have to climb up the highest mountain in Japan. Instead, we spent the day reading Kabayashi Issa's haiku, and climbing anyway. *A cloudburst and then, right away, Fifth Month rain... The same sound, as water boiling, Fifth Month rain... O snail, Climb Mount Fuji But slowly, slowly... Rainstorm, a naked rider, on a naked horse... Young buck, when he starts to make love, mountain rain... Spring rain, at night, too, making love on Mount Matchi... A night, for pounding the love-making clothes, hut's stone... Shaking her body, in the summer rain, maiden*

172

flower... My sleepy mind, counting cherry blossoms, a rainy night...Morning rain, a butterfly, licks it up... In one morning, I climb around ten, Mount Fujis.

Japanese handsaws work on the pull rather than the push. The more Kimi and I pulled on each other, the more we knew we were severing our bond. If the rain ever lifted, she would go back to Tokyo, and I would hitchhike down the narrow road south. We sat up long enough to eat raw eggs and seaweed and ferns for breakfast, and prayed for rain. It continued, like applause.

In late afternoon Mama-san knocked on our door with no small enthusiasm, given the reservation we'd come to expect from her.

"John Rain." She said. Kimi looked at me. I shrugged.

"John Wayne?" I asked.

"Hai." She said. "John Rain." And she took us into the family room. Sure enough, it was John Wayne, playing U.S. Marshall 'Rooster' Cogburn, in *True Grit*. I had never heard John Wayne speaking Japanese before, and the effect was, as I remember it, transcendental. I had always thought of Wayne as a swagger stick of American expansionism, from the *Sands of Iwo Jima* to the barbarian in *The Barbarian and the Geisha*. I didn't quite understand why the Japanese would have had any affection for him, given what I thought he represented to them and their history. But when Emperor Hirohito visited the US in 1975, he asked to the icon of his country's former enemy. Western Village, an animatronics theme park not far from where Kimi and I were experiencing our Fifth Month rains, featured a robotic version of the Duke, shirt later pulled open to expose his electronic innards. It was a suitably synchronous sunset, as we had stolen their myths to make our own. Kurosawa's *Seven Samurai* was the template for *The Magnificent Seven*, Kurosawa's *Yojimbo* had spawned Sergio Leone's *A Fistful of Dollars*, and his *Hidden Fortress* had been wholly lifted by George Lucas to make *Star Wars*. But the cowboy cross-pollination, as we were about to discover, cut both ways.

Five truck drivers from Kyushu appeared in the lounge after checking in. They shared a watermelon, and watch the rest of the movie. But when Mama-san left, the congeniality disappeared with the laughter. The warning came when one of them told Kimi he loved her. This made us uncomfortable. The others nodded their approval. This made us wary. When they brought out their pornographic magazines for my encouraged enjoyment, and their eyes and hands began marching toward Kimi, this made us leave. In my Asian travels so far, I had heard stories of Japanese male psychopathy. I had read the history of Korean 'comfort' women, and what had happened to allied nurses during the war. I had met round and wide-eyed single Western girls who began as Rising Sunbeam English teachers, and ended as Fallen Angel escorts and prostitutes, dismayed in Japan. It was a not-so-secret induction hazard of trying to experience real Japanese society. Like the difference in our handsaws, some of them were pulled, but some of them had clearly been pushed, and it made me wonder which of us were the barbarians.

We crashed like the thunder outside. Her tears ran down my shoulder like the rain.

'Even in warmest
glow
how cold my shadow'
Kobayashi Issa

The Route of Seeing

'From this day forth
I shall be called a wanderer,
Leaving on a journey
Thus among the early showers'
Basho, *Records of a Travel-worn Satchel*

I awoke to Mount Fuji, looking in on us. Kimi was stretched out on the futon foreground, smiling.

Mama-san bowed us *sayonara*, and we walked along the narrow road to the junction at Shoji Lake, where she cried again.

"My trip and I are not on speaking terms." She said, holding on. The Japanese stared and Fuji pulled in her clouds from embarrassment.

I had staked out this hitching post on a rainy day walk two days earlier. It was like she had been, a beautiful inside curve with firm shoulders, a 5° incline, and all the adjacent parts covered. My thumb was a razor.

"Would you like me get you a ride?" I said to ease the guilt. "Yes." She said. And I flagged down the first truck, and she was gone.

My second arc caught a samurai schoolboy and his two high-pitched *moekko* girlfriends in a van. The clutch dropped in my lap and we were off to Kofu, accompanied by pidgin English, sexual innuendo, and Coca-Colas. Less than a minute after they dropped me at the Expressway onramp, a lone executive *sararīman* offered me a ride to Nagoya in his maroon wagon. We broke the language barrier on the other side of the Central Alps. After noodles at a 'toiret stop,' he let me off just inside the Kyoto city limits.

The last ride was the best of the day. Yuji was a landscape architect, driving his decaled Datsun back to Kyushu. He had

175

a fantastic tape collection, and stories of how he hitched around America, and dropped acid on a California commune. We had coffee overlooking Lake Biwa, and I left him at the tollgate on the southern part of the city. And there the need for speed disintegrated. Maybe it was because the sun had come out. I walked unhurriedly, trying to put some context back into my contact. The early summer warmth soaked into my face. I passed Japanese women with white bonnets and bare ankles, planting rice in tiny fields, salt granules peppered among the high-rises. On one side was a gigantic alabaster facsimile of Frank, a Brobdingnagian bust of Buddha in a warehouse parking lot. The imposing pagoda of Tō-ji Kyō-ō-gokoku-ji hove into view, and pretty girls on city buses waved to me with white gloves. After ten kilometers, I stopped for an ice cream, and a phone call to Mrs. Uno's Machiyo Inn.

"One-o people-o?" She asked.

"One-o people-o." I said.

"OK." She said. "You-o come-o." The way my Japanese was improving, I figured I'd be speaking *hyōjungo* like a native in no time.

"G'day Mate." Said Sleek Deek, as I arrived under the rattan blinds. An older woman with a cataract checked me into a single room adjacent to the kitchen for ¥1400 per night. *One-o people-o.*

I stowed Serendipity and Deek took me on brief tour of my new neighborhood- the temple, the bathhouse, cheap eateries, supermarket and bank, and we returned to meet the other inmates: Liz, a 25 year-old chubby Swiss Miss, and her friend Jan, a 22-year-old orphaned nurse from New Zealand; Anov, a red-haired Israeli comedian peddling hash to finance his research into global prostitution; Mike, an Irish-Puerto Rican Chicagoan, multilingual, on the road now for six years and still trying to get out of Japan; his sidekick, Dudley, a Kiwi pharmacist, had spent two years in the subcontinent; and other veterans of foreign wars, who knew better than to exchange addresses. We adjourned to a cozy neighborhood bar across the canal, losing the girls and their French gigolo on the way- leaving Deek and Dudley and Mike and I sharing an evening of sake and stories, down the narrow road path of philosophy. The Japanese students around the counter, and the mama-sans behind it, seemed to appreciate our eccentricity, and bid us goodnight with sincere bows and smiles. Deek woke the girls with a bottle of sake on our return, and we drifted into the small hours, playing guitar and telling tales.

Kyoto had been the Imperial Capital of Japan for over a thousand years, until the bloody pitched battles between samurai factions spilled into its streets in 1869, burning down thirty thousand houses, and shifting the seat of power to Tokyo. But there were still 2000 religious shrines, as well as palaces, gardens and other architectural marvels to behold and, like I had suffered in Florence, Stendhal Syndrome virus lay around every corner. The man to blame for this was Henry L. Stimson, Truman's Secretary of War, who refused to allow an atomic bomb to fall on it. I had three days to see why.

Next morning I hit the ground running, through the eastern part of the city. Under the large orange *torii* crossbars to the Halloween-colored Heian Shrine, to the exquisitely muted elegance of the Chion-in temple, with the three hollyhock leaves of the Tokagawa family crest carved into the ends of the roof beams, the umbrella in the rafters to bring rain and ward off fire, and the squeaky floor boards, inlaid with metal ends to detect any unwanted intruders during the night. I marveled at the split-faced monk, and the screen depicting barbarian travelers in the Kyoto National Museum. In the Sanjūsangendō *Hall of the Lotus King*, were a 1001 thousand-armed Kannon statues, one of which was supposed to look like me. Inside, headaches were cured by the touch of a sacred branch on the head, in the Rite of the Willow. Outside, in 1604, Japan's most famous undefeated warrior, Miyamoto Musashi, took out the leader of the Yoshioka-ryū school of

swordsmanship, Yoshioka Denshichirō, with a single blow.
I returned through the narrowest lanes I could find, catching wafts of traditional music floating across sunlit roan entrances, and glimpses of kimono-clad *mayo* apprentice geishas, but the roar of modern Japan drowned these appreciations completely. A coffee bar on my way back to the neighborhood advertised its name on a signpost outside. *My Sweet Road.*

Back at Numerous Uno, I availed myself of the sauna, and the warm, hot and cold pools of the *sent* bathhouse. It appeared that my room had been singled out for congregating in, and the congregations got larger as the days went by. I met Ian, an English, a cytologist working in Saudi, Dr. Frank and his lovely wife from Minneapolis whom I had met in Burma, and an Indonesian-born Flying Dutchman with an earring and a guitar. Anov brought out his hashish, which made the sake superfluous.

The morning of the second day began at what had been one of the mental images that sustained my hope and desire, during the long cold winter of my internship year. The photo of a few silent islands of rock in a white gravel sea had produced, for me, a deafening existential noise. And I sat on the wooden veranda, and looked out over the Ryan-ji *Temple of the Dragon at Peace.* And I was. At peace, and aware that, as much as we had learned in the five hundred year interval that this *karesansui* dry landscape Zen rock garden had not changed, we had also not advanced beyond this. The garden had been designed so that one could only see fourteen of the fifteen boulders from any vantage point. Only by attaining enlightenment could you see them all at once. The water running in the nearby low stone basin requires the thirsty to bend their knee, in humility, and to allow them to read the inscription. *I only know what is enough.*

My northwest circuit continued via the Zen Garden of Emptiness, to the Kinkaku-ji *Deer Garden* Golden Temple, topped with a bronze phoenix, and sitting over the Kyōko-chi

178

Mirror Pond, which contained four stones in a straight line, representing sailboats anchored at night, bound for the Chinese mythological *Isle of Eternal Life*. The place was jammed like Hangzhou on a Sunday afternoon. A novice monk with a persecution complex had burned the original down in 1950. He may have been onto something.

More tranquility was to be found in the Ryōgen-in Zen garden pebbles at the Daitoku-ji Buddhist temple, linked to the realm of the Japanese tea ceremony, and its master, Sen no Rikyū. The whiskers on the white dragon screen were venerable.

Through the small silk factories in Nimjen, I arrived at Nijō flatland castle, decorated in gold leaf and elaborate wood carvings, to demonstrate the power of the shogun. The fortress had been constructed with nails to create *uguisubari* 'nightingale floors' in the corridors, which squeaked like birds when anyone walked on them, so as to also protect the occupants from assassin sneak attacks. The crenulations in the rock walls of the moat looked like old grey cheddar.

On the third day, I walked to the tall Tō-ji Temple that had greeted my Kyoto arrival. The sign in the gardens outside pointed to *The Route of Seeing*. The Nishi and Higashi Hongan-ji, the Western and Eastern *Temples of the Primal Vow* were as massive, as the Kiyomizu-dera, built without a single nail in the entire structure, and with its interior waterfall, was magnificent. The long hot trek that took me to the grounds of Nanzen-ji, and the Path of Philosophy that followed, led to my saturation point. I returned to Uno House, for the more mundane and the less meaningful- mending my shoes, washing my clothes, playing chess, and primal vowing that I would never visit another temple.

In my last night in Kyoto, there was a fond fondue farewell party for me on the tatami mats in my room. I played the Flying Dutchman's guitar while he played his harmonica, Swiss Miss and Jan lit candles and sang harmony, Anov and Dudley altered minds, Sleek Deek played chess with the

Norwegian, and Dr. Frank expostulated on Bilharzia variants. I was looking forward to the dawn. As wonderful as the shrines of Kyoto had been, I needed to move. Instead of following in the footsteps of the men of old, I knew how much more fulfilling it was, seeking what they had sought.

'Even in Kyoto
Hearing the cuckoo's cry
I long for Kyoto'
Matsuo Bashō

*   *   *

'The temple bell stops but I still hear the sound
coming out of the flowers.'
Matsuo Bashō

I hiked out past a row of sixteen flowerpots, behind which stood a girls bicycle and three large statues- a Buddha, a Kannon *Goddess of Mercy*, and a Shinto monk, up against a concrete wall, under an air conditioner. I could hear the sound coming out of the flowers.
Fifteen minutes later I got my first ride. Ed was a Californian financial whiz kid, with a weakness for Oriental antiquities and fast cars. But in his haste to leave an impression, he dropped me smack dab on the Hanshin Expressway. Thanks, Ed.
I stood stunned like the statues I had passed earlier that morning. An hour went by and, exactly on the hour, a concerned-looking uniformed tollbooth attendant approached, nodding and bowing, as I did in return. He was wearing white gloves. I think he asked where I was going.
"Himeji." I tolled him. He bowed, and went back to his

180

booth. The next truck he stopped was still grumbling when it pulled over next to me. But the driver took me to Himeji, as I wondered what his original destination had been. This was a recurring event for me in Japan. When any highway official noticed me, he stopped and instructed the next vehicle to take me to where I was heading. I had to be very careful not to abuse this, but I'm sure one driver went a hundred kilometers out of his way. Kerouac should have given France a miss.

I had come to Himeji to see the White Egret, the finest surviving example of Japanese castle architecture. Originally built in 1333, it still looked like a bird taking flight. Its defenses were impressive. If an attacker managed to get across the three moats, he would be forced into a complex spiral around the outer walls, made out of white fire-resistant plaster. A thousand 'loopholes' allowed the use of matchlocks or bows without exposing the defender. Angled chutes were strategically placed, for dropping stones or boiling oil. There were 33 interior wells. The narrow road to the interior was a steep maze, and the number of apparent stories from the outside didn't correspond to the actual number of floors within the castle. Inside were small, enclosed hiding places, where soldiers could ambush otherwise unsuspecting invaders. It was brilliant.

I hadn't come to Himeji to see the Baskin-Robbins but, like the animatronics version of John Wayne, there it was. I entered it like I had entered the golden arches on leaving East Berlin, with a mixture of disgust and exhilaration. I pointed to what I wanted.

"You have Locky Load?" She asked.

"Yeah, honey." I said. "I have Locky Load."

Back outside, it began plum raining. That's how big the drops were. They pruned my fingertips by the time I got smart enough to take the two-hour slow train to Kurashiki. At the information counter in the station, was an American couple, also seeking directions to the hostel. Charles was a graduate major in Far Eastern studies and business, and Becky was an ICU nurse from Tennessee. At the hostel we met Fern, an artist from Toronto, and together, found a teppanyaki place for dinner, and returned to the hostel early.

I wasn't ready for what I found in the bathroom mirror. It was my father's face, almost how I remembered his. I hadn't seen him for almost four years, but his words were still with me. '*Don't lose your Medicine... Don't expect me to bail you out of some Bolivian jail... Don't come back with Herpes... A man is at thirty what he is for the rest of his life...*' I was thirty. And alone. And indigent. Locky Load.

After a polite breakfast farewell, and a lightning tour of two Folkcraft Museum streets, I snagged a short ride to Fukiyama from a young quiet guy in a hotrod, followed by a ride to Mihara from a Japanese couple, the female half of which, yammered at me nonstop, in Nihongo. To this day, I don't think she realized that there were some out there like me, and possibly others, who didn't speak her native tongue.

I stood outside Mihara for five minutes at the most, before a big Fuso truck almost lurched into the railing trying to stop. And a big fat *domo arigato* to you, Suzuki-san. A classic knight of the road, 52-year-old family man, porn on the dash, dash on the gas, and gas all the way to Kyushu.

We broke the language barrier around Hiroshima, and stopped near Otake for some *ramen*, so he could show me off to Mama-san and the other drivers, and catnap for an hour. And we drove into the night, through the tunnel to Kitakyushu, another noodle stop where I paid and blew his mind, and on to Kurume, where I helped him unload his truck around 3 am. We finished by sunup, and were on the road to finally part ways after breakfast at Yatsushiro at dawn. So long Suzuki-san. May your engine never overheat.

'Thoughts in time and out of season
The Hitchhiker
Stood by the side of the road
And leveled his thumb
In the calm calculus of reason.'
The Doors, *Hitchhiker*

*   *   *

'I've never really wanted to go to Japan. Simply because I don't like
eating fish. And I know that's very popular out there in Africa.'
Britney Spears

I watched him bank across three lanes of traffic, and pitch up
onto the shoulder in front of me. Another inch and I would
have been one with his paint. He rolled down the window.
"Where are you going?" He asked. Through the smoke of the
dangling cigarette, I could just make out a mop of black hair
and a beard. He looked like Belushi in *Samurai Delicatessen*,
with two big round glass lenses.
"Kagoshima, onegai shimasu." I said.
"Mimimata?" He offered. I checked my map and figured,
what the hell, it was going to be a slow day anyway. And to
think I almost turned down a kindred soul. I put Serendipity
in the back, and got in.
"You going to work?" I asked.
"Hai." He said.
"What do you do?" I asked.
"Doctor." He said.
"Me too." I offered. In return, I got a raised Belushi eyebrow,
which climbed even higher when I brought out my world
map. His name was Kenji, a 33-year-old chain-smoking
neurosurgeon, on his way to his clinic. Pure Land Buddhist.
We stopped at the hospital to find out the best onward route

for me to hitchhike and, when we couldn't find a place for coffee, drove back to his clinic. We played video golf and smoked, and ogled the nurses.

"You in a hurry?" He asked.

"I have to be in Okinawa for my boat to Taiwan Friday." I said.

"Will you drink with me tonight? I like to drink with you." Kenji offered.

"If you do not enter the tiger's cave, you will not catch its cub." I said. And he grinned like Belushi.

An evening of revelry in Minimata was a promise of incoordination, numbness, muscle weakness, visual field defects, hearing and speech damage, insanity, paralysis, coma, and death. And that was just from the food.

It had started with the cats. In 1950 they began 'dancing' in the streets, then strangely going mad, convulsing, collapsing and dying. The locals called it the Cat Dancing Disease, sometimes falling into the sea, in communal 'cat suicides.' Crows plummeted from the sky, seaweed disappeared from the seabed, and fish floated dead on the surface of the ocean. Friends and family members started to slur their speech, shout uncontrollably, or drop their chopsticks at dinner.

In 1932, the Chisso Corporation began to manufacture acetaldehyde, used to produce plastics. Mercury-saturated industrial wastewater spilled into the bay for more than 30 years. The 2 kg of mercury pollution per ton of sediment found at the mouth of the wastewater canal was so heavy, that Chisso would eventually find it economically viable to mine. Its bioaccumulation, as organic methyl mercury chloride, in shellfish and fish, worked its way further up the food chain, until over two thousand people were afflicted with an 'epidemic of an unknown disease of the central nervous system,' quarantined, and their homes disinfected. When a British neurologist finally linked Minamata Disease to the 'Mad Hatters'' organic mercury beaver skin hat makers poisonings of the last century, Chisso fought back with denial and harassment. One woman had her family's fishing nets cut, and human feces thrown at her in the street.

I spent a full day wandering around Mercuryville, changing money, shopping for desperately need clothes and toiletries, and dodging raindrops.

At 5 pm, Kenji emerged from his clinic and we drove over to the apartment he kept for medical and illicit purposes. After a shower and a beer, we went out to eat.

"No fish, Kenji." I insisted. He laughed. But the mercury rose anyway and we ate a fantastic five course Japanese meal of tofu, beef sushi, fish, and salad, accompanied by beer and shōchū.

We continued in the local bar owned by a Kenji's retired sumo friend, and already inhabited by two more of his companions, sitting at the long wooden counter lined with oversized sake bottles, under paper box lanterns, and a string of blue banners.

"Kenji-san!" They shouted, flooding both of us with shōchū and hospitality. First the man takes a drink; then the drink takes a drink; then the drink takes the man.

Karaoke is something you should only do drunk. This was not a problem. A microphone appeared before me, and then the background music and the foreground lyrics, thankfully both in *hiragana* and hyphenated Engrish. I didn't actually know the tunes. Again this was not a problem. I did know the tune to *Ue o Muite Arukō*. They brought me backup vocals and I brought them to tears.

Then they sang, and taught me their songs, gifted me with film and a delicious fish caught by one of the regulars, and made toasts to me, and my odyssey. *Pausing between clouds the moon rests in the eyes of its beholders.* Kenji and I packed it in around midnight, and drifted home to unconsciousness.

The next morning he presented me with a melon, coffee, a packet of *Seven Stars*, and a new shirt, and drove me to the highway, to say goodbye. It was bittersweet, bitterly lonely, sweetly reminiscent of what some humanity is still capable of.

And then the day dragged, for what could compete with that? I snagged a long ride from two rich Fukuoka businessmen going fishing, after a short one from a lost teenager; another from a marine engineer who dropped me off after a bowl of ramen, between Sendai and Ijuin. I walked a long way through humid rice fields, until she stopped in front of the bamboo box of purples irises.

Yoko was a 28-year-old law student from Sendai. She slowed only long enough to collect me, put on Jackson Browne, tell me she wanted to go to Canada, and drive the rest of the way to Kagoshima. She dropped me at the New Port to buy my ticket to Okinawa, and went off to class. She returned an hour before I was to board, for a brief interlude under the bamboo in Iso Gardens. When my boat pulled away from the Naples of the Eastern World, under the cloud-covered stratovolcanic shadow of Sakurajima, I looked back at the wake tip of my boat. She was waving.

'Memories are like karaoke-where... you didn't know even half the lyrics... Only afterwards... do you realize that... you read more into it than maybe existed... it's better to not know the lyrics to your life.'

Douglas Coupland, *The Gum Thief*

Spiders and Snakes

'Summer night--
even the stars
are whispering to each other.'
Kobayashi Issa

The stars were more than whispering. I needed to get out of the sub-polar temperatures of the Japanese high-tech aircon in the steerage class rug room. My twenty-five hours on the ferry to Okinawa would alternate between fire and ice. Outside, on deck, Orion had appeared in the East at sunset. In Japan, the *Yowatashi Boshi* 'Passing the Night' stars symbolized many things. From his trapezoidal hourglass shape, he was regarded as a Japanese drum, or kimono sleeves. His three *Mitsu Boshi* belt stars were recognized as occupational tools, a ruler of liner measurement for land managers, bamboo joints for pole makers, thread-making machine parts for weavers, or a spear for fishermen. For farmers they were a balance, tipping in one direction for the millet season, and the other when it was time to plant rice. They represented the three fundamental values of Japanese consciousness- filial duty, strength and courage, and a will to persevere, though chased by ogres across the heavens.

The ogres were waiting for me in New Naha port. The first was the torpid heat of Okinawa at noon. This left me drenched in sweat by the time I disembarked. The second was the price I paid for an onward ticket on the Arumuri clipper to Taipei. This left me poor, with two days in Naha. A friendly local gave me a lift further into the ogre metropolis. I asked him why they houses were and made of concrete, and their windows were barred.

"Typhoon." He said. I asked him what the worst one had been.

"Kou no kaze." He said. "Typhoon of Steel." The Americans

had called the Battle of Okinawa *Operation Iceberg*. It had been the largest amphibious assault of the Pacific war, resulting in the highest number of casualties. More than 1500 planes and land-based motorboats made ferocious one-way *kamikaze* attacks on the American fleet. Over 100,000 Japanese soldiers, and a quarter of the civilian population, were killed, captured or forced to commit mass suicide. Ninety per cent of all buildings were destroyed. Monsoon rains turned the tropical landscape into a vast sodden morass of garbage and graveyard. Unburied bodies decayed, sank, and dissolved into a noxious stew. Soldiers sliding down the greasy slopes arrived at the bottom with their pockets full of maggots. The official American military history remarked that the military value of Okinawa 'exceeded all hope.'

Hope continued to be exceeded with almost twenty percent of the island converted to a US strategic launch pad for B-29 bombing missions over Korea and China during the Korean War, B-52 attacks on Vietnam, Cambodia and Laos during the Vietnam War, and thousands of aggravated and sexual assaults on local inhabitants by U.S. servicemen, still ongoing. Not to mention the noise pollution, environmental degradation, aircraft accidents, crowding, and interference with the local economy. Or the bonus stockpile of nuclear weapons.

We passed over the Meiji Bridge, flanked by tanks on one side and a sign on the other. *American army installation-Trespassers will be prosecuted under Japanese law.*

"Do you think the Americans will ever leave?" I asked. He pursed his lips and averted his eyes.

"In this world we walk on the roof of hell, gazing at flowers." He said, letting me off on the mile-long Kokusai-dōri *International Street*. Oldies blared from the *Shakey's* across from the *McDonald's*, down from the *Dunkin' Donuts*, next to the *A&W*.

'Hushabye Hushabye
Oh my darlin' don't you cry
Guardian angels up above
Take care of the one I love.'

The lullaby is the spell whereby the mother attempts to transform herself back from an ogre to a saint. I asked two Americans where the Makishi Public market was.

"Hell, I don't even know what a Makishi is." He said. I asked two Mormon clones.

"Gee, I dunno. I've only been here a week." He said.

I was back inside the Panama Canal Zone Baskin-Robbins, except that it was an entire island of American Graffiti. Locky Load.

A black Nissan van, carrying white flags with big red dots, and a garbled megaphone monologue of right-wing extremist mania, went by slowly. I asked one of the bandanas marching alongside, and received a bow, and polite directions in American English.

"Hey buddy, be careful you don't get ripped off in that place, y'hear?" I heard, but I had trouble believing the disconnect between my eyes and ears.

It was in this way that I found one of the grottiest stuffiest mosquito-infested little shitholes on the planet. The alcoholic, shirtless 'man-a-ja,' playing his classical guitar badly, hadn't washed the bedding in so long, it cut the back of your throat like a runny cheese with a terminal disease. He offered me a choice between the humid swamp and mosquitoes in a top bunk or a sour sweat mattress next to the *tak-tak* fan on the floor. *The butterfly perfuming its wings fans the orchid.* I took the bunk.

Five times as many Okinawans live to be a hundred as in the rest of Japan, and the Japanese are the longest-lived nationality in the world. This longevity is apparently attributable to their diet, low-stress lifestyle, caring community, activity, and spirituality of the inhabitants. Except for the caring community part, the inhabitants of the

189

Ikura pension were definitely not in the game. But it was enough.

Osaka-san was a venerable old man, whose reason for being in Naha I never learned. Kanjo was a young hotel worker, who cooked me up a batch of sand-crunchy abalone. And Hirosh was a single 42-year-old construction worker from Hokkaido. He had travelled in Europe in his youth but was now a sad, lonely, directionless, but stoic victim of unrequited love. I noticed he drank a bit, between laughs.

He drank the local beer, *Orion 'Zero Life.'*

"For your happy time." He laughed. It was the company motto. I told Hirosh about another of Orion's classical Japanese images, the trapezoidal *Sakamasu Boshi* alcohol cup measurer, chasing the drunken *Supai* Pleiades across the Western sky, for not paying. We talked until late, until I had to ascend into my fetid bunk. It didn't last. Halfway through the night, blistered in bites and one with the swamp humidity, I climbed down to the sour sweat mattress, next to the *tak-tak* fan on the floor. And slept. *There is nothing you can see that is not a flower; There is nothing you can think that is not the moon.*

The next morning I set out to find the Okinawan market essence, but even in the covered Heiwa-dōri, everything was either expensive or inauthentic, or both. I found a beautiful teapot from Kyoto, but I couldn't afford the forty-two dollar price tag. None of the shopkeepers were very friendly, not that I could blame them. I spent a good part of the day in Shakey's, soaking up 20 per cent of the authentic Ryukyu hybrid culture, and sipping Orion. At dusk I returned to the Ikura for a wash. The shower wasn't much, just a galvanized tin shed, with an old soiled aquamarine-colored synthetic drape for a door. There was no light inside, and no flower on the shower, just an open pipe, over a dirt floor. There was one cartwheel garden tap handle, halfway up the conduit, which produced one temperature of water in the subtropical enclosure. I stripped down and turned the tap hard clockwise. The tap handle twirled off to the right, and scurried up onto the roof. An eight-legged dharmachacra, an Okinawan brown huntsman spider, had his world turned round, in my search for purification. The total war I conducted later on the popping roaches was also a defeat, in the sweltering evening heat. The Japanese had a legend about spiders, Jorōgumo, who seduces unsuspecting travelers as a beautiful women until, distracted by her *biwa* lute playing, wraps up her victim for later dining. It wasn't going to happen.

I took Hirosh out for breakfast next morning, and told him about the brown huntsman.

"Too bad." He said. "Morning spider good luck. Evening spider bad." We hugged each other goodbye, and I left for Naha port. The counter dumpling put a voice on a telephone that spoke passable English.

"Ship may not go today." He Said.

"Why not?" I asked.

"Typhoon." He said. My blood turned cold.

"When will you know?" I asked.

"I call you back at 4 pm." Right. So I sat in that room eating my groceries until the confirmation came through.

"So what am I supposed to do?" I asked.

"Fly." He said. It was the only thing with six or eight legs I had not encountered on Okinawa. *Don't weep, insects - Lovers, stars themselves, Must part.*

They offered me a taxi to the airport. I took it. Sometimes you just have to get out of Dodge. Sanity before sawbucks.

The three most famous exports of Okinawa were karate, a rice alcohol called *awamori*, and a three-stringed instrument called a *sanshin*, made from python skins. But the real snakes were on the other side of the next airport. And they weren't whispering.

'When you have completed 95% of your journey you are halfway there.'
Japanese Proverb

*   *   *

191

'A mighty dragon cannot subdue a local snake.'
Chinese Proverb

"Howdy." He said. "Ron. Ron Bowie. But my friends call me Ronbo."

I shook his hand. It felt like it had been fed on corn syrup and beef. Mostly beef.

"Wink." I said. My relief to have the last standby seat on the plane was tempered by the volume of the American I got to sit next to. And the amplitude of his gold watch and knuckle rings, the wrist and fingers they ornamented, his suit, and what filled it, was large.

"What kind of name is Wink?" He asked, elbowing my ribs. "That's just weird." I asked him what he did for a living.

"Everyone I can, and the good ones twice." He said, shuffling in his seat, and pulling out a business card. It had his name, his Mid-western address, and his occupation. Import-Export. *Entrepreneur* had been misspelled.

"Kansas City?" I said.

"Kansas City." He said, with another elbow. "KC. KCMO. Cowtown. Barbeque Capital of the World. Paris of the Plains."

"Bonsoir." I said.

"What the hell?" I told him it was a French greeting. But Ron didn't have much use for frogs, or niggers, or kikes, or gooks. I asked him how he could stand to do business with the gooks.

"Business is business." He said, setting it with a grim sneer. The stewardess had reached our outpost.

"Scotch." He said. "Make it a double. He'll have the same." I didn't feel like a scotch but, after the scotch, I didn't feel much at all. And this helped me to understand Ron better. It turned out that Nixon had been a great president after all, and Ron did have an appreciation of some aspects of Asian

192

culture. He liked 'the ones that bow and show respect,' and underage

'little gook girls,' for their enthusiasm. Back in Kansas City, he was president of the American Tae-Kwan-Do Association, because he 'believed in those kids.' He ordered us another scotch. It calmed the nausea.

"You know what the meaning of life is, Wink?" He asked. I assured him that I didn't.

"Three 'P's." He said. "Profit, power, and pussy." Marx, Nietzsche, and Freud. The pilot announced our descent into Taipei, and I breathed relief, in anticipation of my imminent escape.

"Hey, I have an idea." He said. "Why don't you come to the hotel with me and you can call the hostel from there?" I had just flown over one typhoon, and into another.

The Portuguese had originally named our destination 'Ilha Formosa,' *Beautiful Island*, but it was dark, and raining. Ron and I grabbed a cab to the Embassy Hotel, where he checked both of us into a big room. I thanked him, but I wasn't really sure it was a good idea.

"It's only because you didn't ask." He said. "Besides, we can get ourselves some girls and have some fun." Then I was sure.

We had only closed the door, when it knocked. I opened it to a middle aged Chinese businessman.

"That's Frank Lin." Ron shouted, and cracked my bottle of Jonny Walker Black duty free. "He's one of the good Chinks." Frank just smiled, and took a seat, and the full glass that was handed him. Frank was a 'partner,' but if it hadn't been for money, you could sense that he would have stomped Ron to death. He and Ron threw some numbers around the room, and Frank melted back into the rain.

"Let's go out and get some." Ron said combing his remaining hair over his lack of hair. A mysterious change seems to come over Americans when they go to a foreign land. I was reasonably sure than Ron enjoyed some form of community respect back in his Kansas City circles, but here in the Far East, on unfamiliar ground, his circle was broken. We drifted to a series of watering holes with cover charges, and were admitted to each under the pretext of Ron looking for his brother. Outside the last one he met Lisa, dressed in red, and desperate. Ron promised her a trip to Sun Moon Lake, and she began to follow us, offering her soul in return. I was quite fed up with all of this, and was planning an escape, when she suddenly and unexpected became violent to me. She broke the strap on my Jerusalem bag, and the front of Kenji's shirt. She wouldn't let go, and Ron laughed loudly, drawing a crowd. I asked one of the onlookers if he would ask her to leave me alone, but he shook his head and looked away.

"Looks like she's all yours now, 'ol buddy." Said Ron. She was eventually detached by the security in the Embassy lobby. Ronbo laughed all the way up the elevator, and ate the food I had brought from Okinawa, while I slept.

I awoke to him shouting at a book-toting teenybopper, outside our window.

"Hey." He called. "Meet me later for ice cream." I dressed quickly, while he told me about how he had raped several schoolgirls 'right here in this room.' I told him I would see him later that afternoon, and left.

The hostel I found was just the sort of travelers haven I needed. Golden Eagle travel booked me a standby flight on Singapore Airlines to Hong Kong for the next day, and I spent this one trying to fill the previous days wounds with some higher purpose.

Taiwan seemed to exist for escaping serpents, although it had enough endemic poisonous species of its own. In 1931, Chiang Kai-shek's Nationalist Government gave the order to evacuate the Beijing Palace Museum's collection, to prevent it from falling into the hands of the Imperial Japanese Army. It took two years to pack it into over thirteen thousand boxes, and two trainloads, to transport it from the Gate of Divine Might, across the Taiwan Strait, to a sugar cane factory on the island. The collection finally landed in Taipei's National Palace Museum, as did I. Although it accounted for only a quarter of the items originally transported from the mainland, the collection was still unimaginably immense, and the source of buckets of Beijing bile. Almost 700,000 pieces of ancient Chinese art and artifact, spanning eight thousand years of Chinese history, meant that I would only see the one per cent of the collection exhibited at any given time. What I saw was stunning, particularly the carvings. There was an intricately detailed cabbage head of translucent jade, with a small grasshopper camouflaged in its leaves, a piece of jasper pork, so real you could taste the soy sauce, and a tiny olive pip, sculpted into a boat with movable windows, a covered deck, and an interior, with chairs, dishes and eight figures. The calligraphy section was also magnificent, but I eventually drowned in an overwhelming sea of porcelain, bronzes, landscape paintings, jade, coins, textiles and history.

That evening I went to the snake market. I remember the bar monkey, a resident chimpanzee dressed in the tavern's t-shirt, hopping from patron to patron, serving turtle meat and deer-penis wine. But the real action was in the hanging serpents and incandescent bulbs of Wanhua's Snake Alley red light district, two blocks long. I watched an old Chinese man order a cobra, from one of the cages under the multicolored signs of a night market stall. The owner grabbed it by the head and, with one quick zip of a knife, had it stunned, hung, skinned alive, and dripping every drop of carotid blood into a small shot glass, sitting on the stainless steel counter. The customer added a few drops from one of the numerous small bottles of condiments, tossed it back in one go, paid for his renewed tumescence, and disappeared back into an adjacent brothel. I looked at the owner. He flexed his bicep, and grinned. Fifteen years later Viagra would kill his business, and save the snakes. Back at the hostel I reencountered Guy, the young Pakistani Brit from Mary's Beijing clique. I asked after her health.

195

"Oh, Mary's in Hong Kong." He said. "She's on the 13th floor of 'D' block in Chungking Mansions, looking for a job. You might meet her there tomorrow." We played chess.

And, in the land of snakes, I remembered the Japanese legend of Jorōgumo the spider, seducing unsuspecting travelers as a beautiful women until, distracted, would wrap up her victims for later dining. It wasn't going to happen.

The typhoon was still a deluge next day. I called the travel agency to confirm my flight, but the Golden Eagle girl hung up on me three times. At the airport, I learned that Singapore Airlines had cancelled their flight, and it took me several more hours to get back to the agency, and find the manager. He was contrite and efficient, and managed to get me on a Japan-Asia flight for later that evening. Back at the airport, I checked in and went through Security, recognizing the official that had greeted Ronbo and I on our arrival. Unfortunately he recognized me as well. The Paiwan aborigines of Taiwan had not been well treated by any of their invaders. The Qing Chinese ate and traded in their flesh. The Japanese launched over 160 battles to exterminate them, which is likely why they beheaded the fifty-four crew of an Okinawan vessel that was shipwrecked on the southern tip in 1871. The Security officer must have had some aboriginal DNA memory of all this, or maybe he had judged Ronbo correctly, and me not so much. He went through Serendipity with a meticulous and malicious intent, and finally found something that produced a smile. My butane gas canister had been minding its own business at the bottom of my pack. The loud hissing of its long death rattle filled the departure lounge.

Be are All Abailable

'Filipinos want beauty. I have to look beautiful so that the poor
Filipinos will have a star to look at from their slums.'

Imeda Marcos

"You're still not mad at me, are you?"
She was exactly where Guy said she'd be, on the 13th floor of
'D' block, in Chungking Mansions. I told her no, and I
wasn't. Maybe it was her new haircut or her sudden pastiness,
but I wasn't anything at her at all. Mary led me to find an old
friend from Ghorapani, Pokhara, and a medieval banquet in
Kathmandu. Bruce was happy for the reacquaintance. He and
I left her, and walked down Nathan Road for a beer.
Next morning I booked onward flights to Singapore via
Manila at *Time Travel*, and made a phone call home. My
parents sounded older, and spoke with soft and gentle
sentences. There may have been tears. An impromptu jam
session waited back at the hostel. Marc lent me his guitar, and
Bruce and Mary, three Israelis, and a French girl named
Beatrice congregated in our room. Bruce was enamored with
one of the Israeli girls, Revhot. She and Beatrice joined Bruce
and I later, for falafels.
On my final day in The Pearl, I wandered the bookstores and
Chinese emporia in Kowloon, paid for my flight ticket, and
picked up my photos of Japan. I met Beatrice just before
midnight. She told me about her plans to go to Canada to get
married, and saving for the fare by selling bogus student cards
to China-bound travelers. We strolled to the rooftop of the
Mansions, and then along the harbor's edge. The sign above
us was a final warning. *Persons getting close do so at their own risk.*
We risked it. I used my anorak to shield us from the others in
the dorm. They slept noisily, as we didn't.

197

She said goodbye to me at the airport bus next morning. In my daze, I forgot my anorak.

"This is only good for the body." Said Ninoy Aquino, about his own bulletproof vest, before he was shot in the head, on the tarmac of Manila International Airport, less than a year before I arrived. I fared better.

"How long are you staying, Sir?" Asked the immigration officer.

"A week." I said.

"You would enjoy Boracay very much." He said.

"OK." I said. And thanked him.

I had landed in the industrial waste and smog of the most densely populated city in the world, its rivers as biologically as dead as Aquino, and the district of Ermita the most air polluted in the city. An air-conditioned bus took me there, to the Malate Pensionne on Adriatico Street... *definitely THE place to come home to in Manila... Since its humble beginning in 1974, captures the hearts of its visitors... offers the romance of old Manila combined with the convenience of today's modern metropolis... an ambience of rustic charm.* And it seemed to attract just that kind of clientele- Peace Corps volunteers, bible-bashing evangelicals, and old Western perverts looking for cheap sex with Asian women, although the first rule of the house was that stray hookers were not allowed in the rooms. My new dorm mate, Don, was a Kiwi widower who didn't mind giving his 'girls' taxi money, but 'nothing more.'

My international flight ticket on Philippine Airlines allowed me a discount on any further domestic trips I might purchase, but I hadn't anticipated the magnitude of the discount I was entitled to, at their office around the corner. I reconfirmed my onward flight to Singapore, and booked a plane to Kalibo, for nine dollars. I had to ask the counter staff twice.

"Oh, yes Sir." She said. "Nine dollars." And then she changed my money, at the black market rate, in the national airline office. I almost pinched myself, but I was already starting to like the Philippines.

I left for the domestic terminal early next morning. The pretty girls giggling at the Malate reception desk wished me a 'good time,' with almost too much sparkle. The turboprop flight to Kalibo on Panay Island was bumpy, but you couldn't expect much for nine bucks. A tricycle driver took to the jeepney stand, where an elaborately decorated customized conveyance, as flamboyant as it was crowded, rocketed off along the gravel road to Caticlan. Halfway there, two soldiers, dressed in camouflage and carrying loaded M-16s, jumped on top. If it hadn't been for the rice fields, I could have been back in El Salvador. We rolled up beside the covered Borocay boat launch, at dusk. Hurricane lamps glowed and hissed above the unlevel benches on the dirt floor. The silhouette of a European lady left with an Australian and his Filipina girlfriend, on the first sailing of the small catamaran, *Rea*, across the two-kilometer strait to the Cagban jetty.

I waited in the darkness for the boat to return, and a second voyage. The crossing was quietly magical, as was the frond-lit march across the jungle kilometer of the dog bone-shaped island, to the nearest west-facing hillside shacks from our landing point. I settled into one and shared my first night in paradise with rice, eggs and beans, and a magnificent solitude, serenity, and silence.

It had been a long time.

'We practically own everything in the Philippines.'
Imelda Marcos

*　　　*　　　*

'I know everyone in the Philippines is happy.'
Manny Pacquiao

Manny's happy country is an archipelago of 7,107 islands. It was pouring rain on the one I woke up on, courtesy of the southwest monsoon. The natives called it *Habagat* season. I called it unfortunate.

After eggs and some coffee, I donned the West Point jacket that Ron had given me, and trekked barefoot through the surf, past a group of local women sitting on the veranda of a large guesthouse.

"Be are all abailable!" Shouted one of the ladies, and the others broke into wild laughter. I waved at their enthusiasm, and walked on a little further, to White Beach cottages. It was as good a place as any. One of the girls showed me a woven rattan hut in the compound, next to another inhabited by a Swiss farmer. I asked about his pens of pigs and chickens, and his potted plants.

"He has been here for awhile." She said. I asked her how long.

"Fibe years." She said. I gave her forty pesos, and a request to remind me when three days were up. My arrival had been greeted by curious kids and dogs. The light from the rain shone the leaves of the papaya tree outside my window.

Two Aussies approached my steps with beer. I told them it was a little early.

"I'm a bong man, myself." Said Greg, not entirely convincing, from the way he cracked and downed the beverage he had offered only a moment ago. His friend, Tim, made the same hissing sound, and polished off his tinny with the same alacrity.

"No worries." Tim said. Because, apparently, they were equipped with more from where those had just come from. Two more hisses announced their intent to converse. And Greg told me that the Angeles City call girl he had brought to

Boracay at his own 'bloody expense,' was no longer performing as anticipated. With the velocity at which he appeared to be drowning his disappointment, his memory of it would arrive in oblivion before the rest of him. And Tim was not faring any better with his goo-goo doll. It took me awhile to convince them to leave.

But as they did, the tropical sun came out, and the silhouette from the previous night took form on the step of a nearby hut. She was an obviously older woman with a tan-colored paisley sarong and a powder blue floral-patterned cotton blouse, long brown hair, elegant features, very fine. Timeless. I couldn't place her nationality. She paid the young girl for her shelter, and slipped inside. It was obvious she wanted to be alone. I was intrigued but not entranced. The flying foxes came out at dusk. And the next morning, when I emerged from under my mosquito net, she was gone.

The island was a seven-kilometer long coconut palm-lined stretch of white powder sand and crystalline water, intensifying from onshore clear through limestone islets to azure on the horizon and, even with the humidity and billowing clouds and intermittent monsoon rainsqualls, and the beach detritus, it was bliss.

Far too perfect for the Cathouse Club set, I thought, the Aussie and Swiss degenerates with their Filipina femme fatales, playing them back better than they thought they were playing the girls. But I wasted a day with them, swimming, and recharging, and playing guitar for them in the evening. I met two Dutch girls, who I convinced to stay and extra day.

The dogs were already waiting for me on my stoop, the morning of my third day. I decided to hike down the length of their dog bone, to the mythical village of Bulabog. The hounds came with me as far as the stream, but I had to turn back a short time later because of a downpour. Two German girls called me over to their porch to dry off, and we shifted next door to the café, as the cloudbursts went back into labor.

201

And the older European woman was at the other table. We all had a beer and introduced ourselves and, as the deluge intensified, the fräuleins excused themselves.

I found myself alone with this mature Madonna, and uncomfortable. She was clever, quiet, coy, striking - and she made me work to find out anything I wasn't really sure I wanted to know. Her name was Regina. And I wondered what kind of queen. She was Swiss-Israeli. And I rolled that combination around for a while. Ten years divorced.

She had money. That much was clear; she also didn't like it, never used it, and tried to hide it. That was obvious as well. She told me she was 40, but she changed like light through a broken prism, and it was hard to know how old she really was. I could see how she was at 20; I could see how she would be at 60- and it was pure witchcraft the way she shimmered between the two.

Her priorities were also hard to figure- vegetarian, pacifist, feminist, but intensely maternal, vixen-virgin, too intensely diamond hard for her espoused baby Buddha beliefs, lonely self-sufficiency, loyal but elusive, I never knew what were the predominant forces or if there were any. But she would always be there and she made me ambivalent like I had been before. I didn't want her but I had to have her. Sometimes I thought I couldn't get away fast enough; sometimes she would leave my bedroom early in the morning and I would wake up empty; sometimes I thought if she were 20 years younger I'd marry her on my knees; sometimes I was able to not think of her, but not often. She was an aching enigma, a visitation, and avenging angel, an omen, a past and future bond, an Oedipal indulgence, a religious revelation, a Kabbalistic reincarnation, Rebecca, Ruth, Rachel, Regina, queen. And the emotions she aroused were subtle, but penetrating- guilt, love, obedience, protectiveness, aggressiveness, submissiveness, tenderness. Swiss cold blue eyes layered with Semitic sensitivity. She controlled me from the beginning, deeply. I couldn't touch bottom, and she wouldn't let me. We both knew I'd drown.

I returned to my hut to find the Dutch girls waiting. Regina was sitting at the next table. It was witchcraft, and I felt my deep tendons and cords tighten reflexively. The Dutch girls let it slide, as I knew they would, and I yielded to the queen. The flying foxes flew overhead.

* * *

'The Philippines is a terrible name, coming from Spain. Phillip II was the father of the inquisition, who I believe died of syphilis. It is my great regret that we didn't change the name of our country.'

Imelda Marcos

She was gone in the morning and I was very confused, but relieved in a way. But I had the same feeling when she returned. We had checked out some cottages at Willy's Place the previous afternoon, and I had agreed to move to what Regina had considered a more authentic environment.

Serendipity rode my shoulders on the stroll down to our new home- two cottages at Salazar's next-door, because Willy's was too expensive. I learned later of her displeasure with getting two cottages, but I thought it was what she wanted at the time.

The authenticity that Regina thought she had discovered, was a death spiral. The new acquaintances we had met at the Beachcomber, so vibrant on our first encounter, were broken, and failing.

Miguel was a Cuban New Yorker in his mid-thirties, and the longtime alpha male goatee of the colony. Regina felt threatened by his strutting machismo. I trounced him in chess when I was bored, and trounced him in chess when I wasn't. His Swiss lover, René, attended to his every visceral need. Alma was a proper English rose, and the broken side of the

203

triangle. Her and Miguel had been together before René arrived, and her injured pride was too caught in the headlights to leave. She had had adopted a pack of unruly dogs, and spent every waking hour constructing a plastic flotsam mural on the windbreak, to commemorate her loss. Such were the surrogations and sublimations of the subtropics.

We celebrated the birthday of their Filipino friend, Wilbeck, in typical Latin style, *borachos amigos*, with a band of three local guitarists, a Luzon lady who stripped down to the music and nothing, and a groaning board of Filipino food. We stuffed ourselves on fried *bangus* milkfish and rice, garlic and vinegar pork *adobo* with *pancit* noodles, and coconuts. In the Philippines, they eat with spoons and forks, and not knife and forks. With the look in Ama's eyes, it was just as well for Miguel.

One morning I left Regina early, for breakfast at Mila's. She was my other queen of paradise, with a strong but warm constitution. I sat at a table overlooking the ocean. The sun was out for a morning stroll.

"You hungry, Wink?" She asked.

"Very hungry, Mila." I said.

"You like omelet?" She asked.

"Sure." I said.

"You like mushroom omelet?" She asked.

"Sure." I said.

"You like special mushroom omelet?" She persisted.

"Fine, Mila." I said. "Fine." And Mila brought me my omelet. It was good. But I hadn't counted on it getting better, until it did. The first thing I observed was a silver shimmer that came in with the waves onto the shore. Then it lagged behind a bit, and flowed as jewels in the surf. When it went three dimensional and animated, I became suspicious. The sky flashed purple and pink, and the ocean green, and Frank materialized in the middle, in a new skin of brilliant bronze.

"How you like your omelet?" asked Mila.

"Fine Mila." I said. "Fine."

Four days had gone by on the island paradise of Boracay. And before I knew it or wanted it, it was time for me to leave. I awoke before dawn and ran down the beach with a young puppy, cutting my foot on a stone, and my heart on the sunrise.

It was a long hot passage on the catamaran back across to Caticlan. We flew over liquid glass, stopping only to circle tender sweetly around to pick up one of the brother's hats, and to sell fish, and take on more locals. There was a supercharged jeepney waiting at the quay. I waded ashore and jumped into the back. And an open trap.

There was nothing ambiguous about her. She was stunningly beautiful.

And hip. And dangerous. All the overloaded afferent nerve transmission in my body crackled with her voltage. Ohm's Law, plugged into her Walkman.

I thought she was with the driver at first, but she was far too smooth- headband, embroidered ponytail tie, long gold earrings, and superbly chiseled face and undercarriage. I got a stiff neck from trying to look the other way, but that only gave me a view of the Bible-bred and acne'd Peace Corps Yankee Doodle, so I turned back, and lit her cigarette. An hour later, she offered me one. She asked me if I was French. I told her no, Canadian. An hour later I lit her cigarette again. I asked if she was from Manila. She told me no, Boracay. She didn't look Boracay, she looked Paris.

"But I spent some time in Belgium." She said. And the noise of the engine, and the heat, and the driver's erratic driving, precluded any further conversation, until we hit the paved road. I asked if she knew a place called the 'High Chaparral' in Kalibo. She said she did. And she would show me. And take absolute control over the day. And I would let her.

Her name was Teresa, 22 years old, baby daughter, originally from Manila, with an import-export company in Belgium, multilingual, wealthy (she had a Mercedes and Renault in Belgium, and a maid and security guard and alarms on

Boracay), astonishingly beautiful and knowing it, and tough. All the men we met treated her with a solemn respect, and obeyed her orders without question. She carried a .38 in her purse, which she had opened with her green polished nails, just long enough for me to appreciate. Teresa had survived to rule, and to conquer. I had a peculiar feeling that I was next.

After she checked me into the High Chaparral, we went shopping, and for lunch at her favorite Chinese restaurant. Only then did she check into the room beside me. I had a shower and napped for a couple of hours. When I awoke, the wind had picked up. I left Teresa a note to let her know that I was going to take in a sci-fi movie at the Plaza Cinema, and that I might see her later. She was at the movie house five minutes after I got there. The usher was cowering in her shadow as he brought her to me.

Back on the second floor café balcony terrace of the Chaparral, the owner brought our San Miguels and barbequed chicken himself. I saw more than respect in his eyes. There was fear. Two Brits at an adjacent table tried out their collective charm, but she silenced them with a single stare.

"Let's go." She said, and I wondered where. She took me down several side streets, through a door under a neon sign. It was a go-go bar. We sat and she ordered us drinks. Young girls danced on the stage, and hostesses mingled with the other clientele. She asked me which one I liked. She told me she would pay the 'bar-fine.' I was disoriented now, unsure of her motivation for bringing me here. Was this a test, a trap? I told her that there was no reason to be here. I told her that I had no reason to want to be with anyone else. She took my hand, and we left.

It was after midnight by the time I showered, and met her back out on the café balcony. She was wearing her towel. The stars splashed across the night sky, in appreciation. I showed her Orion, and shared some of his stories.

She told me that, in the Philippines, Orion was also a hunter, named Teduray Seretar. She pointed to where he kept his bolo, in a rattan scabbard. The pattern of Orion's stars had other interpretations as well. They formed the shape of a *balátik* spring trap, for hunting wild pigs, a *gagan-ayan* northern Luzon weaving frame, or cousins who consented to be left behind in the sky, to guide farmers. She mentioned the *Tatlong Maria*, or Spanish 'Tres Marias,' which came to the Philippines with their Catholicism, and I didn't mention my memory of the fourth, flashing me back to Chile, as she periodically unraveled and rewrapped her towel, driving me crazy in her planned process of controlled fusion. The Spaniards hadn't brought bullfighting, but she did. If she was setting her *balátik* spring trap, I was ready to be caught.

She told me to wait until the watchdogs had gone to sleep, and left the key to her room on the table. In a country that ate dogs as appetizers, I would have been a fool to disobey.

I waited an hour. The key opened the door. I woke her gently. It was such a silly thing to have done.

"We have to sleep, Teresa." I begged, hours later, half serious and less awake.

"You can sleep in Manila," She said. It was the same thing that Beatrice had said to me in Hong Kong.

Sometimes there is order, in the chaos of the universe.

'Give me ten thousand Filipino soldiers and I will conquer the world.'
Douglas MacArthur

*   *   *

'Manila is the cradle, the graveyard, the memory. The Mecca, the Cathedral, the bordello. The shopping mall, the urinal, the discotheque. I'm hardly speaking in metaphor. It's the most impermeable of cities.'

Miguel Syjuco, *Ilustrado*

"There is no charge, Sir." Said the desk clerk. "And your trishaw is waiting outside to take you to the airport." Now that wasn't something I hadn't expected.

The sun was shining and the islands glistened underneath, and the plane touched down, and the jeepney dropped me back at the Malate.

"Did you have a good time?" Asked the girls at reception. I told them I had a good time, but I was glad to be back in Manila so I could sleep. They laughed.

"That bill not be so easy." One said. "Be are on the ring of fire."

I did manage an afternoon nap. And then I met Larry. I couldn't quite figure it out at first. A 32 year-old black guy from Detroit, Larry had been working as a Peace Corps volunteer in Cebu for the previous two years. He didn't have a cent to his name. I asked him why he was here, doing what he was doing. He wouldn't way much at first. I bought him a San Miguel, and then I bought him a couple more.

Larry was eighteen when he was drafted. He wound up as a helicopter door gunner in the mission that invaded Laos and Cambodia during the Vietnam War. He told battle stories and jokes, and then, after another beer, he didn't.

"Have you ever killed a man?" He asked. And then he cried.

I had one whole day to explore Manila. Since the earliest 10th century description of the *Ginto* 'Land of Gold' as an Indian kingdom maintaining diplomatic exchanges with Song dynasty China and ancient Japan; Under Sultan Bolkiah of Brunei, it had undergone Islamic transformation five hundred years later, became the source of Spanish Manila Galleon traffic linking Asian silk, gems and spices to Acapulco's silver, and been further transformed through Chinese insurrections, local revolts, British occupation, a Sepoy mutiny, American colonization, Japanese invasion, and American recapture. Manila was the bloodiest battle in the Pacific theatre, and the most devastated city, after Warsaw, during WWII. My tour of historical sites would be mercifully brief.

Through the sinfulness of Ermita, I walked its entire history, past people that lived on its sidewalks, within the walls of

Fort Santiago. I visited the Manila Cathedral, and the Monastery of San Augustin, poignantly decorated by its many modern saints, sleeping under paintings of some man on a cross. Inside, in the Biblioteca, was an original copy of Marco Polo's *Travels*. It was like being back in Mexico.

On my way back to the Malate, I stopped to peruse the string of antique shops, strangely interspersed among the bars and massage parlors. In one of these I found an ancient basket backpack, and the old proprietor who had it for sale.

"It's called a *pasiking*." He said. "This one is very old. It had been woven by the tattooed headhunters, from the Cordilleran region of northern Luzon. The mountain Bontoc Igorot used it as a head basket, for carrying enemy heads. Their bravest warriors drank from the sacred rice wine and human brain beverage, poured from the spoils of a successful hunt.

He attributed its durability to the rattan contracting when wet, making the weave tighter and less prone to splitting, in the monsoon rains.

It was a masterpiece of split rattan, with bamboo reinforcements at the base, and a reddish-brown patina, from years of daily use and soot exposure. I bought it on sight.

He added a Bontoc myth about the constellation, Orion, at no extra cost.

One night, a maiden descended to the earth with her sisters, to cut sugarcane, and bathe in the river. The owner of the field, coming upon them, hid one set of clothes. When the maidens left for the sky, she had to stay behind, because her white robes were missing. The man took her as his wife. Over time, they had three daughters. But the woman wasn't happy, and spent her nights weaving white robes, for herself and her daughters. Finally, on one other night, while the man slept, the woman and her daughters put on their white robes, and flew back to the sky. Today, the Star Maiden and her three daughters comprise the three belt stars of Orion and the Star Maiden. I thought of Terese, and her towel.

"I never told anyone else that before." Larry told me later. I told him it was fine, and we went out to find the evening.

The corner just down from the Malate, had its own chess grandmaster, hustling passerby for 10 pesos per game. I put down my money, and the comic strategy became entertaining. I began well but my opponent played for his livelihood.

"Eating." He said, as he took a pawn.

"Checking." He would say, as he ate my bishop.

"Winning." He said, as he moved in with the queen, I failed to see coming. I was laughing too hard to begrudge him the victory.

Larry and I went for a long walk after my loss, to assuage my pain. We eventually encountered two ladies, not intended and not bad, considering our state of consciousness.

"Aw, come on baby." I heard him say, and we found ourselves in the hotel across the street. I eventually realized that I was in a room with a woman who had just emerged from a yellow dress. She told me she was the wife of one of the police captains, and then asked me if I was a 'butterfly,' a term that I later learned, was a man who cheated on his paramour. It was time to leave town.

Larry helped me pack, and shook my hand heartily, as I grabbed a cab to the airport to make the Singapore connection. Compared to the '*Thrilla in Manila*' bee stings that Smokin' Joe had received at the hands of Mohammed Ali, I had floated like a butterfly.

'I would prefer a Philippines run like hell by Filipinos,
to a Philippines run like heaven by Americans.'
President Manuel L. Quezon

210

"So why are you telling us about the star nursery in the Orion Nebula, Uncle Wink?" Asked Millie, shifting her position on the picnic table.

"Because its not just stars that are born, Mil." Said Uncle Wink." In the interstellar clouds of the smudge, is an even more special star-forming region called the BN/KL nebula, which is being continuously hammered by polarizing radiation. About half the stars in the Trapezium Cluster have what are called protoplanetary disks, revolving and rotating bulging saucers of dense gas and dust grains, containing at least 40 different chemicals, including simple organic molecules like sulfur, phosphorus, ammonia, and formaldehyde. We've also found carbon dioxide, carbon, nitrogen, water, hydrogen, methane, and oxygen. The next four-man capsule, designed to replace the Shuttle, and take us back to the moon, an asteroid, and then to Mars, will have a hydrogen-oxygen or methane-oxygen propelled ascent stage, a nitrogen-oxygen atmosphere, and water, carbon dioxide and carbon. We're going back out with the same matter that got us here."

"But so what if there are simple chemicals in the gas clouds and baby planets." Said Sam.

"Ah, yes, well." Said Uncle Wink. "The continuous ionic radiation bombards those simple molecules into complex organic compounds. The wisps of green, within the nebular clouds, are polycyclic aromatic hydrocarbons. In Orion KL, we've discovered methyl cyanide, dimethyl ether, sugars, and alcohols, particularly methanol, and abundant amounts of warm ethanol.

There's enough alcohol for 300,000 glasses of wine for every person on Earth, every day for the next billion years. Mind you, condensing the gas directly would give you quite a headache next morning, because the clouds contain a lot of cyanide. But there are many other organic molecules in KL we haven't yet identified.

"We're going back out to Orion to drink wine?" Asked Millie.

"No. Mil." Said Uncle Wink. "We're going back out to see why what seems to have happened, has happened. The radiation causes photochemical chiral asymmetry, resulting in the production of left-handed amino acids and nucleobases. Sixty amino acids have been detected, including eight of the twenty necessary for life. So now we have proteins, and nucleotides. The fractal fields that govern cartwheel and tubule formation, buffeted by supernova-generated cosmic shock waves, coalesce these more complex organic molecules into strands of DNA, and with further locally-supplied heat and energy sources, create activated DNA-molecular-protein complexes that begin to function as protoorganisms."

"Protoplanetary disks to protoorganisms." Said Sam.

"So that stellar nurseries are also nuclear wombs of life." Said Uncle Wink.

"But isn't it too rough out there for life?" Asked Millie.

"Not necessarily, Mil." Said Uncle Wink. "Not necessarily."

Rice Mixed with Sand

'Getting to places like Bangkok or Singapore was a hell of a sweat.
But when you got there it was the back of beyond.
It was just a series of small tin sheds.'

David Attenborough

It had come a long way from small tin sheds, although there was still no shortage. Singapore had been named after the Malay *Singapura*, Lion City, although there had never been any. It more likely referred to the wild tigers that had lived in the tropical jungles here, although the last one had been shot right where I was sitting, in the Long Bar of the establishment named for the city's founder. Stamford Raffles had also given his name to the native *Rafflesia* 'corpse flower,' the largest parasitic flowering plant in the world. It stank like rotting meat, dependent as it is on flies, for pollination.

I was eating peanuts, and sipping four dollars worth of lolly water, a concoction of gin, Cherry Heering, Bénédictine, and Sarawak pineapple juice, invented in 1910 by bartender Ngian Tong Boon. It was difficult to believe that Somerset Maugham and Ernie Hemingway had sat here, swilling this foam-topped candy cocktail. I ended up on the luscious garden terrace with two lovely Dutch girls, but they were clearly not dependent on flies for pollination either, and there weren't enough Singapore Slings in the Raffles Long Bar, to have improved my chances.

I was bone tired, landing in this island country, still reeling from the *abailability* I had encountered in the previous one. Singapore was green and humid tropical melting meritocratic hybrid engine of English, Chinese, Malay and Indian aspiration. It was becoming one of the world's leading

213

financial centers, oil refiner, shipping port, and casino gambling market. Lee Kuan Yew had already run the place for the previous twenty-five years, and his largesse had extended to caning vandals and gum-chewers. It was worth it all, for the Peranakan cuisine alone.

"Can I help you with something?" Said the American voice three feet higher than I was, behind me. I told him I was looking for a place to stay.

"There is only one place." He said. "The Airmaster." I wasn't sure what an airmaster was, but I followed his lanky loping frame, to a hostel pretending to be a travel agency. The Lone Ranger was an Oregonian from Hawaii, or the other way around, psychology professor, who had traded it all to trade in electronic devices in Singapore. He introduced me to my other new dorm mate, Eddie, a balding schoolteacher from Utrecht, here because it wasn't anywhere near his ex-wife. Eddie had a moustache, an earring, a pair of glasses, and a gentle demeanor. We all went around the corner for murtabaks.

I watched the master murtabak-maker spin his pastry into a *filo*-thin skin, and shallow fry it in his heavy flattened wok. He poured in a mixture of duck eggs, onions, garlic, scallions, cooked minced beef and seasonings, folded it quickly into a rectangular wrap while it fried, cut it into smaller squares, and presented it to me in a curry sauce. I was ready to immigrate, until the Lone Ranger brought out desert.

It looked like a large spiked medieval battle flail, except for the greenish-brown color, and the stomach-churning odor. It smelled like skunk spray or stale civet vomit or used surgical swabs. And then the Ranger cut through the thorny husk, and released a burning stinking pig-shit sewer of overripe pineapples, turpentine, and gym socks.

"You're not allowed to take these on the subway, or into hotels." He said.

"Quelle surprise." I said, commenting that the ban on durian should extend into all military airspace.

"Taste it." He said. I closed my eyes. It began as acrid rotten onion cream cheese mush, with notes of sweet almond sherry blancmange. And then the garlic kicked in.

"Like slipping a tongue into your dead auntie." Said the Ranger.

"Like corpse flower ice cream." I agreed. And I was ready to immigrate again.

Eddie came with me to the American Express office next morning, where the money my parents had wired me wasn't. I spent the last of what I had on an International phone call, and found out that they had sent it to a branch of their local bank. The steamy sky opened a downpour deluge in celebration, as the last of my savings came over the Royal Bank counter. I treated Eddie to mutton and rice, quail eggs, spiced grilled vegetables, and starfruit juice, at a silverside food stall. I bought some Sore Lee needed underwear and a new blues harp harmonica under the Russian Cyrillic signs along Market Street, and mailed a card home among the Polish parcel package posting parties at the GPO.

Eddie and I decided to travel north to Malaysia together next day, on the one o'clock train to Kuala Lumpur. We took a bus through the downpour to the station, to find that the train didn't leave for another two hours- just enough time to be bored silly by an obese Western Australian in the station restaurant. He told us he didn't like the food.

"Tastes like muck." He said. "No flavor."

I made the suggestion that, if the opportunity ever presented itself, he should try the durian.

*　　　*　　　*

215

The big sign at the Malaysian border carried a message important enough that you didn't want to miss it. *Death Penalty to Drug Dealers.*

From the Airmaster to an air-conditioned dining car, we splurged for prawn rice, Michael Jackson music videos, and frequent bullhorn announcements from the overhead tin speakers.

For Eddie and I were headed into the land of tin. In the 1850s, Raja Abdullah, the Malay Chief of Klang, landed Chinese miners at the confluence of the *Muddy* Lumpur and Klang rivers, and created a frontier town trading post. The tin prospectors inevitably formed two gangs, the Hakka-dominated *Hai San* and the Hokkien-dominated *Ghee Hin.* After their frequent pitched battles for dominance brought tin production to a standstill once too often, the British appointed a Chinese headman *Kapitan*, Hiu Siew, to stabilize the situation. Kuala Lumpur grew enough to be plagued by diseases, and constant fires and floods. A hundred years later, twenty-five before Eddie and I arrived, the city's Malay population murdered 200 ethnic Chinese, in the worst racial riots in Malaysian history, consolidating the *Ketuanan Melayu* dominance that would evolve into future Islamic intolerance. The tourist brochures were already describing the train station as a 'typical Muslim building.'

Our search for affordable accommodation drove us into Chinatown, and the *shophouse* architecture of the Colonial Hotel, headquarters of the Japanese during the occupation.

Eddie and I were handed cozy Room 215, with two double beds, green tea, and cool, even with the ceiling fan off. Later that evening, at a corner restaurant, I showed him how to use chopsticks, on a sliced duck swimming in noodles, and he thought he would show me how to drink Guinness. He eventually learned of the medal of distinction that I had earned in Ireland.

The following morning I pitched up at the Australian Embassy, to pick up my visa. A stocky middle-aged Sapphic Sheila, and her chain-smoking apprentice, informed me from behind bulletproof glass, that they had no record of my application from Tokyo, and that I would have to wait for five days for confirmation. I asked to see someone taller. They told me that Mr. Coglin would see me when he became *avielable*, which he became forty-five minutes later. I showed him my world map, and pointed out the missing bits.

"Aw, mate, I can't find a telex from Tokyo." He said. "But I'll give you the bloody visa." *Aussie Aussie Aussie. Oi Oi Oi.*

Over at the Canadian Embassy, I had mail, including a letter from June, who had discovered it was possible to love two people at the same time. It decided to downpour. When the taxi driver I was trying to take back to the Colonial took me on a tour of the city instead, he didn't feel the love.

In the evening, we met Jackie, a young Kiwi punker, trying to get to Europe on $200, and most of the Chinese pastry that Ed and I had bought for late-night tea.

The entire next day was a write-off. We had intended to visit the Batu caves, but we waited at the wrong bus stop for the wrong bus to the wrong bus station. The ridiculous humidity gave way to ridiculous torrential storms, and we dodged the pickpockets back to the typical Muslim building we had originally arrived in, to wait for our night train to Penang. Egg rotis and Herald crosswords killed time, and slightly injured eternity.

I was tired but happy, pulling into Butterworth about 6 am. Eddie and I rolled across the morning-lit strait, and from the

217

ferry into the ranks of the rickshaws. A Chinese cab driver cleverly conned us out of two dollars worth of Malaysian ringgits, for the short ride to Georgetown, and the last double at the New Chinese Hotel. We crashed until noon. An omelet and a copy of the Straits Times refreshed us enough, for a stroll down Lebuh Chulia to the terrace of the Eng Aun Hotel, where we met Lindsay, a comical Aussie facsimile of John Cleese, who convinced us of the inherent superiority of his lodging, in terms of its humor and company. Eddie went off to tour the island, and I amused myself in the museum, with its collection of Chinese furniture and secret society memorabilia, taxidermy, and art gallery of Berlin Jazz Festival prints.

I met him back on the Eng Aun patio that evening, chatting with Lindsay, a quiet American named Mike, and four hilarious guys, extremely English medical students, working an elective rotation in Penang, still waiting for Malaysian immigration authorization after two weeks already here. I joked with them that the place had been found by a British Captain Light, and that Georgetown was a drained swamp, leveled and filled, and named for the demented George III. Steve reminded them that he had lost America. We were all preparing to enjoy some good witty tête-à-tête tit for tat, when all our têtes were turned, leveled and filled. No breathing occurred, in the time she took to walk through the veranda. Blonde, tanned, perky hot sauce, total control.

"That's the best looking thing I've seen in months." Said Mike, in full exhalation. The medical students' mouths and eyes were stuck open, like they hadn't had their tetanus shots. She beamed a naughty grin in my direction, and dropped into the empty seat beside me. Her name was Eligia, a Polish ingénue, living in Germany. She was vaguely connected with travel business, unattached to anything else, and looking far less than her 33 years. She was dynamite company: proud, authoritarian, omniscient, quick-witted and short-tempered, provocative, flirtatious, and very, very manipulative- my kind

218

of girl. The boys at the table had to keep swallowing hard to keep from drooling. We left them to grab some noodles at a Chinese restaurant up the street. Eligia did all the talking. And we ran through the rain back to the Eng Aun for a late-night coffee, and I bid her goodnight for a downpour stroll back to Eddie, sleeping with the lights on. He awoke, and cried about his ex-wife and son, and I talked him through it into the early hours, until his tears stopped, and he fell asleep exhausted.

We moved over into the Eng Aun next morning, and had a long leisurely breakfast with Lindsay and Mike. I went out to buy my Final Cartwheel ticket on the largest privately owned independent airline in France, *Union de Transports Aériens*: Jakarta-Sydney-Noumea-Auckland-Tahiti-Los Angeles, for $650. Six years later, UTA would be eaten by Air France. I returned to find Eligia sitting with Eddie, waiting for me. We all went to an Indian restaurant for mutton biryani and lemonade, ice cream and sundries in a huge supermarket on Jalan Penang, and a Guinness back at the Eng Aun. The English medical students and Lindsay and Mike joined us later, to watch the stunts of a Chinese strongman. Eddie got into a card game with the Brits, and Eligia and I went upstairs to play chess, in a game I barely prevailed. *Eating... Checking... Winning*. And then she grinned that grin again, and then giggled, and then laughed.

"You know my name in Polish?" She asked. I shook my head. "It means 'to choose.'" She said. "I choose you." And there was nothing else.

I remember the parts of her that were tanned, and the parts of her that weren't, and the blonde blinding light in between.

*   *   *

'This is Malaya. Everything takes a long, a very long time, in Malaya.
Things get done, occasionally, but more often they don't,
and the more in a hurry you are, the quicker you break down.'

Han Suyin

I wasn't prepared to bump in Adera and her parents next morning. I hadn't seen her since Button Nose in Darjeeling, and she hadn't seen me. When Eligia grinned by, she just shook her head.

It was a sightseeing day, and I took in the star-shaped ramparts of Fort Cornwallis, and the moat they finally filled in, when they figured out the malaria. It felt like I'd been infected. After the second of two mosques, in the midst of narrow winding lanes and old houses, I came into the granite paving of Cannon Square, and the Khoo Khonsi clanhouse. The original roof had been so elaborate, it had caught fire the first night it was finished. Its magnificent Dragon Mountain Hall was still the most ornate in the country, with richly ornamented beams, statues, painted lamps, and colored tiles and carvings, but the crowds and joss stick smoke and incensed atmosphere was so thick, I needed air. The pastel colored carvings of the Sri Mahamariamman Temple were as just intricate, more visible, and transported me back to Southern India, if only for awhile.

The boys on the patio were well into their Guinness, and an obvious ebullient mood, when I joined them that evening.

"I say." Said one of the English med students. "How is that invasion of Poland thing progressing?" And they all broke out in howls of laughter, until Eligia followed on in behind me, and they gazed into their stout.

Eddie and I woke around 4 am, and left under the predawn magic of swooping bats and lonely streetlamps, to catch the first ferry to Butterworth, picking up another earringed Dutchman, on the road north. We needed a holiday, and headed to Thailand for a few days. The train to Haat Yai was an Indian lullaby, in its speed, the early morning tropical

220

sticky lethargy, and the soot-colored dining car. I fell asleep for an hour on one of the torn Naugahyde seats. After a brief interrogation at the Thai border, we stopped in the middle of nowhere, while four trucks whistled their cargo through the open windows. I wondered what could possible have been in the big burlaps bags, but with all the death penalty signposts we had just come through, there was no real incentive to ask.

Just after noon, we boarded a second locomotive to Surat Thani, the *City of Good People*. It was another slow rocking-chair journey, with Guilin-like karst limestone scenery, written warnings from the police not to accept drugged drinks from strangers, and a plethora of food vendors, selling grilled chicken and rambutans. Eddie and I caught a bus to Ban Don, where a French couple showed us where to buy tickets on the night boat to Ko Samui.

After some coffee and cake at the hole-in-the-wall across the street, we boarded. I settled on one of the floor mattresses for the night ride, anticipating a good night sleep, at last.

"Hey, crazy boy!" Landed on my head like a Thai coconut. Looking up brought me in line with Eligia's pixie grin. She had motored through southern Thailand in half the time, and picked up an Australian engineer, named Craig, along the way. His specialty was juggling tennis balls, hardly a talent with any survival advantage in the company he was trying to keep.

Eligia rearranged the sleeping arrangements, blew enough around the room to scatter those nearest us, instructed the Captain to extinguish the lights, and snuggled herself into the Gold Kazoo, in front of me. In the moonbeams, she was my silver spoon, bending, and eating right out of the jar. If you think you're free, there's no escape possible.

Everyone else had left the boat when we awoke next morning. Eddie waited for me while I spoke to Eligia. It turned out OK. She seemed disappointed for a few minutes, shrugged her shoulders, and caught the next bemo for Choweng. She blew kisses from the back.

"She would have killed you, mate." Craig Said. I just nodded. He and Eddie and I piled into our own bemo, and hurtled off down palm-lined paved roads to the turquoise blue and shifting billowy cloud shadows floating along the beach. We paid thirty baht for a simple hardwood plank hut, on an almost deserted strand of white powder and coco palms, some so bent down in obeisance to the water, you could sit on their trunks. The women in the huts on either side of us strutted about naked on their porches. I read.

Next morning Eddie and Craig and I hiked in the hot sun, for a jeep into town, and another to Lamai. We checked into the Palm bungalows, a sheltered little place in the corner of the rocks, equipped with a restaurant, guitars, jars of cannabis cookies, and a preponderance of sirens. Three of them came over to talk, almost immediately.

The two Australians faded into the shade of the third.

"Don't I know you from somewhere?" She asked.

"No, I don't think so." I said. But she did, and I didn't recognize her for the change. When I had first met her in Bangkok she was the unremarkable sidekick of the entrancing young guitarist I did remember. But now. But now Jane had blossomed in the Thai sun. She had developed a mature self-confidence, and let her hair and humor go curly. But she was still gun shy from long-lost boyfriend syndrome, and I was a entering a monastic phase on my journey. We spent the next four days bumping clumsily in and out of each other's trajectories, sitting sundowners at The Rock, swimming, playing guitar and chess, eating fruit salads and pancakes, and rice mixed with sand. But I was older and emptier, and my messenger RNA was retooling, forming proteins of purpose and meaning. On my last night in Lamai, we walked down the beach and held each other under a coconut palm, and under the stars, and I felt complete again, but still older. I pointed out Orion, and the remaining way East, to regain my vision.

On the 24th of July, 1984, I said farewell to Ed and Craig from the back of my jeep, and left Ko Samui. After a sad, dusky wait to board the night boat for the mainland. I slept, despite myself, and when we docked at 4 am, caught a bemo and a bus to Haat Yai, where I met a Swiss fellow named Andy. He was in a hurry to expedite a visa renewal, and offered to share a cab all the way back to Penang. At the taxi stand we picked up Kevin, a bearded Queenslander, and two Chinese girls. We had to bribe the Thai officials to work overtime. It was 1 pm. The Malaysian border guards asked Kevin point blank if he was carrying heroin. He told them he wasn't a 'bloody idiot,' and that he wasn't smuggling anything. They didn't think of asking the Chinese girls. They should have.

After a long drive south we crossed over to Georgetown on the ferry. They let me off at the Eng Aun, where I found Mike and the English med students, exactly where I had left them. They were still working, still waiting for their visas. They were clearly disappointed that I had not brought Eligia back with me. We all went out, past the Ah Choo Medical Hall, to the Taj for Guinness and murtabaks, and a final night of camaraderie.

But it was strange night. I couldn't sleep again. The mosquitoes were bad and the cockroaches were worse. I decapitated one with my flip-flop and was shocked into a twilight terror- both halves carried on as if nothing had happened. I fed the back half to the ants and finally dropped off around four. When I awoke, I discovered that it had crawled all the way across the room to just under my bed, although by now I was certain he was quite dead.

'You do not need to leave your room... Do not even listen only wait. Do not even wait, be wholly still and alone. The world will present itself to you for its unmasking, it has no choice, it will writhe in ecstasy at your feet.'

Franz Kafka

Eating the Wind and Moon

'The older you get the stronger the wind gets-
and it's always in your face.'

Pablo Picasso

My plane climbed quickly next morning, *Saya Makanangin*. Eating the Wind.

The flight took thirty minutes, just enough time to swallow a processed cheese slice and a maraschino cherry on a slice of white bread, between nods to the other four passengers. There was a fidgety Austrian schoolteacher, my bearded American guitar-toting carpenter friend, Steve, and two lovely French twin sisters of Madagascar-German extraction, who extracted all of our attention on the entire parabolic flight path.

We landed on the sixth largest island in the world. Almost seven hundred years after Marco Polo, some things hadn't changed, and some things hadn't yet happened. I arrived between them.

Sumatra had been the fabled Swarnadwīpa *Island of Gold*, named in Sanskrit for its highland mineral wealth, and capturing more western imaginations with mythical stories of giant rats, orangutans and rhinos and elephants and tigers and sun bears and clouded leopards, and exotic flora and cultures. Almost seven hundred years before Marco Polo, the Tang Dynasty Buddhist monk, Yijing, had described the local Malays as having 'curly hair, dark bodies, bare feet, and wearing sarongs.' The 52 different languages they spoke were only one of the challenges that Dutch East India company ambitions had to contend with, in its exploitation of the island's pepper, rubber, and oil.

Just after I left, the Asia Pulp and Paper Company Limited began to go unlimited, constructing illegal roads through prime tiger habitat, and destroying 50% of the island's tropical rain forest cover in less than 35 years. Moslem procreation would add to the destruction, turning Sumatra into the fourth most populous island in the world. The monstrous tsunami, that hit its western coast and islands twenty years after me, would kill almost a quarter of a million people.

But I had landed in the middle, and Sumatra was still an enchantment. The immigration officers were too busy playing Steve's guitar, to give me any trouble. The French twins were heading north to visit the orangutan colonies, but I had planned to explore the Batak highlands before turning south, through the lands of the matriarchic Minangkabau, for an onward boat to Java. In that unique sadness of enamored travelers on diverging paths, we exchanged addresses. Being delivered from temptation, I could still keep in touch.

Steve and I caught a pedal-powered *becek* to the bus stand, intent on getting to Lake Toba by nightfall. I played harmonica for some local Moslem boys, who exhibited far too much repressed and raging testosterone.

"Back in weasel country." Said Steve. When the bus came we sat up front. It broke down three times before we stopped for lunch. We ate stringy chicken and rice with our fingers, and were charged twice as much as the other passengers.

"Back in weasel country." I agreed.

Lake Toba was formed with the eruption of a supervolcano about 70,000 years ago. It was the largest explosion anywhere on the planet in the last 25 million years, ejecting ten billion tons of sulfuric acid into the atmosphere, and layering South Asia with six inches of ash. The resultant volcanic winter killed most humans then alive and, according to mitochondrial DNA evidence, created a profound genetic bottleneck, in our evolution as a species. The bus driver's indolence, and our subsequent arrival in the pouring rain of Prapat, two hours late, seemed to confirm the theory. A young tout named John provided shelter. After playing some guitar, Steve and I collapsed, exhausted.

We awoke to a spectacular view of the lake. The sun glinted

off the tin domes above the slate roof of the ivory mosque, and its attached tall square minaret. John drove us in his jeep to the boat dock, and the two-hour trip across to Samosir, the largest island within and island, and the fifth largest lake in the world. We approached the small village shore of Tuk Tuk, and a scene of large boat-shaped Batak houses, built on pillars and beams, and dominated by their steep upsweeping saddle back thatched roof ridges. The front gables extended out further than the rear ones, intricately carved and painted with suns and stars and cockerels, and red, white, and black geometric motifs. Cheerful young boys swam around our boat as we docked.

Steve and I climbed up past palms and pines and hanging vines towards Ambarita, along paths lined with water buffalo and chickens. The reflections of the puff clouds in the blue water below us were ridiculous.

"I hear these people used to be cannibals." Said Steve. He was right. It was noted by Marco Polo, who had only heard about the inland hill tribe 'man-eaters.'

'They suffocate him. And when he is dead they have him cooked, and gather together all the dead man's kin, and eat him. And I assure you they do suck the very bones till not a particle of marrow remains in them....And so they eat him up stump and rump. And when they have thus eaten him they collect his bones and put them in fine chests, and carry them away, and place them in caverns among the mountains where no beast nor other creature can get at them. And you must know also that if they take prisoner a man of another country, and he cannot pay a ransom in coin, they kill him and eat him straightway.'

In the 1820s, Sir Thomas Stamford Raffles wrote about the Batak eating their parents when they were too old to work, consuming their flesh 'raw or grilled, with lime, salt, and a little rice.' Twenty years later, a German physician refined the reasons, noting that 'they eat human flesh only in wartime, when they are enraged, and in a few legal instances,' including theft, adultery, spying, or treason. As a sign that they accepted the verdict of the community, and not thinking of revenge, the relatives of the victim had to provide the salt, red peppers, and lemons. In 1852, on her second trip around the world, Austrian explorer Ida Pfeiffer was told that:

'Prisoners of war are tied to a tree and beheaded at once; but the blood is carefully preserved for drinking, and sometimes made into a kind of pudding with boiled rice. The body is then distributed; the ears, the nose, and the soles of the feet are the exclusive property of the Rajah, who has besides a claim on other portions. The palms of the hands, the soles of the feet, the flesh of the head, and the heart and liver, are reckoned peculiar delicacies, and the flesh in general is roasted and eaten with salt. The Regents assured me, with a certain air of relish, that it was very good food, and that they had not the least objection to eat it. The women are not allowed to take part in these grand public dinners.'

The blood-red betel-stained bouche of the ancient Batak beauty at the crest of the trail would have had something to say about any such attempt at exclusion. She called from on high. The sweet smell of the coconut oil in her hair wafted on down to greet us.

"Come and stay my place." She said, hands planted firmly on the hips of her sarong. Steve and I looked up to a terrace of female travelers sunning themselves. Shrug followed shrug.

Mama Rudi gave us a bungalow at the top of the hill.

We had two Belgian girls for neighbors, Edwig, a tall blonde with a kidney ailment and a Michigan scholarship, and Katrina, her quiet chain-smoking friend, both majoring in economics and timidity.

Steve and I spent the afternoon playing guitar, going for walks, and meeting the permanent weasel fixtures in the restaurant. One of them told me I looked like Gaddafi. I took it as a compliment.

But the evening was fun. Steve and I joined the company of Hedwig, Katrina, Sandy, and Julia, a 19-year-old English beauty from Bristol, on her way home after working for six months in Tonga. Beneath her short dark hair, full cream complexion, and bright eyes, was a woman still half girl, with a penchant for all things French and romantic. Steve and I played guitar, and amused them with our prodigious appetites. Steve left to talk to the Belgians, and I left to sleep. I had found an old leather-bound book in German, published in 1925, lying flat on a shelf in Mama Rudi's restaurant. The title was interesting enough: 'Die Toba-Batak auf Sumatra in Gesunden und Kranken Tagen.' *The Toba Batak of Sumatra in Days of Health and Sickness.* The author, a medical missionary of the Rheinische Missionsgesellschaft, was more intriguing yet. His name, written in gold on the spine, looked familiar. *Doctor Winkler.*

*   *   *

'Yet either Orion's doing cartwheels or our lives are passing by.
Because one day he's fully upright,
Bow and arrow ready to take down the moon,
The next he's fully prostrate, an old, brittle man, unable to move...
Being trapped in the terrestrial never helped the cause.
Never truly inspired anyone to accomplish anything.'
    Matt Marro, *Either Orion's Doing Cartwheels or Life is Passing By*

Mama Rudi danced in the stern of the ferry, all the way across to the market in Prapat next morning, holding a mango in each hand. The same ridiculous white fluff hung between the blue of the sky and the water. Julia, Steve and I walked to the bus station to say goodbye to Sandy, and booked our own onward tickets to Bukittinggi for three days later. Steve disappeared into a maze of sun-splashed umbrellas and shaded betel-stained vendors, selling rambutans and passion fruit, and baby bananas and live piglets. Julia and I ate cornmeal pancakes and bitter beans, and drank sweet tea and each other's light. She had withdrawn well back into the group by evening, and I fell asleep wishing I was younger.

We had all signed up for the weekly Sunday boat tour around the island. The open upper deck was already bursting when we boarded, but there was room for another two hours of recruitment. A rainbow roared out of the lake in front of us, just before we docked at our first attraction. The curved rooflines of the Batak Museum reflected the full song from the church on the hill. The girls from Mama Rudi's were amused by my shave in the hot pools. When we reached Ambarita, Julia discovered a stall of curios, where I almost tripped over it. Down among the other hardwood folk art, was a thick rustic box, with two carved idols sitting up out of its sliding cover. Inside was a folding *pustaha* tree-bark book, the work of a *datu* Batak medicine man, and the subject of Dr. Winkler's obsession, sixty years earlier.

"What's it about?" Asked Julia.

"It's about magic and divination, and the datu's authority in the Batak religious belief that governs its use." I said, sliding open the cover, and removing the bark accordion.

"What did they believe?" She asked.

"They believed in higher gods of Hindu origin, and in ghosts, demons, and ancestors. But most importantly, they believed in the cult of the *tondi*." I said.

"What's the tondi?" She asked.

"The tondi is the soul." I said. "Every Batak seeks to competitively enrich their own tondi at the expense of all others. This determines how and what and whom they eat, sacrifice, prayer, and even marriage. When a person dies, their tondi turns into a soul of the dead, a *begu*, and feared even more."

"So what does that have to do with this bark book, and your namesake?" She asked. I unfolded the accordion slowly, and pointed to the different parts.

"Doctor Winkler discovered that these pustahas were divided into three sections." I said. "The first was a treatise on the Art of Preserving Life, containing details of diagnosis, domestic remedies, magic medicine antidotes against poison and hostile sorcery, amulets, charms, and other protection devices. Illness originated from the unfulfilled wishes of the human soul, and was cured by eating the tondi of others.

The second part was black magic, the Art of Destroying Life, the preparation of poisons, and the making of *pangulubalangs*, spirit champions against the community's enemies.

To obtain a pangulubalang, a child was kidnapped from a hostile village, and held prisoner in the communal house for several months. He was fed with the best food, including gold-colored rice, spiced meat, and sour fish, and the livers of apes and other game. A buffalo horn with a hole in its end, was used to pour palm wine into his mouth. When the tondi of the child had been properly propitiated, and he was old enough to answer questions but still young enough to be unsuspecting, he was led blindfolded and placed it in a ditch with earth around it, so that only his head remained above ground.

The datu would explain the situation. 'I am going to send you to destroy my enemy. Wherever I send you, there must you go. You must never, however, reveal either your or my name to anyone, nor the manner of your death.' When the child agreed to be sent, the datu put food in his mouth, and spoke to him soothingly. 'Here, take this special meat, take this sour rice, take this ginger, take this roasted rice kernel, take this palm wine and be obedient.' And then the datu placed the point of the palm wine drinking horn into the child's mouth. And poured in the molten lead. The vow that the child took with his last words had bound his tondi, and the village had obtained a willing and obedient ghost ally in the fight against the enemy. The child was dismembered, its body parts charred with other magical ingredients, and filtered to make *pupuk*, a magical substance used as a therapeutic unguent, and to smear 'soulfulness' onto the village images and idols.

"That's terrible." Julia said. "I'm not sure I want to hear about the third section." I flipped through the remaining pleats of bark.

"Divination." I said. "Oracles. Doctor Winkler found out that the desire to know the future is as universal a human need as defense against disease and malice, or the ability to punish and take revenge on your enemies. The Batak had oracles to find out the wishes of the soul, through palmistry, or the pattern of the inside of hen's eggs, or the involuntary actions of muscles. There were oracles for detecting the decrees of gods and ancestors, using eviscerated hanging roosters or double strings. Finally there were astrological oracles, many involving sky dragons." Julia pointed at an illustration of the moon and the adjacent image of a giant serpent.

"Who's he?" She asked. I looked up to find the stall owner getting restless.

"He is the cosmic snake that periodically devours the moon." I said. "The Lake Toba Batak call him 'Hala na Godang.' It's their myth to explain the lunar phases." *One day a shepherd threw stones, and shattered the eggs being brooded by the snake. When she discovered the offence, the snake pursued the shepherd into the heavens, where he hid behind the moon. When the serpent explained the crime to the moon and the sun, they recommended that the shepherd be given a fine. The snake refused to accept this, so the moon offered to sacrifice himself, instead. The terms were accepted, and every month, the moon is devoured.*

"The stars of the snake look familiar." Said Julia.

"It's Orion." I said. "The Batak seasons are regulated by the conjunctions of Scorpio with the moon, chasing Orion across the sky."

"That Doctor Winkler was a man before his time." She laughed.

"And this Dr. Winkler may have arrived too late." I said, folding the bark accordion book back into its carved receptacle, and sliding its lid back on. I bought the pustaha, in the humid highlands of northern Sumatra. Eight thousand miles and thirty years away, I can no longer open the cover, fused as it has become, with its internal magic and time.

*   *   *

'If you enter a goat stable, bleat;
If you enter a water buffalo stable, bellow.'
Indonesian Proverb

Even beyond the shores of northern Sumatra, in the annals of ordeals in time and space and thermodynamics, the bus trip to Bukittinggi was a legend. It wasn't because of the time, although in the eighteen plus hours that it took to make the journey, time was a definite variable, and we were already an hour late. It wasn't because of the spatial dynamics outside the tin bluebird, although the narrow dimensions and continuously changing elevation of the rutted track, and the crazy dangerous drivers who were always in the middle of it, were terrifying enough. The trip was notorious because of what happened *inside* the Bukittinggi bus.

First, there was no space. The seats had been retrofitted retrogressively, three across in three dimensions on both sides of a pencil-thin aisle, to maximize the number of thin Malay bodies per cubic meter. In our row, Steve rode shotgun, while Julia and I found ourselves on the tiny window and in the middle, over a wheel, behind one of the welded bars that randomly crisscrossed the interior. The welder had clearly been in a manic phase in his enthusiasm to cut off every last chance for comfort, or escape. Across our four-foot wide row, we had to sit sideways, and there were still random body parts pressing into our faces and sides. Secondly, the heat that was supposed to be outside couldn't find a way out, because the heat from the inside had already baked us into a milky sweat. Third, where there was Malay heat, there was smoke. Every male on the bus lit up as we left, and whatever oxygen molecules had remained, cowering in confined cornices, were ruthlessly dispatched. Fourth, the smoke wasn't just tobacco smoke, it was the smoke of *Gudang Garam*, cigarettes made with cloves and rubber sap, called *kretek* because of the noise made by the crackling sound of burning cloves. Inside the Bukittinggi bluebird, the kretek noise was deafening. Death seemed certain. And finally, I had consumed an extra *kopi pahit* black coffee back in Prapat, before boarding. Our first stop wouldn't be for six hours.

It arrived in a booming town of delicious ten-cent pineapples, not-so-delicious rice flour biscuits, and throngs of curious locals. By late afternoon we were losing the first two European passengers, a histrionic Italian couple, in a lengthy grand display of mutual resuscitation, while we remained immobilized inside on the side of the road. They got off the bus for good in Sibolga, and we had our first rich taste of delicious Padang food.

Dozens of small dishes, filled with beef *rendang*, succulent coconut milk curried fish, boiled cassava leaf, simmered young jackfruit, chili eggplant, curried water buffalo liver, tripe, foot tendons, fried beef lung, *ketupat* compressed rice, and *sambal*, arrived on our table.

"Welcome to Minangkabau country." I said. "This is *hidang* style. We only pay for what we eat." Steve drained a bowl of water with a floating lime slice.

"That was the *kobokan*." I said. "Its for washing your hands."

"Where's the cutlery?" He asked.

"You eat with your hands." I said. "Hence the bowl of water."

Thus fortified, we reboarded the legend, and off again into the night. Ten minutes later Julia's head descended onto my right shoulder. I put my arm around her, and she nestled in for the long uncomfortable ride. At the next stop, around 3 am, the weasels reached in, to pinch and prod her through the window. The last one nearly lost his hand. We drank teh, and ate cakes, and chatted with some Spaniards. As the red dawn rose to our left, Julia migrated from nestling to nuzzling, and sharing secrets.

"I'd never thought I'd change my mind." She said.

"What made you?" I asked.

"You." She said. And it was all clear and wonderful and I shone and beamed with the rising sun. The gears ground between the volcanoes of Mount Singgalang and active Mount Marapi, into the cool highland climate of what had been the Dutch colonial outpost of Fort de Kock, and the headquarters of the Japanese 25th army, during the WWII occupation. It felt good to breathe and stretch, and hike the hills of Bukittinggi, in our search for a bed. Julia and I dropped Steve off at the *wisma* next door to the more upmarket Benteng Hotel. I reemerged from its lobby, and told her I had organized a second floor double with a view.

"You're not angry?" I asked. She nodded her head, and took a shower, while I rearranged the furniture, to block off what I thought was all the Moslem peepholes. And then there was nothing else to do.

Steve was waiting for us next door about 6 pm, and we shuffled down to the coffee house for chicken, fried potatoes, vegetables and pineapple juice. We left him to stroll around the market, and return to our refuge. Julia lit candles and put on her Samba tapes and told stories of her life in Tonga stories, before she didn't.

We were quiet later when I looked up to find a yellow laser piercing the air above my head. It came from a small pinpoint hole in the adjacent wall. I put a finger to Julia's lips, and then my own, rolled away under the beam, and moved quietly into the dark hallway. The door to the next room was ajar. I kicked it in, and grabbed the head that was attached to the near wall. It belonged to the manager who had checked us in.

"And what do you think you're doing?" I said. Or something like that. He jumped so high I though I would lose him at first, but he landed weakly.

"I was just fixing the light switch." He protested.

"In the dark? At midnight? On the other side of the room?" I marched him downstairs, and humiliated him in front of his staff.

"But I am a married man." He whined. I asked him if I should speak to his wife. Everyone promised to stay downstairs.

Back in our room, Julia had pulled the mattress and the pillows onto the floor, below the lines of sight. Later she told me she was hungry. All I could find was a can of tomato juice, with a 21 per cent service charge. I told the weasel we couldn't have asked for more attentive service.

Twenty-four years after Julia and I checked into the Benteng, the Bukittinggi city administration banned Valentine's Day as contrary to Minangkabau tradition, and Islam. They declared that it lead to 'immoral acts,' such as young couples hugging and kissing. They could have saved themselves the trouble, and just sent the hotel manager, or some other giant rat of Sumatra.

'...the giant rat of Sumatra, a story for which
the world is not yet prepared.'
Arthur Conan Doyle, *The Sussex Vampire*

*   *   *

'By the time I get to Bangkok, I'll know how my trip's going.'
Steve, Pasir Putuh, West Sumatra

The only memory that Julia may still have from our next day together may be the bracelet I bought her in the Bukittinggi Wednesday market. We had moved earlier from the Benteng to the Gangga, and our warm reception at the latter's reception must have been previously broadcast, as we were provided with the most private of rooms, and a guarantee that we would not be disturbed. I offered to put Julia on a flight to Singapore from Padang, an offer that she initially refused but, on reflection, and after being harassed at the unfortunate zoo by a more unfortunate weasel with a monster-sized Burkitt's lymphoma, accepted.

We awoke early next morning, for a tour of the matrilineal Minangkabau, mostly culturally Islamic, but with vestiges of *adat* animist influence. Their name literally meant 'victorious buffalo,' after a legend older than the Bukittinggi bluebird. *The Minangkabau had a territorial dispute with a neighboring prince, and agreed to resolve it with a fight to the death between two water buffalo. The prince produced the largest, meanest, and most aggressive buffalo, but he Minangkabau produced a hungry baby buffalo with its small horns ground to be as sharp as knives. Seeing the adult buffalo across the field, the baby ran forward, hoping for milk. The big buffalo saw no threat and paid no attention to it, looking around for a worthy*

237

opponent. But when the baby thrust his head under the big bull's belly, looking for an udder, the sharpened horns punctured and killed the bull, and the Minangkabau won. The rooflines of their houses curve upward from the middle and end in sharp points, in imitation of water buffalo horns.

The tour bemo arrived for Steve and Julia and I around 8:30, and quickly filled with other travelers. David was a 33-year-old expat living in Paris. The shaving soap behind his ears, and the skull thickness in between, immediately gave him away as English. Nell was a chatty 51-year-old Dutch sculptress, intense and shoe-leather tough, dragging her 16-year-old Egyptian son through Indonesia. The Cockney-accented weasel tour guide brought a broad beamed young German girl mutant, and made sure we knew that the hickey on her neck belonged to him. He cranked up the reggae as we set off.

It was a full day. The morning was for industrial appreciation. We began with a visit to a family-run water buffalo-powered sugarcane press and molasses factory, a rice mill with an unusual cambered pounding machine, and a hum-ho weaving cottage. A fascinating colony of giant flying foxes flapped over our river swim downstream from the cassava fields, and an exorbitant Padang lakeside lunch.

We got more information about the Queen's Palace and Minangkabau culture from the handwritten signs inside than from our guide. They seemed to begin in some kind of English before the translator became tired or bored. Julia and I were intrigued by the

Box of Heritagous Things

Heritagous- thing is a loom that is very high its value for a group of clan. Therefore, it should be taken care of and should be- preserved accurately, then it will be made a place to keep it. This box is one of place to keep the heritagous-things can be kept inside this box are provision of the war.

and in awe of the

Bridal Bed

During the wedding is proceeding at the Bride's house is prepared a bridal bed is a lace to sit down side by side for both bride and groom.

Its shape is four sided which is carved with clothes of many colours and it is embroidered with gold thread and silver. Right and left is put on tabir and above is put on langit and tirai kolam.

If the wedding party is great by slaughtering cow or buffalo then its banta gadang should sit down side by side both bride and groom.

There will be king and queen for a day who is surrounded by ladies in waiting. The place to bed the bride groom is called 'Kalelambu'. It has a layer and it also can be seven walls.

In front of this bridal bed is put on cerano that contents sirih pinang completely and dulang for keeping food is covered withwith tudung saji and dalamak.

We finished with a 'typical' village encounter, in a room far too small to contain the hundred Minangkabau congregated on their floor cushions, smoking kreteks and posing for photos. It poured buckets around the bemo, on our way back.

Cold Guinness and sweet and sour pork waited, in the company of lively conversation, at the Mona Lisa restaurant. David expressed an interest in traveling to Padang with Julia and I the next day.

We ended up sharing a big black Mercedes, for the same price as the bus would have been. The driver watched a Hong Kong video, dubbed in English and subtitled in Indonesian, in between the curves. Four hours, and as many warnings to slow down, deposited us in Padang.

And then I plunked down a hundred bucks at the Garuda office, to fly her out of my life. Steve and David met us downstairs at the Hang Tuah hotel, for her last supper. We wandered down the main street, for satays, murtabaks, and orange syrup on ice, a promenade around the market, and munching rambutans. Julia and I eventually left, to speak French in sadness.

And I took her to the airport by bemo at dawn, and bought her sweet bread and tea for her breakfast, and hard-boiled eggs for her flight. *Maybe not today, maybe not tomorrow, but soon, and for the rest of your life.* And she smiled, and waved, and blew a kiss, and walked out of mine. The tsunami that rolled over Padang twenty years later put the boats moored in the Arau River far onto dry land, including a two hundred ton sailing ship, which was deposited a kilometer upstream. That was just about the way it felt.

On a hot and muggy Sumatran morning, Steve and David and I hired a bemo to Pasir Putih, a perfect pristine beach to wait the two days for Pelni's weekly big German boat to Jakarta.

The choice of accommodation was restricted to either a *losman*, with chicken coop Robinson Crusoe hut, waterless *mandi*, and a scrawny mama cook who would have poisoned us, or a concrete bunker run by a plump matriarch. We knew enough to choose the chubby one.

Our days were occupied with swimming, and playing guitar, and sipping cold drinks made from avocados and chocolate and condensed milk, and our evenings were for rambles from the fishing boat lantern-lit dusk, via the music of 'hello mister,' to the nocturnal noodle shop for *nasi goreng* and durian and bananas. And in my dreams I wished for tighter muscles, quicker reflexes, a slower heartbeat, deeper breaths, higher spirits, and a sweeter mouth. In the hurricane lamps of my Final Cartwheel, I was only going to get older East of Sumatra, eating the wind.

Shadow Puppets

'Different fields, different grasshoppers; different seas, different fish'
Indonesian Proverb

It was perched on the southern shore, like a parrot in a pigeon coop. The bemo driver had evicted a group of uniformed schoolgirls, to whisk us to the Pelni harbor, with fresh mangosteens and bananas. From our ultimate vantage point near the midmorning sun, we focused our gazed downwards, onto swarming ant colonies of boarding Sumatrans. The contrast between the ship and its passengers was extreme. In a hospital-white cabin on the newly minted German liner, Sir David and Steve and I played with the nightlights over plush bunks, the lockers (minus the keys, which had been lost), and the taps in our shower stall. Hot water came out. I read Sartre, until the waves rolled me off to sleep.

Breakfast was a mundane German version of Padang cooking- eggs encrusted in granular fire, vulcanized fish and horse meat, vegetables pickled in an ammonia brine, and Nazi helmet scoops of chisel-proof sticky white rice.

Through the Sunda Strait, our boat passed an island with a legend about ghosts crying, actually orangutans dying. Groups of human skeletons on rafts of volcanic pumice had floated across the Indian Ocean, and washed up on the east coast of Africa, a year for over a year after the event. It produced the loudest sound in modern history, heard three thousand miles from its point of origin. World climate did not return to normal for five years.

"There she is." Said Steve, pointing. And there she was.

When Krakatoa exploded in 1883, the blast energy was equivalent to two hundred megatons of TNT, or about

13,000 times the impact of the nuclear bomb that devastated Hiroshima. The tsunamis alone were responsible for the deaths of more than a hundred thousand people.

We were bound for the world's most populous island, and one of the most densely populated places on the globe. It's vary name conjured up black, hot, steaming excitement. *Java*.

By the time we docked in Jakarta around dusk, Steve and Sir David and I had decided we were headed in separate directions. I squeezed into a sardine can van with two priests, Andreas and Ulli, for a marathon ride through murky slumlight, before being discharged at Gambir Station. The third class train to Yogyakarta left at 7:40 pm. I gave up my seat, to let the priests lean on each other, and spent the trip standing up, eating black bananas. In the subdued radiance of our dawn arrival, I was the first one out of the train. Two small urchins helped me, through the ghetto convolutions near the station, to Losman Saittia, a dark green cavern of Gang II, where I secured a small streetside closet just off the veranda.

When I awoke, my head was still heavier than the tropical air. A splash in the communal mandi revived me enough, to propel my flip-flops in search of food. It was called Superman's, a red, white and blue banana pancake travelers haunt in Gang I. I took a seat with the priests.

"You are from the train." She said, from the next table. Her name was Sabine, a dark intense feline, traveling with her friend, Barbara, another Viennese, taller, with longer frizzy hair. They joined us. Freud would reemerge from his grave.

We all left a little later to the Hotel Bagus, and three other travelers, assembled around a guitar in the back.

"I haff sree chobs." Said Robert, a Swiss farmer, truck driver, and mechanic. There was a chubby Swedish girl named Eva, and another David, a newly manufactured engineer from San Francisco. We recruited them into our company, down the Gang to Mama's, for some delicious tofu *gado gado*, cold beers, lively conversation, and Mama herself, who looked like she did ads for a Javanese cigar company. I escorted the Austrian girls back to their losman late.

The rumblings of the intolerant old Muslim owner, and his three mutant sons, could have rivaled any volcano on the island. It could have been a misunderstanding, rather than a collective psychosis. But as I left I looked up above the door, at the losman sign of the most misnamed hotel in the world, I really didn't think so. *Gandhi's.*

I met the priests on my way to Superman's next morning and, they informed me that Sir David was waiting for me. His nose was there when I walked in, more elevated than I remembered. We exchange banalities until Barbara and Sabine arrived, joined by the Frisco David, Eva, and Robert.

"You are able to keep track of all these searchers after truth?" Asked Sir David.

He came with me to Purnomo's gallery, where I fell in love with his batik of Rama, Sita and Hanuman, painted in traditional colors. The artist wanted more than I could afford, so I bought Sir David lunch at Superman's instead.

I left him later to secure a ticket for Sunday's bone-grinding bus trip to the ferry to Bali, and to stop off in Gandhi's courtyard, to visit Barbara and Sabine. They were glad to see me, and anxious to relate the mistreatment they had experienced at the hands of the XYY Muslim sons the previous night. I told them I was sure it was a 'boys will be boys' phenomenon. And then Sabine accidently broke a glass. And the lid blew back off the volcano. The sons began cursing and banging and bashing inanimate objects within their immediate reach and then, more menacingly, more adamantly, turned their focus on me. For my part, I tried to stay calm and rational, which frustrated their need for immediate histrionic self-righteous indignation even more. I left with the girls, after they pushed me once too often (and just before I would have retaliated unwisely).

"They seem to have a problem with impulse control." I said.

Sabine actually blamed me for not being submissive enough, for not being fast enough on exiting, and for not kicking the schizoshit out of the lot of them. They had wanted it all ways. Waltzing with weasels. I was indignant that the insane had done the inexcusable to the indefensible, and that I was being cast as the catalyst. By the end of a fruit salad at Mama's, they decided to move out of Gandhi's and into Saittia. My landlady, already aware of the situation through the grapevine, agreed to let them move in the next day.

They were on my doorstep at 5:30 next morning. We woke up Sir David and Robert, and walked twenty minutes, to pick up the first of three buses to Borobudur. We arrived before it opened, with time enough for a breakfast of chicken, eggs, and a gravel suspension masquerading as coffee. Another 200 rupees got us a comical rickshaw ride to the main gate.

Hidden for centuries under volcanic ash and luxuriant jungle, it had been rediscovered in 1814 by Sir Thomas Raffles, who named it for the nearby town of Bore, likely after one too many Singapore slings.

Constructed in the 9th century, Borobudur was four years down the road, a pilgrimage to the ultimate Buddhist tollgate on the Final Cartwheel, and the last of my ancient monuments before the homecoming. Strange how my odyssey milestones ran like the road itself- many at first, fewer and fewer out into the hinterlands and then, as I got closer to returning, they begin appearing out of somewhere already seen.

From the air Borobudur appears as a step pyramid in the form of a giant tantric mandala, with a large central bell-shaped dome, surrounded by 72 stone Buddha statues, each seated its own perforated stone stupa rock lattice cockpit. It was a splendid place- miles of bas-reliefs under a soap bubble sunrise on the giant dome.

From the base of the shrine, I followed a climbing circumambulating path, up through the three levels of Buddhist cosmology, the Kāmadhātu *World of Desire*, the

Rupadhatu *World of Forms*, and the Arupadhatu *World of Formlessness*. Nirvana.

The ascent took me through a system of stairways and corridors, the walls and balustrades decorated with over a thousand exquisite narrative scenes of daily existence in 8th century Java, a full panoramic depiction of the endless *samsara* cycle of life and death: kings and queens, princes and noblemen, courtiers and soldiers, and servants and priests living a courtly palace life, hermits in the forest, and commoners in the village. Here were temples, marketplaces, flora and fauna, native architecture, a famous double outrigger ship, and mythical Buddhist spirits. The pains of hell and the pleasure of heaven were illustrated in stone, the punishment of blameworthy activities, from gossip to murder, and the rewards for praiseworthy activities, like charity and pilgrimage.

Five months after my visit, followers of a blind Moslem preacher made a pilgrimage with nine bombs, reemphasizing, in case anyone had forgotten, the absence of accommodation for nirvana in the religion of peace. The day I was there, they were being assisted by the caretakers, fastidiously scrubbing the unsightly definition off the sculptures with their wire brushes.

Robert and Sir David and I made the journey in reverse, hiring two rickshaws for an express trip back to Superman's for lunch. I left them to visit the market, where a transvestite in chartreuse finery tried to sell me a self-portrait. It really didn't do him justice.

"Excuse me." She said from behind me. "Do you speak English?" I answered in the affirmative.

"Do you think you could help us?" Asked her friend. "That man is harassing us. Could you ask him to stop?" A long-haired weasel leered, and nodded to me from nearby. I was polite and firm and he backed off, but only just.

"He's still following us". Said the first one. This time I grabbed him and outlined his options. His sense of self-preservation proved more compelling than his sense of erotic adventure. I bought them tea. The first one told me that he had hit them each across the face for refusing his boundless charm. So, what to make of it? In the preceding thirty-six hours, two friends had been robbed, two others psychopathically abused, and two strangers slapped in the face, for simply trying to preserve their distance and freedom of choice. The faith was not the problem. The problem was the faithful.

I returned to Losman Saittia, for a nap, and awoke, to the fleidernymphs and the priests. We headed over to Mama's, where Ulli and Andreas's tales of their visit to the Dieng plateau were so full of enthusiasm for the subtlety of the place, I decided to give it a miss. Sir David arrived in time to ogle the Austrian girls indecently enough, that they asked me to accompany them back to the losman.

"I don't want to find out you went back and had a party without me." He said.

"You won't." I said. And we did.

The big billboard sign at the Borobudur exit had said 'For Your Healthy Always Drink.'

Sabine pulled out a bottle of ugly Indonesian whiskey, and we proceeded to discuss Wittgenstein und Popper und Adler und Schauberger, und the Austrian philosophers of the Vienna Circle. No, that isn't true. We proceeded to discuss life's choices, and how they had decided that Sabine would be the one to go for the walk. And she did.

And Barbara lit candles. To light a candle is to cast a shadow, and shadows owe their birth to light. One of the classical Javanese fine arts was Wayang shadow puppet theatre. In a tiny losman in Yogjakarta, sixteen years back into the last century, time flew over Barbara and I, leaving our breath and shadows behind. Poetry is an echo, asking a shadow to dance. And we did.

*　　*　　*

'David Attenborough has said that Bali is the most beautiful place in the world, but he must have been there longer than we were, and seen different bits, because most of what we saw in the couple of days we were there sorting out our travel arrangements was awful. It was just the tourist area, i.e., that part of Bali which has been made almost exactly the same as everywhere else in the world for the sake of people who have come all this way to see Bali.'

Douglas Adams, *Last Chance to See*

For our last day in Yogya, we hired an illegal rickshaw driver. He cycled us the wrong way through narrow lanes, to the slime green decay of the Kraton Sultan's Palace water pools, and to the profusion of avian life in the bird market.

"Come and see this huge eagle." Said Sabine.

"That's a turkey, Sabine." I said. She argued that it wasn't, and almost convinced me, as only Austrian girls can.

It had occurred either during the cheese and vegetable omelet, or the squishy mud coffee earlier that morning. Barbara convinced Sabine to abandon their plans to climb Mount Bromo, for the sensuous pleasures of Bali.

On the way back to Saittia's, I took the girls to look at the Purnomo batik I had fallen in love with. They told me to buy it, and I remembered the words of Elliot Kravitz, long-bearded world traveler and Internal Medicine resident on the Canadian prairie, who told me one night before I left that, if I ever saw something I fell in love with, I should either buy it, or marry it. We settled on two hundred dollars, and moved on to a poor amateurish wing-flapping imitation drama of the Ramayana. I wondered if they even knew the story, and took my place near the dancers. I had become enamored with the gamelan, and the feeling of God's presence, or the steppingstone meditative state its interference beats represented. The way the old palace veterans corrected the positions of their younger apprenticed dancers filled me with warmth.

The ancient Javanese had said that 'It is not official until the gong is hung.' We were hung.

247

I fainted into a coma, until Barbara half woke me later, snuggling in one of the rusting candle tapir-welded corners of the boat, half asleep under the twinkling canopy, watching Bali's lights waxing off the port bow.

We looked up into the night sky. Orion lay on his side. I showed her how the rice farmers of equatorial rural Java had seen him as a plough, and a calendar for the phases of rice cultivation. Through the millennia, the first dawn rising of *Bentang kidang* over the western horizon had been the cue signal for planting.

'When kidang first appears, a chopping knife should be used;
When kidang appears in a position similar to that of the sun at 8.00-10.00 am, vegetation should be burned;
When kidang appears overhead or sideways to the west, rice should be planted;
When kidang disappears, insect pests will appear, and rice planting should stop.'

It was the sun that rose over the last three hours of our voyage to Denpassar. The weasels I though we had left behind in Muslim Sumatra and Java, came screaming to intercept us for selection, like boxcars opening at Auschwitz.

"Kuta! Kuta! Kuta!" They shouted, from every point on the compass. Kuta was where most of the accommodation, restaurants, and nightclubs were being built at a furious pace. Any doubt about their catering primarily to Australian surfing package tourists was shot in the temple by the new *Redgum* reggae song blaring out of multiple speakers, in a bus full of glowing ultraviolet blacklight radiation.

'Got a ride out to Kuta in the back of a truck
Cost me twenty dollars and it wasn't worth a buck
Hustled to a losman down in Poppy's Lane
By a Javanese guy in a tropical rainstorm,
Lock up your daughters
I've been to Bali too.'

But in the early Balinese morning, Poppie's Gang seemed to be a quiet and serene laneway in a sophisticated little fishing village, with a long beautiful sandy beach on the western side of a peninsula.

We trudged our packs up from the surf to enquire about accommodation, but most places were full. I found a room in a small losman, a hundred meters from Barbara and Sabine, and took them up the lane for breakfast at a lovely unpronounceable yellow attic, open to the sky on all four sides of the second floor terrace, with coconut palms and Bougainvillea and frangipanis and good music. We ate black rice pudding, fruit salads, and omelets, and drank Nescafé and tropical sea air. It pulled us onto the beach for the rest of the morning, for massages by uniformed old Balinese ladies, sales pitches from vendors of all descriptions, hot sun, high surf, and acres of half-clad bodies- the naked and the dead on the Asian Riviera.

The afternoon ended up on cool sheets with Barbara, and electromagnetic dream frequencies. The sun went down between them.

Two things would eventually come out of the Kuta night-geckos and evil. The first one half woke us with his slap-padding around the walls, and then brought us bolt upright with his first chirping. For the size of this striped rubber monster, he should have been contributing to the rent. The noise he made running across the ceiling woke us frequently during out stay. His ability to walk on it with ease was due to Van der Waals forces of his toepads. He had no eyelids. He would shit on his enemies from a mighty height. The evil in the Kuta night would behave the same way. It would have no eyelids. And the forces would be more explosive. Barbara and Sabine and I went out, to discover its genesis.

Everywhere was gone. Paradise had been lost. In place of that bucolic little town of the morning was Gomorrah.

Its first assault was on the ears. Disco blasted out of every orifice and seam and aperture along Caddesi Street, multiple mindless metronome subwoofers head-pounding my tympanics into my thalamus.

"Den-pass-ar, maaan?" Shouted hustling two-stroke bemo drivers, as they roared by. There were hundreds of Kawasakis, every one in high-revving testosterone overdrive. This is where I learned to hate motorcycles.

The second offense was visual. Moving headlights and neon signs and strobe flashes lit up the chic fur shops beside the hamburger joints beside the pirate cassette stores beside the taco stands beside the photo labs, beside myself.

There were odors of diesel, and burning pig fat and sizzling hormones, and cheap perfume. And my brain synthesized all this electrical efferent sensory overload, into an overwhelmingly odious impression of excess.

We found Robert in a Swiss restaurant halfway down the carnival. He introduced us to the owner, a friend of his from the old country. I didn't get his name. It didn't matter. He pumped my hand hello, and held forth about how he was bringing civilization to the savages. I asked him if he didn't feel like a bit of a mercenary in Illyria, and whether he thought there would ever come a day when there would blowback for his civilizing influence. He just stared at me.

> 'You've been to Paris and you've been to Boston
> You've been to Fiji and you've been to London
> But you can't impress me
> 'Cause I've been to Bali too.'

Back out on the street, the weasels went by, their latest Australian girlfriend shadow puppets on the back of their bikes. *Vroom-vroom.*

There was no point in trying to sleep. We wandered down the epicenter of the cultural cross-pollination, an Aussie bar named Paddy's Pub, on Legian street.

Compared to the rest of Bali's elegant world of myths and symbols and spiritual beliefs, the inside of Paddy's was a visceral swamp.

There are three main narratives favored in *wayang kulit* shadow puppet performances. Two derive from the great epic Indo-Javanese tradition contained in the Mahabarata and the Ramayana, and the *datang* puppet master's ability to poke fun at everyone through the mouths of buffoons is of utmost importance. He keeps the heroes on the right, and the villains on the left. But the third shadow puppet show behind the white screen and large lamp, the *Serat Menak*, is about the 6th century paternal uncle and foster brother of the Prophet Muhammad (Peace be upon Him), Hamza ibn 'Abdul-Muttalib, who used his energy in the cause of Islam, and earned the title of 'Chief of the Martyrs.'

Even in 1984, you could see this thing coming. Eighteen years later, three men walked into a Yamaha dealership, and bought a brand new bike. They asked how much they could resell it for, if they returned it in a few days.

> 'Life is tragic hanging out at Kuta
> If you haven't got a car, a bike or a scooter
> Show me the bike shop
> I've been to Bali too.'

Imron drove the bike to plant a small bomb outside the U.S. consulate. It had been filled with human excrement. He returned to pick up two suicide bombers in a Mitsubishi van, while Idris rode the bike alongside. The first suicide bomber donned an explosive vest and headed into Paddy's Pub. The second armed the 94 electric detonators and the TNT booster, connected by five hundred feet of detonating cord, to the twelve filing cabinets filled with a ton of aluminum powder, potassium chlorate, and sulfur. He had only learned to drive in a straight line, far enough to get the vehicle a parking spot across the street from Paddy's. What he didn't know was that the van had been also rigged for detonation by remote control, in case he had a sudden change of heart. Idris picked up Imron on the Yamaha and drove back to

Denpassar. He dialed the number of the Nokia to detonate the consulate device.

At 23:05 the suicide bomber inside Paddy's Pub detonated his backpack, causing many patrons, with and without injuries, to flee into the street. Twenty seconds later, the second suicide bomber, with or without redundancy, detonated the car bomb, killing over 200 people, injuring 240 more, destroying neighboring buildings, shattering windows several blocks away, and leaving a crater over a meter deep.

The local hospital was so overwhelmed that some of the injured had to be placed in hotel swimming pools, to ease the pain of their burns.

It happened again in almost the same way three years later, except that most deaths and injuries were due to the ball bearing shrapnel, rather than the chemical explosion. The police found the six legs and three heads of the perpetrators. The chief Jemaah Islamiyah suspect had a doctorate degree from the University of Reading.

In the 1930s, anthropologist Margaret Mead and others had created a western image of Bali as 'an enchanted land of aesthetes at peace with themselves and nature.' I picked up and read a tourist brochure off the counter at Paddy's.

"Indonesia's national motto, 'Bhinneka Tunggal Ika,' *Many, yet one*, articulates the diversity that shapes the country." It said. The deejay was playing the new Aussie reggae hit.

> 'Tourists from Holland, Britain and France
> Late night puppet shows, legong dance
> Want to see my slides?
> I've been to Bali too.'

I remembered the name of the album. *Frontline.*

Barbara and I left them. We sat on the beach, feeling the crash of the luminescent surf, and the twinkling deep silence above. Beside the power of the universe, the two-stroke intrusions were but flies on the last Balinese tiger. Still, their lights would always dim ours.

'As long as Muslims were confident they could not be defeated, but now we are just puppets.'

Abu Baker Basher

*   *   *

'The shadow should be the same length as the body'
Indonesian proverb

What finally prodded me out of Kuta beach, on a random Thursday, was not previously known to the species. Most people would have traded their souls for a holiday in Bali. I was willing to do a Faustian deal, for a vacation from it. I had decided on elevation. After many years of nomadic perfection, I had learned that when there was a need to satisfy the senses, I hit a beach; when there was a need to satisfy the spirit, a mountain. In Bali as well, the demons live in the most unclean places in and near the sea, whereas the temples, where gods and ancestors live, are in the sacred spaces on the mountain. And so, after breakfast with my fleidernymphs, and a mutually trial separation, I set off for Ubud.

Located among the steep ravines and forests, and rivers and rice paddies of the central Gianyar regency foothills, Ubud was named after the Balinese word for 'medicine.' So far, so good. When the Russian ethnic German art teacher Walter Spies arrived in the 1920s, Noel Coward, Charlie Chaplin, H.G. Wells, and other luminaries joined with the local crab-eating macaques, to recreate Ubud as the cultural Mecca of Bali. Or so the profuse tourist literature proclaimed.

A minibus, trishaw, and bemo later, I was looking for accommodation among the rice paddies with a young French law student, new at this game, who eventually demonstrated his gratitude by taking the room I had booked. But I found the Lasi Erawati pension for 2000 rupees, checked in, showered, and ventured out to partake of the culture. The museum was empty, save for a mixture of Gauguin and Bosch, and a nervous, camera-happy skirmish in the arcade. She had been clearly too oppressed by the hydrostatic tonnage of her Kuta experience, to ever trust a stranger again. I could hear her heart in the echoes. So I smiled, and made my exit to play with the more spontaneous Balinese boys on the lawn outside, immensely proud of their own peculiar handicraft. From broken green rush reeds, they had fashioned perfect replicas of M-16 assault rifles, oblivious as to how much their games had been influenced, and how close they were to the real thing. I shot one of them with my Olympus XA, they fired back, and we waved to each other over the rise. *Salaam Aleichem. Aleichem Salaam.*

But I was still hungry for more of this culture the tourist brochures had been so effusive about. I determined to make for the residence of one renowned artist-in-residence, who was, or so it said the guidebooks, open to receiving visitors.

Don Antonio Maria Blanco was 72 years old, and still had 15 more years left in him, when I visited in 1984. Born in the Philippines of Spanish and American parents, he pulled out of Florida and California, and was headed in Gauguin's footsteps to Tahiti, when he tripped on Bali, and married a traditional local dancer named Ni Ronji. He stayed, converted to Hinduism, and painted naked women for a living, transforming himself into a 'maestro of the romantic-expressive.' His work was collected by Michael Jackson, and numerous other world dictators.

Blanco had built an ostentatious castle on a hill over the river, on land gifted him by the King of Ubud. I set out on the climb to meet the maestro, innocently assuming, in my weakness for eccentrics, that there would be some kind of magical exchange of kindred spirit syrup, if and when I persevered up to his aerie. But it smelled bad from the beginning.

His residence appeared constructed to keep the world out and not allow any beauty in, as if he was under siege.

A wary young Balinese servant asked me to wait beside an elaborate sentry post, and rematerialized after a few minutes, with two admission tickets. I dutifully paid, my curiosity aroused at this point, and followed a curved tile path past another suspicious attendant, into a dark narrow gallery. The work was good, a mixture of Impressionism and Pop, distempered with gallons or galleons of Iberian mad detail. A contralto voice bounced off the skylights and startled me, and I turned to face a tall, doughy woman in a long colored silk dressing gown, painted in oil like a few of the hanging portraits she appeared in, on the wall.

"Good day." she said, forcing a half smile, and I felt like they been caught rummaging through the drawers in the Queen's bedroom. On closer examination, it appeared she was the Queen, a haughty fallen brown angel reduced to spending her fading medieval days receiving common interlopers into her *palacio-* to pay the bills. It was all a pretentious operatic drama. She made it immediately clear that she was normally above this sort of forced labor. I tried on my best ambassadorial greeting but, after she established my nationality, it was as far as I was going to get. She told me of another Canadian, who had apparently robbed Blanco of his most prized earlier works for less than they would be worth, and who owned some grocery store in Vancouver. Despite the obvious resentment in her sagging face, she told me of my good fortune this day. The Master was even now in his studio next door, and I would be given an audience. She pointed me towards a set of double doors, and vanished off the pastel edge of the canvas.

The portal opened, onto another painted scene. A larger room in the same colors, but how could the skylight let in so much darkness? In the far corner of the studio sat a short shriveled gnarly orc with a black beret, in baggy pants and shiny black toreador shoes, arms wrapped around one crossed leg, lecturing a starry-eyed German honeymooning couple, with a gravelly authoritarianism and eye-bugging intensity.

He seemed more Franco than Picasso, more Guernica than the Barcelona he had claimed as his hometown. He was hardly distracted, but visibly annoyed, at my entry. I had disturbed his momentum, apparently, but he barely dropped a beat in the lecture. When I finally made the distance, all the way across the room to sit at his feet with the others, he stopped briefly, to ask my nationality.

A bitter smile reflected the loss of income he had apparently experienced, at the hands of the other Canadian. He began to expostulate, in graphic detail, his client's predilection for prepubescent virgins, and stared at me as if I had been somehow afflicted with the same perversity, like it was a national trait.

"I'm not sure you can pigeonhole people by their nationality." I offered, still looking for some sort of alternative engagement.

"Yes, my dear." He sneered, immediately redirecting his attention back towards his newlywed disciples. When he finally paused to draw a breath several minutes later, I asked him where he thought his roots were.

"I'm from Barcelona, my dear." He scoffed, seemingly insulted. "Do you miss Ramblas?" I asked. He answered by ignoring me, by speaking of ribald things, and then raised his hand, to indicate that the audience was over. I thanked him for the indulgence.

"Goodbye, my dear." He said, brusque and glaring. And I left.

His derision followed me back into town like a stray cur. Sabine and Barbara were in the small café near the bemo stand, seeking solitude. The only remaining art came in the form of the old rag a stoned American freak pulled out of his daypack.

256

"Yeah man, like I bought this magnificent old batik in Solo, and it only cost me seven bucks." I went back to my art shop farm losman for a nap.

In the evening I hiked up to Chanderi's, for a quiet evening repast. I joined Sir David, sitting with a Swedish girl and an older Swiss guy. Birle was an attractive nurse from Gothenburg, but much too enamored with her own femininity, and her Scandinavian liberal narcissism, to pay any attention to. Hans, on the other hand, was a kindred soul, a 55-year-old engineer who had worked and traveled in different parts of the globe. He was honest about his own obsessive-compulsive culture, the myopia inherent in 'settling down,' and the dangers of the American dream. The American baton twirler who had joined us, took exception to non-Americans criticizing her country's 'preeminence in World affairs.' The classical traveler confrontation emerged through smiles and niceties, and I switched off, as the customary stalemate was enacted. It was late, the Ubud dogs were barking, and I bid them sweet dreams, to walk the moonlit sonata rice fields home, and into the dreams of the shadow puppets.

Next morning Sir David and I hiked up into the green hills and their enclosed pink rice terraces, to the real Bali of flowers and sunlight, and temples and waterfalls. We ended up at a typical Balinese house, for a typical Balinese meal, with twenty tourists in tow. 'Welcome to our typical Balinese feast' was sign-posted over the table. The raki and fried jackfruit, gado gado, and saté duck, chicken, and tripe were good but the gluttony of the tourists made digestion difficult. We left early.

I spent my final day in Ubud, at the Café Lotus and the Nomad Wine Bar, with Hans. He wanted me to come with him to a more deserted island off Lombok, but I told him I was running out of money and patience and eastern vectors. For me, it was time to turn north and east and south. I had just mailed the postcard home that day.

257

Salamat tingal,
After three weeks in Sumatra and Java, Bali is a shot of palm-waving narcolepsy. Indonesia is seething with contrasts: Batak Christians in impenetrable jungle, 100 million Muslims squeezed into the beautiful squalor of Java, and the last vestiges of garlanded Hinduism on this jet set paradise. It's the last shot of adrenaline before the pavement stomping Down Under. I fly into Sydney on September 3 at four o'clock in the morning- the final phase of the Odyssey and the beginning of my reconstruction. One long overdue, but worth the exile. Nothing I do the rest of my life will ever again drive me so intensely or teach me so much. All other lifestyles, after this, seem dark and cold and sleepy, like a hibernating bear. But for now I still have a little time, a few stars and sunsets, tropical fruit smiles on brown faces and one more dawn-lit volcano to climb [Mt Bromo] on the way to the airport.

Jalan-jalan, Wink

'Well, I wandered off to Ubud, just a little up the track
One week there didn't want to come back
Listening to gamelan and playing guitar
Tjanderi's tacos, Hotel Menara, two month visa
I've been to Bali too.'

*   *   *

'You won't get lost, I know, being a person so complete in strength
and weakness, hardness and softness, experience and unspoildness,
cleverness and knowledge and… of course, a fool and an idiot at the
same time.'

Eva, *Letter from Lovina* 30 August 1984

After my banana pancake, fruit salad and coffee, Serendipity and I dusted down the long and winding, past a dawdling Sir David to the bemo stand, for a too many rupee ride to Klungklung. It was here in 1908 that the Dutch massacred hundreds of Balinese marching to their deaths in a suicidal *puputan* defensive assault, rather that face the humiliation of surrender. The same scene had played out two years earlier in Sanur, with the thousands of members of the royal family and their followers. As far as genocidal colonialism would travel in Indonesia, The Dutch East India Company's mission statement made ample provision for everyone going Dutch.

My bemo broke down just outside the massacre site, and I walked the remaining two kilometers, to catch another ride to Siliguiri. The length of the trip was broken by the burnt out volcanic views of Mount Batur, and the long green descent to the northern coast. The next vehicle I caught at the bemo stand was only going to Lovina 'Station,' so I boarded another, laden with hot smelly fish, for the rest of the journey.

My first epiphany was that Lovina had been discovered. After an exhausting reconnaissance along the five-kilometer beach, I found another Settia's, a small losman where the mama of the house agreed to let me sleep on her front porch for the night.

I left to discover the seventy-five cent battered fish at Battia's restaurant, which hooked me into loyal patronage for the next three weeks. It was here I met Franz, whose painful predicament had matured on the black sand strand. His longstanding girlfriend had taken up with a smooth-talking weasel and, as a New Age Northern European male, Franz had no choice but to accept this as a consequence of their 'mature' relationship. I wished him luck.

I was enjoying the same fish for dinner that evening, when a bearded middle-aged American broke my concentration.

"Excuse me." He said. "My wife has scurvy. Do you think you could spare your limes?" His name was Gene, a 53 year-old marine biologist, married to pigtailed Heather for twenty years, and living in Australia for the past fourteen. I told him that it was my next port of call.

"You won't like it, Wink." He said. "I never had a close friend there." Gene and Heather were giving up their calm lives to travel overland to Spain, where they hoped to 'settle in a little place on the Costa da Sol.' I quoted him Ken Brower, from *The Starship and the Canoe*.

'I had encountered a similar wish before, in other solitary people. Someday they would all have a place in the country, they would gather a sympathetic group of people, and human relations would run smoothly. I had daydreamed that myself.'

It was the beginning of a month-long friendship, but not that evening.

I met Franz again, and we walked along the beach, discussing the views on human evolution, Marxism, and the role of women in society. When we stopped for a drink at the Sunset, his girlfriend's role was all too obvious.

"There are some things that are not for sharing." I said, and spent the next hour trying to rebuild his self-esteem. We parted around 2 am, and I returned to my porch under the stars. Mama's cat chased the cricket chirps all night long. Lovina eventually had her way with me. I loved collecting shells on her sand in the morning solitude, swimming with the dolphins, and snorkeling on the reef. I reread *Great Expectations*, ate battered fish until my skin took on the same golden deep fried appearance, shared sunsets and played guitar on the beach with Gary and Captain Arak and other new friends, and enjoyed evening meals with Gene and Heather, discussing marine biology, and the meaning of it all.

Under the sun's parabolas, I dug my toes into the black sand, gazing at time and space. With more time, a pattern formed in the space. Every morning, while I collected shells, she passed me. In the afternoon, she would park her towel at a distance appropriate to the primal territorial laws of the beach. It was the blush that gave her away. She had long red hair, and a primitive Germanic tribal magnetic rounded ripeness, that generated voltage as it spun. After three days of this, I had to find out what would have happened. I approached, when she was sitting with two of her Dutch friends. Her name was Eva, a nurse from Munich. She would meet me at Battia's later, for battered fish.

When she arrived, there was no fish, Gene was off on a political tangent, the Dutch girls were off with him, and only Heather was aware of the voltage. The next morning on the beach, she showed me pictures of her boyfriend. There are some things that are not for sharing.

The night before I left Lovina, Eva reappeared in Battia's. We had fish and she told me she missed me, and we went to the beach to sit under the stars, and spoke of what was in the sky, and in our hearts. There are some things that are not for sharing. And there are some things that are unavoidable.

Heather, Gene and I bid Lovina goodbye, on a night bus to the north coat of East Java on August 31st. We left behind the Badia family, Gary, Captain Arak, an Aussie doctor and his Italian concubine, my T-shirt making tattoo man, a Romanian hairdresser, and a world of stasis. We got nasi campur, bananas and bottled teh on the bus, exchanged crackling kreteks with a German schoolteacher on the ferry, and spent a short night drifting in and out of gear changes on the trans-Javan highway. The bus dropped us in Probolinggo about 1:30 am and I mobilized a coffee, baggage storage, and a private van, for us, and a French couple. The bargaining session woke most of the town. It got cold, starry and high very quickly. I remember the thwack of my flip-flops climbing the cobblestones to Mount Bromo.

Sitting in the vast plain of the Sea of Sand, the active volcano appeared as a gigantic scoop of chocolate ice cream, with the radial ribbing on the sides indicating it had been made with way too much cocoa powder. Its name derives from the Javanese pronunciation of the Hindu god of creation, Brahma. It seemed a little mislabeled. In the 15th century, a childless couple beseeched the mountain gods for fertility. The gods granted them 24 children but stipulated that the 25th must be thrown into the volcano as a human sacrifice. Unlike the simple fun that Abraham and Isaac had experienced, the couple apparently complied. This has resulted in the Hindu festival of Yadnya Kasada, when the people of Probolinggo hike up the volcano to throw offerings of fruit and rice and vegetables and flowers and livestock into the caldera. Some locals climb down into the crater to retrieve the sacrificed goods, in the belief it will bring them luck. Sometimes, especially after the three eruptions since 2004, the luck is bad. There is now a two-kilometer exclusion zone around the volcano.

But back in 1984, a man could walk right down into the valley of the shadow, onto the softness of the ash carpet, where one lone Arctic clad local was collecting sulfur. There was an intense tranquility in the transience of the sunrise and the volcanoes and their interactions.

Gene and Heather and I walked around the crater rim to a higher vantage point, and another volcano signaled puffs of welcome over the hill- green on yellow, gray on blue, tired and hungry and high. We walked down for breakfast in a mountain town, and caught a van stuffed with seventeen more people, the three hours back to Probolinggo, and another longbox to Surabaya.

I made a reservation on the Bima Express to Jakarta for the next day, and checked into the Travelers Inn. After treating Gene and Heather to a beer at the Garden Hotel next door, I crashed, dog tired.

Surabaya is named after a shark and a crocodile, symbols of an ancient battle between Mongol and Hindu forces. It seemed that history was fond of battles here. The Battle of Surabaya was one of the most important conflicts of the Indonesian revolution in 1945. When the Dutch red-white-and-blue flag was torn off the Yamato Hotel's tower, only the current Indonesian national red-white flag came off it. Dolly is the biggest *lakilisasi* red-light district in Southeast Asia is Surabaya, but the threats being made by local Islamists threatens to eclipse any previous warfare.

In the morning we took a bemo to see the Makassar schooners, past an ugly giant sculpture of Suharto, and miles of garbage. The heat was too intense for more than a brief foray. After lunch in a local Chinese restaurant, with repeated coldwater topups for our tired lemons, Gene and Heather walked me to the station, for goodbye hugs and best wishes. I boarded my last Asian train. It was a good journey, as train journeys go. I sat with some educated Jakartans, who gave me more insights into the lives of the common man than I had been able to appreciate as a nomad.

The express pulled into the most populous city in Southeast Asia next morning. In Sanskrit it had been called 'complete act,' the Dutch had named it Batavia, but my new acquaintances from the train referred to it as the 'Big Durian.' Outside the station I met George, a fellow MIT alumnus, on his way back to Boston with a newly purchased gamelan. We shared a cab to the airport and I spent the day there doing crosswords, eating expensive food, and waiting for the UTA counter to open.

The flight took off at midnight. A volcano erupted under my window as we soared over central Java. I was looking forward to a little shuteye before we crossed the Wallace line, but it was not on the radar. Not only were the flora and fauna about to drastically change, but the light switches would flick in reverse, Corioli's forces would spin water down the drain clockwise, motorists would drive on the other side of the road, and Orion would turn upside down in his Final Cartwheel. I was going to land somewhere between the Lucky Country and the Fatal Shore.

> Q. "So Gary, where do you want to be for the winter?"
> A. "Where it's the warmest."
>
> Gary, Lovina Beach, Bali 26 August 84

Fair Dinkum

'At my lowest point, when things were at their most desperate and uncomfortable, I always found myself in the company of Australians, who were like a reminder that I'd touched bottom.'

Paul Theroux, *Great Railway Bazaar*

Even the Romans had a legend about *Terra Australis Incognita*, the unknown land of the South. For me it still was.

The entry formalities were formidable, and costly. The Health People gave me a card indicating that my Australian address was inadequate, the Immigration People were pleasant enough (to me, but not to my Papuan friend, a reporter returning the circuitous route from Port Moresby to Irian Jaya to Port Moresby to Sydney, to disclose his adventures with the Indonesian experiment in noble savagery), and the Customs People, well they were just insane.

Australia is home to many dangerous animals, including some of the most venomous snakes in the world. The viper that attacked me for my Asian seed collection had hands like the Reverend Harry Powell. There was 'L-O-V-E' tattooed on the knuckles of his right hand, and 'H-A-T-E' tattooed on the knuckles of his left. Harry had been an itinerant preacher, con artist, and serial killer. He used to wave his fingers around in his sermons, spreading the gospel of the eternal struggle between good and evil, up and down the Ohio River in the late 1920s. He did God's work, in his fanatical hatred of women and sex, by marrying wealthy widows, and killing them for their money. This tattooed Customs guy must have thought he was doing God's work as well, when he stole my traveler's cheques. Hell, I hadn't been in a country founded by guards and criminals ten minutes, and I'd already experienced both, in a welcoming committee of one.

But no worries, as they say. *She'll be right.* I was in the land of

'Eora,' what the British had originally called the indigenous people here, because, when they asked them where they came from, the Eora had replied 'Eora.' *Here*. This was, of course, before La Perouse brought a French expedition into Botany Bay in 1789, with a cargo of smallpox, and the Eora ended up bobbing up and down in Sydney Harbour. *Here*. And before Governor Macquarie began his initiative to 'civilize, Christianize, and educate' the few that had survived, by removing them from their clans. *Here*. I was in the 'Big Smoke,' the 'Siren City of the South,' the 'Athens of Australia,' and I was eager to interact with my new Sydneysider mates. I asked one at the baggage carousel if he knew the time.

"Fuck off." He said.

But no worries. She'll be right. I walked out into the Arrivals lounge and there was Julie, a rose in every cheek, smiling like the same happy little Vegemite I had first met in the wee hours of the Cairo airport, when she was traveling with Destiny. We drove back to her flat in Bexley, for gin and tonics, and a phone call to Robyn in New Zealand, who informed me she was flying over in two days time. I took Julie out for a seafood lunch at the Botany Bay restaurant. After my year in Asia, the bill flattened me like a lizard on a rock, but I tried not to let on. Back at the apartment I was introduced to Julie's handlebar moustache boyfriend, Mark, and a fireman pal named Wayne. I almost cried myself to sleep, from the sheer joy of being back in the West.

The next couple of days were filled with trying to retrieve my traveler's cheques, and job hunting. Because of the AMEC exam qualification requirement for physicians in New South Wales, it appeared that I might have to go directly on to New Zealand to find employment as a physician, when Jules showed me an ad for locum work in Hobart. I called the number. The woman on the other end of the line told me that they 'desperately need a doctor,' and that a Mr. Lancaster would call me back later.

Jules and I went out to the airport to pick up Robyn. At first I wasn't sure who was waving at me, but I was sure I didn't know who was waving at me. Her face looked familiar, but I didn't recognize the coral colored business suit, or the matching lipstick and nail polish, or the short wavy perm. Destiny had been an ethereal gypsy, dressed in peasant garments made of natural materials and colors. I had memories of her long curls and clavicles and lithe figure gliding, when she moved. She had been my Hope Savage. Whoever was waving at me in this airport, moved like she was corporate, and meant business.

But it was her, and I should have expected that, after a year back in the real world, she would have adjusted to, reassembled, and resembled it. And when she called, it was the same voice from the Golden Temple and Naggar Castle, and the Thorong La.

We had all arrived back at Julie's, when Mr. Lancaster called from Hobart. He offered me a position in the After Hours Medical Clinic, and asked if I could start immediately. The terms seemed reasonable. Possibly because of the G&T's, in a recreation of our first encounter on Egypt Air, I didn't ask as many questions as I might have, but I agreed to be in Hobart in a week's time. This would give Robyn and I a decent opportunity to rekindle, with the few days and little money I had left. As it turned out, I had more days than money, but both were used to good advantage. I borrowed Mark's clothes, to take her out for dinners and shows. I got her a birthday present, and one day I bought her an ice cream, and waited for over an hour, while she decided which pair of red shoes would go with her business suit. This would clearly take some getting used to. We toured the blue harbor and the white Opera House and took Julie and Mark on the Manley ferry, for a picnic, on orange and yellow checked blankets that we had spread over the rocks. *Seven miles from Sydney and a thousand miles from Care.*

We drank Bailey's, and Jules let me wear the same glasses

she had worn in India, the ones with the pink heart-shaped lenses. And our shadows grew long and we watched the sun set, as the time came when Robyn had to catch her return flight to Auckland. I spent my last day at Julie's playing chess with Mark, and looking over my India slides. I was more than nervous. I hadn't worked as a physician for a year and a half, and in less than a week I would need to demonstrate to Mother Nature, and the citizens of Tasmania, that I was the Gord Strewth bonza ridgie didge, and that I still knew what I was doing.

'Don't worry about the world coming to an end today. It is already tomorrow in Australia.'

Charles M. Schulz

*   *   *

'Hold me now, hold me now Till this hour has gone around
And I'm gone on the rising tide For to face Van Diemen's Land'
U2, *Van Diemen's Land*

My voyage to Hobart began with an overnight ordeal to Melbourne, on Ansett Pioneer bus lines. I started at the back beside an unsavory skinhead, until I saw what was tattooed on his knuckles. The front seat next to the Myers girl was better. I told her I might go to Antarctica, if things didn't work out in Tassie.

My eyes, and the head they peered out from, were tired and gritty by the time we reached the Yarra River estuary, and entered the Cultural Capital of Australia. In the 1880s, as a result of the Victorian gold rush boom, Melbourne had been the richest city in the world. You wouldn't have suspected either of these triumphs from the bargain basement clothes emporium I unearthed my work gear in, although you may have found no small evidence of its Chinese heritage. I took in a Soviet space exhibit at the museum, and tried unsuccessfully to find a used manual of medical therapeutics. The highlight of the Empress of Australia night passage was the five-dollar fish and chips, before I crawled into the Gold Kazoo at the back of the lounge. It was 140 miles across the treacherous Bass Strait, although most of the treachery would prove to be on the other side.

"I almost tripped over you last night." Said a corrugated crone, who aggressively exhaled a cloud of smoke at me in the same reprimand.

Tasmania only left mainland Australia 9,000 years before I did, when Ice Age glaciers ground away the land bridge. Koalas and dingoes were stopped cold on the new shoreline, and the island became an ark. The road kill is limited to wallabies, possums, wombats, Tasmanian devils, quolls, and three kinds of fatal snakebites. The planet's oldest living organism, King's holly or *Lamatia tasmanica*, has grown on the south coast as long as the oldest human habitation, 40,000 years or 570 lifetimes. Because of its isolation, and the Roaring Forties blowing all the way from Cape Horn, Tasmania has the purest air and cleanest rainwater in the World. Its daylight torments with a ferocious melancholy. The western half is still wilderness. I was coming to a 'sometimes forgotten teardrop,' a land of secrets and distortion. Rarely visited, it had always been described in extremes, either as Paradise or Purgatory, Heaven or Hell.

The heavenly part usually related to its untrammeled natural beauty. Almost every landscape was a watercolor.

'It is most extraordinary to see that these dense forests, ancient daughters of nature and time, where the noise of the axe is never heard and where the vegetation is richer every day from its own products, can extend unimpeded everywhere; and when at the other end of the world one happens to see forests exclusively composed of trees unknown in Europe, of plants strange in form and various in their productions, one's interest becomes more keen and more pronounced.'
Nicolas Baudin, 1802

In 1870, the Marquis de Beauvoir described it as a 'smaller Switzerland,' and three years later Anthony Trollope had written that 'everything in Tasmania is more English than is England herself.' I had landed on the Apple Isle.
The Hell was human.

'And it was in this paradise that the yellow-liveried convicts were landed, and the corps-bandits quartered, and the wanton slaughter of the kangaroo-chasing black innocents consummated.'

Mark Twain, 1895

Tasmania was haunted by extinction. The last *thylacine* Tasmanian tiger, and every single native aboriginal had been annihilated by 1876. It was the site of the worst atrocities against the black man, the place of bread buttered with arsenic for the unsuspecting, and the terminal Black Line beating, in the hunt for the last survivors. It is said that the cry of yellow-tailed black cockatoo is a lament for dead aboriginal children.

And similar treatment was meted out to 76,000 convicts, mostly thieves, who received an average sentence of seven years, eight months from England 'beyond the seas.' It was Alcatraz rather than Arcadia in the Albania of the Antipodes, the most felonious of felons sunk below depravity into cannibalism in, according to Robert Hughes, 'the Paestums of an extraordinary time- an effort to exile en masses a whole class.' These were the monuments of Australia, but the Australians projected everything they loath about themselves- racism, parochialism, homophobia onto Tasmania- so backward and inbred, visitors were advised to grow an extra head.

'The first day that we landed upon that fatal shore,
The planters gathered around us, they might be twenty score,
They ranked us off like horses and sold us out of hand,
They yoked us to a plough, brave boys, to plough Van Diemen's Land.'

Upon Van Diemen's Land

And I was heading to be yoked.

The bus service was my first indication of the untouched state of the island. It followed the old coach roads, as sedately as the old coaches. The driver made sure all the old girls had used the dunny and, in his plodding dialect, provided en route commentary about the history and the local characters. It turned out they were one and the same.

"That's Misery guts Murray's place over there on the Tamar." He would say. "1858. Madder than a two bob watch." It took us two hours to get to Launceston. Settled in 1806, its inhabitants had founded Melbourne, and were the first in the country to have hydroelectric lights and underground sewers. The first use of anesthetic in the Southern Hemisphere occurred here although, with the pace of speech I'd encountered, it wouldn't have taken much. In coming weeks I would learn however, that despite the fact that some Tasmanians spoke 'too slow to keep worms in a tin,' to judge their wit by their cadence would hurt you.

After an hour's tea break in a café, we boarded for the last few hours drive through the midlands, which reminded me of the north of England.

Like the island, Hobart Town had also been, and would be again, both Heaven and Hell.

Charles Darwin had visited, in February 1836.

'The lower parts of the hills which skirt the bay are cleared; and the bright yellow fields of corn, and dark green ones of potatoes, appear very luxuriant... I was chiefly struck with the comparative fewness of the large houses, either built or building... If I was obliged to emigrate I certainly should prefer this place: the climate and aspect of the country almost alone would determine me... All on board like this place better than Sydney – the uncultivated parts here have the same aspect as there; but from the climate being damper, resemble England. To a person not particularly attached to any particular kind (such as literary, scientific) of society and bringing out his family, it is a most admirable place of emigration. With care and a very small capital, he is sure to gain a competence, and may if he likes, die wealthy.'

Charles Darwin, *Voyage of the Beagle*

Errol Flynn's predominant recollection was 'of its apples, its jams, its rose-cheeked girls.' And when Mount Wellington hove into view, still incongruously snow-capped in November, I felt the accuracy of Mark Twain's description of the place, in 1895.

'Suddenly Mount Wellington, massive and noble like his brother Etna, literally heaves in sight, sternly guarded on either hand by Mounts Nelson and Rumney; and presently we arrive at... Hobart. It is an attractive town. It sits on low hills that slope to the harbour – a harbour that looks like a river, and is as smooth as one. Its still surface is pictured with dainty reflections of boats and grassy banks and luxuriant foliage... How beautiful is the whole region, for form, and grouping, and opulence and freshness of foliage, and variety of colour, and grace and shapeliness of the hills, the capes, the promontories; and then, the splendour of the sunlight, the dim rich distances, the charm of the water-glimpses!'

But Mount Wellington was a volcano that had not yet erupted. Six hundred million years ago, Hobart had been eight degrees north of the equator, and heading south ever since. Which is partly why it was also an outpost bolthole, like Casablanca, to where you escaped, when everything went *cods wallop*. Like it would anyway.

He was waiting for me as I got off the bus. An older fellow with graying hair, the most remarkable thing about his was his artificial left eye. It was where I chose to focus, as the other one refused to stay in one place.

"Lancaster." He said, hand outstretched. "I'm the manager." He drove to the hotel he had booked me into, and bought us a couple of whiskeys in the bar downstairs. I had a feeling he could have had more. He chain-smoked Winston's, and told me about how he used to own the After Hours Medical Service, until his partner split with the money, and he was taken over by a local hospital and put on a two-year contract.

"Commission." He said. "Way of the world." He told me that I would need to find a place to stay, and a vehicle. He had arranged an interview for me at the Medical Council of

Tasmania, without whose blessing, I would be unable to work.

"Get yourself a girlfriend." He said. I told him I already had a girlfriend in New Zealand.

"Get yourself one here." He told me that Tasmania was the ABC isle. "Apples, beer, and c*nt." He said. "Cider, Cascade, and Cadbury's."

And then he paid, and I could see how painful it had been. And then he left.

*   *   *

> 'It isn't what they say about you, it's what they whisper.'
> Errol Flynn

What Lancaster hadn't known, and what I didn't tell him, was that I already had friends in Hobart. Robyn's sister, Debbie, and her husband, J.B., were the reason I had found my Destiny in the first place. We had traveled to Quetta, in Pakistan, to meet them coming overland on their Top Deck tour through Asia. I hadn't seen them since then but, except for the taxi business and the bridal gallery, they were still the same old 'Debs and J.B.'

"Faaiir Dinkum, mate." He said, languorous on the other end of the phone. I made a mental note never to call long distance. Debs picked me up next day, and we went across the Tasman Bridge to Montague Bay, to plan strategy. She introduced me as Robbie's boyfriend to J.B.'s mother, a refined elderly lady with an angelic smile and quiet demeanor. I would never see her without her white hair perfectly coiffeused, pearls around her neck, and every garment thread where it was supposed to be. She had a spark.

"In my day, Wink," She said. "I would have given you a go myself." Fair dinkum. And we all drank tea. Debs helped me place an ad for accommodation in the *Mercury*.

273

'YOUNG professional requires furnished bachelor flat with fireplace in Battery Pt or Sandy Bay for immediate occupancy. Call 44 1569 after 6 pm.'

And I found one for a vehicle that would fit my needs.

'Corona sedan reg. No BE4912 as is $430.'

Then she drove me down to my appointment at the Medical Council of Tasmania, where I was ushered in to meet Mr. Lemon, the Secretary. He was a big man, with Scrooge spectacles, and a patronizing affect, like he was doing a favor he was not quite committed to. For my part, I felt more like George Robinson, the Wesleyan bricklayer appointed by Governor Arthur in 1832, to negotiate with the aborigine, Tongerlongetter.

'I went up to the chiefs and shook hands with them. I then explained in the aborigines' dialects the purpose of my visit amongst them... They evinced considerable astonishment on hearing me address them in their own tongue and from henceforward place themselves entirely under my control.'

Mr. Lemon, flicking through his registration guidelines, was having none of it.
"It doesn't appear, that the medical school you say you attended, actually exists." He said, sneering over his half lenses. I told him that was impossible. Queen's was one of the most respected institutions in the country.
"Its not here." Said Mr. Lemon. "And if its not here, it doesn't exist." I asked him if I could have a look. He turned the ancient ledger around. There was Dalhousie and Toronto, one that had gone extinct, and one that had never existed. I looked at the date on the bottom of the page. *1947*. Jared Diamond once remarked that 'Tasmanian history is a study of human isolation unprecedented except in science fiction-

namely, complete isolation from other humans for 10,000 years.' Mr. Lemon was bringing up the rear.

"There are ten medical schools in Canada." I said. "The one I attended has a long and illustrious reputation. Perhaps there is someone you can call." I could tell, from his reaction, that in the pantheon of Tasmanian guard and convict ancestors, Mr. Lemon's stock had all been guards. He half agreed to look into it, and set up a more important appointment, for the following day, with the president of the Council. I would need to do better.

In the evening I went off to look at the Toyota. It had a hundred thousand on the clock, but it ran well. Besides, it was white and had white-walled tyres, light blue upholstery, a white fluff rug on the dash, and matching pom-poms hanging from the mirror. I named her Betsy. My last four hundred bucks fell into the large hand of the owner. Until the petrol ran out, I was mobile.

My ad for accommodation had made it into the Mercury, and the next morning I had a call from a local family physician. Rob had recently bought a beautiful old villa in Battery Point, but wasn't quite ready to move in yet. We agreed to meet later that afternoon, to have a look.

I parked Betsy across from the shiny brass plaque of the

Medical Council of Tasmania   Office Hours 10 am- 1pm

Inside, the President was waiting for me. I was ushered in to meet a churlish old gynecologist. In the land of ABC, he hadn't specialized in apples or beer. He shuffled through my application.

"I guess one might say you're something of a medical hobo." He said. "Hmmph."

"That is not correct." I answered. "I travel a great deal but I never wander."

"Then I assume that you move about with direction." He said. "What is your usual destination?" I gave him Tom Robbins.

"The source." I said. "I am always voyaging back to the source."

In the end he told me he would grant me 'provisional registration,' which would have to be ratified by the membership at the next general council meeting. He told me to be discreet. He didn't tell me about the case of scotch. I had legitimacy, or so I thought.

I drove Betsy to meet Rob, at 2 Dewitt Street, in Battery Point. He was a breath of fresh air, after Mr. Lemon and the grinch gynecologist, guarding the standards of medical care in the state. We hit it off, and came to a mutually satisfactory arrangement for the big empty rambling old white villa. It had two noble square white chimneys with round terra cotta pipe extensions, perforating the multiple slopes of the red-tiled roof, scalloped gingerbread dormers, a large rear garden patio, raised beds of red and white roses in the front, and a terrible haunted secret, which I would only discover after Destiny arrived.

"She'll be apples." He said. I had shelter.

Lancaster answered his phone on the first ring.

"002-231026. Home and hosed. Done and dusted " I said, checking the rest of the list for him.

"You'll also need to pick up the CB radio." He said.

"CB radio?" I asked.

"I may not have mentioned it." He said. After you finish at the After Hours, you'll be doing house calls in your vehicle. You start tomorrow. You'll need a map of Hobart."

What I really needed was the whole book of revelations, but that would only arrive with Doctor Syntax.

*   *   *

276

'I verily begin to think there is some peculiarity in the atmosphere around Van Diemen's Land which is adverse to the transmission of truth, for somehow all or other accounts carried home partake of the same distorted or wholly imaginative character.'

Louisa Meredith, *My Home in Tasmania*

The After Hours Medical Service operated within the original limestone domicile of Hobart's first surgeon, the last white Georgian mansion on MacQuarrie Street. There was a sign hanging from a gallows outside, like some of the convicts that had built the place, and an old coach lantern above the polished brass, on the large black door.

I was a one-man show, responsible for checking in the patients, finding the diagnosis and prescribing treatment, collecting the money, and answering the phone. I needed to answer the phone to find out where Betsy and I would go after each clinic, on my appointed round of house calls. I needed the CB radio, because Lancaster would bomb me with additional house calls, while I was trying to figure out where I was going. Which is why I needed the map.

My first evening in the clinic was a bit of a learning curve, not the least of which was due to my poor grasp of the language. I had asked my first patient why he had come.

"I'm, uh, crook." He said.

"OK." I said, and asked him again what his problem was.

"I'm, uh, crook." He said, again. I told him I didn't care about his avocation, only why he thought he needed medical attention. At which point he went off on what the locals call a 'barney.'

I looked forward to my 'tea break,' after my first few hours of yoked ploughing. Debs would bring down one of her magnificent roast dinners, which I would 'scoff' in the twenty minutes I had before my house calls.

I needed an extra hand I didn't have, for the house calls. My coordination was a bit off, driving Betsy on the wrong side of the road, CB receiver in one hand, cigar in the other, and the map of Hobart in the middle. One poor fellow must have seen me run over the 'Keep Left' sign, at the top of his cul-de-sac. At first it seemed like he didn't want to answer the door.

"Did you call for a doctor?" I asked.

"It's alright, mate. I'm feeling better now." He said. Sometimes I found grace, sometimes I found tragedy, and sometimes I found both. One night I was called to the house of a poor old woman, nursing her husband's last palliated gasps. I told her I didn't think I had anything to offer. She told me she had called because she didn't want to be alone when he died. My other calls waited.

I got better at everything as the days went by. My driving improved, and I became more accurate and efficient at the clinic and on my house calls. I noticed that Lancaster was smoking less, and cracking the odd smile. I began running again, to Sandy Bay, and along the headlands. My kitchen in Battery point began to acquire utensils, and the rest of the house had the odd piece of furniture. I still didn't have a bed though, and slept in the big living room. Inside the Gold Kazoo, I still hadn't noticed the smell.

On my rare days off, I would go walkabout, in the weekly market in Salamanca place, admiring the exotic wares, and the convoluted patterns of exterior plumbing on the 19th century warehouses. I paid a visit to the oldest synagogue in Australia, a rare surviving example of Egyptian Revival, like the rare surviving examples of worshippers that patronized it. Betsy and I would tour parts of the island, to Wine Glass Bay, or the Freyecinet Peninsula, or down to the old convict settlement of Port Arthur. I ate bread from Coleman's Convict Bakery in Taranna, and watched Tasmanian devils mating and shrieking, or just shrieking, in a private pen in someone's back yard.

"Bet you wish you we're doin' that?" Said the owner to another visitor.

"Naw, mate. Looks bloody dangerous."

I developed a passion for the wild costal scenery, with its

278

holes in the rocks and southern light and tortuous trees with their high foliage flattened into Byzantine profiles.

'The mountainous southern coast of Van Diemen's Land! It is a soft blue day; soft airs, laden with all the fragrances of those antarctic woods, weave an atmosphere of ambrosia around me. As we coast along over the placid waters, passing promontory after promontory, wooded to the water's edge, and 'glassing their ancient glories in the flood' both sea and land seem to bask and rejoice in the sunshine.'

John Mitchell, 1850

It reminded me of South America, and so it should have. These Southern beech and leatherwoods were found in the Andes, the only relative of the Tasmanian cave spider was living in Chile, and the only other place on the planet where a fossilized platypus tooth had been discovered was in Patagonia.

I was even closer to Antarctica, and Hobart, with its deep Derwent estuary, had been the epicenter of the Southern Ocean whaling and the sealing trade, and the homeport of the French and Australian Antarctic operations. I applied to, and was interviewed for, a post as base physician. The questions were challenging, and I'm not sure I rang all their bells. I actually hadn't had experience draining an epidural hematoma in the frozen wop wops. But their final question backpedalled me out the door.

"And you have no concern about the two-year commitment?" Asked the older one.

"Two years?" I exclaimed. That was more than a third of the average convict sentence handed out in the original penal colony. Two years was too long, and Betsy and I limped back to Montague Bay, for dinner.

"Does your sister cook as well as you, Debs?" I asked.

"Oh yes." She said. "Robyn's a great cook." As I would find out.

After I paid Lancaster and my rent, I had sent the rest to Robyn, to pay for a flight to Hobart. She had quit her job in

Auckland and, decorporatized, arrived off the plane more like the sprite I had fallen in love with in India. But her taste had clearly become more sophisticated, and her first impression of Betsy, and the white-carpeted dash and pompoms, was dispiriting. She was more enthusiastic about the digs in Battery Point, and got stuck into cleaning it like she meant to stay.

We had a grand dinner with Wyn and Debs and J.B. that evening, and it looked, for all the world, like we had arrived with our bums in butter. J.B. teased us, and grizzled comically about bloody immigrants, until I reminded him of Robert Muldoon's observation that 'New Zealanders who emigrated to Australia raised the IQ of both countries.' We left them to return to the Gold Kazoo, and the big expanse of carpet on the living room floor. Later that night, Robyn sat upright. "What's that smell?" She asked. And that was only the beginning.

*　　*　　*

'Often when I slumber, I have a pleasant dream,
　I'm lying on the cold green grass down by your purling stream,
　Oh, wondering through the maid of fair with my sweetheart by the hand,
　Then I awaken broken-hearted upon Van Diemen's Land.'
Upon Van Diemen's Land

The notification came in the post about six weeks after landfall. Robyn and I had been doing just fine. Nice house, new friends, discovering restaurants, and rediscovering ourselves. But the Tasmanian devil's in the details, and the detail that had been missing is that the president of the Medical Council of Tasmania had overstepped his authority by granting me provisional registration. Lancaster had apparently thought he was sealing a deal when he gave him the case of scotch. Instead, he was sealing my fate. When the other guards flocked in to their general meeting, the uproar was deafening. Rob apparently tried to come to my defense, but the righteous indignation generated by an alien being granted registration without their approval, would result in expulsion from my new tribe. Some were offended that they would have been rejected if they had applied for a similar position in Canada, some were protecting their turf, and some were just right bastards.

During that week, I had also been doing a locum for a Henry Wolanski, who had neglected to tell me that his wife also worked in the practice. I arrived at his surgery the first day, to find a day sheet with 70 names on it. I asked his two nurses how they had expected me to see as many patients as both of them.

"Dunno." They said. But I did, and I was lucky I didn't miss anything, although I would have missed an acute retrocecal appendix, if my nose hadn't been twitching from the adrenalin. I called Rob when I got the Council letter and he met me at a pub called Doctor Syntax, in Sandy Bay. I asked him about the Aussie *Fair Go*, the *Fair Crack of the Whip*, *Fair Suck of the Sav*, *Fair Dinkum*. He looked down into his Cascade.

"The answer isn't in there, Rob." I said. And I told him I was fed up to the back teeth. And I went troppo, off like a frog in a sock. I wasn't going to sit there like a stunned mullet. I chucked a spaz, a wobbly, on for young and old. I was going to fight this. And I asked him what he thought my chances were.

"Buckleys and Nunn." He said. "You have to understand, Wink. You're not just up against bureaucrats. You're up against Tasmanian bureaucrats. They have a two hundred year head start on conflict resolution and population control. They're experts at beating their captives to death."

I told him it was on the nose and, speaking of which, I mentioned that the missus had been curious about what the odor was in his living room.

"Oh, that's Mabel." He said.

281

"Mabel?" I inquired.

"Yep, Mabel." He said. Mabel had been the previous owner. They had found Mabel in the living room, after no one had seen her for several months. When Robyn and I finally opened the living room curtains in the late afternoon, we could see her silhouette on the carpet, right down to her shoe buckles.

"I don't like civilization anymore." I said. It doesn't agree with me."

I had also called Lancaster, and we met. And he told me, between chain-smoking puffs on his Winston's, that the only thing he was really concerned about was, when he passed on, and he thought that day was not far away, his wife would be financially secure. And I was almost angry with the small-mindedness of the man, for who would have such restricted horizons, goals so mean and minute. This was, of course, before I had reached his vintage, and realized that the small nobilities were the most worthy.

The ABC was in our back garden next afternoon, but it wasn't the apples, beer and that other thing, it was the Australian Broadcasting Corporation. I had called them, in my righteous indignation and, like all good Aussie media, they had come over immediately, in their love for the smell of blood. They played it to the hilt, the David and Goliath shtick. How dare this monopolistic monolith kick the legs out from under an impressionable young altruist, whose only purpose on the planet, was to minister to the needs of sick Tasmanians. But Rob had been right. The Medical Council was expert in disassembling criticism, and they portrayed me as an interloper, who would only undermine the standards of care that Tasmanians had a right to expect, should I be allowed to continue in my role as usurper. There was no mention of single malt.

And that is how we lost. And I sold Betsy to Patrick, our Irish border, for twenty dollars more than I paid for her, and even that was too little. And I packed Serendipity. And Rob came by, with a donation from some concerned members of the Medical Council, 'in the spirit of a loan.' And he took me back out to Doctor Syntax, so we could both have closure. But it was fine. I reassured him that I never had any intention of staying in Tassie, and he told me he knew that, and his only wish was that they had treated me better. But I told him that I hadn't expected anything more than more than half the population, and the seals, and the whales had experienced. And he smiled.

Robyn and I went over to Montague Bay next morning, to say goodbye to Wyn. It turned out that, in all the secrets that Tasmania kept hidden, she had one too. J.B. was her only son, but she had also had a daughter, and one night Lucille had disappeared. And everyone, or almost everyone knew what had happened, but like so many other things that had happened in Tasmania, nothing had happened. For like Louisa Meredith had said, there is some peculiarity in the atmosphere around Van Diemen's Land, which is adverse to the transmission of truth. And a man can't live without truth. So on the 24th of November 1984, Robyn and I left Hobart, quiet for most of the trip. We admired the occasional farmhouse, but I never looked back after crossing the Tasman Bridge. We were headed north, closer to mainland Australia, and farther from each other.

'How hard it is to escape from places! However carefully one goes, they hold you- you leave little bits of yourself fluttering on the fences, little rags and shreds of your very life.'

Katherine Mansfield

Beyond the Black Stump

'Australia is an outdoor country. People only go inside to use the toilet. And that's only a recent development.'

Barry Humphries

I love a sunburnt country. But this was absurd. Big mistake. No cars, no shade, no truck stop, and the first road I'd ever seen paved with dead lizard skin. And the only other things that moved, when the wind didn't, were the blowflies. All of the biomass, that hadn't been turned into dead lizard skin, had been heavily invested in blowflies.

It had only been two days since Robyn and I had rented a car, and given rides to an American and Kiwi hitchhiker, dropping them at the Launceston airport. We fed our leftover picnic of chicken to the seagulls at Mersey Point in Devonport, during the long wait for the Empress of Australia's return night voyage to Melbourne. The cafeteria had apple compote, coffee vending machines, and servers with tattooed knuckles. I fell asleep between the seats, and Robyn woke later. She said I had been screaming. We could only guess at what. Now that I think of it again, I had never checked to see whether Mr. Lemon's knuckles had any blue messages of love and hate on their outside.

When we docked next morning, the cacophony of French and American and Australian got on the bus to Spencer Station, while I put Robyn on one to the airport. She was going home to wait for me again, and I went off to see the Red Centre. The *Back o' Bourke*, the *Back of Beyond*, the *Never-Never*. She told me she understood. She was good like that.

For some bizarre reason, the suburban train I took out to Albion was reminiscent of my ride to hitchhike out of Kyoto. But where I found myself, after miles of walking, was nothing like Kyoto. I asked the first upright wildlife in several hours.

285

"Which way to Adelaide, mate?" I asked. And he pissed himself laughing.

My first ride came in the form of Tony, a longhaired half-deaf freak floor layer, hauling a load of sand casting moulds to Ballarat. We talked about hitching, women, and the meaning of life, the usual. I help him unload, drank a soda, and stood under the welcome shade on the outskirts of town. I'd been there a few moments when a big black Falcon pulled over and offered to take me to Adelaide. I wondered a bit about the driver, a young Kiwi guy with a black mustache and two earrings, and a dirty face two-year-old boy in a fully packed car. He didn't want to talk at first and, when he started, he didn't want to stop. He told me that his wife had left, pregnant by a family friend. Rod was absconding with their young son to Darwin, or so he said. Which made me an accessory to a kidnapping, traveling with a fugitive across a state line. I spent the trip playing and feeding little Ricky, but the novelty had worn off by the time we pulled into the hills of Adelaide. After sleeping through the cold rainy night in the back seat, I thought better of continuing with them 'up through the guts.' We wished each other luck.

I had hiked about ten kilometers when a young paint salesman took me as far as the Shell station in Wakefield, I had a shower and chicken and chips. An elderly couple picked me up on the wattle-lined boulevard, and dropped me three miles down the road in the blistering sun. Five minutes later, a born-again schoolteacher took me to Murray Corners. She was about to undergo surgery for her kidney disease, and 'just wanted to tell you about Jesus.' My last ride of the day, although I didn't know it, was from a 'Been-to-the-Philippines' Casanova roofer, who scooped me up in his Jaguar, on his way to a fishing trip in Port Augusta. The sign he dropped me beside would make an impression. *Pimba 170... Glendambo 284... Coober Pedy 640... Alice Springs 1366.* Several hitchhikers had written their impressions on the back, none of which were encouraging. One of them said '*Help! I need a lift. Now.*' The last letter, agonizingly trailing off the bottom of the sign, didn't look good. And neither did the company. Not far from the back of the sign was another hitchhiker, who had already been there a day.

"This spot's taken, mate." He growled, threateningly. I wondered how far I would have to trek before it was no longer his spot.

It turned out to be around five miles. To a wattle grove, where the last petrol station in the world lived. A cop car, looking like something out of Mad Max, stopped to check my ID.

"How long does it usually take to hitchhike out of here?" I asked. He wasn't especially encouraging.

"Could take two days." He said. "Could take three weeks." The lady behind the counter in the petrol station was even less so.

"We're thinking of building a shed in the back." She said.

Just along sundown, my growling mate from the sign rocked up. We bought each other a coffee and commiserated. His name was Chris. An hour later we gave up trying to get a ride, and threw our sleeping bags out into the wattle grove. There appeared to be a local version of sport among the jacked up V8 owners, whose idea of fun was to try and run over sleeping hitchhikers in the wattle grove or, failing that, at least spiral in a load of gravel and abuse.

"Tinny short of a six pack." Said Chris. I believe my comment was different.

Three trucks heading north woke us at dawn, but we were too slow to even get their attention. It was a beautiful day in Port Augusta. The sun was rising, the roosters crowing, and the commuter was on his way to work. But there was otherwise no traffic. Under a 'Southwark Bitter' sign and early morning cloud cover, beside a forlorn petrol pump and barbeque pit, my remorse for the demise of a one magic thumb got lost, in the desiccated droning haze of wind and flies.

'The Wanderlust has lured me to the seven lonely seas,
Has dumped me on the tailing-piles of dearth;
The Wanderlust has haled me from the morris chairs of ease,
Has hurled me to the ends of all the earth.
How bitterly I've cursed it, oh, the Painted Desert knows,
The wraithlike heights that hug the pallid plain,
The all-but-fluid silence, -- yet the longing grows and grows,
And I've got to glut the Wanderlust again.'

Robert Service, *The Wanderlust*

The term 'outback' was first used in print in 1869, when the writer had referred to anything west of Wagga Wagga. The Outback was located '*Beyond the Black Stump,*' named after the Black Stump Wine Saloon that once served Coolah, NSW, on the Gunnedah Road. Chris and I weren't in New South Wales, but what we were in, was deep.

We had just given up and were enjoying the sun on all the shoulders when a station wagon pulled up in front of us. At first we didn't even look up.

"Think it's a ride?" I asked.

"Dunno, mate." Said Chris.

"Well." I said, peeking out from under my bush hat. "I think it's a ride." And we pulled a silent movie double take on each other, and jumped to the car.

"Where ya goin', mate?" Asked the driver.

"Coober Pedy." I said.

"So are we." He said. "Hop in." Chris and I had snagged two local Lutheran ministers, off to convert the opal miners. We settled in for the long ride, and the attempted conversion of our score. We stopped only twice. The first was to allow me to shoot a photo of my first kangaroo. The second was for tucker.

It looked closed, although there was a hand-scrawled message in marker, on the plywood wall that held the buzzer. *Press only* *once for night service- when its dark out. Fuel or tenting. Opening fee $3.00.*

It was midday. The reverend father pressed the button.

"Can't you mongrels fuckin' read?" Came the clearly annoyed voice from inside the shack.

"Sorry." Said the minister. "We just didn't want you to miss an opportunity for some business."

"If I was a fucking' businessman, d'ya think I'd 'a chose to live in this shithole?" He said. "Whadever youse wankers want, we've only got steak sandwiches, but that should matter much to dickheads that can't read signs, because they're one sandwich short of a picnic anyway." Despite the welcoming local color, the steak sandwiches were cracker, although I still can't get my head around the sight of a sliced beet trying to ride a fried egg. I made the mistake of telling the chef that this was my first time to the Outback.

"Welcome to the fuckin' Outback, ya bloody Wog." He said. Made me even warmer all over.

Chris was clearly enjoying this, and taking his time. The preachers were ready to leave.

"Gotta use the thunder box." Said Chris.

"Gotta shoot through, mate. Let's hit the frog and toad."

It could have been worse. They could have tried to communicate in French.

The *bitumen* ran out quickly and the trees weren't far behind. But, in the rapture of the linear motion, I was oblivious to the scenery, not that there was really any to be oblivious to.

The better part of a thousand kilometers north of Adelaide, on the Stuart Highway, we were all grateful to see Coober Pedy at the end of a long day. What you could see of it anyway, because most of it was below ground. Its name actually came from the local aboriginal description of their observation that the new neighbors couldn't hack the scorching forty-degree daytime heat. The cost of a three-bedroom dugout *kupa-puta* 'white man's hole,' with lounge, kitchen, and bathroom was the same as it would have taken to build it on the surface, except for the cost of the air-con. The only tree sat on the hilltop over the town, welded out of scrap iron. The locals played golf at night, with fluorescent orange balls. They each had their own small piece of 'turf,' for teeing off. Their Aussie rules football club's nearest match is a thousand kilometers, roundtrip, and they only tar-sealed the Stuart Highway three years after I got there. By fifteen years after I had hitched through, there were a quarter million mine shaft entrances and a law discouraging large-scale mining. Each prospector had a fifteen square meter claim. For Coober Pedy was the *Opal Capital of the World*, and definitely an exceptional place.

A crossroads of Greek and Yugoslav diggers and restaurant owners, Chinese buyers, Aboriginal vagrants (with their 'own bar' in the back of the hotel), tour groups, local Ockers, and the world's most depressed hitchhikers, Coober Pedy's layout was randomly slipshod, and testimony to its 'rough as guts' stillbirth. The dog's breakfast ring of tailing piles, that encircled the town, was as haphazard as everything else.

The preachers dropped me at the Opal Bar, a travel office-hotel-cum youth hostel where a limping local, looking a little like Festus out of the old black-and-white *Gunsmoke* television series, introduced me to a four bunk room, a shower, at $.20 a minute, and the Yugoslav caretaker, who also wouldn't be out of place in any photo of miners in the Old West. I dumped Serendipity for a look around.

For an amorphous form of silica, not that different from common quartz, opal seemed to generate a lot of fanatical obsession, and money. Maybe it was the money, although it was my Scorpio birthstone. Almost thirty years before I walked into George Pagnagliarno's place, an eleven-inch long 'Eight Mile' opal came in at two and a half million Aussie dollars. The two I picked at from George were a little more modest. I met Chris outside, who'd given up on hitching out that day. We went to the pub.

Now I'd been to several unusual watering holes on my

odyssey by now, but the taproom in this most remote of mining outposts in South Australia was indescribable. So I will try. Even before we entered, we had to run a gauntlet of complimentary Aboriginal marijuana mouthparts, offering a cloud of weed exhaust to every potential patron, as they entered. *Welcome to the fuckin' Outback.* Physically, inside, it was not that dissimilar to every other public tavern in Godzone, constructed of painted block and tiled floors imperious to bodily acids, a dartboard, wall telephone, pool table, blackboard, and Foster's Lager banner...*Now at the bar.* The place was chock-a-block. The long-bearded miner in a coma under the banner, beside his empty takeaway foam fossils, had likely been holding the fire extinguisher for several days now. The ones still conscious at the actual bar counter were taking turns, expressing their erudite opinions, and punching each other in the face. The smoke was at eye level, and the beer taps seem stuck in the down position. A table of aboriginal women, was breaking all the rules of every country. Even the air was black and blue. All of Ripper Rita's barmaid's tips would have been in her bra, if she'd had one, so all of Rita's tips were her bra. She was well-padded but, strangely, still accessible. The few tourists that had ventured inside were keeping their heads down. And then I pulled out my opals. There were a dozen languages that went up an octave, and each one had a different opinion of how much I had been ripped off by George. It had been worth every penny of the price of admission. I had previously been made aware of the insecurity that some Aussies had felt over the fact that most of their immigrants had come from overseas, and some of them did not partake, and even frowned upon, the personal ingestion of alcohol. It was in Coober Pedy that I made peace with the fact that these new settlers, in particular, wouldn't stand a proverbial Aussie shit show.

*   *   *

'Arabs have the custom of showing their emotions and hiding their women. Australians show their women and hide their emotions.'
                                        Ted Simon, *Jupiter's Travels*

I didn't feel like lingering much the next morning, so I packed up Serendipity, bought a three-dollar bottle of water, and began the long march to the highway. I was at peace for some inexplicable reason- stuck miles from anywhere, in some of the most hostile country on earth, watching Land Cruiser loads of Yugoslav miners drift by, drinking my expensive water and picking through tailing piles, waiting for the rain, chatting briefly with the ministers (who paid me a social visit on their rounds), and waiting for a ride. It was surprisingly prompt, and interesting.

A Holden wagon pulled over, with a yellow front and white rear, and two Norton bikes in the back bed. The longhaired fork-bearded sun-blistered tattooed driver was still shaking his head, when they came to a stop. His door was held on with rope. His name was Neville, but I didn't get it from him. He never spoke a word to me the entire time I was with them. I got it from her.

From Lee, a most fascinating creature in anyone's book, but even more so in mine: big green Irish eyes, black hair, left shoulder tattoo, gentle, smiling, and deeply in love with everything, and everyone. If Mother Teresa had lived up to her potential, been a bit more compassionate, and worn a leather jacket, Mother Teresa could have been Lee. Although she wouldn't have done anywhere near the same justice, to the leopard skin top and black shorts.

Lee wasted no time in telling me about herself. Mother had played and traveled, with too many paramours for Lee to know which one had been her father. Or maybe even her birth mother.

"Never mind." She said. Meanwhile, Neville had finished shifting enough of the interior around, to make room for me in the Holden. He had bought the car for a thousand bucks in

Adelaide, and this was the test drive home 'up through the guts.'

I noticed a blur in the rear view mirror, growing on the horizon. It was the first running version of Chris I had seen. He had overslept, and now he was trying to overtake.

All we heard was the crash, as he leaped headlong, ass over teakettle, into the space he thought might have existed between the two bikes. It hadn't.

"You know him?" Asked Lee.

"He's a recent acquaintance." I said. "Bit grumpy."

"Not as grumpy as he's going to be." She said. And we looked round to see Neville holding him up at eye level, pack still on his back, with one hand. And we couldn't see where he landed but it was likely quite far, if the Doppler shift of his scream was any indication. I waved my empathy through the rear window, as we pulled away from the tailing piles of dearth.

Lee resumed right where she had left off, relating how she had quit school at fourteen, and biked around Aussie, in an artistic search for life's meaning. I got a quizzical glance, returned a nod, and got back a smile. She was not uneducated, just self-taught. In between the tarot cards and the road signs, she had read the Zen and Sufi classics, and Carlos Castaneda. Her feet may have been firmly planted on the ground, but she allowed her head to float into the clouds. Lee wrote her own poetry, read some, and then recited *Dust Devils* from Aleister Crowley, and memory.

'In the window of the mind arises the turbulence called I.
It breaks; down shower the barren thoughts.
All life is choked.
This desert is the abyss wherein is the universe.
The stars are but thistles in that waste.
Yet this desert is but one spot accursed in a word of bliss.
Now and again travelers cross the desert; they come
From the Great Sea, and to the Great Sea they go.'

293

"There's one other thing you need to know." She said.

"What's that?" I asked.

"I'm a one-man woman." She said, running her hands through her hair, and shaking her head with a laugh. The only deterrent I might have needed, was already receding in the red dust behind me.

Gradually, the ice broke off the corrugated road, and Lee and I filled the grooves with enough enthusiasm for the three of us. At high noon, we stopped at a huge windmill. It was missing vanes, but its rainwater tank was full. Lee pulled everything off and jumped in, motioning for me to follow.

"Beautiful." She said. And she was. I looked at Neville. He shrugged. The tank was big enough to do laps, if you managed to keep your head down. I was coming back in my next life as a shark. In the Outback.

Neville had done his homework before buying the Holden, but it hadn't been enough. The smoke signal was an inauspicious sign, and a message that the adventure would now begin.

"Tranny?" Asked Lee, and Neville nodded. She flagged down three Germans in a rented van, and went down the road to get transmission fluid. Neville and I played chess. He was good. A cab stopped to give us enough transmission fluid to get within twenty miles of Mount Willoughby. We stopped near a sign promoting the local color. *Persons from or traveling to Aboriginal Lands will not be served liquor.* Another game of chess, and an hour later, saw Lee come rumbling back with three more liters of transmission liquor.

We headed out onto the great Northern Highway, lined with burnt out car wrecks, semi tires, beer bottles, and fine red dust. It was a magnificent journey. First, we lost the muffler, and tied the remaining section of the tailpipe to the passenger door handle, when we lost the lights. We stopped to put in more transmission fluid, to retie the exhaust, and to stretch and gaze at the star-speckled empty silence of the late-night desert. Neville plodded along about twenty kilometers an hour, not daring to go any faster on such a miserable track. The night, the boredom and the torpor grew until, finally, just before midnight, we hit the bitumen, and Neville put the pedal to the floor, all the way to Kilgara.

I had a coffee, followed by a Foster's, followed by an offer from the three Germans in the rented van for a lift to 'The Rock,' followed by a shower, and an unsuccessful attempt to sleep. The mosquitoes were voracious and disgusting, and I only got to sleep about four am, under my jacket and the Gold Kazoo.

Lee gave me a big hug this morning, long enough for the message, but not long enough to get me killed. Neville begrudgingly shook my hand, and I left them, richer in opals and experience, in fire and doubt- would I make it back to Sydney in time for my flight? In the red center of my green-eyed experience, I had found the true blue.

'In Australia, not reading poetry is the national pastime.'
Phyllis McGinley

*   *   *

'Australia is the most isolated continent.'
Jared Diamond

The mosquitoes hovering closest to the ground in Kilgara were trained commandos. They broke through the combined heat and thickness of my black jacket and the Gold Kazoo.

My new ride providers were nervous at first, but it may simply have been because of Neville's resemblance to Mel Gibson. There was Claud, a very German mustached systems engineer from Frankfurt, Michael, nursing a painful lost love in Deutschland, and Lothar, a chubby bearded nice guy, with a Teutonic sense of slapstick, if there had ever been such a thing.

"If you smoke, you know, I am low-tar." He said. They had rented the camper van for 'a good deal,' but the close heat inside made conversation very expensive. Our later discovery that the van would only kick over with a push start would be even more disappointing.

It was nearly four pm when the view we had all been waiting for, pulled into the sunset vantage point. A grey overcast sky, the width of the cosmos, shone a diffuse white light stream through a cloud hole. The illuminated pure red coral sand receded into patches of jade green desert scrub, behind which loomed a gigantic mauve sea cucumber. We had made Ayer's Rock.

In 1984, it was not only acceptable to climb the eleven hundred foot sandstone inselberg, it was *de rigeur*, a must for any serious traveler of substance. The aboriginal name, Uluru, hadn't yet caught on, and it was still acceptable to take photographs. I paid the eight bucks it cost for all of us to enter, and we started up, on the hour-long trudge, through the blowflies, and the vertigo. Thankfully, there was a chain to hang onto, but my heart was pounding, and my breath ran off the rock like a violent sirocco. The views from the top were African, almost Namibian, if the German tribute bubbling around me could have been reconciled with the experience.

We took photos, signed our names in the guest book, and made the descent a lot more quickly than we went up. I made a brief diversion through a grove to some aboriginal paintings, but the flies and my own exhaustion drove me back. We were all a little further towards dying, after having to push-start the combie again. Lothar handed me a cold VB, as we drove a victory lap around the lot.

They dropped me seventeen kilometers down the track, at the Yulara village complex. The five-star Sheraton that would open the day I arrived, along with the Four Seasons sister, was designed to close down all the cheaper accommodation a few weeks later, and turn 'the village' into 'the resort.' I paid seven bucks for a bunk in the Ayer's Rock Lodge dormitory, had a welcome shower, and went down to the barbeque area to get something to eat. It cost me three dollars for two hamburgers, and twenty cents for the use of the electric barbeque, but the price of admission also bought me a grill space and a picnic table with two other Canadians.

Phil was a modest Bluenoser with big biceps, who had begun traveling east around the world about a year and a half before I arrived. Uncle Ron was a wealthy well-traveled hardworking 38-year-old Alberta farmer with a subtle sense of humor.

As an American journalist filled us in on the history of the complex, a lean, low-slung white shiny canine slinked through the camp.

"I wonder who that dog belongs to." Phil said. "Should be on a leash."

"Good luck with that one." I said. *"Canis lupus dingo.* Maybe the one that killed Azaria Chamberlain not far from here." And we talked about that in hushed tones.

Phil was excited about the grand opening of the hotel so, knackered as I was, the decision was made to whoop it up in the wop wops. The Sheraton was celebrating with a square dancing party. We escaped to the raucous pub in the Four Seasons. The band was good, and a little rangerette in a white blouse had all the Ockers drooling in their two-dollar beers.

A good time was had. Uncle Ron and Phil and I left after midnight, with the little majorette in tow. She had described her ride home like the images we had formed of the dingo, romantic at the beginning, demonic at the end.

"He had a few roos loose in the top paddock." She said. I gave her my sleeping bag and crashed.

After breakfast with Uncle Ron the next morning, I walked out to Yulara Junction, for my final hitch to The Springs.

I had waited for about half an hour, before a blue station wagon with new plates pulled over. Mark was a 21 year-old Swiss traveler doing Aussie on his own, before returning to the Army, and a job on the railway. He had been driving alone for several weeks, and it was beginning to show. We stopped to pick up dessert melons. He was nervous, suspicious, and very lonely. When he finally dropped me at Eridunda Junction, he came out to the road with me, to share his cold pizza.

A car full of black faces drove by, and I yelled out "Alice!" at them, and turned to hear Mark finish his sentence. He pointed up the road to where they had stopped, and I shouted a goodbye and good luck, as I ran to catch up with the big yellow V8.

I entered a dark ocean of white teeth. They didn't say anything at first, but I was instantly mesmerized by their gestures, a complicated system of finger-pointing and hand actions. When they did finally speak, their language was totally *k-k-ng taka ooah* exotic. But what I truly marveled at, was their ability to drive at such breakneck speed, after consuming one case of beer, and starting in on their second. One came over the seat for me, followed by cigarettes, and another Victoria Bitter. Their clothes hadn't been washed in eons. Their matted hair was streaked with red and blond, and the car was strewn with debris, despite their having just bought it from a dealer, the day before. The drivers name was Noonga, a schoolteacher from Annabella, $400 fortnightly, relaxed and immediately trustworthy. He warned me about the vagaries of the other two, however, whose names I was able to pronounce but couldn't remember, stockman on their way for a wild weekend in Alice.

We finally broke the ice, after a stop for water at Curtin Springs. I showed them my map and told them about *Orion's Cartwheels.* Noonga was from Arnhem Land. He told me the Yolngu story of *two brothers who went fishing, and caught and ate a forbidden fish. The Sun became angry, and sent a waterspout that carried the two brothers and their canoe up into the sky, where they became Julpan, the Orion constellation.*

He asked me about white men, prejudice, and Africa, and acknowledged personal problems, with alcohol, and self-esteem. It was a great ride. I played harmonica and they sang the songs and harmony in return. They were magnificent hosts- they knew every tree, rock and dry riverbed along the way, showed me an eagle eating a dead kangaroo, and entering Alice, demonstrated a quiet pride in the aboriginal presence of its accommodation, schooling, and medical services. They took me all the way down to the Stuart Arms, introduced me to few of the brothers, and shook my hand goodbye, like they meant it. And I checked into the hotel. There was a note for me from Uncle Ron at the desk, and I went up to see how his flight from the Rock had been. As he opened his door, the air-con just about knocked me for a sixer.

"Christ, that was fast." He said. "I've only been here twenty minutes."

"Royal Flying Doctor Service." I said. "Put the billy on."

Bearing the Southern Cross

'When you see the Southern Cross
For the first time
You understand now
Why you came this way.'
Crosby, Stills, Nash and Young, *Southern Cross*

In five days, I had traveled the 1800 miles From Melbourne to Alice, with a diversion to Ayer's Rock. At the stroke of midnight, on the first of December, 1984, I was wide awake in a seven dollar sweatbox, two floors under Uncle Ron's air-conditioning. He had told me earlier that I was insane.

"Why would you try to hitchhike all the way through Tennant Creek and Mt. Isa to Townsville, on a road that sees more camel trains than cars when, for the price of a cheap flight, you could be lying poolside at the Caravella Hostel in Cairns, drinking shandies, and chatting up the Scandinavian girls?" He asked. Writhing in my own perspiration, with a week of the same on the horizon, I began to take his point. The watery diarrhea only assisted. We had consumed a beer in Melba's Piano Bar, after a few lanes in the air-con bowling alley, a beer in the front lounge Abo bar, the old goal, and the Flying Doctor HQ. On a Sunday in Alice, we could have painted the town red, if it hadn't already been there.

"I'm coming with you." I told him next morning. His grin lit up the breakfast nook. A Lebanese taxi driver, off of Todd Street, took us to the airport. A hundred and fifty bucks got me halfway across the continent by two in the afternoon. Where the mangrove swamps had been filled in with dried mud, local sawmill sawdust, and Edge Hill quarry ballast, sat the Caravella Hostel, and Uncle Ron found ourselves poolside, a thousand miles from Ayer's Rock, surrounded by sunshine, young fillies, and good music.

I decided to fall in love with Anne, a 21 year-old corpulent Madonna from Copenhagen, waiting for her Israeli boyfriend to arrive from Townsville. We played with Jasper, a Danish carpenter looking for work, Carolyn, a young girl from Perth, Mike, a Scot on the local dole, Cathy, a marijuana saleslady with absentee boyfriend, John, a Sydney plumber with a penile compass needle, and Liz, an obnoxious Ohio freelance photographer. That night the Southern Cross transfixed the night sky above us.

Ron and I awoke for a greasy breakfast, and the twenty-dollar reef trip. Despite the company of an American loudmouth, the snorkeling was superb. The Michelmas bird sanctuary was our first stop. After sandwiches, we cruised to the outer reef, located in the Coral Sea, visible from outer space, and the world's biggest single structure made by living organisms. I got my flipper caught in a huge clam, and marveled at the parrot fish, sea cucumbers that released red dye, a groper that came after Uncle Ron and I, and clownfish in the anemones. I couldn't believe how brown I had become, in just one day on the then pristine reef, compared the mass bleaching of the coral that would follow, with the pollution, the shipping accidents, the overfishing, and the Crown-of-Thorns starfish invasion.

John and Liz were heading south to Townsville next morning. They invited me to come, I discovered en route, to pay for the petrol.

"That'll be ten dollars, Wink." Said John, at the pump.

Neither he nor I said another word the whole trip, but it wouldn't have been possible anyway. Liz jabbered nonstop, about nutrition and the evils of scientific medicine, for every minute of the entire ordeal. Whatever John was plumbing must have been subterranean. For my ten bucks, they dropped me in the middle of nowhere. It was all good.

A half hour later, an army regular, working in Papua New Guinea, drove me into a place for a drink and a salad roll. A few minutes later I got a lift in a brown station wagon with

Patrick, a 19-year-old station hand from Northern Territory, who dropped me at a petrol station on the other side of Ayr. I waited out the rest of the day there, drinking coffee and trying to catch a ride from the truckies. They told me that hitchhiking had changed forever in Queensland.

"Insurance." One said. "Ratshit for you, ratshit for me."

A Kiwi couple, Steve and Rosie, gave me a lift, after dark.

"We're the wetbacks of the outback." Said Steve.

They were picking tomatoes in Bowen, and took me as far as they were going, the Harbour Lights Caravan Park.

"Home, sweet home." Said Rosie. Twenty bucks got me a trailer, a tin of beans, and some bread and cheese.

Early next morning Steve gave me a lift to the highway. It was two hours before Joe pulled over, in his yellow Torana. He'd been working on contract, as an electrician in Townsville, and was heading down to Keppel Island on his way back to Brisbane. He was good company, and I bought him a beer in the Rockhampton pub, before he dropped me on the outskirts. I was trying to finish my melting cheese sandwich, on the roadside, when a Swiss Ocker stopped to chat, and tried far to desperately to sell me his Land Rover.

"Mate, if I had that kind of money I wouldn't be standing on the side of this fucking highway, would I." And Joe came along to rescue me, an additional 170 kilometers down the track at the junction of Calliope and oblivion, where I spent a couple of hours of solitude, writing poetry on eucalyptus bark, and preparing myself to spend the night.

'On the side of the road one learns the most about which direction to go.'
Jct 1 and 39, Calliope and Gladstone, Queensland, 06 Dec 1984

I read Georgie Sinclair's Haiku, on the back of another road sign.

'Remaining centered
With arms extended
Cartwheel forward.'

303

A brown mirage pulled out of the hazy heat, and the driver kicked open his station wagon passenger door.

"Get in." He said. "We're going to Sydney." Pat had mashed his right hand in a mixer on a station months before, and was going back to New South Wales for 'another op and some compo.' He was in a hurry. We got a speeding ticket in the sticks of central Queensland.

"Outback Australia, huh!" Said the cop.

"A hundred is a poxy fucking speed to drive at." Pat told him.

We blew through the fruit towns with gigantic fiberglass shrines to their main local industry, featuring a 'big banana' in Coff's Harbour, and Woombye, with a giant pineapple.

"We'll stop when we see a giant tinnie." He said.

And we kept at it, driving through the night, past Brisbane, and Surfer's Paradise along the Gold Coast, into New South Wales, and on, and on south.

"Best way for you to have seen this country, mate." Pat said, as we pulled into Sydney. "Manchester with a harbour backdrop."

It was late afternoon, when he dropped me on the other side of the bridge, and I set off in the rain with a Korean cab driver for Beethoven Lodge, a place I'd heard about somewhere, some other time. I checked in, showered and adjourned to the TV room, met Jutte, a blonde Berliner teacher I had known from Lovina Beach. We went down the road for a couple of donor kebabs, and crashed out exhausted.

In the morning I cleaned the tearoom, went up to see the New South Wales Museum, and wandered around King's Cross. It was too much to bear. I called Julie, and she told me how to take the train to Koogarah station. When Mark got home we went out for Lebanese and to see Pink Floyd's *The Wall*. It reminded me of a tragic Chinese poet. On my final day in Australia, I took them out for a seafood platter at Doyle's, and they grilled me a steak for dinner. We partied with friends until three, and then Jules took me out to the airport, a few hours later. I was two hours from Nouméa, and as many flights to Destiny.

'God bless America. God save the Queen. God defend New Zealand and thank Christ for Australia."

*   *   *

'In a way Australia is like Catholicism. The company is sometimes questionable and the landscape is grotesque. But you always come back.'

Thomas Keneally

Australia wasn't that much like Catholicism. But New Caledonia was. Just over nine hundred kilometers from Oz and twelve thousand from France, the archipelago had been named by Captain James Cook, for its resemblance to Scotland. He had obviously been gone a long time.

The native land and sea clans of the Kanaks had been cannibals, but the Catholics were far more dangerous. Like most Papist colonization, they came first for your resources, then your labor, and then for your soul. The French took the sandalwood trees and, when the trade in sandalwood declined, they took their muscles. 'Blackbirding' was a lucrative form of enslavement, and transported tens of thousands of Melanesians onto the sugar cane plantations of Fiji and Queensland. When they were returned, after their 'use by' date, the Marist missionaries began to arrive in the 1840s, to collect what was left. Twenty years later, New Caledonia became a penal colony, and when nickel was discovered in 1864, the circle was joined. When I arrived, there was serious Kanak discord, and even the occasional evacuation from Nouméa, although you would never have know it, by the string section of topless young nubile French girls lying along Anse Vata, in the Grande Terre sunshine. But I hadn't made it there yet.

I was still at the airport, in a bottlenecked queue to get through immigration, then to pick up Serendipity, and then to hitch a lift into town. The first guy took the longest, and dropped me at the turnoff, but the second ride came along inside of three minutes. Her name was Sylvie, a 38 year-old Parisienne schoolteacher, recently divorced, understandably wary. But not enough, I guess. She drove me around the scenic viewpoints of Nouméa, and then home for a shower. The Catholicism kicked back in at dinner. We went to the L'Eau Vive du Pacifique Restaurant, run by the local nuns. The Ave Maria prayer appetizer was a little heavy, but the seafood provençale that followed was magnificent. We left for a Perrier and lime (the water was 26,000 times the price of the limes) at Hotel Vanata, and the casino piano bar, for some quiet entertainment. It was bizarre to speak French after coming from Australia, but lovely to hear it again. I slept in the adjacent room, with the mosquitoes and the heat and the cat.

The next morning we ended up underwater, snorkeling, holding each others hands and breaths. She left me on the beach, while she went to ride her horse. Old men played boules, and naked young lovelies roasted on their imaginary rotisseries, like they were lying on the shore in St. Tropez.

Sylvie returned with a bottle of Beaujolais, and we had a colorful sunset pique-nique of roast beef and smoked fish.

New Caledonia can claim the world's largest tree fern and pigeon and skink and gecko. Because of the differences between the forces of attraction and repulsion that Sylvie and I were experiencing, it also had the world's most unfortunate timing. But that was fine. We still gave what we could to each other, and it was enough.

After bearing the world's most southern croissants next morning, from the 'Praline' patisserie, she drove me into the country for views from a chalet on Mt. Kirigi, and then to the airport, for my flight to Auckland.

And what Kipling had said about Auckland, would equally apply to my Destiny.

Last, loneliest, loveliest, exquisite, apart...

'What heaven brought you and me, cannot be forgotten.
I have been around the world, lookin' for that woman,
Who knows love can endure. And you know it will.
And you know it will.'
          Crosby, Stills, Nash and Young, *Southern Cross*

'It is impossible to imagine a more complete fusion with nature than that of the Gypsy.'
          Franz Liszt

"Are you saying that life came from outer space, Uncle Wink?" Asked Sam.

"Since, we're also in outer space, that goes without saying." Said Uncle Wink. "What I'm saying is even more fascinating. Its not that hard to imagine that, after several billion years within nebular environments, constantly being resupplied with energy and all the necessary ingredients for life, that self-replicating proto-cellular organisms, equipped with DNA, could be fashioned, giving rise to life.

In 1958, physicists discovered clouds of bacteria, over a billion per quart, thriving in pools of radioactive waste directly exposed to ionizing radiation, and radiation levels millions of times greater than could have ever before been experienced on this planet. Prior to 1945, poisonous pools of radioactive waste did not even exist on Earth. The world's first artificial nuclear reactor had not even existed until 1942. And yet, over a dozen different species of microbe seem to have inherited the genes which enable them to survive conditions which for the previous 4.5 billion years could have only been experienced in space.

In 1956 experiments were performed to determine if canned food could be sterilized using high doses of gamma radiation. A tin of meat was exposed to a dose of radiation that was thought to kill all known forms of life, but the meat subsequently spoiled, and a bacterium was isolated.

Deinococcus radiodurans is the world's most radioresistant organism, capable of withstanding an acute dose of ionizing radiation a thousand times more than would kill a human. Known as a *polyextremophile*, D. radiodurans is capable of surviving cold, dehydration, vacuum, and acid and, as the world's toughest bacterium, has earned the nickname, *Conan the Bacterium*."

"So how does it survive the radiation, Uncle Wink?" Millie asked.

"Good question, Mil." Said Uncle Wink. "It turns out that

the DNA in D. radiodurans is organized into tightly packed cartwheels, which seems to facilitate self-repair of both single and double stranded breaks, possibly because of a gene which increases nitric oxide production with increased UV radiation exposure. So maybe the Orion Nebula, and others like it is not only the nursery for new stars, but a life raft for the dissemination of life through the universe. Some scientists think that the radioresistence of D. Radiodurans had a Martian origin, and that it was delivered to us on a meteorite. Others have used the bug as a means of storing information, as hardware that would survive a nuclear catastrophe. They translated the song *It's a Small World* into a series of DNA segments 150 base pairs long, inserted these into the bacteria, and were able to retrieve them without errors a hundred generations later."

"How many bacteria needed to arrive on Earth to have created life here?" Asked Sam.

"One." Said Uncle Wink. "One replicon. But here's the exciting part. We know that prokaryotic bacteria evolved, as some point, into eukaryotic cells, containing a nucleus. The skeletal structure of both kinds of life, is based on the centriole. The primary, ancient function of this organelle is to generate flagella and cilia, filaments used for motility and sensing. However, in animal cells centrioles are also used to organize the microtubule network, a kind of 'motorway' system, used for transporting proteins and important during cell division. And here's the punchline. The shape of the centriole, like the matter and skeletal structure in the rest of the universe 'fractal at all scales,' is a cartwheel, with nine spokes radiating from every symmetrical   centre."

"Why does it have nine spokes, Uncle Wink?" Asked Millie.

"Don't know, Mil." Said Uncle Wink. "Still working on that."

Coromandel Gold

'Kaore te kumara e korero mo tona reta.'
The kumara does not say how sweet it is.
Maori Proverb

Somewhere below me, along the Land of the Long White Cloud, between the Hauraki Gulf to the east and the Pacific to the west, the Hunua Ranges to the southeast, Manukau Harbor to the southwest, and the Waitakere Ranges to the west and northwest, sometime just before midnight, I landed in the City of Sails. Most of my odyssey lay behind me. High Street, Queen Street, Ponsonby and Karangahape Roads, Newmarket and Parnell, and Destiny lay on the other side of the door. Immigration and Customs took five minutes. Agricultural inspection took almost an hour. This, together with the comedian in the shorts and long socks, who had bounced his twin spray cans down the aisle of the plane before we were allowed to move, had been my first introduction to how serious the Kiwis were in preventing any noxious foreign life forms from penetrating their force field. When I breached the door, it was already too late. Green eyes and angelic Antipodean amour, was on the other side.

It took another hour for Robyn and I to get out of the parking lot. She drove us to her new digs at 40 Turakina Road, in Grey Lynn. The old villa belonged to Rosie, a sweet hotel receptionist, and Graham, a quiet, fair-complexioned *cordon bleu* chef, and part owner of the Number Five Restaurant. They welcomed me with a J and G and T's, and the rest of the hospitality alphabet, and Robbie and I nodded off peacefully, into Kiwi land.

The back cover of the phone book that greeted me, on my side of the bed next morning, was a wake up. *In a violent earthquake... In a rising flood... When a bad storm threatens... In an eruption... When a tsunami warning is issued...*

311

I awoke to Vogel's toast and Kiwi butter and Manuka honey, and French pressed coffee with full cream from thick glass bottles. It was a preview of what else was to come- of mussels and scallops and crayfish and snapper and flounder and whitebait fritters, roast lamb and kumara, Nana Pitcon's pickled onions and beets, lemon Paeroa, pavlova, hokey pokey ice cream, and passion fruit and feijoas, and pineapple lumps.

There were a few pineapple lumps at the New Zealand Medical Association next morning, but nothing like the chunky grenades lobbed by their Tasmanian cousins.

"They're a bit of a backwater down there." Said Dr. Cole, an honorable gentleman, and dean of the medical school. He confided cautionary tales of several pretenders who had illicitly acquired registration. The sign outside was also intriguing. *Costley Patients Drop Zone.*

I had already met Debs, Robbie's middle sibling, in Hobart, but that evening I was introduced to her youngest sister, Nikki, just as effervescent, and boyfriend Patrick, a pretentious rich kid studying hotel management, who acted as if he already owned some. The night of the party, at his parent's house in Takapuna, I found out why the term 'North Shore' was more of a marker for money than manners.

We took Nikki's yellow Honda Civic down the road to Huntly for the weekend, to meet Robyn's parents. I took an instant liking to Ron, a quiet, gentle bricklayer with a strong Kiwi joker sense of fair play, and a generous soul. He entertained us on his banjo, with songs a generation older than I would have expected. Ancient vehicles ran on narrow rural roads, and the entire country, in fact, seemed time-warped in the 1950's, or before. All the old codgers were a rugged, industrious problem-solving lot, and there was nothing that couldn't be fixed with Kiwi ingenuity and 'a bit of number eight fencing wire.' Modesty was not only expected, but enforced, through the 'Tall Poppy Syndrome' cure, which involved harsh criticism for *skiting* high achievers.

New Zealanders had no particular use for intellectuals. Their heroes climbed Everest, or played rugby, or rescued sailors, or hunted pigs, or caught the biggest kingfish. They may have been proud of the fact the physicist Ernest Rutherford had been a countryman, but they were still a bit suspicious about that business he had gotten himself involved with. It is now all a bygone age, but I'll always remember it as a better one.

Robyn's mother, Patty, took longer to take to, even though, or because, she doted on me from the moment I arrived. There were no gaps in the conversation, and no question there was no answer for. If anyone veered near one, the answer was simply 'Never mind.'

At the Auckland Medical Bureau on Monday, a delightful well-traveled widow, named Jeanne, put me onto a few contacts for locum work. The medical exam insisted on by the Immigration Department, was performed by Dr. Chunn. It's only because Dr. Chunn is now dead that I can reveal the fact that many of Dr. Chunn's patients had likely ended up preceding him. I'm not sure he had ever actually seen a stethoscope, before he used one on me.

The week passed further into the bureaucratic doldrums, and it was looking more and more that I wouldn't have approval to begin work until after New Year's. We celebrated this by inviting Rosie and Graham and their friend, Vivacious Vivienne, out for Mexican food one Friday night. Robbie and I spent a few days playing Scrabble, stuffing ourselves with the wintergreen guava feijoas off the big tree in the Grey Lynn villa's back yard, and walking the shops of K Road, and beyond.

Christmas was with Ron and Patty, at their *bach* in Port Waikato. Ron had built it from old war surplus and scratch, on stilts, near the dunes on the Tasman Sea. The Port had been an important anchorage during the Maori Land Wars of the 19th century, but the old wharf store was the only latent remnant. We awoke to singing carolers, congregated in the back beds of their *utes,* and the milkman, exchanging our crystal clean glass bottles glinting in the sunlight, for ones of frosted opalescence. We took the dogs for long walks over the sand dunes, played chess with the many Christmas visitors, and went fishing with Ron off the rocks and surf, smoking the kohawai we caught by the carload, with the tea tree we had cut by the cord. Robyn related stories of waking in the night to go floundering by lamplight. We strolled the sunsets on the dunes, and ate well. Patty droned on incessantly, but you could tune out the frequency easily enough. They gave me presents, and a feeling of home I hadn't experienced for years.

Robbie and I hitched back to Auckland with a couple of local sheep farmers and had a beer at the turnoff. They told us they got two dollars for each lamb. We discussed how many they needed to sell, to buy an old car, and how they thought they still lived the good life.

"You don't know how lucky you are." Said one.

The wine steward from Graham's restaurant gave us a ride the rest of way, and the weekend disappeared into vagrancy.

$$* \quad * \quad *$$

'Hitchhikers don't hold hands.'
Robyn, hitching Auckland to Coromandel

Jeanne called from the Auckland Medical Bureau on Monday morning. A doctor named Murty, in Rotorua, was looking for a four-week locum, beginning the second week of January. I gave him a ring, and it turned out precious, long before Tolkien's version had been transported down under.

"Alright Dr. Winkler." He said "We'll see you on the seventh." There was relief in his voice, and in mine.

Robbie and I had decided to spend New Years tramping and camping, in the rugged isolated bush of the Coromandel.

The eighty-five kilometer long peninsula was named for the British Royal Navy *HMS Coromandel*, which had stopped at a

314

harbor here in 1820, to purchase giant spars of native kauri, and was itself named after India's Coromandel Coast. The coast here was dotted with stunning beaches and amazing views. The uninhabited interior was steep and hilly, covered in subtropical rain forest, and backboned by the volcanic vertebrae of the Coromandel Range, rising over half a mile above the ancient colossal contortions of gnarled Pohutakawas, and their crimson clouds of round paintbrush flowers, lining the shoreline below. It was a mystical place born of diggers of gold and kauri gum, and the hippies that followed them, in the countercultural environmental backlash movements of the 1970's.

The four rides it took us, to get as far down as the Thames turnoff, were all different. There was a boilermaker from Manchester, a Maori couple who didn't say a word, a far-to-serious Evangelical, and a plump and pleasant Cook Island lady. We scored a ride on the open wooden flatbed of an old truck, to Thames Junction and, after a cheese and egg salad sandwich and a fruit juice, grabbed a lift with a young local in an old new car to Taurarua Junction. It took one more ride from a vanload of grannies up Torurki Road, and we found ourselves on a gravel track past the *punga* tree ferns along the sunlit river, and the beginning of the trailhead.

The first day's tramp was a trial. We hadn't left Auckand particularly late, but our arrival had been delayed by the vagaries implicit in any hitchhiking endeavor. The hut we were headed for, at Waiwawa, was not that far off, but the path was muddy, claustrophobic and poorly marked, and Robyn and I had taken a few wrong turns along the way. We were hot and tired and closed in by the ferny foliage and the wild goats and the tannic rock pools, and we had only fifteen minutes to spare before sunset, when we found a campsite by the creek. But it was beautiful and calm, and the white noise over the stones of the river made our macaroni and cheese taste sumptuous. Our sleep would be just as delicious, but we sat for a long while, watching the fireflies illuminate the stream bank pungas, and triangulating to the hooting of the tiny *morepork* owls, looking down on us. I smoked a small bowl of green *Amphora* in my meerschaum. It seemed like the right color for the occasion.

When Captain Cook had first anchored off the shores of New Zealand, his crew plugged their ears with wick, at sunrise. The dawn chorus of the world's largest bird sanctuary, with no history of predation, had been that dangerously deafening. Our own dawn chorus was of a lesser decibel level, but no less impressive. And then we had a visitor. He and his brothers from further up the peninsula lived semi-permanently in Waiwawa hut. He had come to tell us that we were camped within a stone's throw of where we had been making for. I asked him why he hadn't thought to provide this potentially valuable information the previous evening.

"You looked comfortable enough." He said. And we broke camp and shared a coffee and some stories in their derelict refuge, just up the riverbed from the rest of the world. They gave us some jerky, and advice about the bogginess on Table Mountain, before we ascended through the dense ferns and Kauris to the Wainora turnoff. It was a marvelous walk after the insecure trail seeking of the previous day and we stopped to admire the streams we crossed, in the shadow of Table Mountain, and the birdsong it emitted. We emerged onto a crowded scene of scores of poorer holidaymakers tents, crammed with the tidings of the season, so we pushed on up the river to our own isolated spot, to ring in the New Year. Beside the reflections of a deep swimming hole in the tree fern grotto, I built a campfire, for warmth and chili con carne. On the other side of the planet, almost an entire day later, tens of thousands of people in Time's Square would have fireworks and champagne and neon and noise. But in the deep interior of the Coromandel, in the company of kingfishers and moreporks and fireflies, beside the large stones of the river, on our hard tent floor, Robyn and I had the happiest New Year's Eve in the world.

Time went slower next day. We had nowhere more special we could go. We made a foray to an old uphill waterfall gold mining sluice, but it was just as delightful to return to our own pool, tent hovel, gas stove, and fireplace. Another *Amphora* pipe full of contemplation took me to an epiphany. I liked this country. It wasn't as materially wealthy as Australia or Canada, but the horizons were enough, and more idyllic, the people seemingly more honest and secure, the pretensions, those that existed, more manageable. I hadn't heard the 'she'll be right' slogan that much, possibly because it already was.

Robyn and I watched the meteors flash across the Southern Cross that night.

"Maybe someday." I said.

"Maybe someday what?" She asked.

"Maybe someday, I'll buy you a place with a gold mine, in the Coromandel." I said. She gave me that harsh glare that Kiwi's reserve for *skiting* high achievers. And the fireflies danced anyway.

On the morning of the second of January, we hiked out and along the Kauraunga River Road. It was raining hard but the walk was invigorating. A camper van stopped to pick us up after about an hour. He was kind enough to drop us at our cheese and egg salad Junction, where, after a modest feed and half an hour in the downpour, a young Milk Board driver took us all the way to Auckland. He said goodbye at the junction of K Road and C U Later.

The day before we were to meet Doctor Murty in Rotorua, Nikki drove us to the bus station, where Robyn and I took a two-hour coach trip to Huntly. We spent the day rummaging through the mementoes of her world trip, and the evening watching telly, and eating fish and chips in a local newspaper, on the living room floor.

❀ ❀ ❀ ❀

317

Sulfur and Molasses

'New Zealand is not a small country but a large village.'
Peter Jackson

I had heard of Rotorua. It was the biggest tourist attraction in the country, home of the Māori of the Te Arawa *iwi*, and an active geothermal area of mud pools and geysers. The lakeshore had been a major scene of skirmishes, during the New Zealand Wars of the 1860s.

In the morning we had planned on getting there by taking another bus, but Robyn miscalculated the schedule, and we ended up hitching. It didn't go very well.

A talkative cow-cocky and his mate drove us to the outskirts of Hamilton, a hippie traveler carpenter and his wife moved us a little further, to where a Jehovah's Witness family a yellow van took us to the Taupo-Rotorua turnoff. This was the 'didn't go well' part.

We stood there for about an hour and a half. It looked like we might not make it in time to meet Murty. Robyn threw stones, when cars refused to stop. This was unhelpful. Finally, Jeff and Nina pulled over, and brought us the rest of the way. He was a tall thin computer jock, with travel tales of questionable authenticity. She was a short fair plump Aussie. They were moving to Rotorua, and took a few minutes to drive past the Māori church and *marae*, the impressive Tudor manor house of the lawn bowling club, and show us around some of the other attractions in their new hometown.

"That's Pill Hill." Said Nina. "Where all the rich doctors live." It didn't look that bad. They dropped us at the Rotorua International Hotel, and I called the doctor to inform him that we had arrived. A few minutes later, a dark thin handsome East Indian, quiet and well-spoken, arrived in a yellow Honda Civic.

"Sati Murty." He said, extending a hand. "I expected you a little earlier."

"We had a little trouble with the hitchhiking." I said. A subtle look of concern drove itself across his face.

"Hitchhiking?" He said, not quite sure he had said it. "Where is your luggage?"

"Here." Robyn said, pointing to Serendipity on my back. The look of concern on his face drove around in circles.

"This is all you have with you?" He asked.

"No." I said, and his look of concern pulled into a parking stall. "This is all I have in the world."

I understood his unease. He was a respected member of the community. His wife and son, Sanjay, had been in India for two months, and he was flying out that day to join them, and leaving his home and car and medical practice to some hitchhiker with all his worldly possessions on his back.

"Don't worry, Sati." I said. I travel a great deal, but I never wander." And he relaxed.

Sati was from Andrah Pradesh, and had trained in New Zealand in Medicine for three years, before opening his practice. He took us to what would become our new home for the next month, a modest rancher with a central patio overlooking the lake. *9 Aquarius Drive.*

"They call this Pill Hill." He said. And he introduced us to Ringo, the cat, and how to feed the goldfish and the video player. We left Robbie to play house, and drove down to the surgery, to meet the staff. It wasn't much to look at from the outside, honeycomb-colored Huntly brick and white painted clapboard, in a tiny shopping plaza. He introduced me to Shirley, one of his nursing sisters, and Marion, his jumpy equestrinanny chain-smoking receptionist. Both quickly tuned me into their stations, and told me to come 'loaded for one of those Canadian bears' on Monday morning.

"You have Wednesday afternoon off, and Thursday night on call." Said Sati. Then he said goodbye, and I drove home, for the first time in my life.

Marion was on fire Monday morning, no-nonsense ironfisted velvet-gloved, no 'mucking around.' Shirley was off, but Sati's other nurse Mary, was excellent, short, petite, still in love with husband Arthur after forty-five years, smile starting to wrinkle, but the beam still strong. The work was stimulating, too much Obstetrics and Gynecology and Pediatrics for my liking, but I saw 27 patients the first day, with a morning and afternoon tea break, and an hours respite, for Robyn's Chinese lunch at home. Rosie and Graham came through on Wednesday, and we went out to a pub with them, and Jeff and Nina, for dinner. My first Thursday night on call, I hospitalized an asthmatic, and met the first of many patients who were to become favorites. Sweet old Mrs. Penny, with her gout slippers, drooping cigarette, and big warm stoic Māori heart, was a delight.

"I'm worried about you smoking too much, Mrs. Penny." I said.

"Too much worry will kill you faster, Dr. Winkler." She replied. At the end of the week, Marion gave me the cash proceeds of my efforts, and I walked into 9 Aquarius Drive, and threw a thousand dollars into the living room air.

Robyn and I settled into our newfound Utopian domesticity, like a sub on the sea bottom. I was the consummate professional, driving my car between suburban practice and lakeside home. Robbie became a model wife, perfecting recipes, keeping house, and taking to the sewing machine like a kamikaze pilot to a carrier deck. In three weeks she had completed as many new projects, a shirt, a pair of pants, and a track suit, punctuated with 'here, try this on' sessions that turned me into a voodoo object d'art.

I had finally unraveled the intricate workings of the mysterious newfangled video device, and some evenings ran through *Casablanca, Blade Runner, Bolero,* and *Chariots of Fire.* Others were filled with playing squash, smuggling our wine into a private spa at the Polynesian Pools, or the twirling white balls of the *kapa haka* poi dances on *hangi* entertainment nights at the THC. It was there I ate my first, and last, mutton bird.

"It needs to decide if it wants to be a fish or a chicken." I said.

We got to know our immediate neighbors, Cecil and May, and invited each other for home-cooked dinners. One night we found a hedgehog in our garage, and named him Bruce. Ringo was rechristened Sniveler, after my cat in Cape Town. On the weekends, we would make daytrips to the Buried Village and other museums, picnic out at the Blue and Green Lakes, or inhale the fire and brimstone of the local geothermal attractions at Whakarewarewa. Hell's Gate. We treaded careful paths through lethal acres of greenish-yellow crystalline talc, penetrated by steam vents and boiling soup and tar pits of plopping thick bubbles of mud. It was in the air, and in our throats. The fumigating monoxide that crept into some motel rooms and killed the guests in their sleep was odorless, but our lives reeked of heated sulfur, and tasted of match heads and gunpowder. Our momentum had moderated into the slow spice of blackstrap molasses.

*   *   *

~ Home Sweet Home ~
09/02/85

'Terrible tragedy of the south seas. Three million people trapped alive.'

Thomas Jefferson Scott

Half the patients in Murty's practice were *Pākehās*, no
different from other white patients of European descent I
had treated in other parts of the world. The men lived lives of
quiet desperation, and the women, or the ones I got to see,
had a spectrum of neuroses that afflicted those who had no
escape from living with those men. And this was paradise.
Mr. Kalomanski was a hyperhypochondriacal Hungarian who
would appear every second day with a new justification for a
permanent sickness benefit. He had the wrong doctor.
Murty's accountant had a variegated obsessive-compulsive
disorder that was hard to keep track of. One of the surgical
registrars laparotomized Mrs. Rogers on just my say so, and
thankfully for good cause, and Mr. Talbott unfortunately
ignored his chest pain for too long, to not wind up in heart
failure. On any given clinic day, I saw the usual parade of
menorrhagias, snotty noses, and runny ears and bowels.

But the most interesting patients to me were the other half.
The Māori had a spunky irreverence, an aboriginal *joie de vivre*,
a calm resignation and playful humor, reminiscent of my
Cape Colored patients, in South Africa. Māori means 'normal'
or 'ordinary,' and that appellation certainly applied to the
men, who presented with the standard ailments of venereal
disease, lower back injuries, and work excuses. Hone Kinita
told me he couldn't work because he had all three. There was
an ex-heroin addict, toughing it out so hard you could feel his
bones grinding. But the most fun was with the aging Māori
women, like Mrs. Penny who, no matter how bad things were
getting, stuck to the deliberate mischief codified in their
cultural playbook.

Mrs. Penny was the culmination of almost eight hundred
years of Eastern Polynesian settlement in Aotearoa. The
mitochondrial DNA evidence that would come to New
Zealand after me, would prove that her ancestors had been

Taiwanese aboriginals, before the Chinese had arrived. The bone samples and rat-gnawed seed cases had dated their first arrival, on the shores north of Dunedin in South Island, to 1280 AD. They came in large ocean-going *waka*, from what they believed was their mythical homeland of Hawaiki, in several waves. Wherever it was from (and I still think it was from Ra'iatea), they wreaked major havoc on the place, after making landfall. It only took them 200 years to wipe out the large moas, killing an average of nine per week, each bird providing a hundred pounds of meat. They burned down half the forest on the islands, flushing them out, and searching in vain for the quick regrowth of young shoots that would have normally occurred on the warmer Polynesian islands they had arrived from. The bitter roots of cabbage trees were baked in *umu-ti* pit ovens instead. The climate cooling that was coming would begin to drive them all north, in pursuit of 36 types of small and sparse food plants, many that required up to a day's cooking time, just to detoxify the poor nutritional value they contained. There was no food suitable for feeding young children. Mothers breastfed their toddlers until they were five. They usually died before they were 30 years old, because their teeth were worn to their gumlines, or from broken bones, or other trauma, or sepsis. Earthquakes and tsunamis reduced their numbers further. In their quest for protein and calories and survival, they took 32 species of birds to extinction, including the giant Haast's Eagle, which preyed on the moa. The fortified pā hilltop citadels and elaborately carved war canoes and meeting houses and *pounamu* weapons and ornaments, that traveled from the Archaic into the Classical period, got there on half-empty stomachs, that would be filled with warfare and cannibalism. The quaint Haka ritual at the beginning of every All Blacks rugby match was the equivalent of saying grace.

Ringa pakia!	Slap the hands against the thighs!
Uma tiraha!	Puff out the chest.
Turi whatia!	Bend the knees!
Hope whai ake!	Let the hip follow!
Waewae takahia kia kino!	Stomp the feet as hard as you can!
Ka mate, ka mate	I die, I die,
Ka ora' Ka ora'	I live, I live
Ka mate, ka mate	I die, I die,
Ka ora' Ka ora'	I live, I live,
Tēnei te tangata pūhuruhuru	This is the hairy man
Nāna i tiki mai whakawhiti te rā	Who caused the sun to shine again for me
A Upane! Ka Upane!	Up the ladder, Up the ladder
Upane Kaupane"	Up to the top
Whiti te rā!	The sun shines!
Hī!	Rise!

The fighting *hapu* units that won the battle of land or *mana* soul-essence, would eat their conquered enemies. The first Pākehā that encountered them didn't take long to figure out why they were picking their teeth, an insult and insinuation that their ancestors had eaten yours.

The Māori had been 'the last major human community on earth untouched and unaffected by the wider world.' The admixture of American and European whalers and sealers and ship deserters, Australian escaped convicts, Christian missionaries, Western diseases, muskets, and exposure to French colonial ambitions didn't make them any prettier. In 1840, William Hobson, acting on a request for protection from a number of these influences, signed the Treaty of Waitangi with 500 *rangatira* chiefs, bringing the two cultures as together as the new colony and their innate differences would allow.

Almost 150 years after her forefather had signed the agreement, Mrs. Penny wasn't allowing me very much.

*   *   *

325

'I've never been to New Zealand before. But one of my role models, Xena, the warrior princess, comes from there.'

Madeleine Albright

Sometimes there are omens that portend the end of domesticity. One evening we got a strange phone call from a Mary in Texas, passing along a message to Sati, that a relative had been committed by the husband, to avoid impending divorce proceedings.

Robyn and I could feel our own remaining time contracting. For me to hitchhike my South Island cartwheel, we would need to become unhitched. Our connubial bliss was taking a beating, and the bruises were beginning to show. In the stagnation of uncertainty, Robyn was finding boredom.

'And then, there was me. I had wound down to neutral. I needed a wash. The Talmud said that there were three gates to purgatory, and one of them was Jerusalem. There I was, in all my aromatic Aramaic glory- waiting for Steve and redemption.'

So that's where we went for the weekend. Jerusalem had been an important *kainga* fishing village on the Whanganui River, where a Catholic mission had been established in 1854. Thirty-eight years later, Suzanne Aubert had founded the congregation of the Sisters of Compassion. By the time that Robyn and I had arrived in Sati's yellow Honda, the sisters had left town, and taken it all with them.

The day had started well enough, at the cerulean splendor of Huka Falls. On through Tongariro, it began to rain. When we passed through Raetihii, I decided I wanted to drive and, by the time we reached Jerusalem, the flax had unraveled. The place was also known for the community that the deranged poet James Kier Baxter had formed there in 1970, and where he was buried. *And so these two old fools are left, A rosy pair in the evening light, To question Heaven's dubious gift, To hag and grumble, growl and fight: The love they kill won't let them rest, Two birds that peck in one fouled nest.'*

326

'I thought of our strange lives, the grinding cycle
Of death and renewal come full circle,
And of man's heart, that blind Rosetta stone.
Mad as the polar moon, decipherable by none.'

We continued to Puripiki, and along the Wanganui River further into Taranaki. The atmosphere lightened a bit but driving north again the rain returned. We finally stopped in some motel flats for a thirty-dollar silent night, and next morning it was a long quiet drive to the Cape Egmont lighthouse, New Plymouth, Ohura and the other depressed towns on the way back to Rotorua.

Sniveler was my only friend and companion that evening until just before midnight, when Robyn told me that she didn't want to go back to Auckland. And, for a while longer, we were fused and welded and bonded and one.

On the last Thursday I took my clinic staff out for the lunch smorgasbord at THC. We arrived back in Marion's car a little tipsy, to find several patients waiting, with chest pain.

It was a nice balanced lifestyle but it ended far too quickly. Sati had called from India, and asked if I could work an extra week, but he made his first flight connections, and Robyn and I, after a farewell libation at Cecil and Mays, melted into Robbie's cousin's car, and decamped to Leanne and Dave's trailer on Blue Lake. We were gutted, having risen so quickly to an apex of quintessential domestication, only to have it all dashed by the return of this interloper. It had all been an illusion, of course. One doesn't acquire that happy a trail's end, without the sweat and dedication in accomplishing the long rocky ascent. Still, it gave us a horizon, and a benchmark.

We spent two days above the rhyolite and pumice bottom of the Blue Lake bed, playing chess, and enjoying family barbecues. Ron and Patty arrived with their Japanese exchange student, Shoko, Robbie's aunt and uncle, Nettie and Albie, and all the children that had come after.

Destiny and I took an evening walk around the lake, listening to the tuis and the serenity, whispering nothings, and watching a wasp make off with a dragonfly's head.

I had arranged another weeklong locum with Ish Morar, and called to confirm it with him, before we all drove, watching the pungas go by, up to Mount Maunganui, for the weekend. It was a full two days, visiting the Sinclairs on their Kiwi fruit farm, losing at billiards and eating ten dollar dinners at the RSA after climbing The Mount, and breaking even at just more game of Boggle with Nettie. Albie and Leanne drove us back to Rotorua late Sunday.

The week went quick. Ish also had a house overlooking Lake Rotorua but it wasn't like Murty's. His practice was more central, downtown in the Plunkett building, and he hadn't cultivated a clientele. I attended a Kiwi guy's reactive lymphadenopathy, a Canadian girl's conjunctivitis, an Australian girl's flu, a Maori girl's hemangioma, a Singapore girl's anorexia and insomnia, and a Rotoruan girl's breast abscess. We had dinner with Cecil and May, for old time's sake. At the end of the week, Ish took us to the highway, where we caught a lift with an old matron to Hamilton, a busload of river runners to Huntly, where Ron and Patty took us the rest of the way back to Rosie and Graham's, in Grey Lynn. We spent a weekend on the hippie isle retreat of Waiheke, with Terry and Lydia and their cat, Mata, at Hekerua House, with Paul and Meg for an Italian dinner at 'Our House,' and eating peaches off the trees, on a country road on Onetangi Beach. They tell me the place has changed.

The Waters of Greenstone

'If it would not look too much like showing off, I would tell the reader
where New Zealand is.'

Mark Twain, 1897

It had been 1661 days since he first drove me across the
Mexican border to Tijuana, 1114 days since he arrived in
Israel, and 740 days since he came to visit me in Denmark.
Emerging from the gate of UTA 582 from LA was Steve of
the Jacuzzi, a little balder, a little older, and fully geared up to
help me finish the Final Cartwheel. His arrival was a
prophetic reminder of two worlds in collision. The world I
currently lived in was a green lush fern and water world, a
world of love and trust and simplicity, responsibility without
cross-references, a family world, a tea cozy and too cozy
world, a world without avarice or nuclear weapons.

The older white and cold world I would be heading back to,
and had come from, flooded the tarmac with speed and
strangers, pretentious display and concreted conquest,
Kentucky fried confusion and Midas muffled abstraction. It
was a world, unreal and ungentle, insincere and insecure.
Steve and I hugged like the brothers we were, and I took him
back to Rosie and Grahams, for Robyn's roast lamb dinner.
There was kumara on his glasses. He liked it.

Early next morning Steve and I hoisted our packs, and
hitched our first ride, with a reproductive physiologist to
Papakura. An English 'manager' took us through Huntly, to
the other side of Hamilton, where a Dutch grape farmer got
us to the driver of a seven-ton truck, and Lake Taupo, where
our luck ran out.

We watched the cars drive by in droves, while we ate our fish
and chips. A Dutch couple with a three-legged dog took us 3
miles out of town, and we walked and walked along the lake

and setting sun and rising moon to complete exhaustion and ice cream and peaches and an eighteen dollar cabin, at the Windsor Motel, in the center of nowhere.

To our northeast bubbled hot springs with *extremophile* microorganisms, capable of surviving in exceedingly hot environments. Each of the two torrid suns setting over Taupo that night, had their own revolving planet. Revolutions of past perfect, or past imperfect and future conditional. Two worlds in collision.

In the morning Steve awoke with a low-grade fever, and diarrhea. We walked down the road apiece from Waitahanui, and set up our thumb stand. A logging truck soon rolled to a stop in front of us and took us twenty-five kilometers down the road to Turangi-Taupo. We watched him remove his hubometer, roar off down a logging road and waited patiently for a couple of hours, as the sheep fornicated obliviously in the adjacent pasture.

We needed a change of scenery, and hiked to the next petrol station. An American girl named Robyn invited us into her old villa, for tea and to meet her cynical boyfriend, Austrian Joe. When they hitched off to the dentist in Taupo, Steve and I settled in, feeding the horse, nibbling on meat pies, and clocking the hours. It was about three in the afternoon that a local friend of theirs piled us in the back of his truck, and rattled us, and his *dags*, down the Turangi road to pick up one of his mates, and back down to almost where we started, near our original petrol station.

"What was that all about?" Said Steve.

"If it wasn't sex. It must have been companionship." I said.

It was getting later and colder. The sun had dropped, the wind had whipped up, and it seemed as if we would be sleeping in oblivion that night, continuing our roadside ketchup travel tales of the grey blowing afternoon. And then it happened in a green blurred instant.

Dave the Knight Rider, swerved his brand new lime Citation in a 180° return pass, a man of character and conscience and

330

magic right foot. He had just flown up from Napier to buy his 327 Special in Auckland, for $7500, and was now making for Otaki at just under light speed. He made a tiny perturbation to pick up dazzling Dave the Younger, tweaked the heavy metal in and around the sound system, and beamed us all into hyperspace through Tongariro's desert downpour, blasting sonic booms back into the clouds along the way. We stopped for burgers and that's about all, and found ourselves perched over a beer in Otaki's Railway Hotel three short hours later.

When the bus to Wellington failed to materialize, Dave was outraged at the implausibility of it all. We piled back into the gunship and, after collecting three of his mates and a case of beer, teleported down to Wellington, in less than an hour. The ferry to Picton had already departed, so he helped us find the Rowena guesthouse, and flew off into the darkness and out of our lives forever. Godspeed, but he really didn't need it. Dave the Younger, Steve and I ended up in Rowena's triple room, everyone Grateful Dead for the Knight and the night ride.

Steve and I left Dave the Younger dead on the floor next morning, to make the ferry to the South Island. It rolled and pitched and yawed our newspaper and breakfast. Our views of the Marlborough Sounds were watered down. We raced out of Picton to the motorway, south to Christchurch, in our mission to see Frank and Bev, who we had met almost three years earlier, in Athens. But that would be the wrong direction.

An old farmer, his dog, Radar, and a radio crooning Country and Western, stopped long enough to transport our hopes to the near side of Blenheim, long before it would become the wine capital of the country. Its main agricultural commodities were still wheat, and the compost produced from dead hitchhikers. The decomposition was well underway, after the five hours that Steve and I stood where we had been abandoned. We walked into the nearby Fawlty Towers motel restaurant out of desperation, and hunger. I had forgotten about Steve's culinary capriciousness. He couldn't decide what he wanted.

"Steve." I said. "They have curry and rice, and rice and curry. You can't go wrong." I forced him into a hesitant commitment. We ended up in Newman's Coach Depot, and placed a call to Frank and Bev, to let them know we would be late. As it turned out, they were away for the weekend, and there was a bus leaving for sunny Nelson, in the other direction, at 6:30 pm. And we were on it, weaving a pastoral tapestry through the mountains. The sun went down, Steve wasn't far behind, and I was left with the thrill of a new direction on an old road. Nelson was the second oldest city in the country, and named in honor of Horatio's exploits at the Battle of Trafalgar, thirty-six years earlier. The first immigrant ships of the London-based New Zealand Company had arrived in 1841, claiming more accommodation than they had actually purchased from the local Māori. This resulted in the Wairau Affray, where 22 settlers died. Steve and I were too tired for any of that, and settled for the iconic Queenslander architecture of the Metropolitan Hotel, a shower, and a Speight's or more, in the pub downstairs. Steve carried on a passable conversation with a new deaf mute mate, until he couldn't. Until we were eaten quickly by our pillows.

*   *   *

'If the people of New Zealand want to be part of our world, I believe they should hop off their islands, and push them closer.'

Lewis Black

Ao*tea*roa. That's what the sign said. *Land of the Long White Cloud.* It was painted on the bottom of an interior wall of a rust-colored rammed earth house, with two white-trimmed windows half-open to an expansive view of the Marlborough Sounds. The window latches were those beautiful old brass sliders with the thumbscrew stops. The mural shone on the side of a shop in the morning sun, as we headed out of town. We left late, because Steve had to call home to confirm his identity, and we had run out of money. It was hard at first.

After a manic hike through Nelson's outskirts, we picked up a short ride to the beach. A tattooed young Shiela, who 'always picks up hitchhikers,' took us to a printer in an old Hunter, who took us back to Richmond, on his march through the South to Appleby.

And then it suddenly got easy. Dave the Younger had just gone by for the second time when a Maui van containing a couple of Aussie physiotherapists, Italian Eddy and Viterie, pulled over to the rescue. It was an enjoyable day, crisscrossing the island, swimming in the cool ocean, and almost running out of petrol. We stopped for a drink and to take a photo of a cutout of an old gold rush digger with his thumb out, in Westport, before continuing south across the Buller River, down State Highway 6. After several detours, along magnificently expansive white wave-cresting beaches to the Pancake Rocks, the Aussies said goodbye. They had left us in a land that was literally founded and foundered on the rocks, first Māori *pounamu* jade, then gold, and then coal. South Island had originally been known as Te Wai Pounamu, *The Waters of Greenstone.*

They had left us in a land of sandflies, a romantic word for the black fly assassins related to my own youthful torment, in Northern Ontario. The Māoris had been more acquiescent to these clouds of bastards, and even had a positive spin legend for why they should have some respect. *When the god Tu-te-raki-whanoa created Fiordland, the landscape was so stunning, that people stopped working. They just stood around gazing at the beauty instead. The goddess Hinenuitepo became so angry that she created the sandfly, to get them moving.* I wasn't buying it.

They had left us in the land of the west coast wind, which

was the only way I could tolerate the sandflies. We had almost given up all hope, when a diesel mechanic offered us a ride in his Land into Greymouth. Brett droved us past large coal trains, via an off-road slip that had demolished a coalmine. Twenty-five years after Steve and I went through, an explosion here would trap 29 miners. That had been initial hope that, with the employment of the same sophisticated technology that had just rescued a similar number of Chilean copper miners, they could all be saved. After all, this was New Zealand, and we weren't racist or anything, but if the Chileans could pull it off, how hard could it be? But this wasn't a copper mine. This was a coalmine, with methane gas. A second explosion probably killed them all. If the Kiwis hadn't already had a Gallipoli, this would have been it.

Brett dropped us at the Greymouth Cobb & Co., a California gold miner '49er kind of eatery and watering hole. We sauntered through town, until we found a charming little guesthouse named the Westhaven.

"Don't mind the bugs." I thought I heard him say.

"No mate." Said Pops. "Bunks. Looks like you've already met the bugs." After a shower, Steve and I went down to the King's Court Motel, for dinner. I asked the waitress what the go was.

"I'd have the fisherman's basket." She said. I nodded.

"And for you?" She turned to Steve. The menu was two pages. I just hung my head, while Steve begin his pilgrimage through the ingredients of every dish he didn't understand. She began to look around at her other tables, and the exits.

"Two fisherman's baskets." I said. "And a bottle of Cook's Chasseur." Steve was offended at my rudeness but, for my part, I thought that if he hadn't developed a more efficient way of determining his preferences, or some proficiency in decisiveness, he should had at least realized that even moves in chess have time limits.

Ultimately, he was not disappointed. Two huge steaming baskets, spilling over with scallops and mussels and fish and whitebait, with chips and salad, landed on our shores. They didn't charge us for the wine or the pavlova. We played pool with the locals, and dreamed, like you can only dream after an overdose of seafood.

Pops had prepared breakfast for us around 7 am, and we had to rush to catch it. He apologized for not having sausage. We apologized for being late, and paid him.

"Good as gold." He said. And it had been. We were back out on State Highway 6 for less than five minutes, when Chris came along in his combie. He was a Telecomm technician from Melbourne, and took us down to the Franz Josef glacier, the legendary frozen trail of tears of a Māori maiden whose lover had been swept away by an avalanche. Nice. The year Steve and I were there, its rate of advancement was ten times that of other typical glaciers, over two feet a day. It is now receding. No more tears.

Chris let us off in Fox Glacier, where Steve and I checked into the Fox Glacier hotel, and walked up across the swing bridge and the climb along Glacier Road to the terminal face of a monstrous ice field. The brown triangular sign we walked beyond, had bold yellow letters. *AREA UNSTABLE DANGER*. A hundred tons of ice fell on two Aussie girls in 2009. It is still advancing, Australia fair.

We hitched a lift back with an English couple to the Ngai Tu walk, a peaceful hike with waterfalls and a little rifleman that came out to greet us.

Steve and I returned to the guest lounge of the Fox Glacier Hotel, in the mists of the late afternoon. We ate cheese and *bickies*, and sipped our *Steinies*, spellbound by the long white clouds, coming down from the mountains. Just as they made it to ground level, she made her entrance into the lounge.

"I'm allergic to cheese and onions." She said, to no one in particular, although Steve thought she was looking at him, the way that I thought she was looking at me.

*   *   *

335

'When nationalities have traits, the women are always worse.'
Priscilla Figbottom

That wasn't her name, of course. That's just the name Steve gave her, in case something exotic happened, to keep it light. In the 17th century, a horse was regarded as 'figged,' if it carried its tail well and its back end moved lively, after ginger had been applied to the relevant parts. In Priscilla's case, watching her move, the name may not have been misapplied at all.

She had been working as a Jillaroo in Australia for three years, and had that freckled ruddy, dilated, healthy glow that transplanted English girls seem to develop in warm countries. Lucky horse, I thought.

First contact actually came next morning, as Steve and I were singing golden oldies at our hitching post on State Highway 6. Her cherubic smile figged over to wish us luck, but it was for naught.

We didn't get a ride at all that day, except from Italian Eddy and Viterie, who took us down Glacier Road for a change of scenery. Steve and I had a game of chess, spoke to a hard luck Christchurch lady, living in a bus down a park road with four dogs, whose boyfriend was painting the Vacation Hotel, and slapped at the sandflies until 3 pm, when we gave up and strolled back into town. The manager of the Vacation Hotel had been friendly earlier in the day so we checked in, did some laundry, played the piano, and ate an early dinner of smoked salmon, venison ragu, and a glass of claret, in the restaurant. Steve and I went over to the Fox Hotel club to play pool. Priscilla was sitting with Kay, an Aussie musicologist, and Jo, an older French woman, and the owner of the Fox Hostel, who was allowing the ladies to sleep on the floor of his house, as well as shouting all the rounds. Priscilla told us of the glowworm grotto.

"Its like a Bob Dylan concert." She said, and Steve seemed to have developed a sudden and uncharacteristic interest in entomology. But it was not to be, because I told Steve we were committed to getting out of Fox next morning, and he needed his rest. He wasn't happy.

We checked out next morning just after dawn and burned out to the highway in an attempt to catch the first ride. The one lone Caltex pump at the petrol station was one more pump than any ride we would see. We had bet Priscilla a beer that we would make it to Queenstown by that evening. When she came down to check on us later that morning, we made a mutual decision to abort and catch the bus.

When it pulled into the hotel, Allison seemed to want to sit with me, but Steve grabbed the front seat beside her. He ended up delivering the mail for the driver, which turned into a frequently comical task, considering the rainfall squalls south of Fox, although didn't seem to have dampened his ardor much. We stop for some fried fish, changed drivers, and motored into Otago and spectacular sunny views of Lake Wanaka and further south. With a brief diversion into Arrowtown, and two more driver changes, one in the middle of nowhere, we finally pulled along Queenstown Bay on Lake Wakatipu, the mountain backdrop of Remarkables precisely named, and into Queenstown at dusk.

A three-man cabin in the motor camp was perched up a steep hill. Steve rearranged the furniture, and we showered and set off into the town center to find some tucker. Priscilla's allergies to cheese and onions seemed to have been cured by the Mexican food at Saguaro's. We paid, and walked through the picket line, and into the raucous bar at the Mountaineer, and then Ekhart's for final jug, before returning home to a troubled sleep. While Steve worked on the rivets with his snoring, my own respirations were stuffy from a cold, and Priscilla's breathing was too close for comfort.

She made porridge and coffee for us in the morning, before Steve and I left to book the 'triple thriller' helicopter ride, jet boat, and class three rapids rafting trip for the day after.

We meandered through the mall, changing money, trying on hats, and checking out the details of the Routeburn trek. We met Priscilla an apple and spiced crepe and coffee, and I escorted my cold back to the bunkroom, to crash for a couple of hours.

I awoke to find Priscilla preparing dinner, after which she and Steve went out for the evening to pan for Queenstown gold dust.

My nose, plugged with rubber cement, didn't let me sleep at first, and Steve's snoring woke me later. Priscilla was rustling her sleeping bag and giggling at Steve's grunting almost as loud.

"You okay?" I asked.

"Can't sleep." She said. Oh. Sweet Jesus.

And I found out how the two Aussie girls felt, when the hundred tons of ice fell on them.

Steve and I exchanged glances in the mirror, while shaving next morning.

"You were in fine form last night, old buddy." I said, trying to break some of the glacial ice.

"So were you." Said Steve. And we both laughed so loud, I was almost sure that she had heard us.

After a pancake breakfast, Steve and I were informed that the 'triple thriller' we signed up for had been reduced to a 'double delight. Something about the jetboat operator needing an operation of his own. We were driven to the helipad on the Shotover River. The pilot flew us over Skippers Canyon, upstream to Arthur's Point, where Shania Twain would later buy up most of the countryside, and over the rapids we were about to run.

We changed into our wet suits, life vests and helmets, and were given a quick briefing on left and right paddle, digging in, high siding, and the white water position, by our guide, Hamish. He warned us about the pitfalls of each four sets of rapids we would run: *Mother, Jaws, Oh-shit rock,* and *The Tunnel.* Cascading between the rocks he told stories three fingered

Pete, Circular rock, and the Shotover itself, the second-largest gold bearing river after the Klondike. We passed a dredge barge was still earning $2 million a year, and finished through the 560 foot Oxenbridge Tunnel, a failed attempt by the brothers it had been named after, to divert the river to recover the alluvial gold on the bottom.

I went off to find a chicken and oranges, and returned to the bunkhouse to cook dinner. We ended up in the Mountaineer that evening, but I didn't get home until after midnight, and had to wake Steve to get in.

Our last day in Queenstown was set aside for provisioning ourselves for the Routeburn trek. Steve and I bought toques and gloves, boot socks, film, and freeze-dried food. In the afternoon we met Priscilla for a cruise on the snow white 'Lady of the Lake,' the *TSS Earnslaw*, a 1912 coal-fired steamship with teak furnishing, brass portholes, and a bright red forty foot funnel, out of which belched voluminous amounts of black smoke. We were issued period songbooks, and sang ourselves around Lake Wakitipu in Edwardian style.

Steve took us out to the Ming restaurant for a delicious meal of pork and cashews, scallops and vegetable, and beef in black bean sauce. Later than night, when he began belching voluminous amounts of the right sound, Priscilla had another attack of insomnia. It took most of the night to remedy, and restore her healthy glow.

*　　*　　*

'Cross that rules the Southern Sky!
Stars that sweep, and turn, and fly
Hear the Lovers' Litany: -
'Love like ours can never die!'
Rudyard Kipling, *Collected Poems*

The bus driver was a '*dag.*' The term actually referred to the feculent material hanging off a sheep's back end, but only the Kiwis would have turned it into an affectionate appellation for a character with exceptional personality.

The motor camp proprietress *shouted* us all breakfast next morning. While Steve and I hustled his pack down to NZR, to meet us in Te Anau, at the end of the Routeburn, Priscilla toddled about in a fog, and almost missed the bus.

The driver related his version of the Māori legend about the formation of Lake Wakitipu.

"The giant that had been killed by a hero warrior, left his heart at the bottom of the lake, beating the three-minute periodic rise and fall of the water line." He said. "And the rest of the Māoris sat around in their Mark IVs, drinking their DBs to celebrate." In the PC world of today, he would have lost his job, quick smart, but in 1984, it was just innocent Kiwi humor.

We carried on for forty-five kilometers, down the winding road from Queenstown, to where Peter Jackson would film Isengard, from the first book of *Lord of the Rings*, a quarter century later. He told us how to predict the weather in Glenorchy.

"If you come out of the pub and you can see the hill, it's going to rain." He said. "If you come out of the pub and you can't see the hill, it's raining." We stopped briefly in Kinloch at the northern end of the lake, and the eastern side of the Southern Alps, 'to feed the sandflies,' before he finally dropped us at the roads end, to begin the Routeburn Track.

Across the swing bridge, it was marvelous to be on the trail again, Serendipity on my back, blood and river running in the sun, trying to keep up through the red and mountain beech leaves. Up a gently rising sidle over Sugarloaf stream and under the Bridal Veil waterfall, we climbed steeply above the gorge to the site of an old blacksmith camp, at Forge Flats. The only sounds that kept up with my breathing were the bellbirds and my heartbeat- up, up, up- stopping for fantails and icy aquamarine pools and mountain views. The valley opened up and recrossed the Routeburn, where Pricilla and I sought refuge from the sandflies in an embrace, past Eagle

Bluff and Emily creek, where a major slip would slide an entire beech forest from around our footsteps two years later. But there were still no clear views of Mt. Somnus and Mt Momus, and we ascended steadily towards the Routeburn Falls Hut.

We got bunks, had a wash in the sink, and chatted with the other two trampers- Goliath, an American Rockwell engineer, tossing it in for the grand tour with a two hundred-pound pack, and a Danish-speaking Briton. I sat to draw for a while and then put on the freeze-dried lamb and peas. The trampers were entertaining a lone kea outside who was too busy with their offerings, to care about dismembering our boots. The sunset and stars over the Routeburn Valley were breathtaking, otherworldly in the truest sense of it, and I showed Steve and Priscilla the *Te Punga* Southern Cross, anchoring *Tama-rereti's waka* Milky Way, with the two Pointer stars as his rope. And a familiar companion, still inverted.

The track become narrower next morning, climbing under bluffs as it edged around Lake Harris. There were vistas up the 'Valley of Trolls' towards the Routeburn source of Lake Wilson, and the Serpentine Range. Step by step, we ascended into the chamomile and azure colors of the Harris saddle, the border between the two National Parks of Mount Aspiring and Fiordland. At an altitude approaching cobalt, our horizons stretched far into the ether of the surrounding Humboldt ridges and ranges. We climbed the 5000 foot peak of Conical Hill and I was back in the Nepal, above the clouds, reaching out to touch the stone cairns and snowcapped timeless backbone of the universe, eye to eye with my soul yet one more time.

We descended the western aspect sadly, as all descents are, stopped for some trail mix and an orange, and turned onto the track southwards, traversing the Hollyford face, with expansive views out to Martins Bay and the Tasman Sea. They flanked us on our right for the next two hours, until we climbed a ridge for a vertiginous panorama of jade and emerald Lake McKenzie, and a descent on a steep chain of zigzags to a bunk in Lake Mackenzie Hut. I was overcome with a sudden unexpected urgency of inner rumblings that resulted in an unsuccessful running descent for the shelter's long drop. It was a gorgeous place, though, nestled between the sunlit mountains and a gemstone lake, and the days trek accomplished by three tired Routeburners.

A circus of six cheeky keas played a game of noisy tag on the roof, when they weren't undoing the shoelaces on Steve's boots, or stealing food out of our pack. As much fun as the antics of these mountain clowns were to watch, and as beautiful as their alpine parrot olive-green and yellow and red and black and blue and brilliant orange colors made them, keas were two pounds of curved beak and clawed mischief. Only forty per cent of them would live to see a year, although there were some that made it over fifty. Perhaps if they hadn't been hardwired to tear apart the rubber parts of cars, steal passports, and rip the fat from under the woolly backs of sheep, they might not have been as endangered. They were still year off receiving the full protection of the law, and even the ranger was throwing rocks at the ones on our hut.

"How'd they get their name?" Steve asked.

"Ke-a... ke-a... ke-a." They cried.

"Oh." Steve said.

"Eats, roots, shoots and leaves." Said the ranger.

"Kind of like my buddy here." Said Steve. The keas continued their keaing outside the hut, we all played rummy in the evening under the hurricane lamp, and Priscilla nuzzled in, when the stars took over later.

Sunrise on the peaks set us off at a phenomenal pace, playing tag across a small flat, climbing to the bushline, and descending beyond the ribbonwood 'Orchard,' dodging the six hundred foot spray of the Earland Falls, and dancing with the sandflies at Howden hut. We all caught up with each other at Key Summit, and tramped down together to the Milford roadhead at the Divide. The weather was changing quickly in the Hollyford Valley, and we flagged down a lift with a vacationing couple from Hastings, just in time. Harry was an ex-logger turned cray fisherman, and his dog, Fred, was much quieter than his wife seemed to be. They drove us through the fog of sandflies, to what Kipling had called the eighth wonder of the world. Milford Sound was all that. We made the one o'clock sailing of the SS Milford Haven, along the steep 4000 foot cliff faces, the fifteen-kilometer length of the fiord, past the peaks of Mitre and the Elephant and the Lion, Stirling and Lady Bowen Falls, and hundreds of temporary cascades, fed by rainwater-drenched moss, some never reaching the bottom, drifting away in the wind, some falling skywards in the updrafts. Milford was one of the wettest places in the world, with over twenty feet of rainfall a year. The rain came down like the cliffs went up and, except for the odd basking seal and the bored Captain's commentary, it could have been the planet's largest cold shower.

We stopped for kiwifruit ice cream on the three-hour bus ride to Te Anau. All the accommodation was booked out, except for the dorms at the motor camp. Steve picked up his pack at the bus hut, and played a few games of snooker at the pub, before returning to the snoring trolls in our bunkhouse. In the middle of the night, I stole outside, and under the Milky Way and an upside down Orion and the Southern Cross, Priscilla and I said goodbye.

'Oh to owe not anyone nothing
to be not here but here forsaking equatorial bliss
who walked through the callow mist dressed in scraps who walked
the curve of the world
whose bone scraped whose flesh unfurled who grieves not
anyone gone to greet lame the inspired sky
amazed to stumble where gods get lost beneath the Southern Cross.'
                    Patti Smith, *Beneath the Southern Cross*

Glowing Skies

'The United States invented the space shuttle, the atomic bomb and Disneyland. We have 35 times more land than New Zealand, 80 times the population, 144 times the gross national product and 220 times as many people in jail. Many of our big cities have more kilometers of freeway than all of New Zealand, our 10 biggest metropolises each have more people than all of New Zealand, and metropolitan Detroit has more cars on the road than all of New Zealand. So how come a superpower of 270 million got routed in the America's Cup, the world's most technically oriented yacht race, by a country of 3.5 million that outproduces us only in sheep manure?'

Eric Sharp, 1995

Steve found it in the Southland paper that someone had left on the bus. We had left for Invercargill just before noon, and there was no mistaking the enthusiasm in his voice.

"It's going to be in Bluff today!" He said. "Where the hell is Bluff." Which only started the bluff series of jokes.

"It's twenty miles from Invercargill." I said. "What's going to be there?"

"The Enterprise." He said, hardly able to contain himself.

"The aircraft carrier or the starship?" I asked, thinking he may have just started to slip a bit.

"Neither." Said Steve. "The Enterprise New Zealand."

"Which is?" I asked.

"Which is Digby Taylor's racing sloop entry in the America's Cup." He said. "I guess you don't get out much." And then he realized how silly that sounded. I called his bluff.

"So, let's say that we actually get to Invercargill, and let's say we can actually find a very expensive taxi, to take us to the Enterprise, and let's say it hasn't left, and let's say that the esteemed Mr. Taylor agrees to take us on this trip. Then what?" The driver was droning on about 10 sheep per acre, the Winton lady who pierced babies' fontanels, and the size of the trout caught by the Mossberg shopkeeper's son the previous day.

"Then we ride." He said. And it was so.

After the Routeburn, Invercargill descended on us like New York, with its mile of car dealers and late Georgian architecture. We cruised down Esk Street, looking for the government tourist bureau, finally finding out there wasn't one, and dropping into Thomas Cook, where we found out that, yes, the Enterprise was in Bluff and a taxi would cost us twenty bucks. We paid it and the chubby driver's unceasing commentary ran through profound insights into the Homestead and Paradise Escorts, eventually arriving at the mast of the Enterprise. We got Digby Taylor at the helm, no life jackets, and two hours of hanging on for dear life - out through the rip beyond the Foveaux Strait oyster fleet, and eight-foot swells around Dog Island. My head position, in the navigation room picture, was at a serious angle. The return leg was sixteen knots, smooth as silk and blinded with sunlight off the port side.

"They may give us a run for our money." Said Steve. "But we've got more money."

"Sometimes money doesn't buy you happiness." I said.

"The America's cup has nothing to do with happiness." He said. And who was to know.

A clockmaker gave us a ride back into Invercargill, where Steve was interviewed by a local newsman.

"What did you think of your first trip aboard a world-class yacht?" He asked.

"Excellent." Said Steve. "And I'm not even from New Zealand."

The second treat of the day was the Railway Hotel, a turn of the century red and white Italianate, Queen Anne, and Dutch-influenced Baroque Revival hybrid gingerbread ornament, itself worth the trip to Invercargill. Mrs. Gerrard greeted us warmly, and gave us incredibly cozy Edwardian rooms on the second and third floor, after delicately expressing her envy at our Enterprise trip. After a bath and a change of clothes, Steve and I met the bartender, Mitch, in an exquisitely decorated bar. He showed us his sailing memorabilia and I played some jazz on the baby grand, before a delicious meal of smoked salmon, *steak au poivre* and cherry cake. The house red left something to be desired but, after the events of the day, there wasn't much more to be desired.

"Nightlife." Said Steve.

"Steve." I said. "This is Invercargill, ass end of the country, and one of the southernmost cities in the world. It's flat and cold and populated by Scots. They're just getting over forty years of prohibition. Its streets are named for rivers north of Hadrian's Wall, for Christ sake. Just where do you think they're hiding the dancing girls, this close to Antarctica?" But this was no lost American sailor, this was Steve of the Jacuzzi. Failure, and reason, was not an option.

We set out down the main drag to the Homestead. To describe it as sparsely populated would be to offend space and time. The only three female denizens were tractor retreads, but Steve assured me it was early. The only two patrons that arrived later were two local army enlistees, who fascinated us with obscure details of the ANZUS treaty, and what a man could do with a sheep and a pair of gumboots, when the major was away. The Homestead shut at ten pm, mercifully, and Steve and I stumbled home in the biting wind. I asked the desk clerk if there were any good books lying about. He told me he had just finished a brilliant read, and he would send it up to my room. Just before midnight, I had a knock at my door.

"You're in luck." He said. "I found the King James version."

'It'll go up there on the mantle with all the rest.'
Mercury Bay Yacht Club Manager,
(when asked which position of honor the America's Cup would have)

*   *   *

347

'I myself prefer my New Zealand eggs for breakfast.'
Elizabeth II

The eggs were the inflection point. In the dining room of the South Sea Hotel in Oban, on Stewart Island, anything I put in my mouth after these morsels, would be navigating a northerly trajectory. I looked down at the placemat, and then up at the owner. *The Southern-most hotel in the World.*
"Its not true, Bruce." I said.
"What's not true?" He asked.
"You don't have the most southern hotel in the world." I said. "Ushuaia does."
"Where the bloody hell is that?" He asked. And I realized, it really didn't matter.
Steve and I had paid Mrs. Gerrard for our rooms at the Railway, and took in the sights of Invercargill. It had a decent enough museum, two hundred acres of Queen's Park, and an intricate old Victorian brick water tower, built in 1889 to pressurize the city's water supply, that looked like one of the dilapidated pagodas I had seen in China. Mrs. Gerrard called the same loquacious chubby taxi driver of the previous day. He took us to the airport, for the twenty-minute flight on a geriatric British twin prop monoplane, to Stewart Island.
Thirty miles south of South Island, the Māori had called it Rakiura, *Glowing Skies*, possibly because of its sunsets or, more likely, because of the *Aurora australis*, the southern lights sister to the *borealis* that danced over me when I was a kid, on freezing winter nights in Canada. Every kind of tree on Stewart Island, unlike Steve and I, had arrived in the belly of a seabird, and not the wind, although you could quibble the point. The forests were dense with podocarps, and hardwood species of rata, kamahi, and manuka. Because of the absence of the human-delivered predatory cats and rats and stoats and ferrets and weasels that infested the other islands, Stewart still had reasonable populations of wekas and kakapos and kākās

and kiwis. But the cats and rats and possums were on their way. There were large populations of Sooty Shearwaters and my least favorite fish chicken, the muttonbird, as well as fantails and silvereyes and the fabled albatross.

Steve and I had landed at the aerodrome near the only settlement of Oban, on Halfmoon Bay. The only other passenger asked me to mail her postcards, when I got to 'town.' Town was one general store, twelve miles of road, one hotel, one pub and 20 oyster boats. Electricity came from diesel generators. Steve asked me what we were doing here.

"Looks like we're mailing postcards." I said. And we did.

There were older postcards that we bought at The Fernery, after a hike to Observation Point and another bay, back in the hamlet. We wrote them in the tearoom, and then the pub, before Mad Murray, a carpet cleaner from Invercargill, demonstrated his prowess on the piano, and the poisonous potential of DB bitter stout. *TODAY'S GREAT BEER.* Or so said the sign outside, like there would be no tomorrow.

We had signed up for dinner in the hotel dining room that evening. Steve and I were half-attended to by the bucktoothed waitress, the hickey on her neck a mark of local supply side economics, and a perfect compliment to our canned cream of chicken soup, mutton and salad, and cheesecake and coffee. We adjourned to the TV room watch Elliot Ness, before retiring to the Spartan room to digest the day.

We had the Queen's breakfast next morning.

"Box o' birds." Said the waitress, when we asked how she was. From the new road sign on her neck, she had been an early one, catching the worm.

Steve and I tramped out to Acker's Point, played with the wekas in the underbrush, one of which was more than happy with the core of my stolen apple, and hiked back to fetch our packs.

In the postcard I had sent home, I wrote to my parents that I would see them in a month's time. I hadn't seen them for almost five years, and I wondered what we would make of each other. I wondered a lot more, actually, but I still had a month not to think about it.

"And now for a little music in the waiting lounge." Said the van driver, parked beside our Southland Air plane at the airfield. No one had to be anywhere, in any kind of a hurry.

Back on the other side of the Foveaux Strait, Steve and I begin a trek to the outskirts of Invercargill. We didn't make it all the way. Our purchase of a couple of overripe bananas at a roadside dairy, got us an offer of a ride from a basketball playing lady lawyer, who took us to Gore, via an interesting account of her experiences with Southland prejudices. Our next ride was just as fast.

Raylene took us up to Balclutha with flashing eyes, gambling stories and questions about the outside world.

A jacked up Maorimobile, containing three tired young workers from the local freezing works, dropped us off in Milton. For two hours it really looked like the end of the road, and the sign on the side of the highway wasn't particularly propitious. *Have you visited our motor camp?* Finally, about 7 pm, three young guys picked us up in a decrepit old Hunter, and took us the rest of the way to Dunedin, dropping us on Princess Street south of the Octagon. Entering the lobby of the Excelsior, we enquired about accommodation from the potted proprietor. He convincingly redirected us to the YWCA.

"You'll be with your own kind." He said.

The Wizard of Was

'A country of inveterate, backwoods, thick-headed, egotistic philistines'
Vladimir Lenin, 1909

Because of the discovery of gold at Gabriel's Gully in 1861, Dunedin had been the largest city in New Zealand for the next forty years. Julius Vogel, the Jewish baker whose bread recipe had evolved to compliment the local butter and manuka honey and Robyn's Kiwi identity so perfectly, had also, as Prime Minister, devised an development scheme to attract thousands more to settle the nascent Otago metropolis. He certainly nailed Steve and I, a hundred years later.

We set off for Moray Place, to check into Kinnard House, with our own kind. A Russian Natasha, bangled to the elbows on both arms, registered us for two nights, and a shower and shave, upstairs in Spartan quarters, before we headed out to find midweek nightlife in Dunedin.

Foxy's was a club at Robbie Burns, that a friend had told us about. We arrived after a lamb dinner elsewhere. Out of boredom we drew each other's caricatures, and attracted the attention of two housewives from Gore, who seemed desperate to talk about the ANZUS treaty, an unpredictably popular topic, since Steve and I had arrived in the South Island. We were relieved when they left, and we followed, shortly thereafter.

We were late for the tour next morning, but it was fantastic. Olveston was a grand old Arts and Crafts-influenced mansion on the hill, built for 'a jolly bouncy little man who liked a bit of swank perhaps but was kindly and quite without side.' David Theomin was a wealthy piano importer, who had built and furnished the 35 room, fourteen thousand square foot Jacobean brick manor, rendered in Moeraki gravel, Oamaru stone facings and Marseilles tile roofings, with central heating, an internal telephone system, a service lift, a food mixer, and an electric toaster. The elevated internal balcony was an aerie from which to watch the dancing in the ballroom below. The Japanese collection of curios was exquisite, but only a small component of what was on display. I was volunteered to demonstrate the grand piano but I would've much rather attempted the two ton billiard table in the parlor. One of the most exquisitely constructed places I've seen anywhere in the world, my awe was shared by our tour guide, who obviously also loved the place.

Steve and I backtracked down George Street to the University bookstore, and the Otago museum, containing an impressive collection of Maori and Island curios, well presented. We went to the Captain Cook for lunch, some poor scallops and a surfeit of chips, and I went home to catch up on my sleep. The pork with capers, olives and onions later, at Foxy's, was good but we ended up with the cashier and her noxious friend, still recovering after being thrown down a flight of stairs, in what was paradoxically referred to, in these parts, as a 'domestic.' After two hours of our trying to empathize with her situation, we decided that it may have simply all been self-defense.

Steve and I left Dunedin next morning, on a bus to Pine Hills, and the highway north.

The Maori driver was a nice old guy, and took us to the turnoff. But it was tough going- it was after ten, when we got our first ride, a fish factory worker heading to Moeraki to visit his parents for the weekend, in a battered old Mini.

He dropped us off at the Moeraki Boulders, the unusually large, grey, symmetrical cannonball mudstones, some over seven septate feet in diameter, lying along Koekohe Beach, on the wave-cut Otago coast. Ten minutes after Steve and I were ready to move on, Nick pulled over in his weaving Maorimobile. He was from Gisborne, on vacation in South Island, and asked if I could drive.

"I like to sit in the back seat and enjoy myself." He said, cracking open another beer. So I got behind the wheel and immediately discovered that, not only was there no steering, there were no brakes.

"It's not very good, is it, mate?" He asked.

"No, Nick." I said. "It's not very good." But we eventually got to our turnoff north of Omaru, and bid him bon voyage. An elderly woman pulled over for us, a fair while later. Her husband was a farmer, admitted to hospital that day, for a bleeding gastric ulcer. She needed the company, and showed us some ancient Maori rock paintings on a limestone outcrop, and took us into Kurow. Steve and I thanked her, and paused for grilled sandwiches and hokey pokey ice cream. Robyn loved hokey pokey for dessert, like she loved Vogel's and Kiwi butter and manuka honey for breakfast. Maybe it was the quality of the vanilla ice cream, or maybe it was the lumps of honeycomb toffee. Maybe it came from the Italian 'O, che poco.' *Oh, how little.* Or, maybe it didn't. Or maybe, as I would learn from my niece twenty-five years later, it was the meaning of life.

Steve and I fell asleep on the roadside in the hot afternoon sun. It looked like we were going to sleep there that night, in our hokey pokey slaver. But then, around dusk, a Timaru farming couple slowed long enough to offer us a ride all the way to Omarama, by the dam at Lake Benmore. The left us with a box of shortbread. We were good.

Omarama is Māori for 'Place of Light,' an apparent reference to its extraordinarily pure clear sky. Since Jenny pulled over with her dog, Spud, over a quarter century ago, and secured us a cabin in the local motor camp, it has become a destination resort, for anglers, artists, and astronomers from all over the world. Spud had a wristwatch attached to his collar.

"He's a watchdog." Said Jennie.

Jenny was the proprietress of the Stagecoach, a local restaurant, and for her and Steve and I, in the pub that

353

evening, Omarama was a destination resort for meat pies and Speight's, exactly perfect for where it was, and when.

* * *

'Climb the mountain not to plant your flag, but to embrace the challenge, enjoy the air and behold the view. Climb it so you can see the world, not so the world can see you.'
David McCullough Jr., Wellesley High School 2012

Jenny hosted Steve and I over at her café next morning, for a wonderful breakfast. There were kisses on cheeks, before we left for the road. A diabetic caretaker picked us up. He and his wife were traveling to Twizel, to see the doctor about his leg. There was gangrene, and I was quiet about my training, and his prognosis.

Steve and I walked to Mount Cook. It was a long way from anywhere else in the world but for us, it was only nine kilometers from the turnoff. For the time we waited to hook a ride, it may have as well been Mars. It was just before noon before Leon, an agricultural student from Wanaka, stopped for just a nanosecond, and transported us all the way to the Hermitage. The highest mountain in New Zealand, and despite all the more recent politics, I knew Mount Cook as the 'Cloud Piercer,' a romantic rendering of the probable real name the original Māori knew it by.

Steve and I checked into motel flat number 34, at the Glencoe, with spectacular sunny views of Mount Wakefield and Sebastopol. We walked out to Kea Point, to find Mt. Cook and Sefton.

The sun fell behind Aorangi, and my dreams became more vivid. I had been experiencing flashbacks. A healthy

354

apprehension about finally returning home, had become a phobia. For the first time, in almost five years of traveling, I was apprehensive.

The sun was still shining when Steve began sputtering. Familiar sonorous engine knock fell quickly behind the glaciated mountain backdrop of Mount Cook and, after a nothing evening dinner at the Glencoe and an expensive beer and a couple of chess games at the Hermitage, we stumbled down the starlit path home to bed.

We set up our packs on the highway next morning, past three waiting hikers, moving up, immediately after they all got a lift in one car. A few short minutes later, one of the rescue rangers stopped and drove us up to the turnoff. He told us of the rigors, and satisfactions, of his job. Of the fact that most fatalities on the Copland, which he hikes to get home to the West Coast, are Australians; of the experienced mountaineers stranded for 14 days, who lost their legs; of the THC monopoly at the mountain; and of the Blue haired swivel-heads that constitute the bus tours he had to protect from dying at altitude.

We waited for over an hour at the turnoff. but it was unimportant. The sun was shining and we were alone in the Sierra, except for the odd passing car. It was the odd one that finally pulled over.

"How far you going?" I asked.

"Auckland." He said, which was way beyond what we were aiming for. And we piled in our bags and bodies in the golden Holden, and met George, a 50-year-old carpenter from Takapuna, who drove like the wind for three solid hours, pausing only to show us the stunning view of Lake Tekapo and the mountain backdrop, from the altar window of the Church of the Good Shepherd, timeless stone on an ultramarine backwash, and the bronze statue of the iconic neighboring New Zealand Collie sheepdog. He told stories of Maoris and Pakehas, of mythical matches between All Blacks and rugby-challenged Poms, of lesser Aussies, and of his own unique Antipodean nobility. When he dropped us on the outskirts of Christchurch, a mere ten kilometers from the city center, we were almost jet-lagged, to have made it in so short a time. Steve and I grabbed a burger and Just Juice at the service station, and began a short hike into Hornby. A young woman screeched to a halt, rolled a bale of hay off of her backseat, and took us to the Cathedral in the Square, twenty-five years before it fell into pieces.

They drove down to Cathedral Square to pick us up. Steve and I hadn't seen Frank and Bev since Athens, three years earlier. Ever the quintessential Canuck, he still looked like Sergeant Preston of the Yukon.

"Banished from the Garden of Eden, Wink?" Asked Frank, with a chuckle. I remembered Heracles, flexing his muscles on the wine label, and we hugged. Frank and Bev had gotten hitched while I was hitching, not long after we met them, and it seemed that married life had been treating them well. But the seemed to be having a little more trouble with my itinerant state than I was with their conjugal one, and I caught a glimmer of wanderlust residue in Frank's eyes, as we shook hands.

We drove off to meet Cath, a lovely Cantabrian lady, who continuously teased Frank, and he teased her back. When she placed a large jar of Vegemite in front of him one morning, Frank gave her the correct Canadian response.

"It's like lifting a horses tail, pouring on a salt shaker, and giving it a big sloppy kiss."

Cath handed me a message from Destiny, concerning a telegram that had arrived from my medical residency program director in Canada.

I hadn't slept much the night before. A black and white horror film, about the end of my travels and beginning of my travails, had been double-billed on my retinas.

I called Robyn, who told me that I needed to call Emy, the secretary of the new program director. I found a phone, and Emy put me through to a seriously nasal voice, with a faux bonhomie. He asked me if I had any reservations about accepting the position he was offering, that of a second year resident in Internal Medicine.

"None." I said. He asked me what efforts I had made, to keep up with the medical literature.

"None." I said. He told me I needed to send him a telegram to confirm my acceptance of the offer, and fired a final shot across my bow.

"Everyone that knew you here had told me you had been some kind of hotshot." He said. "What kind of guarantee do I have that they were telling me the truth?"

"None." I said.

And I sent the telegram. Each man is a hero and an oracle to somebody.

*　　*　　*

'I find it hard to say, because when I was there it seemed to be shut.'
Sir Clement Freud, 1978

The old codger was getting *agro* with my apparent ignorance.

"How can you tell you're in Christchurch on a Sunday?" He asked. I confessed I didn't know.

"You can fire a cannonball down Colombo Street, and not hit a bloody thing." I smiled.

"How can you tell you're in Christchurch at any time?" He persisted. I shook my head.

"Every day feels like Sunday."

There had been so many entertainers and speakers in the Square when Steve and I first arrived, you could have sworn you were in Hyde Park. Among the punks and Jesus freaks and Maoris, were the Birdman, the Bible lady, and an ambidextrous alcoholic, deliriously trembling his *delirium tremens*, while simultaneously campaigning for Ethiopian starvation. He seemed to be in favor.

There were half a dozen other opinions on soapboxes around the plaza, but we had come to see just one.

In the oldest established city in New Zealand, Steve and I had awoken early. We spent the morning watching the punters poling their boats down the Avon, hunting down a poster of Reagan carrying Thatcher, in a parody of Rhett Butler and Scarlet in *Gone with the Wind*, climbing the 133 stairs of the Anglican Cathedral tower, and drinking coffee and eating souvlaki.

He approached, clad all in black, from his beret to his shoes. A silver medallion with a large central blue stone hung in the middle of his chest, halfway to his silver belt buckle. Long black hair, tinged with the same silver, flowed out from under his beret, trying to stay away from his exuberant goatee. He was carrying a travel trunk and an old wooden ladder, festooned with handbills and decals. A bugle hung off the top. He climbed halfway up the ladder, blew a few soap bubbles, and then his bugle.

"Welcome to my city." He said. The Jesus freaks went wild, and the ambidextrous alcoholic began to heckle. Total calm control prevailed.

The wizard was wine for the soul. He began by presenting several amusing but well-reasoned arguments about the sources of wickedness- any state without a monarchy is evil, women are evil through their shopping habits, education is evil, and Jesus was evil. The freaks hurled abuse.

"Miracles are evil." He said, notably guilty for a few of his own. There were legends of drought-breaking rain dances in Auckland, Canterbury and the Australian outback, and would be another, twenty years after Steve and I saw him, in the form of a successful spell, that dispersed the fog that was preventing the first flight from landing, at the reopening of the Oamaru airport.

He convincingly presented his cosmological 'Theory of

358

Everything,' with elements derived from Sheldrake and Jantsch and Parsons and Whitehead and Prigogine. He was 53 years old, the same age as my mother, and he was great.

He had been born Ian Brankenbury Channell, in London, and had served as a pilot-officer navigator in the Royal Air Force, before acquiring a double honors degree in psychology and sociology, from Leeds. He joined the teaching staff at the University of New South Wales where, during the student upheavals of the late 1960's, he created a movement called Action for Love and Freedom, and implemented this as the 'Fun Revolution.' The Sydney Morning Herald loved the new 'university that swings,' but the Head of his department, convinced he was insane, fired him without consultation. And then he went rogue.

Channell allowed his passport, driving license, social security ID, and other important documents, to lapse. He reinvented himself as a fictional character, and an art form. He began to experiment, and was given a small honorarium by the vice chancellor, to become the university wizard. He became the 'Cosmologer and Shaman' at Melbourne University. The Director of the National Gallery accepted the offer of his live body as a living work of art (on extended loan).

In 1974, he migrated to Christchurch, and began to orate, on his ladder in cathedral Square. City Council tried to have him arrested, but he had become so popular that he was featured in guidebooks, and the Square had become a venue for public speaking. Three years before Steve and I arrived, the same City Council appointed him Wizard of Christchurch, and seven years after we left, the Prime Minister would designate him the Wizard of New Zealand.

On his recommendation, Steve and I had an apple juice in the *Albatross*, while the participating vehicles in the antique car rally parade drove by. Later than evening we took Frank and Bev out to a vegetarian restaurant. It was far better fare than that of the Māori restaurant we treated them to the next evening, after a slow day out on the Banks Peninsula, at the

French settlement of Akaroa. Surrounded by craggy volcanic hills, the sheltered harbor, with its running dolphins, was serenely beautiful. Steve and I sat and reminisced.

We spoke of legacies, both his and mine. Of the limitless frontier of space, of the limits of our individual biology, and of the love that provided meaning to both. Our bloodstreams had always run together, and deep. He told me how he may have misjudged his first impressions of my odyssey as an 'empty life.'

"But you're going back to a world you no longer belong to." He said. "You'll never again have as much freedom of choice as you do now."

"I know." I said. And told him how my circle was closing too fast, locking me in, and shutting me off.

"Or, maybe it's a door." He offered.

"Yeah, maybe." I said. "Its hard to predict."

The Wizard of Christchurch, for all his miracles and magic, and potions and predictive powers, didn't see the real evil coming. He didn't see the arson that would destroy his wooden house in 2003, and his narrow escape from the fire. He didn't see the vandalism of his Wizardmobile, which he had lovingly constructed from the front halves of two VW Beetles. And he didn't see the earthquakes and the aftershocks that would destroy his city, the 184 fatalities, and the fear and liquefaction. From the air, I would see photos of the Cathedral, collapsed in Cathedral Square, and realize that the shape of the square was actually a crucifix. The Jesus freaks went wild.

"You can fire a cannonball down Colombo Street, and not hit a bloody thing." The old codger had said. And so you still can. Frank and Bev separated not long after Steve and I left Christchurch.

Some evils you can argue against eloquently. But prediction is very difficult, especially if it's about the future.

"The first European to find NZ was a Dutch sea-captain who was looking for something else ... It takes its name from a province of Holland to which it does not bear the remotest likeness, and is usually regarded as the antipodes of England, but is not. Taken possession of by an English navigator, whose action was afterwards reversed by his country's rulers, it was only annexed by the English Government which did not want it, to keep it from the French who did."

William Pember Reeves, 1898

Tiki Tour

'New Zealand is a country of thirty thousand million sheep,
three million of whom think they are human.'
Barry Humphries

'Altogether too many sheep'
George Bernard Shaw, 1934

Steve and I flew out of Christchurch on time next morning, after saying goodbye to Frank and Bev. The Dash-7 flight was delightfully smooth, with friendly stewardesses, birds-eye views of the Southern Alps, the Kaikura Range, Mount Egmont, and Tongariro's sunken nipple cones. Rotorua was hot and sunny, and I heard our names paged just outside the airport. Cecil had driven down to meet us, took us home to drop off our packs and, after a tour of the Forest Research Institute, loaned us his car for the afternoon. I steered Steve around to the usual tourist sites, Blue and Green lakes, Buried Village, and back to Whaka, for the thermal activity and Maori tour bus carvings. After a brief visit to the museum, we picked up Cecil, and returned to Pill Hill to meet May and their sons, and a sumptuous dinner of roast beef and Yorkshire pudding. After a glass of Rémy Martin in the backyard, I wandered over to the fence line, to meet Sati again, for the first time. He asked about Robyn, and introduced me to his wife, Padma, and son, Sanjay. I offered to pay the unanticipated sixteen-dollar surcharge on our phone bill, but he refused.
I suspect it was the smoking that got him. Sati is gone now, but his Aquarius Drive house will always contain the fondest memories of my Kiwi Destiny.
We all made a mid-evening diversion to meet Bob, an old

cane grower in Burma, and his Sabah wife, Trudy, who layered on the trout, wine, and tiki tour stories. When we returned to Cecil and Mays, Robyn called from Auckland, to remind me to convert 'our money' into traveler's cheques. I realized that I had only a little over a thousand dollars from all my hard work, as much as I had escaped Tasmania with, four months earlier.

"Its enough to get back." I told Steve.

"Hard to know, if you don't know where that is." He said. And I agreed.

The next day Cecil took us around to the various thermal attractions of the Wai-O-Tapu *Sacred Waters,* in the Okataina volcanic zone, just north of the Reporoa caldera, by roads he wasn't quite sure of himself. We stopped for a naked soak in Kerosene Creek, a look at the boiling mud volcanoes, and around to the Artist's Palette, Champagne Pool, Bridal Falls and Lady Knox Geyser.

After a brief lunch of asparagus rolls, Cecil drove us over to the Agrodome, for the sheep spectacle. The game show Aussie cow cockie, dripping sweat and saliva, hosted a tawdry display of shearing, and stick-and-carrot maneuvering of sheep dogs into various poses. It was a sad farce, but the blue hair swivel-heads ate it up.

The evening was better, but not as special as I remember from when Robyn and I lived in Rotorua. Cecil took Steve and I down to the THC for the hāngi. The oven-minders uncovered the earth from the pit, pulled the burlap sacks from the hot stones, and lifted out steaming baskets of mussels, kumara, lamb, and muttonbird. Steve loved it as much as I did.

At one point a Japanese elder tried to take over the microphone, in a misguided effort to help out the Māori minstrel, but was thwarted by his family, with the help of some burly security from the front desk.

The three of us overindulged in the smoked eel and salad and kiwifruit wine, likely the reason for our jump in the adjacent hot pools after the performance. There was further encouragement to 'get the gear off,' from the female Australian tour group, but there wasn't enough kiwifruit wine on the planet to have accomplished that sort of compliance.

Saturday began more slowly, however, and Cecil only dropped us at the Ngagata turnoff after nine, and hugs all round.

It looked like we were going to be there forever. The clouds came over and my anticipated Future Shock almost wanted it to happen. But, finally, a kidney specialist from Melbourne, in a rental car, pulled over and took us all the way to the Big Smoke. John had been attending a conference in Taupo, and was glad for the company, especially a colleague from the other side of the world. We shared stories, impressions and Benson & Hedges all the way to Ponsonby. Steve had been *whinging* about the lack of real Amurrican burgers, so we dropped in at Hamburger Heaven on our hike home, so he could get mayo on his glasses.

We had a great homecoming back at Rosie and Grahams' in Grey Lynn. Robyn had snow-white pants, and a red top, smiling, and radiant with anticipation. She put on a great spread for dinner and the night passed slowly in a magical haze.

"Where are you going tomorrow?" Rosie asked. I pushed everyone aside.

"Up the boohai shooting pukekos with a long-handled shovel." I said. Everyone raised a glass.

*   *   *

365

'Super-suburbia of the Southern Seas,
Nature's- and Reason's- true Antipodes,
Hail, dauntless pioneers, intrepid souls,
Who cleared the Bush- to make a lawn for bowls,
And smashed the noble Maori to ensure
The second-rate were socially secure!
Saved by the Wowsers from the Devil's Tricks,
Your shops, your pubs, your minds all close at six.
Your battle-cry's a deep, contented snore,
You voted Labour, then you worked no more.
The Wharfies' Heaven, the gourmet's Purgat'ry.
Ice-cream on mutton, swilled round in tea!
A Maori fisherman, the legends say,
Dredged up New Zealand in a single day.
I've seen the catch, and here's my parting crack-
It's undersized; for God's sake throw it back!'
Wynford Vaughan-Thomas, *Farewell to New Zealand*, 1908

We had no idea how much oil it leaked. But it was inevitable
that we would find out. Robyn had borrowed Nikki's yellow
Honda, to take Steve and I on a final scenic excursion to
Northland.

"What's a tiki?" Steve asked.

"In Polynesian mythology, it's the first man." I said. "Or a
Māori carving of an ancestor, sometimes in greenstone,
sometimes in bone or wood. They wear it around their neck
as an amulet or talisman."

"So what's a tiki tour?" He asked.

"That's what you're on. Steve." Said Robyn, wheeling all the
way around from Takapuna to make sure she hadn't left the
oven on, back at Rosie and Grahams'. It was April Fools
Day, 1985. We picked up another fourteen dollars worth of
engine oil, just in crankcase.

Robby provided a smooth drive up the tar seal to the main
town in the Bay of Islands. Paihia had been inadvertently
named by Reverend Henry Williams, one of the evangelicals
that overran the more innocent parts of the world, in the
early 1800s. He knew the Māori word for 'good,' *pai*, but not

366

much more.

"Pai, here." He said, and so it was. He named his missionary station Marsden Vale, after the prototype proselytizer of the region, Samuel Marsden. *We prepared to go ashore to publish for the first time in New Zealand the glad tidings of the gospel.* Charles Darwin found them all playing cricket on the lawn, less than two decades later. Oh Joy.

Robyn and Steve and I had a wine and cheese picnic on the beach, before moving on the modest white colonial house in Russell, where the Treaty of Waitangi was signed in 1840. Despite all the injustice that has followed on both sides, it was the Māori that had originally written to King William IV, to request protection from the traders, whalers, sealers, and French, the *Tribe of Marion*, all of which had brought muskets and grog and greed. They got their wish.

As the 150 Northern chiefs signed the Treaty, the representative of the British Crown, William Hobson, had made the pronouncement "He iwi tahi tātou." *We are now one people.* Which, given the subsequent land exploitation, the bad blood, the crime, the domestic violence, the pervasive political correctness, and the magnitude of the frivolous but legally lucrative special privilege claims of the Treaty of Waitangi Grievance Industry, he may have been a bit optimistic. Northern Chief Whai had been present at the signing ceremony.

"Yesterday I was cursed by a white man." He said. "Is that the way things are going to be?" Pretty much. Another, Nopera Panakareao, summarized his understanding of the Treaty for some of the other chiefs.

"The shadow of the land is to the Queen." He said. "But the substance remains to us." The British, as they had in most other places around the globe, acquired 'something more than the shadow.'

After its historical signing, the treaty had disappeared for over half a century until, in 1908, it was rediscovered in poor condition, partially eaten by rats. They're still arguing about whether the culprit rodents had been originally brought by the Polynesians or Captain Cook. They were now one species.

We checked out everything available in accommodation before deciding on the Ivanhoe Lodge, a private hostel run by cigar smoking Dave, $20 a double, and a complimentary dinner of Kawai and snapper, salad, and white wine. Dave and I ended up on his back porch with a stogie, and our respective tales of transience. He whistled a long and hard trail of exhaust, after hearing mine.

"You're up the boohai, mate." He said.

"Shooting pukekos with a long-handled shovel." I said. He blew a small smoke ring through a large one, and nodded.

We were up *sparrow fart* next morning. Knowing Steve's love for sailing, Robyn had booked us on a two-masted brig for the day. The water was aquamarine perfection, but the old salt skipper tore a gash in his mainsail, taking us out to one of the islands, where we climbed a hill, and trekked to gather mushrooms, for dinner. The return leg was cloudy, but it did nothing to diminish Robyn's radiance, smiling at me from the stern.

Back at Dave's I grilled a side of steaks to go with our mushrooms, and the three bottles of wine that provided the kind of debate over acceptable Scrabble terms, that made the Treaty of Waitangi look like an alignment of the planets. We played until the words ran out.

After a snapper lunch at the pub in Russell, we piled back into Nikki's oil leak and drove to the sand dunes in overcast Opononi, on the south shore of the Hokianga harbor. We checked into the 'accommodation for hitchhikers,' run by the Māori woman on the lawnmower.

Steve had slept through the trip, and awoke in time to head down to the pub, leaving Robyn and I to get takeaways, and sit on our cottage carpet, talking about how this was our second last night together. She buried herself in *The Snow Leopard* and, when Steve returned, he buried himself in his postcards and headphones, knees bouncing up and down to the music. It seemed like I was the only one left in the here and now. And it didn't feel like a place and time I should be occupying. In three weeks time, the cartwheels were over, five years of revolution and revelation, feast and famine, turmoil and tranquility. I would spin all the way back, and ahead, to where I started. *Get back to where you once belonged.* And I wondered. Did I belong in this culvert, tapering to dementia and death?

*   *   *

'I believe we were all glad to leave New Zealand. It is not a pleasant place. Amongst the natives there is absent that charming simplicity.... and the greater part of the English are the very refuse of society.'

Charles Darwin, 1860

Darwin had been correct about a great many living things, but he was dead wrong about the Kiwis. I had lived in no British culture anywhere, which had gone so out of its way, to make me feel that I had not gone out of mine. I loved their humor and hospitality, and practicality and humility and, yes, I loved their simplicity too. It was an honest reflection of their priorities, not their intellect, and woe to the son of a bitch that got that one wrong. Besides, I was in love with one.

Steve was gleeful enough next morning, and snored all the way through the downpour talk back to Auckland, except for a brief stop to visit Tāne Mahuta, *Lord of the Forest*, the largest living kauri tree in the world. Somewhere between 1250 and 2500 years old, he was the last remnant of the ancient subtropical rainforest that once covered the North Island, before they were all cut down to build, and burn down, San Francisco.

"Someday, I'll plant one for you." I said to Robyn.

"To go with my gold mine on the Coromandel?" She asked.

"Yep." I said, and we drove on south across the Auckland Harbour Bridge into Grey Lynn, and Rosie and Graham and champagne and good vibes.

Our last day in the New Zealand was bittersweet. We did our laundry in the morning, and arranged for all of us to meet Vivacious Vivienne and Joanne at the Exchange Tavern for lunch.

It was a wonderful farewell but the service was slow, and we were all thoroughly potted, by the time our Mediterranean salads arrived. Vivacious Vivienne made a similar entrance, in her red convertible and matching lipstick, and Marilyn Monroe white framed oversized sunglasses and cleavage. She was in a playful mood, hitting Steve broadside, after he turned down another beer.

"Maybe you want your mothaah." She said. He took it well, or she would have come about for another pass. As it was, she drag raced us downtown for a last minute shopping spree. Steve bought a sheepskin while I bought some time with Robyn.

Graham was not only the part owner of the Number Five Restaurant he was the chef. And he had been busy all afternoon, having left us just after lunch from the Exchange. It was all laid on- lamb's tongue salad, chicken breast stuffed with salmon, a Matua Hermitage, and passion fruit torte for dessert. Rosie came for coffee, and to say goodbye, followed by Nikki in the oil-dribbling Honda, late as usual. And before I was ready, Steve and I were in the long queue at the UTA desk, with Ron and Patty, Shoko and Vivacious Vivienne, and Nikki to see us off. And Robyn. And tears.

"A gold mine and a kauri tree." She said.

A man often meets his Destiny on the road he took to avoid it. On that night, on that road, mine told me she loved me. There are still rare but real occasions when it's better to arrive than to travel well.

Millie was getting impatient, as only Millie does.

"I don't get it, Uncle Wink." She said. "What do all these big and little things, connected by cartwheels, have to do with you and Auntie Robbie? That's the story we really want to hear."

"The cartwheel chaos of the cosmos and creation is the reason why Auntie Robbie and I had any chance at all, Mil." Said Uncle Wink. "It was all about chance. The commitment we were in the process of making to each other was a deliberate sacrifice of ego, and both the cause and the cure of the agony generated by our love for each other. It was an ordeal caused by the lance of passion, healed only by the same lance that delivered the wound touching it again, making us one from two.

The only true wisdom lives out in the great loneliness, and can only be reached through suffering. The prime condition of life and the secret cause of suffering is mortality. It cannot be denied if life is to be affirmed.

The brink, the jumping off place to the ocean of transcendence, goes through *being* and *consciousness*, before arriving at *bliss*. Auntie Robbie and I were following the trail, and slowly coming to bliss."

Voyage of the Taporo

'For as this appalling ocean surrounds the verdant land, so in the soul of man there lies one insular Tahiti, full of peace and joy, but encompassed by all the horrors of the half known life. God keep thee! Push not off from that isle, thou canst never return!'

Herman Melville

Languid. Some words are just like that. Even if you're not sure what they mean, they turn out to mean what you think they should mean. A day after our night flight from New Zealand, Steve and I were doing languid.

I had managed to sleep for an hour or so, but Andreas and Erika, who had flown with me from Jakarta to Sydney seven months earlier, sat beside us on the plane, and were anxious to catch up. We flew through the sunrise on the mountainous spires of Mo'orea, and landed at Faa'a airport just before dawn. A trio of local musicians, each with a frangipani behind the ear, provided a Polynesian welcome.

The name Papeete translates as 'water from a basket,' but most of the water had escaped into the air around us, dripping perfume and diesel fumes. We jumped a 90 CFA bus into town, to the ferry dock. Another 600 CFA got us into Darwin's 'picture in a frame,' across the nine miles, and through the coral pass, to the most beautiful island in the world. As the horizon contracted from the ocean, Mo'orea, with Mount Tohi'e'a rising into the clouds from its center, loomed like a backdrop from *King Kong*.

We landed in Vai'are bay, where a Le Truck loaded us into its abdomen with the rest of the boat and, roaring full tilt down the one road around the island, eventually discharged us at the Bank IndoSuez. Steve and I changed a traveler's cheque, and were taken in tow by the cool redheaded proprietress of the Tiahura, who made us wait for her while she did her shopping, and then showed us a bungalow, *complet avec* cuisine, toilet, spiders, geckos, cockroaches, and the occasional mouse. Her manslave, Nicolai, checked us in, and we wandered west, hugging the coconut fronds along the beach, stopping to laze in the water, watching the topless French girls align and rotate their tanning oil-covered palms, umbrellas, towels, and postures, as the sun rode down the afternoon. Languid.

We had mahi-mahi au poivre vert, a chef's salad, and a bottle of Entre-Deux-Mers Chateau Launay 1983, and set off down the beach again to gaze at the southern constellations, under our coconut canopy.

"What do you want to do with your extra day?" he asked, referring to our crossing back over the International Date Line.

"This." I said. And we returned to sleep.

Mo'orea is ten miles wide, two miles for every day Steve and I spent exploring her curves. She was heart-shaped, with 'Ōpūnohu Bay and Pao Pao Bay forming her north shore symmetrical indentations. The latter was also called Cook's Bay, after the place of greatest cultural cross-pollination in Polynesia. It was the epicenter of the wave of romance that followed his voyages back to Europe. The Transit of Venus, that he was sent to record in Matavai Bay on Tahiti, was a backseat Aphrodite, to the bare-breasted brown girls his sailors pulled nails out of the wood they depended on their very existence for, to gain favors. Before the guns and prostitution and venereal disease and alcohol and epidemics of typhus and smallpox and influenza, there had been love, and the myth of Jean Jacques Rousseau's Noble Savage. Cook had arrived almost a thousand years after the progenitor Tahitian Taiwanese, and less than a hundred years from their virtual annihilation.

Steve and I had arrived smack dab in the middle of what would eventually tally as 193 nuclear bomb tests on the outer atolls, and three months before *Opération Satanique*, the French government's clandestine effort to sink the flagship of the Greenpeace fleet in Auckland harbor, for its continuing efforts to prevent further nuclear testing in the region. Authorized all the way up to then French President François Mitterrand, the *agents provocateurs* placed two limpet mines on the hull of the vessel, and detonated them ten minutes apart, miscalculating the dedication of a Portuguese-Dutch photographer, Fernando Perreira, to retrieving his camera equipment. He drowned in the second explosion, and most of the world in collusion, in the company of threats from the French to deny New Zealand export access to agricultural markets in the EU, turned a blind eye to the murder.

'The French Government does not deal with its opponents in such ways.' Was the denial communiqué released by the French embassy, in Wellington. But they had dealt with the knife-wielding Tahitians with guns in the same way, two hundred years earlier.

The Kiwi police caught the two primary perpetrators, who were plea-bargained down from a ten-year sentence to a two-year holiday at home. The other agents, who had removed themselves to Norfolk Island, were picked up by a French submarine, which scuttled the yacht they had escaped on.

Two years after Steve and I were in Tahiti, Jacque Chirac's continued insensitivity and nuclear nonsense resulted in widespread rioting in the streets of Papeete. I had met many Polynesians and Kiwis who disliked the French for silly reasons. This one wasn't one of them.

And it would all be in the future, while Steve and I were still in the present, snorkeling among yellow and white and black-striped angelfish, black sea urchins, parrot fish, a moray eel that just about ate my fins off, zebra fish, butterfly fish, and sea cucumbers, drinking citronade and apple juice, and playing chess and writing postcards.

One night we went to Pimpy's, and danced with Tina and Axel, two Tahitian girls with complex pedigrees. Tina was a mélange of Polynesian and French and Chinese, the most beautiful woman on the planet, cognizant of the fact, and potentially more dangerous than anything Monsieur Chirac was planning to detonate in her backyard. Steve and I backed away slowly, to dreams that were almost as delicious.

But I was uncomfortable with this new easy lifestyle, and yearned for the days of bumpy bus rides, bumpier adventures, worse food, and better biceps. Steve was a great friend, but sometimes it was like being shackled to a stone. He needed contact with the real world, or at least the one he lived in, back in the States. In Tahiti, he found telephones, and instant access. I found this accessibility frightening, with no idea, in 1985, how absolutely insane the technology was about to become. And, in all this High Society Islands scrutiny of the bounty, I missed Robyn.

We spent the rest of our time on Mo'orea snorkeling, eating the *plat du jour*, drinking Hinano, and sighing over the Tahitian beauties. Our chambermaid especially, was always egging me on, but never enough. On our last night, Steve and I bought a baguette and a Camembert and a cucumber and a papaya, and sat outside our bungalow with a two-dollar bottle of *vin ordinaire*, until the sun dragged the last of its red rays underwater.

We left the Tiahura Easter Monday. I played my harmonica for the Tahitian kids and the French soldier in Le Truck, on the way to the ferry.

"Blues." He said.

"Blues." I said.

*   *   *

'French Polynesia embraces a vast ocean area strewn with faraway
outer islands, each with a mystique of its own. The 118 islands and
atolls are scattered over an expanse of water 18 times the size of
California, though in dry land terms the territory is only slightly bigger
than Rhode Island. The distance from one end of the island groups to
another is four times further than from San Francisco to Los Angeles.
Every oceanic island type is represented in these sprawling
archipelagoes positioned midway between California and New Zealand.
The coral atolls of the Tuamotus are so low they're threatened by
rising sea levels, while volcanic Tahiti soars to 2,241 meters. Bora
Bora and Maupiti, also high volcanic islands, rise from the lagoons of
what would otherwise be atolls.'

David Stanley, *Moon Tahiti*

It was raining on the return passage to Papeete, but the
Tahitian passengers were having a party anyway. En route, we
were entertained by two little boys, and traded them our New
Zealand coins for their bonbons. Docking in the harbor,
Steve and I ran across the waterfront esplanade in the
downpour, and up the slippery stairs of the Hotel Pacific, to
see if they could provide us with any information about a
boat to Bora Bora.

"Bonjour!" I said, making a pirouette through the revolving
door.

"Hello." Said the desk clerk.

"Hello?" I asked. "Parlez-vous Anglais, Madame?"

"Oh, yes." She said. "That's all I can speak." Steve and I
looked at each other.

"How can you work in a French-speaking territory, and not
be able to converse in the language?" I asked.

"Its difficult." She said. "But people are very nice."

"And you work at the reception desk." I said. "And the
switchboard?"

"And the switchboard." She said. "Yes."

Miriam was a sixty-two year-old diabetic Hawaiian, who 'sort
of got lost,' on her way to dive the reef in Australia.
"I was more concerned about the language barrier." She

laughed. And we realized that her charm was the source of her daily salvation.

We asked Miriam about a boat to Bora Bora. She suggested checking out the Keke III, back across the street. The ticket booth was closed but, from the Easter congregants, we learned that another boat would be sailing to the outer islands the following day. After poulet and pommes frites from one of the roulotte wagons, we went back across the street to ask Miriam about accommodation. She gave us a room on the top floor with two double beds, and a view of the harbor, and Steve and I set out to see the town.

My first impressions of Papeete were unimpressive. It was sleazy, as only tropical ports can be, and expensive, as only French outposts can be, and dangerous, as only colonial privilege and oppression can make a place. Steve caught up with me, on a side street, in a little red car, with Miriam in the driver's seat. It was a rental, and she was struggling to put the daily fifty-mile allotment on the odometer. We did a tiki tour of the town- Pōmare's tomb, Albert Park, the *Mairie* town hall, the market, a hamburger joint, and around the dock to inquire about the boat. But it was still Easter Monday, and no one was there. She dropped us back at the hotel, and warned us to be careful at night, before driving off, with a wave in her rearview mirror. It was good advice but, like most of that stuff, it went unheeded.

Steve and I watched a spectacular sunset over the harbour, and went out for ham and cheese omelets at one of the wharfside roulottes, and a couple of Hinanos in as many shady watering holes. We decided to end our evening in what seemed, at first, to be a fairly upscale piano bar. No sooner were we seated, than a Tahitian girl grabbed me, stuck her tongue in my mouth, pulled the shirt out of my pants, and tried to drag me onto the dance floor. My problem was not as acute as Steve's, whose assailant was a transvestite, with bigger biceps than both of us. There was a hasty retreat, Miriam's earlier warning flashing behind our eyelids.

We scrambled downstairs early next morning, blowing kisses to Miriam on our way out the door. Our first stop was to the third world ticket office, to pay for our journey to Bora Bora. Our boat had arrived overnight, and Steve and I walked over to inspect what we thought would be a rough facsimile of a cruise ship. And rough it was, an immense red and white cargo vessel, almost six hundred rusty tons, built twenty years earlier in Norway, and looking every year of it. There were two tall yellow cranes at either end of the large open deck that constituted most of the ship, and a small pilothouse at the stern. A name was painted on the hull, just aft of the anchors. *Taporo IV*.

It would almost a day to island hop itself to Bora Bora, with stops at Huahine and Ra'iatea, and all the oily open deck space you could want, fully exposed to all the natural elements, and likely some of the more synthetic ones. The price was right. From there, however, the price went into orbit.

Steve and I stopped for a juice and croissant, at a stand outside the Club Med office. He had a far off stare.

"Bit out of our league, don't you think?" I said.

"You don't ask, you don't get." He replied. So we went into the subzero quiet aircon, and parked ourselves in front of a young desk jockey. He quoted a price for four nights. We rolled our eyes. He quoted a cheaper one. We rolled them a little less. I asked him how many guests he currently had in the Club Med in Bora. He quoted a cheaper price. I offered him a quarter of his original asking price. He said no. We got up to leave. He said yes.

"Which flight should I book you on?" He asked.

"Don't worry." Steve said. "We've got tickets."

We had lunch in a little Chinese place, tried to buy a poster of Galerie Winkler from a Chinese lady, without success, and shelled out a fortune for bananas, tomatoes, starfruit, pork and beans, and a baguette. Back at the hotel we picked up a couple of books, and Miriam took us down to the dock about 3 pm.

"Bon voyage." She waved.

"Miriam." I said. "You've been practicing."

*　　*　　*

'European imperialism long ago made Tahiti a distant suburb of Paris, the missionaries made it a suburb of Christ's kingdom, and the radio made it a suburb of Los Angeles'

Cedric Belfrage

Steve and I staked out a small area on the wooden slatted deck. We left at dusk, into a gently rolling sunset, suffusing through the surrounding palm-fringed islands. We pulled out the bread and wine, the latter of which must have contained some magnetic property, as it immediately attracted a Parisienne artist, who successfully applied her wily feminine charm to score most of the bottle. After a night stop at the dock in Huahine, I pulled the Gold Kazoo further out on the deck, to get some cooler air.

The Taporo made Ra'iatea about 5:30 in the morning, just as the first rays of the sun hit the pastel colored ramshackle colonial houses, with their upper story shuttered windows, bougainvillea, balconies and balustrades, and main floor hanging laundry. We grabbed a coffee in a pleasant little market café, and reboarded for the final stretch to Bora Bora.

When I awoke again it was already on the horizon, as stunning as I'd heard it would be. Soaring almost three thousand feet out of the surrounding dense coconut-forested lagoon and barrier coral reef, Mount Pahia and Otemanu were two peaks from the same extinct volcano. The petroleum and rusted metal smells of the Taporo, were gradually wrestled away by fragrances of coconut oil and frangipanis, and the sweetness of just being there. We made landfall at Vaitape around noon, and disembarked into a truck for a rocking ride to Chez Aime, a downmarket and only backpacker bunkroom on the island.

After the Chinese proprietress got us organized there was Steve and I and a BMW factory worker from Munich, Joseph, in one room, an American Bermudian couple next door, a Danish guy named Svend from Århus bunked in around the corner with two Swedish sisters who were both named Eva, a two meter high German named Rolf, and a token Frenchman named Jean. We became fast friends for the day we were there. Steve and I rented bikes to ride past Otemanu and the old shipwrecks, to a fabulous beach on the other side of Hotel Bora Bora. On the way back we picked up a baguette and some cheese, pate, and wine, and spent the evening trading travel stories and Hinanos.

Our proprietress was most upset next morning, when Steve and I awoke early to leave. I yanked him onto a dump truck I had just thumbed down, through the hail of abuse we received, for only staying one night. But it was no big surprise, compared to what was waiting for us when and where the truck stopped to let us off. Steve and I looked at each other and nodded, before taking the path down past the sign, to the radiating cluster of overwater bungalows on stilts over the Faaopore Bay lagoon, down the hill in front of us. *Club Med Bora Bora.*

"This must be the place." Said Steve.

Bora Bora means 'First born.' The only one awake in the entire complex at that hour, wasn't quite up to the delivery. In the enormous bar under the giant thatched *fare*, sat a thin middle-aged Frenchman, strangled in plastic beads, and furrowed in the only way that middle-aged Frenchmen furrow, chain-smoking Gitannes, and long past his 'due by' date. He was holding his head with one hand, and his Galoise with the other. The ash went the length of the cigarette. It fell off as he looked up. He almost fell off too.

"This is a private club." He said, all indignant.

"We have a reservation." Said Steve. The face grew more furrowed.

"But you must have vouchers." He said. We handed them over. He looked at us, then the vouchers, then us again.

"Its not a dream." I said. "We're real."

"But we are not expecting you until the first plane." He protested, taking an extra long drag on a freshly lit coffin nail.

"We're here." Steve Said.

"But how did you come?" He asked.

"We came on the Taporo." I said.

"You came on the Taporo?" It wasn't so much of a question, as an expletive.

"We came on the Taporo." Said Steve.

"But the Taporo is a cargo ship." He said.

"Well, that would explain the oil stains on our tuxedos." I said. Game, set, and match.

"Hey Smokie, how 'bout a little breakfast." Steve said, eyeing up the now burgeoning buffet.

"Mais oui." He said. "Bien sur." They likely hadn't seen that much destruction on Bora Bora since the last Americans landed, in Operation Bobcat. It wouldn't have been pretty for a man of sophistication like Smokie to watch. He left in a hurry, shortly after directing one of the staff to show us to our bungalow, 'if they ever finish eating.'

After we tried one of everything, one of the attendants took us down to #2, our overwater bungalow, with the fish viewer in the floor.

"Cool." Said Steve. It was cool. We stowed our gear and jumped into an outrigger that took us out to Motu Tapu, *Accursed Island*, one of the recreational options at the club. It was here I had my first windsurfing lesson, but it was less than successful. Antoine, the instructor, was far more interested in lining up lessons of a different sort with one of the Californian cuckholds later, than in teaching me not to kill myself. I wound up with a bumpy shiner on my left eye, and an ice-packed journey back for lunch.

Steve and I had made our second pass of the smorgasbord, and were quietly grazing, when I heard something drop next to me on the table. I looked over to find a package of Dunhills, and up into the same cerulean colours of the lagoon.

"What happened to your eye?" She said, giving me both of her own.

It was all I could do to swallow.

*   *   *

> 'She was makin' for the trades on the outside,
> And the downhill run to Papeete.
> Somebody fine will come along
> Make me forget about loving you.
> At the Southern Cross.'
> Crosby, Stills, Nash and Young, *Southern Cross*

Her name was Ava. She told me she was a 27 year-old psychologist, working for a communications company in Munich. I congratulated her on her skills.

The afternoon was a good one, lying in the sun back on Moto Tapu, listening to Steve's Walkman and outnumbered two to one, watching her watching me.

She was there at dinner that evening, azure eyes glistening like the water, eating quietly, deliberately, controlled. The Club Dedheads held a lip sync contest, and I was nominated one of the judges. It was an exercise in farce, and a little blond completely destroyed *'Diamonds are a Girls Best Friend.'* Not as destroyed as Jim's wife, Dianne, who thought she was lining her next victim, by pouring her beer into my glass. I needed air, and was gone.

I ended up on the very end of the pier, star and fish gazing, until I heard her feet padding up behind me. I knew it was her. And we sat and talked until late, and covering and uncovering some of the most secret parts of our souls. One of the Tahitian loverboys came out, in an attempt to coax Ava into a game of ping-pong. She sent him away, in time for Steve to arrive, with stories of Antoine and the California cuckolds, and the happiness of one too many Hinanos. We said goodnight.

Steve and I had arranged to go snorkeling with a rugged Tahitian strongman, who Steve had nicknamed Conan the Barbarian. I watched him bring in a five-foot shark with a hooked rope and a ten-pound fish as live bait, wrestle it onboard, and open its mouth so we could take a photo. Note to self. Conan eventually took us back to Motu Tapu, where I found Ava, somewhat distant and withdrawn.

But the afternoon was different. We lay on the beach together, listening to Billy Joel, two headphones from one Walkman, trading flowers and shells and fingers.

There was coconut oil on our skin, a magical sunset on the South Pacific and, together at dinner later, Beethoven on the piano.

We were forced into conversing with the other Club Ded prisoners. Jon was a very pleasant bronze sculptor from San Francisco, vacationing with his son; John and Sonia were a kind couple from Auckland, who tried to keep the conversation going. Jim was there as well, back with Dianne who made obnoxious comments about Ava and I, and our decreasingly reluctant attraction. The repeat flying pass that the Tahitian loverboy made, crash-landed with a single glance from Conan.

And so, after drinking water and watching the fish, and drinking more water, Ava suggested a walk to the bridge. We went, slowly and hesitantly.

"What should we do?" She asked, as we reached the last pylon. And, as if in answer, the sky opened up in a deluge.

And we ran to her cabin, and pulled off each other's wet clothes, and fell laughing, succumbing to the rhythm of the tide.

Then, later, she lit two Dunhills. And the water ebbed and flowed under the fare, and into our dreams.

The next three days didn't matter at all, because Ava had left the next morning. She had asked me not to see her off, so I didn't, not wanting to alter the reality of the illusion, or the illusion of reality. In April 1769, Captain James Cook made his first visit to Tahiti, to view the transit of Venus. He had seen his, and I had seen mine.

They were three long-suffering days, of organized Club Med beads and bravado, and competition and condescension, and false 'fun' and friendships, and hype. Steve and I were forced to sit with three bluehairs from LA one night, mutton dressed as lamb. I told the one that kept pinching my cheeks that, if she didn't knock it off, I was going to bring her dead husband back to life.

There were escapes, of course- Conan's prowess with the denizens of the deep on the shark boat, the excellent surprise visit from our group at Chez Aime for the Tahitian dancing, Umberto Eco's *The Name of the Rose*, and best of all, the snorkeling.

Of all the worlds I had visited, the one under the water on Bora Bora was the most peaceful. There were butterfly fish that hovered goggle-eyed around my mask, the parrotfish with their spumoni colors and flick-knife fins, the clown fish safe in the anemones, and angels, devils and urchins of another kind. One afternoon, as I was snorkeling off Motu Tapu, the sky above me went dark, and I looked up at a monster black and white manta ray, flapping in slow motion, like some primeval bat. His departure reminded me breathe.

I walked out of the Bora Bora Club Med at 14:32 hours, Tuesday, April 16, 1985, and never looked back. It was wonderful to see the Taporo again, and Eva Kristina and Eva

Katerina, Svend and Rolf, and the token Frenchman, Jean, to throw out the Gold Kazoo, and read in the shade. The trip was initially slow and unremarkable, but I developed severe stomach cramps the first night, probably a combination of bed bugs and bad wine, on the porch of a midnight shop in Taha. I was running to the head most of the night, like the good old days on the Indian subcontinent. We pulled into Papeete just before two in the morning and, though I managed little sleep, I spent more time watching strange changes in my southern constellations, my sleepless comrades, and the stevedores beginning to load watermelon on the docks. Steve snored through it all peacefully.

They scuttled the Taporo in 2005, in two kilometers of open water between Tahiti and Mo'orea, not only because it had taken a 'heavy list to port,' but because it had apparently always been a fire risk, and threatened to 'sink at any time.' In all the decades that the Taporo had provided a reliable shipping link for the islands Sous-le-Vent, *Under the Wind*, who was to know it was more at home under the water. The president of the 'Heiura-Greens' Green Party spokesman was 'outraged' by the sinking, upset that ships should only be sunk in very specific locations, so that such incidents did not become 'a thorn that remains in the soles of some.' It's not clear whether or not he was including Auckland harbor and the Kiwis, in his remarks.

The Bora Bora Club Med was closed less than four years later.

It had apparently hosted such luminaries as Ringo Starr, Harrison Ford, Meg Ryan, Patrick Swayze, Senator John McCain, Janet Jackson, Pierce Brosnan, Drew Barrymore and Cameron Diaz, but none of them, not a one, had arrived and departed on the Taporo.

Reentry

'The clouds were all fled, the beauty of the tropic day was spread upon Papeete; and the wall of breaking seas upon the reef, and the palms upon the islet, already trembled in the heat.'
Robert Louis Stevenson, *The Ebb-Tide*

'Throughout the island world of the Pacific, scattered men of many European races and from almost every grade of society carry activity and disseminate disease. Some prosper, some vegetate...At the far end of the town of Papeete, three such men were seated on the beach under a purao tree.' Actually two were still asleep, and one was fretting intensely.

Svend woke me about 5:30 am, to ask if his ticket was correct. "It says my flight goes today." He said.

"It's possible." I said. "They also have a flight on Thursday."

And the full, unprepared impact of his traveling 'back to where he once belonged' this very morning hit him like a rock. As the rest of the backpackers awoke, they brought commiseration.

Steve and I strode down the Taporo gangplank, said goodbye to the Chez Amie *amie*, and waded through the Pacific sunrise to the Hotel Pacific. Miriam had reserved us a room, but it wasn't yet ready, so we stowed our packs, took our croissants and *jus d'orange* across to the Mo'orea dock, and walked to our patisserie for an early morning coffee. The day degenerated into shopping. I bought a couple of Galerie Winker posters and some coconut oil soap. Steve and I ate some greasy chicken and chips, before returning to greet Miriam, who unlocked the bed comfort in Room 503.

It was early evening before we ventured out again, this time in search of an Italian restaurant named *Picadou*, suggested by John and Sonya in Bora. We had homed into it, and were about two blocks away, when we noticed a Tahitian guy bearing down on us in the dark, from behind and to the right. "Bonsoir!" he said enthusiastically, ecstatic to see us for the first time. "Picadou? Picadou?"

"Oui, Picadou." I said.

"Venons a manger." He grinned back, patted us affectionately, and introduced himself as Peter. My spider sense was tingling, but he seemed innocuous enough, poor by the appearance of his garments, rich by the demeanor of his experience, smart, hungry, and a survivor.

"Un bord pour trois!" He announced to the waitress, and the bells and buzzers in my forebrain went critical. I watched, as he made sure we were seated in a location ideal for his purposes, near the door, and I explained to the waitress that I wanted separate checks, in subdued French and with a subtle smile. Peter was too distracted ploughing through the bread and New Zealand butter, when I explained to Steve in the best slang I could muster, that Peter would betray us before the cock crowed three courses. Meals on wheels.

The beer landed, as he was blitzkrieging his way through the third loaf of bread, and his seventh pad of butter. The waitress came to take our order of salad and fettuccine carbonara, and Peter's 'steak naturale'- that clinched the diagnosis. I played with him in English, just a little, like a snake charmer who knows just how far he can push his animal's basic nature.

"Hate to eat and run, Peter? Dessert? Should we order a pizza?" And Steve had trouble keeping a straight face as Peter feigned comprehension, just smiling and masticating furiously, as fast as he could. But his shoulders told me that he knew that I knew that he knew.

When I bit into a piece of glass in the fettuccine he scrambled for possession, but I wouldn't make it that easy for him. He winked hard at our server.

"I don't think it's wise to hustle the waitress as well." I said, watching his plot to get the food, the getaway, and the girl. In between bites he fed me, some line about going off to New

Zealand via the Marquesas, and I almost wet myself laughing. When the end game came he became a graceful phantom, shaking our hands, hovering over the pamphlets near the cashier, and easing ever so lightly through the swinging door. My soul yearned to go with him but I had a flight the next day. The staff inquired about his absence a half hour later, and their common bloodline exposed itself, cursing, smiling and nodding in admiration.

"Maybe he was hungry." Shrugged the manager.

"Maybe he was." I agreed. And we all wished him Godspeed.

For his was the story of Tahiti, of Captain Bligh and the Bounty and Pitcairn and Norfolk, of the entire South Pacific, a tale of inequity and greed and betrayal, and conflicted Christianity, and death. It was the story of three questions, and three of the apostles, Peter, John, and Paul.

Peter had already vanished back into the soggy streets of Papeete.

W. John Attwater, Esq. was Robert Louis Stevenson's repugnant and fascinating character in Papeete, where *The Ebb-Tide* began, ruthlessly violent while speaking of Jesus' forgiveness, an azure reflection of Stevenson's own tortured feelings about his religion, and published the same year he died.

And then there was Paul. Gauguin left for Tahiti in 1891, looking for a society more elemental than that of his native France. Seven years later he painted the masterpiece he considered the great consummation of his existence. Rabidly anticlerical by this time, his painting paradoxically posed three questions that were but a simple variation of the catechism he had been inculcated with, while he was a student at the Petit Séminaire de La Chapelle-Saint-Mesmin, outside of Orléans. He was so convinced that the rest of his life, after the painting, would amount to so little, that he vowed to commit suicide when he completed it. In rough wide brush strokes, he painted the title across the top.

'D'ou Venons Nous Que Sommes Nous Où Allons Nous.'
Where Do We Come From What Are We Where Are We Going.

'Will the circle be unbroken
By and by, by and by?
Is a better home awaiting
In the sky, in the sky?'
Ada R. Habershon, 1907

*   *   *

'The final story, the final chapter of western man,
I believe, lies in Los Angeles.'
Phil Ochs

They were big Gautama clouds, cotton wads tinged with gray.
I had slept fitfully, and awoke after five hours or so, in the
sky, Lord, in the sky. And the day following, the Circle would
be unbroken, by and bye, and bye and bye. It would be the
beginning of the end, the finale of five years of struggling and
soaring, deafened by the descent of a DC-10 into LAX. Had
there ever been such an ignominious climax to any other
story, I was unaware of it. I fly economy, therefore I am.

The flight was a clockwork affair- good purser, French food,
even a medical consultation for a blocked myringotomy
grommet, in a Vegas-bound ear, good nap, and a feeling of
leaving my life behind. We started our descent into LAX at
sundown, and when the wheels of our DC-10 touched down,
I felt two points on a vast circle thump and lock into finality,
my spine, and once upon a time. And we deplaned onto
ground that wasn't as solid as I remember, down *'Have a nice
day'* corridors, to line up at US customs.

The immigration fellow crossed his eyes at the stamps in my
passport, shrugged his shoulders, made Steve write down his
Houston address on my card, and set us free.

390

The customs officer's first question was his downfall.

"Where have you been on this trip?" He asked.

"The planet Earth." I said." It has a good reputation."

"More specifically." He said, unimpressed.

"South America, Africa, Europe, Asia, Australia, Oceania." I said. "And here." You could tell he wasn't handling this well, by the crazy long time he was taking to go through baggage that, for the purported duration his client had reported traveling, should have been several orders of magnitude bigger than what he was rummaging around in. His finally realized that his efforts were not going to result in anything painless, and waved us on.

We walked to the final gate up the ramp to meet Steve's girlfriend, pleasant but diffident, murine almost. She drove me into the New World and the freeways and the hype, through the cold smoggy oil-lit night of bygone years.

They dropped me in Seal Beach, outside a place that seemed remotely familiar. Remote had been five years earlier, but it was the same Oakwood Apartments. Charlie was away in Catalina for the weekend, and I had the place all to myself. I put the key in the door. Super 8 memories fell out of the opening.

> 'I spent my time reading his books, playing Charlie's guitar, running on the beach, and shopping for those few 'last minute things' that any Odysseus would need, on a five-year sojourn around the world... Like Don Quixote, I was looking for giants, and surrounded by windmills.'

Inside, I found the mementos that Steve had brought back for me. It was strange, like they belonged to someone else. I spent the evening watching Bible bashers on the small black-and-white TV, and tried to go to bed early. But I couldn't sleep, and ended up in the Jacuzzi at 2 am, leaning back and closing my eyes. Flashes of more silent movies raced on my retinas, flickering through the whole journey, until there was only red and black. My eyes opened, to find Orion, right side up, and leaning south.

I spent two more days, turning Charlie's apartment into a hermitage. In limbo between two lives, and between two pasts and an unsettled future, I needed the vegetable time and space to recalibrate my instruments.

Steve and his girlfriend appeared at designated intervals, to share a late brunch at some Marina, wander around Balboa for a few hours, or take in a movie. Over a seafood salad at TGIF, they tried once again to persuade me to stay with them, but I told them they needed their time together, and I needed mine alone. I spent an afternoon wandering aimlessly through a half-empty mall in Newport. One of the shopkeepers asked me what I was looking for. My outburst of laughter unsettled him.

The problem with limbo is that it offers no guarantee. One can land in Heaven or, depending on the tailwind, more adverse destinations, somewhat further south. On a cold and overcast LA spring morning, Steve and I flew to Houston, and his waterway condo. There I would spend my last night in the States, with him, reminiscing and reflecting on our adventure together, eating ribs and drinking beer. He handed me the final onward ticket he had booked for me, to the final peg in the ground, and the last and first pin in the map. He saw me look down at the name of the airline he had selected, and smile. *Frontier.*

*   *   *

'You never return. Another man finds another town'
Dag Hammerskjold

I flew over and into empty Mid-western space and echoes. Everyone on and off the plane was more quiet and reserved than I thought possible. I could feel their tension, and forced politeness. The immigration guy hardly looked at my passport.

In the hallway beyond the walkway, were two faces I was sure I had once known, but these ones were sallow and rounder. They possessed a fragile delicacy I had either never seen or appreciated, or maybe it had happened while or because I was away. However else they appeared, they appeared relieved of a long suffered and heavy burden. There were tears in six eyes.

"So, how was it?" Asked my father.

"Good." I said. It was as much as he wanted to know. There was so much to say, they was nothing we could say that wouldn't depreciate the value of the volume, so we walked in silence out the airport doors, into the parking lot.

"Still have the old brown caddy, I see." I said.

"Yep."

"Still a gas guzzler?" I asked.

"Not too bad." He said. And they got in the front, and I put Serendipity on the trunk, and climbed into the back seat. It was larger than some rooms I had slept in, on the road. We pulled out into the familiar suburban maze that would take us to the flatlands of the Trans-Canada highway, which would eventually take us into the granite lakes and conifers of my native Canadian Shield.

"So dear, what are your plans?" My mother's turn.

"Dunno." I said. "I have a position as a second year resident beginning July 1st, but I'm not sure I should do it."

"You should do it." My father said.

"You should do it, dear." My mother said. "You'll be closer to home." *Home*. I thought about home.

We passed the haunted humdrum places of the infinite space and time that filled up the gap in my boyhood. Steinbach, Falcon Lake, Minaki, Norman, Keewatin, and finally, home. Hometown. Kenora.

"People have been asking about you, dear." Said my mother.

"You should call them." My father added.

"OK." I said, not meaning to call them.

We had a quiet dinner, and I excused myself to go down to the basement. There were forty-four boxes in the basement, that hadn't been there when I left. I opened them in chronological order, marveling at their textures and colors and even some of their remaining smells. I slept in my old room that night, the one I had slept in since I was twelve, and had hung my model airplanes and aviation posters in. I remember catching hell for the scotch tape. My feet hung over the end of my old bed. My room, like my parents, had become small.

They told me, next morning, at breakfast. They had invited a few of their friends over that evening, and wondered if I was up to presenting a slide show of my travels. I told them it would be a pleasure. But of course it wasn't. The friends all arrived, as friends do, and would leave unaffected, the same way. As I advanced the first slides in the carousel, my mother interrupted.

"Who would like coffee, and who would like tea?" She asked. "Milk? Sugar?" It wasn't anyone's problem but mine. She was the hostess, and I, merely the guest speaker. It was her show. My father was outside, talking football with the guys. And I remembered the words of the seers.

Its your trip, not theirs. Its not that they won't get it, its that it would be fatal to everything they've ever strived for and accomplished, to realize that there may not only be another world view out there, but another world. You would be cruel to inflict it on them.

394

There were no yesterdays on the road, but I had returned to an arena built on yesterdays. I had returned to a tribe who lived in the sun, and didn't waste a lot of time, thinking about their souls. Thomas Mann had it. *If anything is capable of making a poet of a literary man, it is my hometown level of the human, the living and ordinary. All warmth derives from this love, all kindness and all humor. The only way you could describe a human being truly is by describing his imperfections.*

I had come home.

'I arrived there still smelling the smell of sweat and stale urine, of unruly growth and open decay. I was used to faces that showed the imprint of emotion, the stamp of excess. I was accustomed to things being old, worn down, chipped, scratched, scuffed and patched, but real. Where I had been, people and things were forced to show the real stuff they were made of, because the superficial could not survive the battering it got. I was used to the sounds of life: roars of laughter, shouts of anger, whistles, catcalls, bargaining, argument and domestic squabble; to the sight and smell of animals; to old people sunning themselves.

Where I had been, children came running.'

Ted Simon, Jupiter's Travels

Landing

'There are loved ones in the glory
Whose dear forms you often miss.
When you close your earthly story,
Will you join them in their bliss?'
Ada R. Habershon, 1907

The greyhound bus I took back into the city was half empty, with lonely spinsters at the front, and broken alcoholics and native Indians at the back. There were plenty of middle seats.

I had found a cheap apartment, on an elm-lined side street, with a view of the convenience store below. It was spacious, and full of light from the glassed-in balcony on the uneven deck. Underneath the linoleum tile inside was hardwood strip flooring, and the oak doors and decorative trim was magnificent. It had twelve-foot ceilings, a claw foot porcelain bathtub, and a marble fireplace. The price was right.

I negotiated with the landlord to make some improvements. He would provide the paint and materials, if I did the labor. It took me a month to refinish the floors, roll and brush the plastered walls an eggshell white, and acid dip the paint off all the brass trim and fittings. I polished it until it gleamed. I spent long days and nights alone, listening to classical music, working and sleeping in my overalls. I sourced out some second hand furniture and brought out an old oak desk from my parent's basement, and all 44 boxes. My Moroccan rugs and textiles hung where they belonged. The result was arts and crafts, with a touch of Paris.

Robyn arrived from New Zealand via Los Angeles. We took a cab back to the apartment, and walked up the flight of stairs, to a vinegar-soaked Greek salad, and a three dollar-bottle of Hungarian *Szekszárdi*. I lit a fire, and she lit one back.

I took her down to as upscale a restaurant as existed in Osbourne Village at the time, to make up for the Greek salad. The waiter arrived with a faux French accent. He told Robyn about the special of the day.

"Moules." He said. "Mussels." I cringed, remembering the giant green-lipped beauties she served up, in just the right amount of vinegar, in New Zealand.

"I'll have the mussels." She said. I tried, but she insisted.

They came as the three tiny spokes of a Mercedes hood ornament, encircled by a squirt of mayonnaise. The whole assembly was the size of a quarter, on a plate as big as a wall clock. The waiter pirouetted as he landed it, waiting for the gasp of appreciation.

"That's not mussels, mate." She said. "That's bait."

I called my mother to let her know I would be taking the bus down for the weekend, and would be bringing a friend from New Zealand.

"I hope she doesn't have any plans, dear." She said.

"Nope, no plans, Ma." I said. "She just dropped in to say hi."

Robyn wrapped my parents around her little finger, and me around a dilemma. I was flat broke busted, culture shocked, and about to restart a grueling medical residency, in a frozen metropolis I had no special regard for.

I wasn't sure that Robyn would appreciate the hardship. Among her many attributes, was a loyalty and resilience I had rarely encountered. Her mother had sent her over with a collection of knitted woolens that she was delighted not to have to use, during the short hot prairie summer she arrived in. But I thought she would be less buoyant, when the forty below blizzards came to town. I tried to warn her.

'I was doing my residency in Manitoba. For my sins... Both of us were going to have a very flat, very dark, and very cold year. I kept telling myself that there would be no distractions to learning.'

I was wrong, of course. Love is love, and hers was indefatigable. I gave her forty dollars a week, and she would bring home two bags of groceries, hanging off the oversized carrier of my old navy blue Raleigh bike. Some evenings I would splurge at the convenience store downstairs, and bring home a video and two *Oh Henry* bars. One day she came home to find a teddy bear with overalls, the one she had admired in the shop down the street, sitting on the couch, grinning. She called him 'Cheeky.' We found Mama Mia's for pizza, and the cheap Chianti that came in basketed bottles.

We learned that, while we away living our lives, we had missed important news and product development, indispensable to sustaining life in the modern era we had betrayed by our absence. We were punished by their acronyms, the PCs and AIDS and VCRs, and by our ignorance of such vital amenities as email, contact lenses, cellular phones, and microwave ovens. Fact is, we were told by a rheumatologist that no competent professional could consider functioning without at least two microwaves.

My parents would give us their tiny cabin on Lake of the Woods on the weekends. She saw her first bear, and I felt her spine shiver, when she heard the loons. She loved the loons.

When the winter came, she made me take out a loan, to buy a second-hand Hyundai *Pony*, so I didn't have to ride my bicycle out in the snow, when they called me into work, in the middle of the night. We called him HOS, for *'Hunk of Shit.'* Our apartment superintendent would turn the power off to my block heater in the middle of the night. The second worst sound in the world was the *grrrr* made by a starter motor on life support. You had but one chance. The very worst sound in the world was the *cli-i-ck* it made when it died. You had no chance. This was enervating, especially when I was being summoned to the hospital emergently.

On rare weekends off, Robyn and I would still travel to Kenora, to cross-country ski at Rushing River, or to play Scrabble with my mother. We would stop in the middle of nowhere on the highway, in the middle of the night, and watch Orion dance with the shimmering northern lights.

She would eventually burn through the last of her tourist visitor visas, and the immigration agents downtown no longer believed it, when she told them she needed another, because of her fascination with the place. One night I found myself talking to my parents, and long distance to Ron and Patty, sealing my Destiny. We got married in the apartment over the convenience store the following April, and left the revelers for the Fort Garry Hotel, and a short honeymoon in the Yucatan.

> 'There was a beautiful view of blue water on top of puddles of green Caribbean, as we came down the last hill on sunset... The patron let me sleep on the concrete terrace beside several animated Yucatec Mayan-speaking workers. I listened to them swallowing air and returning it with interest.
> "B'ix a bèel?" they asked. *How is your road?'*

Our road was fine.

None of the places that Robyn and I traveled is the same today, as they were in the early 1980s. Some of them no longer exist. Most of the cells in our bodies have turned over, and we're new organisms. We're not the same human beings in other ways as well. The tolerance I set out to acquire on my Cartwheels not only failed to flourish, but also withered faster because of them. A man becomes more judgmental with more exposure. My parents are gone, although to where is the existential question. The consciousness that finally dawned, the restoration of Orion's sight, after five years on the road, was ironically waiting in the form of my father, on my return. He had spent his time giving to his community, and they gave back when he died, by naming the lakefront promenade in his honor. It seemed he had an unusual gait. He may have got it from me. I haven't been to *Winkler's Walk* yet. It's on my bucket list, but I'm not sure I can walk in his footsteps, because of how I tried to force him to walk in mine. It turned out that, to have reached the end of my *father quest*, I didn't need to have hitchhiked anywhere at all.

My readjustment to the rigors of medical residency went as well as could be expected. They tossed me in at the deep end my first day, in charge of a thirty bed clinical teaching unit, and the education of the two interns and three clinical clerks that came with it. My street smarts, and the Socratic method, saved me from disaster. When one of the trainees asked me a question I would ask the one standing next to him what he thought, and the one next to him whether that was correct or not. If the question came from a lone student, I would ask him to save the question for the group. I studied until three am, and got three hours sleep before having to do it all again, and that was on the days I wasn't on call. I learned fast. I met my old trainees, now five years further on in their careers. There was a touch of envy, but it didn't come from me. One of the Internal Medicine attendings upbraided me for chasing rainbows, while he had been working hard.

"Follow your bliss." I said. His bliss turned out to be his loathing.

The new department head was an ambitious but gentle man, who had put the word out that he intended to meet all the residents for some face time, in scheduled one-on-one meetings. On the morning of my turn, I was ushered into the inner sanctum, and shook an outstretched hand that was twice as large as mine. The man had big hands.

"So, tell me Wink." He said. "What is your five-year plan?" I almost fell off my chair. I don't think he understood my answer.

Back out in the hallway I found my house staff, fear written on four faces.

"We're out of control." Said the most senior one. "There are thirty inpatients, five more in emergency, two with no blood pressures, and a lawyer having withdrawal seizures we can't stop. His family is demanding to speak to you. Now." And overhead, out of the heavens, came the all too frequent reverberation.

"Paging Dr. Winkler. Paging Dr. Winkler".

They were always paging Dr. Winkler. Like I didn't have anything else to do.

'Crawling on the Planet's face
Some insects called the human race
Lost in time and lost in space
And meaning…'
Rocky Horror Picture Show

The Southern Cross floated like a kite above the horizon. Young Colville had joined them on the picnic table, because he wanted to be in the story.

Uncle Wink pointed to the farthest of its pointer stars.

"That's Alpha Centauri." He said. "It's the closest star to us, with the nearest exoplanet capable of sustaining life as we know it. It's binary."

"Is this the end of the story?" Asked Millie.

"Yes. Mil." Said Uncle Wink. "Although there is one last cartwheel I need to tell you about."

"Which one is that?" Asked Sam.

"Every line I've written, Sam, has squared and closed a circle I began over thirty years ago." Uncle Wink said. "All cartwheels are connected, and the meaning of life, is there really is one, is the one that happened on the shoreline down there, years before Auntie Robbie and I got the shack here in Otama. Before there was a picnic table, the man that owned this headland was a German neurosurgeon, who specialized in stereotactic surgery, locating parts of the brain in space and time. He used to do naked cartwheels down the beach, not in the search for the meaning of life, but because he was alive. The inner value, the rapture that is associated with being alive, is what it's all about. Life is an experience, not a mental meaning. What is the meaning of a star? Besides, the same year that Vincent was cartwheeling naked down the sand, the Wizard of Was had taught me two words, with the power to make children disappear off a magic picnic table.

"What were the words, Uncle Wink?" They all asked at once.

"Hokey Pokey." Said Uncle Wink. It was the name of their most favorite ice cream, at the Kuaotunu store.

As he left, Uncle Wink looked back at the picnic table, empty under the full starry firmament of the night sky. Alpha Centauri danced. Just a little.

Other Works by Lawrence Winkler

Westwood Lake Chronicles

Cartwheels Quadrilogy
Orion's Cartwheel
Between the Cartwheels
Hind Cartwheel
(The Final Cartwheel)

Stories of the Southern Sea

Wagon Days

Samurai Road

Stout Men

Fire Beyond the Darkness

*   *   *